243-Powell
241
233
P.146
P.170-171
P.217

HEMINGWAY

THE 1930s

HEMINGWAY

THE 1930s

MICHAEL REYNOLDS

W. W. NORTON & COMPANY

NEW YORK LONDON

Excerpt from Ernest Hemingway, *Winner Take Nothing*, reprinted with permission of Scribner, a Division of Simon & Schuster. Copyright 1933 Charles Scribner's Sons. Copyright renewed © 1961 by Mary Hemingway. Excerpt from *Ernest Hemingway: Selected Letters 1917–1961*, ed. Carlos Baker, reprinted with permission of Scribner, a Division of Simon & Schuster. Copyright © 1981 The Ernest Hemingway Foundation, Inc. Excerpt from *Hemingway's Spanish Civil War*, ed. William Braasch Watson, reprinted with the permission of The Ernest Hemingway Foundation, Copyright 1988. All rights reserved. Originally published in *The Hemingway Review*, Volume 7, Number 2. Previously unpublished Hemingway letters are reprinted with permission of The Ernest Hemingway Foundation and copyrighted by them. "The Law of the Jungle," by E. B. White (*The New Yorker*, April 14, 1934) is reprinted with permission of the E. B. White Estate.

For information about permission to reproduce selections from this book, write to Permissions, W. W. Norton & Company, Inc., 500 Fifth Avenue, New York, NY 10110.

The text of this book is composed in Fairfield Light with the display set in Corvinus Skyline. Desktop composition by Tom Ernst. Manufacturing by Courier Companies Inc. Book design by Chris Welch. Cartography by Susan Rensted.

Library of Congress Cataloging-in-Publications Data
Reynolds, Michael S., 1937–
Hemingway : the 1930s / Michael Reynolds.
p. cm.
Includes bibliographical references and index.
ISBN 0-393-04093-3
1. Hemingway, Ernest, 1899–1961—Biography. 2. Spain—History—
Civil War, 1936–1939—Literature and the war. 3. Authors,
American—20th century—Biography. 4. Journalists—United States—
Biography. 5. Depressions—United States. I. Title.
PS3515.E37Z75466 1997
813'.52—dc20
[B]   96-43113
CIP

W. W. Norton & Company, Inc., 500 Fifth Avenue, New York, N.Y. 10110
http://www.wwnorton.com

W. W. Norton & Company Ltd., 10 Coptic Street, London WC1A 1PU
1 2 3 4 5 6 7 8 9 0

Dialectic and bizarre, we traveled on
To Roncesvalles and Blois, to Krasnador,
Caux and Hurtgenwald, Avila and Gijon.
For sharing everything he knew,
For all the meals with wine and laughter,
This is his book, and I, his debtor,
Hold him ever as my standard measure.

In the way you speak
You arrange, the thing is posed.
                        –Wallace Stevens

Even though it is possible to design, manipulate and orchestrate
        one's immortality in advance,
    it never comes to pass the way it has been intended.
                        –Milan Kundera

CONTENTS

MAPS

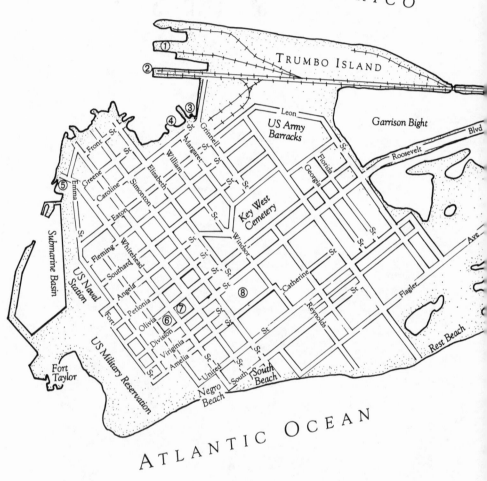

GULF OF MEXICO

TRUMBO ISLAND

Garrison Bight

US Army
Barracks

Leon

Front St.

Greene St.

Emma St.

Caroline

Simonton

Elizabeth

William

Margaret

Grinnell

Roosevelt Blvd

Florida

Georgia

Key West
Cemetery

Windsor

St.

St.

St.

St.

Ave

Flagler

Catherine St.

Reynolds St.

St.

Rest Beach

Submarine Basin

US Naval
Station

Fleming

Whitehead

Southard

Angela

Petronia

Olivia

Division

Virginia

Amelia

United

South

South
Beach

St.

St.

Fort

St.

Fort
Taylor

US Military Reservation

Negro
Beach

ATLANTIC OCEAN

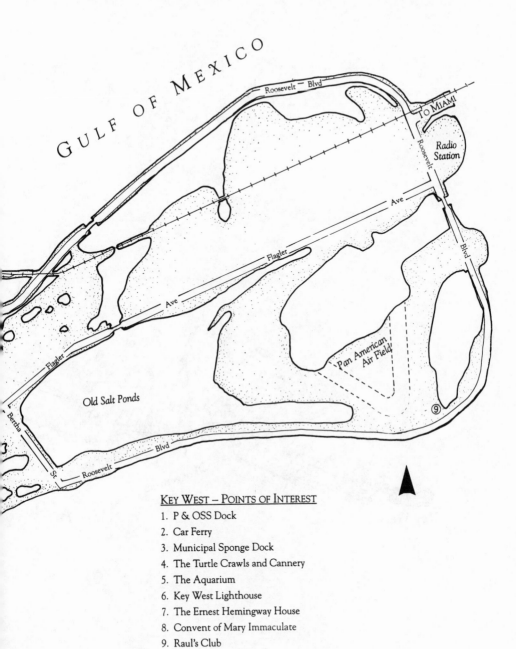

GULF OF MEXICO

Roosevelt Blvd

TO MIAMI

Radio
Station

Roosevelt

Ave

Flagler

Blvd

Ave

Pan American
Air Field

Flagler

⑨

Old Salt Ponds

Bertha

St

Roosevelt

Blvd

KEY WEST – POINTS OF INTEREST

1. P & OSS Dock
2. Car Ferry
3. Municipal Sponge Dock
4. The Turtle Crawls and Cannery
5. The Aquarium
6. Key West Lighthouse
7. The Ernest Hemingway House
8. Convent of Mary Immaculate
9. Raul's Club

Map of Key West c. 1936.

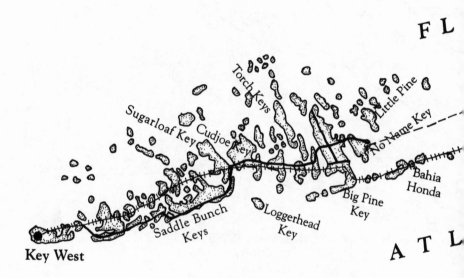

F L

Torch Keys

Little Pine

Sugarloaf Key

Cudjoe Key

No Name Key

Big Pine
Key

Bahia
Honda

Loggerhead
Key

Saddle Bunch
Keys

Key West

A T L

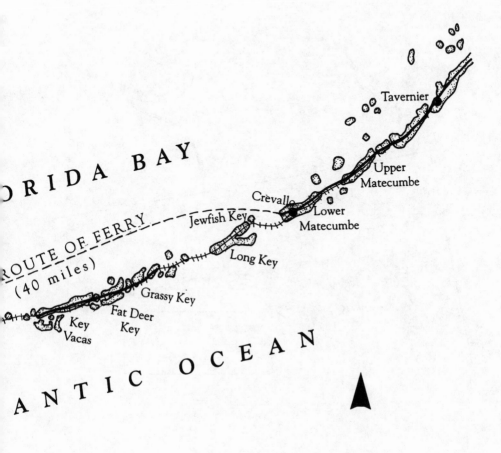

FLORIDA BAY

ROUTE OF FERRY
(40 miles)

Jewfish Key

Long Key

Grassy Key

Key
Vacas

Fat Deer
Key

Crèvalle

Lower
Matecumbe

Upper
Matecumbe

Tavernier

ATLANTIC OCEAN

*Map of the Florida Keys before the 1935 hurricane destroyed the
rail line.*

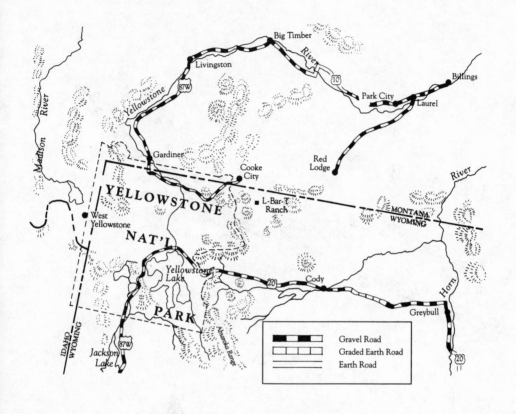

The isolated L-Bar-T Ranch area east of Yellowstone National
Park where the Hemingways fished and hunted throughout the
1930s.

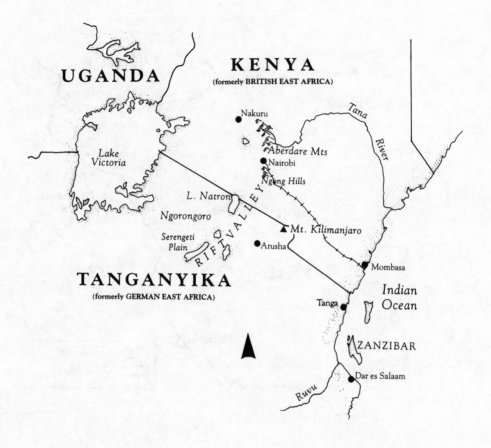

UGANDA

KENYA
(formerly BRITISH EAST AFRICA)

Nakuru

Lake
Victoria

Tana
River

Aberdare Mts

Nairobi

Ngong Hills

L. Natron

Ngorongoro

RIFT VALLEY

Mt. Kilimanjaro

Serengeti
Plain

Arusha

TANGANYIKA
(formerly GERMAN EAST AFRICA)

Mombasa

Indian
Ocean

Tanga

ZANZIBAR

Dar es Salaam

Ruvu

*Area of East Africa where the Hemingways were on safari in
1933–34.*

The 1937 division of Spain during the civil war before Franco's Nationalist forces broke through to the Mediterranean.

PROLOGUE

IN 1918, WHEN young Hemingway passed through New York on his way to the Great War, no one took notice. Nor was anyone interested when he and his bride sailed from New York for France in 1921. Four years later, when he returned to break his contract with Horace Liveright and sign with Scribner's, he attracted little attention outside of the Left Bank. By the time of his first divorce, he had published *The Sun Also Rises* (1926), and there was a small blurb in the *New York Times*. When he came through New York in December of 1928 to deliver the typescript of his new novel, a New York gossip columnist interviewed him but, with no pressing need to run the story, did not use it until three months later:

> *New York, March 8–New York had a visiting novelist this winter who made no effort to be a bright boy at the tea table, spurt epigrams or comment on crude American manners. He was Ernest Hemingway, who has a cherubic moon of a face and a cocoonish mustache and although a product of Chicago, lives in Paris and made his reputation there. . . . Hemingway is one of the fabled writing geniuses in real life who cares nothing about financial rewards of his trade. . . . [He] has just finished a novel promised to a magazine at a big price, but at the last moment was touched by a sentimentality and begged off. He gave it for a very small price to a magazine that bought his first story.[1]*

The gossiper got the story about half right: a draft was typed, but *A Farewell to Arms* was three months from being finished, and the $16,000 *Scribner's Magazine* was paying Hemingway for serial rights was hardly a "small price." Nor had *Scribner's* published his first short story. Nor did Ernest usually make sentimental decisions about money. But who would care or long remember if the story was right or wrong? Its fleeting importance was that it kept Ernest's name before the public, whose appetite for inside information about the famous and the infamous was awakening. Before the approaching decade was out, newsstands would offer *Time, Life,* and uncounted fan magazines to feed that appetite. As the real and fictional lives of cultural figures were becoming public domain, Ernest Hemingway was coming home in time to catch the wave that would carry a few from his generation into the next decade.

As the Twenties drew to a close, many a familiar name was fading from view. Scott Fitzgerald, who claimed to have invented the Twenties "flapper," would be forgotten within ten years, along with others who stayed too long abroad or failed to read right the signs of the time. Literary magazines once the heartbeat of the period were disappearing: gone were the *transatlantic review, Ex Libris, Liberator, Der Querschnitt, The Egoist,* and *Exile. This Quarter* and *Little Review* were fading. Within a year, talking pictures will replace silent stars with fresh faces speaking intelligible English. Within four years, the nation, mired in a economic depression beyond comprehension, will repeal prohibition along with the Republican Party as it embraces Franklin Roosevelt's New Deal. By the end of the Thirties, Ernest Hemingway will be as well known as many sportsmen, movie stars, gangsters, and politicians. In his first eight Paris years, he became a literary cult figure. During the next ten years, he will become an American icon. It is an old American story of promise fulfilled through fortitude and good fortune, a tale of rewards beyond all expectation, a cautionary tale of the Dream and its dark side.

HEMINGWAY

THE 1930s

Chapter One

1 9 2 9

THE MUSIC CHANGES

Paris and Spain

MAY 5, HENDAYE, on the Atlantic coast of France at the Spanish border: the spring season, declared open, brings moneyed Parisians and American tourists to nearby Biarritz but few yet to Hendaye. Where the Bidassoa River edges the town and empties into the Bay of Biscay, there stretches out a gentle, cupped white beach, backed by several small hotels. There are people on the beach, walking or sitting in the morning sun. No one is swimming.

In the breakfast room of the Hotel Barron where he finishes his coffee and brioche, Ernest Hemingway reads the Paris letter from Pauline. Their young son, Patrick, is recovering nicely from the flu, and at the American Hospital, Pauline is having something painful done to her infected sinus cavities which makes everything better. Very soon, she is sure, he should be able to rejoin them. Ever since the influenza epidemic of 1917 drowned soldiers in their own phlegm, Ernest has been mortally afraid of the flu. Pauline said she understood when he left her sick in Paris with their sick son and his insolent sister and his former wife and all the problems of returning to Paris. She is going to get well, she says, and then he will come home.[2] As soon as he can get his head working, he promised her, as soon as the words are right. Four years earlier in Hendaye, alone at the Barron, he finished *The Sun Also Rises*; he has come back to a good writing place, trusting that the luck will return.

Each morning, just as he had done on the *Yorck* crossing from New York, he reopens the typescript for his new novel and rereads the final chapter, at the end of which his narrator, Frederic Henry, tries to explain what happened to himself and several other characters after the Great War. Lamely Frederic concludes, "I would tell what has happened since then but that is the end of the story." In mid-February when Hemingway accepted *Scribner's Magazine's* offer of $16,000 to serialize the novel, he knew he must revise the ending. For three months now, he has tried again and again to get it right. He has tried it complicated, and has tried it plain. Nothing satisfies him.

On July 8, 1918, beside the muddy Piave River on the Venetian plain, a night mortar shell ruined his right knee, filled his legs with shrapnel, and left him with a concussion; after less than a month at the front lines, Hemingway spent the remainder of the war recuperating in a Milan hospital, where he fell in love with a nurse eight years his senior. Ten years after the experience, he has created a war more real than any he had known. He gives his war wound and his nurse to Frederic Henry; to his fictional nurse, he gives his second wife's pregnancy. From his first marriage with Hadley Richardson, he takes their good times at Chamby when the roads were iron-hard and they deeply in love. From maps, books, and close listening, he has made up a war he never saw, described terrain he never walked, and re-created the retreat from Caporetto so accurately that his Italian readers will later say he was present at that national embarrassment.

Begun in Paris and continued on his transatlantic voyage to Key West, the novel moved with Hemingway through the summer of

1928. From Key West to Pauline's home in Piggott, Arkansas, and on to the best hospital in Kansas City, he wrote steadily while Pauline prepared to deliver their son. In the Kansas City hospital, Ernest watched the surgeon perform the cesarean section. At the end of July he left Pauline to recover in Piggott while he drove to Sheridan, Wyoming, where, on August 22, he finished his first draft, 650 hand-written pages.

Over the next four months, Hemingway was steadily on the road: Piggott, Chicago, New York, Chicago, Piggott, Key West, and back to New York to meet his first son, John, arriving from Paris. On December 6, 1928, father and son boarded the train for Key West; outside of Philadelphia, Hemingway received the Oak Park telegram telling him his father was dead. Clarence Hemingway, depressed and ill, had committed suicide. During the week after his father's funeral, Hemingway sorted out his mother's financial problems and revised the first half of his war novel. Returning to Key West, he quickly completed his revisions, and on January 22, 1929, the typed draft was finished except for the ending.

When Ernest and his family sailed for France, the telegram waiting for them at the boat was from Max Perkins wishing them luck and asking Ernest, "If you see Scott in Paris write me soon how he is."[3] Max was worried about his friend's drinking and his marriage, and worried about his publishing company's continuing advances against the Fitzgerald novel that remained only promises. The last letter Hemingway mailed before sailing asked Max not to give Fitzgerald the Hemingways' Paris address: "Last time he was in Paris he got us kicked out of one apartment and in trouble all the time (insulted the landlord, peed on the front porch—tried to break down the door 3-4 and 5 A.M. etc.)."[4] But the Hemingways were too well placed to go unnoticed in St. Germain, and Fitzgerald knew their apartment on rue Férou quite well from 1927. In April, when Scott, Zelda, and their daughter, Scotty, arrived in Paris, they took an apartment on rue Palatine, less than a block around the corner from the Hemingways, whose church, St. Sulpice, was also the parish church where Scotty Fitzgerald was taken to Mass.

Arriving in Paris with too many endings for his novel and none of them right, Hemingway went alone to Hendaye to close the book. Because he had lived in the novel, inventing it day by day, he did not know from the beginning that Frederic, his American ambulance driver on the Italian front, would end up in Switzerland standing over the lifeless body of Catherine, who died giving birth to their stillborn child. Significant characters developed early in the story—the surgeon and the priest—disappear during the retreat from Caporetto, and try as he did to bring them back in the conclusion, every effort is off-key and forced.[5] In his modest room at the Hotel Barron, galleys for the novel's last installment with the still flawed ending wait his attention while in Paris the first installment has appeared in the May issue of *Scribner's Magazine*.

As Hemingway is correcting those last galleys in Hendaye, Owen Wister—author of *The Virginian*, close friend of Hemingway's boyhood hero Teddy Roosevelt, and fellow Scribner's author with whom Hemingway visited the previous summer—has, in Philadelphia, finished reading at Hemingway's request a complete set of the magazine galleys.[6] To the delight of Max Perkins, Hemingway's editor, Wister then writes a wonderful publicity blurb:

> *In Mr. Ernest Hemingway's new novel,* A Farewell to Arms, *landscape, persons, and events are brought to such vividness as to make the reader become a participating witness. This astonishing book is in places so poignant and moving as to touch the limit that human nature can stand, when love and parting are the point. . . . And he, like Defoe, is lucky to be writing in an age that will not stop its ears at the unmuted resonance of a masculine voice.*[7]

In a separate statement to Perkins, Wister voiced his concerns about Hemingway's use of the first-person narrator and the novel's conclusion, suggesting that the nurse's death be softened and that the ending bring together the two themes of love and war. Perkins agrees completely. The book's flaw, he tells Wister, is that the war story and the love do not combine. "It begins as one thing wholly, and ends wholly as the other thing." If only the war were in some way responsible for the nurse's death in childbirth. "As to the third person," Perkins says, "I believe he did intend to attempt it in this book, but abandoned it. I do hope that he may adopt it in the next."[8]

The first letter Ernest received when he returned from Hendaye was a dinner invitation from Scott for Pentecost Sunday or the following Monday holiday.[9] In honor perhaps of the impending Pentecost when fiery tongues once descended upon those huddled in an upstairs room, Scott signed the letter:

> *God Save us, Preserve us, Bless us*
> *Yrs. in Xt.*
> *Fitzg—*

Beneath his signature he drew three crosses upon a hill with a smiling sun above and below a sign: "To Jerusalem, Your Opportunity, 1 Mile." Writing in his slightly paternal, joking voice of 1925, Fitzgerald masked the anxiety he felt about their relationship, which his wife, Zelda, resented, and about his own failed but never forgotten Catholicism.

The day after receiving Fitzgerald's dinner invitation, Hemingway put the final magazine galleys, with the exception of its last page, into the mail, telling Robert Bridges, *Scribner's Magazine* editor, that for ten days he had been revising the last three paragraphs and they were "almost right." He promised to get them on the fast mail boat leaving May 23 and due in New York on May 31.[10] The following day in New York, Max was assuring Ernest by mail that he could continue working on any parts of the story that bothered him, meaning the part that bothered Max: the end of story. If only the physical details of Catherine's pain were reduced, the reader (Max) might not squirm so, losing the thread of the story. Then there is the nagging question: where did the war disappear to? "Love and War," Max said, "combine, to my mind, perfectly to the point where Catherine and Lieutenant Henry get to Switzerland; thereafter the war is almost forgotten by them and by the reader. . . . I can't shake off the feeling that war, which has deeply conditioned this love story—and does so still passively—should still do so actively and decisively."[11]

By that time the Hemingways and Fitzgeralds have exchanged dinners somewhat less than successfully: Zelda cold and distant; Pauline too obviously tolerant; Scott trying too hard; Ernest not hard enough; all uncomfortable. Scott said: "It worked out beautifully didn't it. . . . it was a more irritable Ernest, apprehensively telling me his whereabouts lest I come in on them tight and endanger his lease. The discovery that half a dozen people were familiars there didn't help my self esteem."[12] And Zelda said: "We came back to rue Palatine and you, in a drunken stupor told me a lot of things that I only half understood: but I understood the dinner we had at Ernest's. Only I did not understand that it mattered."[13]

No matter how badly their reunion had gone, Ernest could not refuse Scott when he asked to read the new novel, the typescript of which Fitzgerald took with him to make extensive suggestions for more changes:

Eliminate the opera singers in Milan: "just rather gassy."

Take out the entire chapter where Frederic and Catherine spend the afternoon at the fixed horse races: "dull and slow."

Tighten the overwritten scenes in Switzerland.

Don't let Catherine go on and on about her pregnancy: "This could stand a good cutting. . . . the brave expectant illegitimate mother is an *old situation*."

Catherine's glib speeches could be cut: "Don't try to make her make sense."

"Our poor old friendship," Scott said, "probably won't survive this but there you are—better me than some nobody in the Literary Review that doesn't care about you & your future."[14]

With the novel's first installment published in the May issue of *Scribner's Magazine* and with final magazine galleys corrected and returned, Scott's suggestions served no useful purpose, saying more about his own writing than about Ernest's. After four years of work and continuous promises of finishing, Fitzgerald had barely two chapters to show for his continuous revisions of what would, in

another five years, become *Tender Is the Night*. He completely mis-
understood Ernest's use of the fixed horse race as a deterministic
metaphor for man's condition, and Scott's unsympathetic reading of
the nurse, Catherine, said more about his relationship with Zelda
than it did about Ernest's text. At the bottom of the ninth and final
page, Hemingway wrote: "Kiss my ass."

But Hemingway found enough merit in Scott's suggestion that an
early rhetorical passage be moved to the end to test it: "If people
bring so much courage to this world the world has to kill them to
break them, so of course it kills them. . . . It kills the very good and
the very gentle and the very brave impartially. If you are none of
these you can be sure it will kill you too but there is no special
hurry." Hemingway typed the passage but rejected the solution, perhaps because he did not want to increase his debt to Fitzgerald, on
whose advice three years earlier he had cut the opening eight pages
of *The Sun Also Rises*.[15]

―――

June 23, Paris, Place St. Sulpice. The three-tiered fountain, with
its carved cardinals, mewling stone lions and circling pigeons,
dominates the square where a Sunday morning of parents, grand-
mothers, and small children are entering between hulking gray
stone church towers to attend ten-o'clock Mass. All ivory and gold
the altar, Christ crucified on the left and risen on the right, side
altars cusping the congregation. Church bells are ringing.

―――

Dressed for Mass, Ernest, Pauline, her sister, Jinny, and their uncle,
Augustus Pfeiffer come out the barred door and into the courtyard of 6
rue Férou. As they pass through the iron gate, they are framed by two
white sphinxes that are elevated on either side of the entry. At one end
of the narrow, cobblestoned street stands their parish church; at the
other end, the Musée du Luxembourg: both within a stone's throw and
both reassuring in their complementary ways.

Uncle Gus, thin and grayed, walks younger than he looks, a
pinched-faced man whose smile offsets his sharp eyes. He has been
in Europe for some weeks acquiring new holdings for the Richard

Hudnut Corporation, which is to say for himself, majority owner of the company's stock. He has also found one or two interesting chess sets to add to his rather fine collection. Uncle Gus is married but has no children, a condition which makes his two nieces that much more valuable to him.

On his arm, Jinny listens intently to the old gentleman. When she speaks and he smiles, the family resemblance is strong. Having lived in Paris for more than five years on her trust fund, Virginia Pfeiffer is fluent in French and in the ways of the city. She is a pleasant companion, always ready to do a good turn: take care of Patrick, house-sit the apartment, find someone to fix the furnace. Witty, well-dressed but not flashy, she and Pauline have come a long way from Piggott, Arkansas, where their father moved the family from St. Louis to become a gentleman farmer and village patron. In Piggott, only one or two close friends understood how strange Jinny was in that cotton-field town, but in Paris, where nothing is strange, Jinny is very much at ease. If she prefers the company of women to men, she is far from alone in the city of lights.

Behind uncle and niece walk Ernest and Pauline. Smartly dressed but pale from her illness and the wet spring, Pauline seems fragile beside her husband, who stands almost a foot taller than she. After the pain of her sinus drainage and the lost sleep with fever-ridden Patrick, after all the small but demanding duties that fell to her upon their return to Paris (find a maid, balance accounts, replace lost linen, greet old friends), and after the anxiety of Ernest's inability to finish his novel, she, too, is smiling, for those stresses are behind them. Before them is the promise of another Spanish summer. She is thirty-three years old, wife and mother, securely funded, and married to one of the most interesting men of her generation. Pauline Hemingway has every reason to smile.

Taller and younger than the Pfeiffers around him, Ernest is aging more quickly than some of his peers. At twenty-eight, his receding hairline making prominent his widow's peak, his face looks heavy behind his black mustache, and his bulk fills his dark suit completely. Twice married, twice a father, once divorced, he is becoming the authority figure he imagined himself to be a few years earlier. Soon Pauline will be calling him "Papa." This morning he, too, is smiling, for he has found his novel's conclusion: no explanations, no maundering about lost characters, Catherine and the baby dead in Lausanne, and Frederic alone, walking back to his hotel in the rain. The previous evening, Owen Wister, who was passing through Paris and whose concerns about the ending Ernest knew, was with him for supper. After reading the new ending, Wister said, "Don't touch a thing!"[16] Having exhausted himself in the book for fifteen months, Hemingway's storehouse is empty, his mind briefly at rest.

There is now a misty rain falling lightly in rue Férou: a damper for the first day of the Grande Semaine and the steeplechase at Auteuil perhaps, but a fair Sunday nevertheless as Ernest enjoys that brief moment of well being that comes with a finished book. Soon enough he will face again the certainty that only two conditions exist for a man of letters: either he is writing, or he is not. He might ease his driven need by answering letters, taking notes, or keeping a journal, but no matter what he tells himself, he feels slightly fraudulent until the next book begins. Later Ernest said that the writing of the book should destroy the writer. If there is anything left, he has not worked hard enough. The writer himself does not matter: the book is everything. Others will tell him how much they like the new novel, but their praise will not bring back the wonder of writing it, nor can praise fill up the emptiness left by its departure, nor dull the anxiety of searching for the next book.

Having no other way to put it forcefully, Hemingway said that within the writer there was his death, and that death was the book. Physically, he might survive any number of books, but each one would kill off a part of him, a piece of what he knew, leaving the book with a life of its own.[17] The last five years of steady writing have killed off more of him than he can admit: two novels, one satire (*Torrents of Spring*), and two volumes of short stories. Writing only about what he knew best from his own life and the lives of friends, he has used up the experiences that life had given him as a gift. It was like closing out a bank account in which nothing remains but small change.

9

As soon as the May issue of *Scribner's Magazine* appeared, his new life solidified, irrevocably, leaving behind certain pleasures, while opening possibilities and expectations only dreamed of earlier. Never again will he lack an audience; never again will he read a rejection letter. *The Sun Also Rises* plucked him out of the bush leagues of the small literary magazines and made him a talent worth watching. *A Farewell to Arms* will take him into the major league of best-selling authors, where soon an entourage—lawyer, agent, editor, and publisher—will be continually looking after his and their professional best interests. Soon enough he will need dollar, pound, franc, mark, and peseta accounts at the Morgan Guaranty Bank to accommodate his various royalties. In ten years of continuous work, he has transformed himself from the precocious, war-wounded teenager writing clichéd imitations into one of the best young writers of his generation. At twenty-four he had little to show for all his ambition; at twenty-nine he has written two of his century's best novels.

Possibilities, which he once sought so ardently, now come uninvited for his consideration. Before he could leave Paris for the drunken feria of San Fermin, Janet Flanner insisted on an interview for a *Ladies' Home Journal* article she is writing on expatriates, which he will be in, she says jokingly, whether he cooperates or not.[18] Nino Frank, the editor of *Bifur*, a new literary journal, says that James Joyce told him that Ernest might give him one of his short stories for the premier edition of the journal.[19] *The Forum* wants Ernest to send them a short story: "Two thousand words is the desired length and in any case the stories must not exceed three thousand words. . . . the story must contain narrative or at least plot. . . . not be merely a sketch. . . . We will pay five hundred dollars for the first serial rights."[20] George Antheil wants Ernest to collaborate on a play similar to what young Bert Brecht has done in Berlin with *The Threepenny Opera*. "The composer [Kurt] Weil, who wrote the music, has been begging me to find an American writer who would work out something with us (Weil and I) for Berlin. . . . You are the only boy who could do this thing if you would."[21] Victor Llona wants to translate and publish "Ten Indians" in an anthology of American writers.

The pay is only two hundred francs ($8) but it will be "excellent publicity." Four days later, he says André Maurois has agreed to write the introduction for the story. "Being by Maurois, your introduction will be the most arresting in the Anthology."[22] Paul Johnson wants Ernest to contribute to a "series of six prose pamphlets, each containing an essay or short story . . . boxed together . . . to sell at $10.00 the set . . . . The only rules [are] . . . that the contribution be a short story or literary essay, and that the minimum length be 2000 words. . . . Random House is prepared to pay $200.00 on acceptance." Those invited to compete for the six slots are Sherwood Anderson, Thomas Beer, James Branch Cabell, Willa Cather, Joseph Hergesheimer, Conrad Aiken, Theodore Dreiser, Ellen Glasgow, Ernest Hemingway, and Thornton Wilder.[23]

In early August, Collier's Weekly offered $750 for a thousand-word sketch and more for a five-thousand-word story. "If they like that," Paul Reynolds, Hemingway's would-be agent, told his editor, "they would order more."[24] When Ernest did not respond to the offer, Collier's came back with an offer of $30,000 for the serial rights to his next novel, with a $1,000 down payment for the right of first refusal. "They will pay you twenty-five hundred dollars ($2500) for any short stories of yours that they buy," he was told.[25] Every bait went untouched.

In Conway, Massachusetts, Archibald MacLeish finishes reading the May installment of A Farewell to Arms and writes Ernest that it is so good that it frightens him. "Your book," he says, "starts like Tolstoy—it starts slow and deep & real the way Tolstoy starts—it is like the beginning of a year not the beginning of a book—(& the first chapter is a magnificent poem)—& I am afraid you are not only a fine writer which I have always known but something a lot more than that & it scares me. I can't go on with this. It is murder to talk about it this way."[26] Three days earlier in Boston: "The June issue of Scribner's Magazine was barred from the book stands here yesterday by Michael H. Crowley, superintendent of police, because of objections to an installment of Ernest Hemingway's serial, A Farewell to Arms. It is said that some persons deem part of the installment salacious."[27]

In Paris, while Ernest, Jinny Pfeiffer, and Guy Hickok ready themselves for the two-day drive to the feria of San Fermin, the Grande Semaine finishes its course of fashion displays and featured handicaps at the several racetracks. As the city fills with noisy tourists and its permanent residents leave for country places, the summer seems no different from any other in the Twenties. Some notice that fewer Americans are in Paris, but at the several European entry ports, great ocean liners—*Aquitania, Lancastria, Gripsholm, Ile-de-France, Majestic, President Harding, Deutschland, Mauretania*—continue to disgorge their traffic. Action on the Paris Bourse slows to a crawl. "Midsummer drowsiness is drugging business on the London stock exchange," the *Tribune* reports. "Public apathy is becoming increasingly apparent." On Wall Street, "Indications are for a peaceful summer . . . and a gradual accumulation of strength which should express itself in a rising stock market with the approach of autumn." On Monday morning, a share of U.S. Steel is selling at 179.[28]

The summer *transition* manifesto—signed by Kay Boyle, Harry and Caresse Crosby, and Hart Crane among others—insists that the Left Bank coterie writers are alive and well. Its eleventh article states flatly: "The plain reader be damned."[29] Ernest's name, which two years earlier the revolutionary journal gladly featured, is nowhere in sight. That part of his life—the Left Bank literary life; the *transatlantic, This Quarter, transition* life—is finished. As the *New York Evening Post* reported: "The Hemingway who sat nightly in the Latin Quarter is no more. . . . [*The Sun Also Rises*] marked his permanent exodus from the Dome, the Rotonde, and the rest of the Bohemian resorts in Montparnasse."[30] That summer and fall all appeals for his fiction, all promises of money large and small, go unattended. He and his world are in flux. The plain reader, so roundly damned by *transition*'s elitists, is waiting for a new fiction to be written by plain authors; very soon plain characters will step onto a proletariat stage waiting to be built.

Late that week, the U.S. Secretary of the Treasury announces that the government is ending the fiscal year with a $170 million surplus, and President Hoover predicts that eighteen more years of prosperity will retire the national debt completely. The Democrats are

expected to seize upon these figures to support their demands for fur-
ther tax cuts at the bottom of the scale. They contend that the last tax
reduction voted by Congress benefited big corporations and wealthy
persons far more than it did the small-salaried class. The Republicans
contend that by reducing the tax burdens of wealth and big business,
the Government increased the general prosperity of the country
through development of industry and commerce.[31]

On the big board, U.S. Steel closes the week at 188.

At Pamplona on July 6 precisely at noon, the feast of San Fermin begins with a ceremonial rocket, cannon fire, and music. This summer so many cars arrive that the Plaza de la Constitución and all its side streets are gridlocked. The following morning, the dead awake to a brassy band in the plaza calling them to watch the 7:00-a.m. *encierro*, the running of that day's bulls from their holding pens down barricaded streets to Plaza de Toros. The Hemingway party, arriving early to acclimatize, are strategically housed at Hotel Quintana. From their small balcony, they have an excellent view of the narrow Calle de la Estafeta, down which come young runners wearing red *boinas* and sashes followed closely by bulls clattering on the cobblestones. This year no one is grievously hurt; two are wounded, but walk away. By midmorning the bulls and runners are replaced by the solemn procession of San Fermin led by the Bishop of Navarra followed by mounted Guardia Civil, choirs of children, parish church councils both local and visiting, church and municipal dignitaries, various guilds, and assorted bands of singers and dancers. The spiritual soon gives way to the carnal: flute, drum, and bagpipers leading rowdy street dancers before the procession of gigantic papier-mâché royal couples—Ferdinand and Isabella—and strange *cabezudos*, little people with big heads. And everywhere the Riau Riau clubs were dancing, pulling even overweight newsmen like Guy Hickok into their ritual:

We stood four feet apart, arms up, on tiptoe, waiting for a place in the
music to start. It came and we began. Tum, tum, tum to the left.

Tum, tum, tum to the right. Both of them over again. Then at a shrill tumult in the music we whirled (that is he whirled and I did my best) and began again. It became very involved and it was only by watching his feet and forgetting everything else in the world that I kept in the same dance with him. Sometimes we whirled one way, sometimes another. Twice he leaped in the air, with me in on only the second leap. Once the whirl was preceded by a quick drop to one knee. Then it stopped.[32]

At four-thirty, as the day cools somewhat, bullfights begin, lasting well into evening. Blood stains the sand arena, flowers and full *botas* fall on the heroic, cushions on those who fail. This day a careless banderillero's arm is ripped open by a horn of an Encinas bull. That night on the plaza, Japanese fireworks and illuminated balloons alternate with music, dancing, and always drinking.[33] Guy Hickok described it all for his newspaper:

The whole square is a confusion of unorganized noises for hours before the fireworks begin. An uncountable moving mob mills about the square, plunging into and out of the wine shops under the arcades around it, singing and dancing in groups in the square itself, trying to climb the two greased poles, and never succeeding, trying to ride the two big barrels swung between poles, barrels apparently on ball bearings, so quickly do they turn and throw would-be riders to the ground.[34]

While Guy was sitting with Ernest under the arcade at the Iruña, a magazine writer spotted them

at a table against one of the pillars, with a bottle of beer in front of him, and a newspaper folded to the criticism of yesterday's bull-fight, exchanging idle comments with two friends, heedless of the racket that encompasses him, surveying the crowd with the friendly eye of a man who reads a familiar story, . . . Ernest Hemingway, the author who discovered Pamplona.

He is dressed in loose tweeds, his collar is low and soft and his necktie is pulled awry; he is hatless and one foot is thrust into a clumsy woolen carpet slipper. Somehow he cut his foot a day or so ago. With his dark hair and his dark mustache, his coloring is inconspicuous in the crowd of dark-haired Spaniards; but his poise and his strength are not. The vitality of the man is apparent even when he is motionless; it is an unobtrusive force which manifests itself by no overt gesture, yet it is pervasive and inescapable. . . . Hemingway is real; he is content to be only himself: Pamplona is real, unlike any city but itself. And in Pamplona Hemingway seems at home.[35]

"Discovered Pamplona" was shorthand for saying, "He gave us the drinker's dream, the prohibitionist's nightmare." No matter how experienced a drinker one thought himself, he was likely a novice at the week of San Fermin, where drinking was not an occasion but a steady state, a condition as pervasive as sunlight. By week's end the Pamplona air itself is rich with fumes of rioja consumed from goatskin *botas* worn loosely slung from the neck.

There was plenty of drinking that year at Pamplona, but not so much that they did not see what was happening in the bullring. With Hemingway beside him, Guy was able to write with shrewd, inside knowledge while seeing his first bullfights. During the first five corridas, two matadors were gored and three picadors were seriously hurt when their bulls gored their horses, lifting them up and over on top of the horsemen. There were stunning moments in the ring when Felix Rodríguez danced too close with his bull as he slipped the sword into the killing spot, and with Ernest's help, Hickok saw it:

While he still gripped the sword, the horns caught him under one arm, lifted him and flung him down. The bull lunged at him in a last second of fury, scattering sand as he hooked viciously with right horn and left, bearing down his weight. Others flicked their capes to draw the bull away. Felix Rodríguez was carried to the infirmary. In a quarter of an hour he was back, his neck bandaged and blood showing on his white pleated shirt, but smiling that debonair super-Hollywood smile. He stood ten minutes, then fainted and was carried out again.[36]

Ten days after the feria and safely returned to Paris, Hickok, a happily married expatriate newsman, wrote Hemingway about seeing Jinny Pfeiffer in Paris:

I didn't expect Jinny to look so good without Pernod glasses. I thought . . . I could look at her with indifference. But she came along looking so cool and calm and her eyes so shiny black and everything so nice that . . . it was a God Damned awful experiment in chemistry that you performed down there professor Hemingway. You take a fat forty-one year old innocent and pour him full of everybody's absinthe and bulls blood [Sangre de Torres wine] and trout water and a week of sparks and riau-riau and bombs and keep something like Jin . . . around all the time and what the Hell could you expect to happen. I'll bet a bull I don't get her out of my head inside a year.[37]

Paris, August 1. At the sign of the Black Manikin, where Edward Titus makes his living, his latest publishing venture is in the window—*Kiki's Memoirs*. Everyone on the Left Bank knows Kiki, the most famous model of Montparnasse and wife of enigmatic photographer Man Ray, whose lush nude displays of her body are not the least attraction of the book. "Did you know Kiki?" Ernest asks. "Did you ever see her bare? Did you once see Shelley plain and did he stop and speak to you? I'd rather have seen Kiki than Shelley."[38]

In Santiago de Compostela, the Hotel Suizo is not the ancient town's most resplendent hotel nor its most favored. Stuck into a side street without redeeming qualities, it has no elegant foyer, nor spacious dining room to attract the wealthy. The Suizo's dining room, barely two tables wide, is plain but adequate with starched white tablecloths and a standing array of waiters.[39] It is the class of hotel that Hemingway habitually chooses, neither shabby nor elegant, family-owned and giving good value for its price: "good pension for 10 pesetas, good rooms, wonderful god damned town and fine hilly country, Galicia."[40] The Hemingways have not come to Santiago for the bullfights, which are "all shot to hell," he tells Waldo Peirce.

After the Pamplona feria, Guy Hickok, Pat Morgan, and Jinny Pfeiffer returned by train to Paris, and Pauline joined Ernest at Hendaye to drive to the Valencia feria, where the bullfights were much better than in Pamplona. Now, after a warm month on the road, they are in cooler Santiago, its pilgrims departed, its hotels half empty, and where afternoon showers wash the stone city to a glistening shimmer. Most come, by whatever route, to this sanctuary either to pray or to fish. Ernest has come for both reasons, and another of his own.

Watching him bring a novel to completion is not a new experience for Pauline, for she, as the other woman, was intimately involved with Ernest when he finished *The Sun Also Rises*. She remembers the strain to the breaking point that novel put on his marriage with Hadley. She remembers that he left a wife and son in Paris to finish his fiction alone in Hendaye, and afterward became a stranger to Hadley, arguing about little things and anything. This summer in Spain, without another woman's presence to explain his erratic behavior, Pauline sees the pattern repeat itself in smaller ways. The sexual rush of her dyed blond hair with which she surprised him at Hendaye has worn off, and she is worried. In the cathedral of St. James, she lights her several candles, each for its separate problem.

When they arrived at the Suizo, their baggage contained unfinished stories which Pauline brought with her from Paris,[41] stories to which Ernest now returns but in a mood ill suited to finishing them. Smarting from the avuncular advice of Fitzgerald and Owen Wister, he continues to fret over Max Perkins's failure to support his full usage of the English language. Max restored some of the words deleted by *Scribner's Magazine*—"Jesus Christ," "son of a bitch," "whore," and "whorehound"—but others, like "cocksucker," were impossible to print in 1929 America. No matter that their competition, Remarque's *All Quiet on the Western Front*, was using "the word shit and fart etc. never dragged in for coloring but only used a few times for the thousands of times they are omitted."[42] With the argument settled by blank spaces in his text, Ernest cannot let loose of the issue, for he feels that he has betrayed his dedication to honest writing.

When not writing, he frequently takes their 1929 Ford off by himself to fish one of the several local streams famous for trout. On August 12, with new sunglasses, newspapers, and a sack full of tomatoes and onions for lunch, he spends the day fishing the Río Ulla as far as the upper dam. On the way home along the new railroad bed, he stops to cook the trout with salty country ham. Then, one after the other, two tires go flat. After patching the inner tubes by flashlight, he finally arrives back at the hotel at 11:15 p.m. With Pauline beside him in bed and his beer bottle on the side table, he adds, "No fights for two days."[43] Waking the next morning tired from his excursion, he spends the day quietly in Santiago. While reading of yesterday's bullfights in the newspapers, as he customarily begins his day, he also scans the pages for information on the new Spanish constitution and how the various revolutionary movements fare.

All that August there are signs to be read by the close observer. In Nuremberg, where it eventually would come full circle, the reporter saw what was happening, but misread the equation:

> Rival militant Nationalists of all shades buried the axe today when 120,000 uniformed Hitlerites marched past their leader, Adolph Hitler, beside whom stood Prince August Wilhelm, one of the Kaiser's sons, . . . evidence that a united monarchist bloc is coming into existence in Germany.[44]

U.S. Steel rises to 215, approximately the weight of Florence Martin, better known as Flossie, the "Dowager of the Dôme," the "Duchess of Montparnasse," who was giving up her domain to return to the United States.[45] The financial page might say, "No Midsummer Recession of Business Is Feared in U.S.,"[46] but beneath the surface of the Twenties, tectonic plates are shifting.

Midmorning in Santiago, Ernest gets his hair cut, purchases supplies, and checks with the patrón for mail forwarded from Paris. On $5 a day, he claims they are living cheaper than in Key West.[47] After their late lunch, Pauline works on unanswered letters, writing to Katy Smith that they hope she is soon to be Mrs. Dos Passos. (Ernest underlined that entry in his daybook, thinking perhaps of how much he once wanted Katy and later wrote the story of having her, a story he could never print.)[48] It was a day for marriages: a redirected telegram arrives announcing that Ernest's ambulance-driving friend from the war Bill Horne has married someone called "Bunny."

With the shutters drawn against the afternoon heat and with Pauline writing letters at the desk, Ernest stretches out to read from the pile of books with which he always travels. Today he chooses the Dumas historical novel *Les Quarante-cinq* and D. H. Lawrence's novella *St. Mawr*. Five years later, Dumas will contribute a single line to the text of *Green Hills of Africa*.[49] That evening, he notes in his daybook that at lunch he drank "*1 bottle beer*" costing sixty-five centavos. The underlining is for Pauline's benefit in their continuing disagreements about his drinking, which is causing his fingers to swell. Before turning out the light that night, he adds and underlines: "*3 days without any fights.*"[50] Between books, between countries, he is at odds with himself.

———

September 2, Palencia, Spain. A hotel room with a double bed; on a night table, bullfight tickets, glasses, a bottle of mineral water, a newspaper, and several books. Shutters are closed against the midday heat, but they do not prevent the temperature from rising in this room on the unshaded side of the hotel. On the bed, Ernest is stretched out, reading. Pauline is not in the room. Whenever he shifts position, he winces from a pulled groin muscle. Street noise of a feria and a faint haze of dust hang in the air that seeps into the room.[51]

———

He is always reading current fiction in the way that painters visit galleries or musicians listen to the Victrola, but he also reads to accumulate information in specific areas: military history, biography, travel, and natural history. Like his boyhood idol Theodore Roosevelt, he travels with his own library carefully chosen for divergent moods as a man might lay in specific wines in anticipation of certain meals. In Palencia he is reading to pass the time until the afternoon corrida begins. Yesterday the fights were excellent, and he anticipates another good day. He studies the corrida and its attendant drama with the detachment of a natural historian who, four years earlier, said that he wanted to write "a sort of Doughty's Arabia Deserta of the Bull Ring, a very big book with some wonderful pictures."[52]

From Santiago, he wrote Max Perkins that he had a vague idea about his next book—a collection of sketches of "things and places—not so much about people"—bullfight and fishing sketches; places like Key West, Santiago, Paris, Constantinople: something between essays and reminiscences. He could see three kinds: quiet ones, funny ones, and immoral ones. Maybe the magazine would take the quiet ones. The book itself would be something like W. H. Hudson's *Long Ago and Far Away*. Better to be writing something rather than trying like Scott to write a masterpiece; the next novel would have to wait until his "Goddamned imagination" began to function once again.[53]

Now in his fifth Spanish summer, he is gathering field notes for a book he does not yet understand, a book which will take another two years to complete. When it is finished, it will be a history of the bullfight, a guide to its present performance, a collection of morality tales, a book about writing, a book of natural history with a touch of *Don Quixote*, a book more complex than anything he has yet attempted. To that end he has registered the deaths of several hundred fighting bulls in his well-trained memory, bulls whose color, size, and speed he can remember. What is not in memory is there in the bullfight newspapers and magazines he has collected. For the history, he has recently acquired *Paginas Tauromacas* to add to his growing library.[54]

He is also reading medieval history, a subject in some ways not that far removed from the bullfight.[55] Hemingway is not looking for subject matter; he has plenty of that closer to home. Nor does he have any desire to resuscitate the long ago and far away. Like so many of his generation—the men who went to the Great War to make the world safe for democracy—he is looking for values that remain valid no matter how the stock market fluctuates or which way the political climate turns. One obvious source of stability is the Catholic Church, which has come through almost two millennia with its tenets intact. Having first satirized authors of his generation turning to the church ("The Lord is my shepherd, I shall not want him for long"),[56] Hemingway, too, embraced Catholicism, partially as the price for embracing Pauline Pfeiffer, a dedicated Catholic. If he sometimes seems less concerned about his soul's fate in the *hereafter* and more worried about sustaining himself in the *here and now*, his religious need is no less genuine or deeply seated.

With his conversion to Catholicism, Hemingway was remolding himself and eventually the characters he created. Leaving behind the passive young men of his early period, vulnerable men to whom unfortunate things happened, he was searching in no organized fashion for that man's *other*, the active man who chooses his fate rather than letting it choose him. Outlaws, spies, and revolutionaries are part of his reading, men operating outside the social contract but not without access to its comforts. The bullfighter and the boxer continue to interest him, both as men isolated by their art and as metaphors for the artist. In the background of this search, standing tall, is Chaucer's medieval Knight, his armor stained with usage, his list of battles writ large across his face. The warrior who "loved chivalrie, Trouthe and honour, fredom and curteisie." This knight was God's mercenary, going to all the wars of his time, choosing the side he thought most just. At the end of his tale, Chaucer's Knight laid down two guiding principles which would become central to Hemingway both man and author: to make "virtu of necessitee" and "for a worthy fame, to dyen when that he is best of name."

In his first Paris period, Hemingway sometimes pretended to more extensive war experience than his one month as a Red Cross ambulance driver had actually provided. In fact, he did not speak of the Red Cross, and friends accumulated tall tales of his fictional experience with Italian Arditi who plugged their bullet wounds with cigarette butts and who preferred the knife to the gun.[57] But he had experienced the big wound: the night mortar shell that killed the man standing next to him nearly crippled Ernest for life. Maybe he had not walked "eye deep in hell," but he had come home to the "old men's lies" that Pound described. Raised Republican in Republican Oak Park, he could not support the party that rejected the war and its veterans, nor could he support the Democrats who sent him off to it wearing a blindfold. At postwar conferences at Genoa and Lausanne, he witnessed the old order doing business as usual, protecting business. He listened to their promises and observed the consequences without taking sides. In 1924, his "Earnest Liberal" lamented:

> I know that monks masturbate at night
> That pet cats screw
> That some girls bite
> And yet
> What can I do
> To set things right?[58]

What, in fact, could anyone do in the face of the tourist trade, the Post-Toasties and Lucky Strike marketplace. Europe was more Americanized than ever, he told his mother-in-law. "Coca Cola sold all over Spain. Chewing gum too."[59]

What could a citizen do but place his faith in the market, where U. S. Steel rose fifty points to 257? Who could argue with a 300 percent return on his money in thirty-two days? Brother, take a ride on the Reading. Take a flier on futures. Have confidence in the confidence men running the pools. As the *Tribune* reported,

> Scare after scare in speculative circles has been followed, after a brief recession, by the resumption of an upward movement in the New York stock market that has shattered hopes that the advance had finally been checked. . . . stocks soaring to new heights is regarded as evidence that the Federal Reserve . . . authorities have lost control of the credit situation. While there is considerable unemployment in the big cities, the confidence in business is unimpaired.[60]

Elsewhere, confidence in various cultural establishments waned:

BOMB SET OFF IN BASEMENT OF REICHSTAG
National Social Group Blamed

"The national Socialist gang which has been terrorizing small towns in northern Germany for the past six months" was blamed for the explosion. Chalked on a lamppost they found "the Fascist swastika with the words 'Greater Germany Wake Up.' "[61] In Palestine, disagreement on who could do what at the Western Wall set loose an Arab effort to exterminate the Jews, who, they said, were trying to usurp a homeland in Palestine. The Grand Mufti of Jerusalem incited the bloodletting, which in two days killed thirty Jews and brought British bayonets to town restoring order.[62]

Meanwhile at various bookstores in Paris, London, and New York, the final issue of *Little Review* carried Hemingway's sarcastic "Valentine for Mr. Lee Wilson Dodd and Any of His Friends Who Want It," which concluded with some painful advice for those critics who found his characters too sordid:

> *If you do not like them lads*
> *One thing you can do*
> *Stick them up your —— lads*
> *My Valentine to you.*

In their opening remarks, editors Margaret Anderson and Jane Heap explained why they were closing down *Little Review*, where they first serialized Joyce's *Ulysses* when no one would publish it, closing the review whose contributors included almost every important author of the era. Anderson said, "Even the artist doesn't know what he is talking about. And I can no longer go on publishing a magazine in which no one really knows what he is talking about."[63] That Monday morning, September 2, 1929, the bull market peaked at prices not to be seen again for a quarter of a century. The *Titanic* is sinking, but no one has yet informed the passengers.

In early September, Ernest and Pauline grow weary following the cartels, two days with Sidney Franklin, the Jewish bullfighter from Brooklyn, just then a curiosity in Spain. More arena afternoons, more blood and sand, and afterward a warm hotel room with too much noise outside in the street, and, later, a meal of several courses not ending before midnight. A Madrid street thief picks Hemingway's pocket: passport, *carte d'identité*, *cartes gris* and *verte*, everything but his money. Then, discovering the name of his victim, the thief returns it all to him at his hotel. The summer is finished: time to leave.

On September 12, Ernest and Pauline drive into Hendaye, checking into the Ondarraitz Hotel, with, as advertised, a "splendid view of the sea and the mountains." Six days later, refreshed with late mornings and beach afternoons, they leave Spain to return to Paris. For two months he and Pauline have been each other's best and worst company: no Fitzgerald in their nights; no child in their days, little Patrick summering with his nursemaid in Compiègne. They've had fine afternoons at the bullring and lazy strolls on the Hendaye beach, but many tense, awkward moments as well, with apologies afterward. Unable to touch her husband in his dark times, Pauline has studied the rise and fall of his irregular moodiness, his quick-trigger anger. She and those who know him worry about these unexpected emotional explosions. At the end of the year, Paul Nelson advises him: "I want you to go see Dr. Fortier or Dr. Vannier before leaving. You need to stop burning up what you don't replace. Go ahead. Don't be a thick head. You owe it to us all. It's fine to be down low but you have to go up to go down."[64] This summer, for all its pleasures, has taken its toll: too many road miles, too much dust, too many bottles of red wine, too many heavy Spanish meals too late at night.

Waiting for the publication of his novel has also taken its toll. From Madrid, he sent nagging telegrams to Max Perkins, worrying about getting the text right and worrying about libel. "What did you do about the note in the front?" he asked. "That in the English edition reads—None of the characters in this book is a living person, nor are the units or military organizations mentioned actual units or organizations."[65] When he cannot lose himself in the moment, whenever he starts thinking about the book, he turns edgy, prickly, tense. By mail, Fitzgerald kids him about his "nervous bitterness," and Ernest tries to roll with the joke: "On re-reading your letter I find it *Is Not Snooty at all*. And old Hem wrong again. Evidently a prey to his nervous bitterness!"[66] But words cannot mask the fact that he is anxious about the worth of his new fiction. "That terrible mood of depression," he tells Fitzgerald, ". . . is known as The Artist's Reward. . . . Summer is a discouraging time to work—You don't feel death coming on the way it does in the fall when the boys really put pen to paper."[67] Whether or not this cheers Fitzgerald is unrecorded, but it describes only too well Hemingway's summer. Packed in their back-seat suitcases, along with ticket stubs, hotel bills, and *The History of the Crusades*, are fragments of fiction, stories ragged and unfinished. A year has passed since he completed the first draft of *A Farewell to Arms*, a year of revisions, letters, telegrams, and these unfinished stories. With little patience, the writer is waiting once again on his muse, who is somewhere else this summer.

When he is not writing well, he is liable to all manner of physical problems from a chronic strep throat to minor injuries. As this summer closes, his fingers are swollen from too much wine, he thinks; his pulled groin muscle still pains him; his injured foot, barely healed. When he was the Doctor's son, young Hemingway learned that injuries and sickness brought him attention; at twenty-nine, he buried his father, who from worry, fear, and deep melancholy put a bullet through his brain. Now, the Doctor's son does not seek injury out, but it finds him as if it were his brother. When he hurts, those about him are the first to know. Wife and mother, nurse and lover, Pauline answers his needs with an intensity he seldom experienced from Hadley. She ministers unto his pains and responds to his fantasies. On this day along the river, the wind ruffling her now blond, short-cropped hair, Pauline Hemingway is a woman accomplished: she has wed and bred with a man much desired, giving him a son and taking him to new levels of financial ease and sexual excitement. She shares his anxiety about *A Farewell to Arms*'s incipient reception:

The Sun Also Rises was Hadley's book; this one, while dedicated to Uncle Gus for all his gifts, is, nonetheless, her book.

———

October, Paris in the fall. Rain with a little weak sunlight in the late afternoons. Rain sometimes hard enough to short out the circuits and stall the evening metro. Rain to dull the donkey races and dampen the opium pipes at Harry Crosby's country place, Moulin d'Ermenonville. Rain to take the edge off of the Prix de l'Arc-de-Triomphe, where Peter Pickem (né Harold Stearns) picked Kantar to win. While Paris listened to it on the radio, Ernest and Pauline catch the beauty of the green track from Crosby's box; Harry and Caresse with their two whippets, Narcisse and Clytoris, watch Harry's money on Kantar to win disappear as did so many of his whims. Rain is not the friend of Harry Crosby, worshiper of the sun, whose black tattoo he wears etched between his shoulder blades. Harry, on his way to death, takes Kantar's loss quite well.[68]

———

On Saturday, October 19, panic swept through the American stock market like a cholera plague. Smart ones, like Bernard Baruch, had been quietly reducing their holdings for some time now, but the shoe salesman in Detroit and the cotton broker in Memphis held on as long they could. When the market closed, those on the margin were out of the game and with them ten to fifteen billion dollars of paper profits disappeared as easily as smoke. U.S. Steel closed at 209. That same Saturday, in the street window of Sylvia Beach's Shakespeare and Company, the newly minted *A Farewell to Arms* was on display. Published in New York on September 27, a copy of the book reached Hemingway on October 3. His reaction was immediate: Scribner's was trying to sabotage the book. The reclining woman on the dust jacket was "lousy and completely unattractive decadence, i.e. large misplaced breasts" which would only inflame a censor. His name was so small it could not easily be read, and the title was obscured. He, himself, could not find the book until a clerk pointed it out to him. "All I get out of this book," he said, "is disappointment." He never should have compromised on the language. "The fact that I do it on account of my family is no excuse and I know it. I'm a Professional Writer now—than which there isn't anything lower—I never thought I'd be it and I'm damned if I'm going to do it anymore." All he wants is one copy of the book, even bound, uncorrected galleys, with all the words exactly as he wrote them. That will take "some of the curse off it."

The letter rambles on in convoluted sentences that increasingly slope downhill to the right. Maybe the dust jacket wasn't all that bad. When he first saw *The Sun Also Rises*, his reaction was similar; that novel "looks very fine now—so maybe this one is fine too." There remains the question of "the alibi note." Since his contract holds him responsible for libel suits, the disclaimer, which Scribner's finally put in the second printing, was an insurance policy. Not that anyone could possibly sue, but maybe the Italians would. "Using so many Italian names there must be people with those names." No one in the book was real, and in 1917, the Red Cross hospital "did not exist—there is no possibility of any libel there."[69]

What finally eased the pain of parturition were the book sales. On October 15, Perkins, in answer to Hemingway's letter and telegram asking about sales, wired his worried author that the first printing of thirty thousand copies was sold out and two more printings of ten thousand copies each had been run. "Prospects excellent."[70] On the heels of the telegram, Max wrote Ernest, telling him there were two $3,000 checks in the mail as well as good reviews. He tried to explain "the line of thought that led to the present design" of the dust jacket: the designer was the best in the business; the office was nervous about too much War on the cover. "We wanted no helmets or artillery." What Max was really worried about were the literary wolves ready to snap up a young, hot commodity like Ernest. He was sure, he said, that Ernest would come to him before making a publishing change. Scribner's would go to any length to keep its prize author happy, but Max "did not want anything personal ever to hold you back from it. . . . if you get to feel dissatisfied and thought we could not rectify the trouble, I wouldn't want you to be held back just because I was such a wonder as a Tarpon Fisherman."[71]

On Sunday the Paris *Tribune* review calls *A Farewell to Arms* "technically and stylistically the most interesting novel of the year . . . a blossoming of a most unusual genius." The story was "brutal . . . awesome . . . terrific . . . vulgar . . . beautiful."[72] The Paris reviewer's enthusiasm was redoubled by the New York critics. The day after its publication, the *New York Sun* said parts of the novel were "magnificently done . . . the finest thing Hemingway has yet done."[73] Malcolm Cowley found "a new tenderness" in the story which he called "the most important book" Hemingway had written.[74] *The New Yorker* loved it; *Saturday Review* gushed; *The Nation* said, "It is a real occasion for Patriotic rejoicing."[75] Of course, each reviewer found some flaw, something overdone, underwritten, or undeveloped. For one it was too much dialogue and not enough scenery; for another it was too much detachment and not enough emotion. Some thought it less than *The Sun Also Rises*; others thought it brighter, as if the two books were comparable.

The *Tribune* review, which started so well, could not let the novel go without saying:

> *Ernest Hemingway is the direct blossoming of Gertrude Stein's art. Whether he consciously was influenced by her no one, of course, can say. But he does in "A Farewell to Arms," what Gertrude Stein did in "Three Lives," except that he does it in a longer, more complicated medium and with more certain power. There are whole pages in the new book which might have been written by Gertrude Stein herself, except that, even in their most tortuous intricacies, the reader is perfectly clear about what Mr. Hemingway is saying and why he is saying it that way.*[76]

Who invented young Hemingway? I did, said Ezra, with my blue pencil. Oh, but someone was following me who was always following, said Gertrude, and it certainly looked like Ernest. No, no, wheezed Ford, it was I who set him the proper example, gave him the lesson of the word exact. There would be no end to the question

of influence; he could see that now, but the Gertrude Stein attribu-
tions were irksome. Yes, he had gone to her early for writing lessons,
studied her technique, written his imitations and his parodies. And,
yes, some of what he learned was still apparent, but he knew this
book was so far beyond Gertrude's range that comparisons were
almost funny.

The next evening, it was Gertrude herself whom he literally
bumped into at close, public quarters, where both were polite. His
divorce from Hadley two years earlier also marked the end of his regular afternoons at the Stein-Toklas apartment on rue de Fleurus.
Gertrude and Alice, godmothers to Hemingway's first son, were hurt
by his changing partners; Alice, who never approved of Hemingway,
used the occasion to drive the wedge between the two writers. From
the beginning, Alice told Lovey, as she called Gertrude, that Ernest
was crude, vulgar, and less than virile, a rotten pupil "who never got
past the second lesson." And Gertrude would tell Pussy, as she called
Alice, that it did not matter.[77] That was when he was so attentive,
almost like a courting lover. When those flowers faded, so did
Gertrude's enthusiasm, and Alice ruled. Alice almost always ruled.

On Tuesday morning, Gertrude's note arrived at rue Férou, asking
Hemingway to bring Scott Fitzgerald and Allen Tate to an evening at
her apartment, an invitation which implicitly invited Ernest without
having to say it. He rattled off a note to Fitzgerald, explaining the invitation. "She claims you are the one of all us guys with the most talent,
etc. and wants to see you again."[78] Of course, Gertrude was perfectly
capable of inviting Fitzgerald without benefit of Ernest's help. Scott,
who was Alice's delight, was no stranger to rue du Fleurus, having visited there with and without Ernest several times. Figuring that it was
better to enter the Gorgon's lair with plenty of support, he rounded up
the Fitzgeralds, Ford Madox Ford, John Bishop and his wife, Allen
Tate, and Caroline Gordon to accompany himself and Pauline.[79] If
Hemingway suspected that he was being set up for a public embarrassment, he was not worried. In his pocket he had an invitation from
The Bookman to write, for $200, a "tribute" to Gertrude.[80]

On Wednesday evening, the Hemingways and their accompaniment are met at the door by Alice, the tiny gatekeeper who looks like a gypsy, questions everyone, and forgets nothing. Ushered past mirror and umbrella stand, they move through the studio salon filled with heavy Spanish furniture to the small dais where Gertrude Stein is speaking to other guests. Chinese tea and American cake wait in the back room beside cups and plates as if the century has not yet turned. Then walls of paintings appear, slowly in the lamplight, slower in the candlelight—Braque, Gris, Matisse, Picasso—as closely packed as family photographs. The focal point is a nude girl holding a basket of red flowers, her hair black as pitch, her body dead white, beneath her feet Picasso's signature. Gertrude, seated beneath Picasso's portrait of her that she has come to resemble, her hair now more shortly cropped than Ernest's, begins to laugh infectiously at someone's remark, laughter rolling down the scale until it seems to shake the room.[81]

Ernest, on his best behavior, joins the men circled around Gertrude, who is lecturing on American literature. Emerson, she says, was the first American genius moving toward the elimination of subject matter. Subject matter is European and passé. Hawthorne was impossible, too European. Whitman and Dickinson had their moments, but Henry James, even if he was too European, was the next step forward after Emerson, moving away from experience and toward abstraction. Ford, she says, looking him straight in the eye, will never count at all. This literary genealogy, of course, led straight to Gertrude Stein, who is the climax of American genius.[82]

During the tea and cakes, Hemingway does not take exception when Gertrude chooses to praise Scott to him, does not point out that Scott's long-awaited novel looks to be even longer in its awaiting. She says she likes A Farewell to Arms, but whenever he begins to remember rather than invent, the book is flawed. He does not ask her which parts she thinks he was remembering. Scott, walking up in the middle of their conversation, misunderstands when Stein tells him that he and Ernest burn with unequal flames. Fitzgerald, who is overly sensitive to the two novels Hemingway has written while he has not finished one, is hurt by what he takes to be a slight to his talent. Nothing Hemingway can tell him as they walk homeward can wash the bad taste away. Outside it is a warm October evening. A passing rain has left the air clear and fresh. As the young visitors walk in small groups back toward the Luxembourg, Fitzgerald is somewhat ahead of Allen Tate, who hears Scott repeating to himself, "I have seen Shelley plain."[83]

The next morning Scott's note arrives quite early, asking if Ernest was annoyed by his, Scott's, remarks. (He wants reassurance; he wants Ernest to like him truly, but somehow he always manages to create a scene.) Gertrude, he says, thinks that Hemingway is the superior writer. In what has become an emotionally expensive friendship, Ernest once more plays the older brother. What Scott took for a slight, Ernest tells him, was a Stein compliment; she has never had anything but praise for Scott. She was trying to say that he, Ernest, had the smaller talent, had to work harder for his results. Comparisons and talk of superiority are all "horseshit." Scott is "touchy" because his novel is not finished. Ernest understands and does not mind. Writers, he tells Scott, "are all in the same boat. Competition within that boat—which is headed toward death—is as silly as deck sports are."[84]

Six hours later in New York City, someone noticed that water was pouring into the hold of the good ship Wall Street:

GREATEST OF ALL STOCK
MARKET CRASHES WIPES OUT
BILLIONS IN SELLING HYSTERIA

It came today—the supreme crash in the stock market that the financial Jeremiahs predicted last year when the Babylon of paper prosperity was soaring to undreamed heights.

It came with a vengeance, the long delayed reckoning, and it surpassed anything that the most gloomy had predicted.[85]

New York bankers, pooling their money to shore up the damage, were barely able to stop the ship from going down. President Hoover announced that the business of the nation was sound, that conspicuous consumption was a healthy sign. U.S. Steel rode out that day's panic, closing at 204.[86] On Friday the market rallied as professionals picked over the remains, looking for bargains. Bernard Baruch bought 5,500 shares of American Smelting. The following Tuesday even Baruch abandoned ship, selling when he could find a buyer as the market dropped into an abyss without apparent bottom. In Paris, Americans, who arrived secure in their paper profits, were jamming the steamship lines seeking cheap passage home. U.S. Steel closed that day at 174, an offer with no takers. "I hope to Christ you weren't caught in the market," Hemingway wrote to Max Perkins on the last day of the month. Like most Americans, Ernest thought the "slump" momentary; by election time in 1932, Hoover would have brought the economy back. Meanwhile, in New York at the Hotel Pennsylvania, George Olsen was singing a new lyric, "Happy Days Are Here Again," to a less than enthusiastic audience.[87]

———

Berlin, November 15. After the six-day bike races and negotiations with Rowohlt for serializing *A Farewell to Arms* in German, he stops at Alfred Flechtheim's gallery on Konigsallee, where he is stunned once more by a small Klee watercolor, its disturbing face and its outrageous price. He makes a down payment in marks, the remainder to be paid at Flecthheim's Galerie Simon in Paris. The Mussolini-like face, under construction, two tiny men with baskets climbing ladders across its surface, is an unlovely but accurate metaphor: all across Europe tyrants are rising.[88]

———

On the stuffy night train to Berlin, Ernest could not let go of his letter to Max without scrawling across the back of the last page: "Remember O[wen] W[ister] et al wanting me to tone down or cut out some of the last chapter? That's why they're reading the damn book. It's no fun for me on acct. of the blanks. Now I can never say shit in a book. Precedent. When you make your own precedent once you make the wrong precedent you're just as badly stuck with it. It takes away from the interest in writing fiction."[89]

By the end of the summer he began signing his letters "E. Cantwork Hemingstein," which was not entirely true. He finished a made-to-order essay on bullfighting for the newly formed *Fortune* magazine, where Archie MacLeish was now working. Picking up $2,000 while practicing for his book on Spain was a safe thing to do, offending nobody. He was working now on an introduction that Edward Titus, a Left Bank bookseller and sometime publisher, asked for the English translation of *Kiki's Memoirs*. Hemingway wrote that the era of Montparnasse was "definitely marked as closed when she, Kiki, published this book. . . . although nobody knows when they start everybody is pretty sure when they are over and when, in one year, Kiki became monumental and Montparnasse became rich, prosperous, brightly lighted, dancinged, shredded-wheated, grape-nuts-ed or grapenutted . . . and they sold caviar at the Dôme, well, the Era for what it was worth, and personally I don't think it was worth much, was over."[90] He never thought much of the Montpar-nasse crowd of talkers who never got around to writing or painting what they talked about so well, so late, so long. As for "rich, prosper-ous, brightly lighted," who but Ernest and Pauline fit that farewell.

Edward Titus was also responsible for a story that Ernest was writ-ing, a story *Scribner's Magazine* would never publish. Earlier in the fall, Titus, who had resuscitated Ernest Walsh's defunct periodical, *This Quarter*, challenged bisexual and infamous gossip Robert McAl-mon and recently arrived Canadian writer Morley Callaghan to a lit-erary contest: each was to write a story about two homosexuals. McAlmon, married to a lesbian, defaulted; Callaghan, a protégé of Hemingway's, wrote "Now That April's Here," in which a male homo-sexual leaves his lover for a woman. Without formally becoming part of the challenge match, Hemingway was working on a story in which a writer's female lover leaves him for another woman, a story he called "The Sea Change."[91] It was a very quiet story without offending words and almost no action, a strange story rich in understatement.

———

Christmas Eve, Montana-Vermala, Switzerland. The Palace Hotel for consumptives—a pale stone building with many balconies fac-ing east to catch the morning sun. Inside the Murphys' parlor there are white fur rugs on the floor, several chairs, a spirit lamp heating wine seasoned with cinnamon and lemons. On a low table sits a wind-up phonograph, but there is no music playing.

———

From the balcony, looking out over the frozen valley of the Rhône fifteen hundred feet below them, the guests can see snowfields glowing blue-white in the moonlight. Wrapped in heavy coats and muffled against the constant chill, those in the room speak in whispers. Ernest and Pauline Hemingway, Pauline's sister, Virginia Pfeiffer, Scott and Zelda Fitzgerald, John and Katy Dos Passos, Dorothy Parker, and Donald Ogden Stewart have gathered to support Gerald and Sara Murphy in the attempt to save their oldest son, Patrick, who has contracted the frequently incurable tuberculosis. These are the Murphys whose Villa America at Antibes summered so many of the beautiful people during the Twenties: Cole Porter, Pablo Picasso, the Fitzgeralds, and the Hemingways. Gerald collaborated with Porter on a comic opera, studied with Fernand Leger, and in his own Paris studio painted beautifully flattened consumer products on large canvases. Sara organized and cared for her brood and all who visited, providing meals for the hungry and a shoulder for the weepers. These two have never before encountered an obstacle their money or their intelligence could not overcome. Now they face their son's illness with the same diligence and good humor with which they earlier planned beach parties.

The Murphys occupy six rooms, having brought themselves to the mountain with their three children, maid and chauffeur, an automobile, three dogs, eleven trunks, and seventeen suitcases, not to mention accouterments purchased locally. Each evening they and their old friends assemble to drink quiet gluhwein toasts while Patrick sleeps in the adjoining room, his infected lung collapsed by gas injections.[92] Turning to Sara, Scott says, "I don't suppose you have ever known despair?" Sara turns away, too angry to answer and too polite to show it.[93] No matter how charming Gerald and Sara appear, they cannot completely mask their distracted hearts, nor can their chilled guests evade the pall that fills the room. Of the four novelists and two humorists in the room, not one of them will ever write publicly about that evening or any other in the Palace Hotel, not even Fitzgerald, who has appropriated Sara and Gerald as characters for his novel in progress.

Two weeks earlier, in a borrowed New York City studio, the compulsive Harry Crosby lay down with a small pistol beside a consenting lover, whom he shot before putting a bullet into his own brain. Two days later, Archie MacLeish, after standing night vigil over Harry's body, wrote, "Recklessness and freedom of soul are dangerous things and those who condemn them condemn them with reason. As those who love them suffer for them. But without those fires lighted sometimes in the world it would be a dark and hopeless place."[94]

Chapter Two

1930

THE ARTIST'S REWARD

Key West, Cooke City, and Billings

S EVENTEEN UNPLEASANT DAYS at sea in a small
ship, heaving and rolling through heavy swells, bring the
Hemingways finally to freezing New York long enough to visit
Ada MacLeish in the hospital, Max Perkins in his office, Henry
Strater in his painter's studio, and one or two lawyers for good measure.[1] New York was full of literary gossip, which Ernest loved, and
Max, laconic as ever, tried to ignore. With the pale blue eyes of a
dreamer, his hat ever present indoors and out, its brim set back to
amplify conversation for his poor hearing, Max Perkins was an
unlikely man to edit Ernest Hemingway. In fact, he did little editing,
which is why they got along as well as they did. Instead he was
Ernest's corporate protector, confidant, banker, and private book
buyer. When an advance was needed, Max signed the deposit slip;
when Ernest raged against the realities of commerce, Max always
responded in a lower register. With his inability to spell or punctuate

correctly, Max seemed ill suited to his trade, but his passion for literature and his uncanny ability to bond with his authors made him the perfect editor for Hemingway. During this New York visit, Hemingway needed Max's help, but not with literary matters. With a loan from Uncle Gus and royalties from the first sixty thousand copies of *A Farewell to Arms*, Ernest established a trust fund for his mother, who once berated him for having overdrawn his emotional bank account with her.

At every turn in the city, someone wants a piece of him, for Ernest Hemingway is now a considerable property. The *New York Times Book Review* carried Scribner's block advertisement featuring *A Farewell to Arms* and Tom Wolfe's *Look Homeward, Angel*. Hemingway's novel, the ad said, "should have had a publishing season to itself. . . . It is so great a book that praise of it sounds like empty babbling." Despite the Wall Street panic, sales of the novel passed eighty thousand copies before Hemingway arrived.[2] Ernest's sometime literary agent, Paul Reynolds, is negotiating the theater version of the novel with the lawyer of playwright Lawrence Stallings and the lawyer of the producer Al Woods. This is the new country, the artist's reward, all quite flattering but not without its potential loss of freedom. With editor, publisher, lawyer, agent, wives and children, mother and siblings dependent upon his writing, he can feel the trap of responsibility beginning to close around him. Part of him still admires the fine homes and families of Oak Park, seeks the responsibility, wants to be called "Papa," the provider of largess, the giver of names, the man in the house. The other side of him is never easy in any place called home.

Two days in and out of New York with the *Bourdannais*, stopping only a day in Havana, they arrive finally in Key West on February 2.[3] While they and Henrietta Lechuer, Patrick's French nanny, move luggage into a rented frame house on Pearl Street, the sun is setting, and lights are coming on in kitchen windows. At Joe Russell's place near the waterfront, sailors are lining up at the bar; on Division Street, a Jesuit priest is patiently holding his fast in order to say evening Mass; on Amelia Street, the last cockfight is over and bets are being paid off. Black washerwomen leaving the Casa Marina Hotel, grizzled fishermen drinking cold beer at the Thompson Ice-house, children playing capture-the-flag in the Bayview park, grandfathers gathering at the Cuban consulate for dominoes, and sailors from the battleship *Maine* resting in the graveyard at the foot of Pauline Street: it is an ordinary evening, warm and without incident, in Key West. On Pearl Street, Ernest and Pauline sort out their scant belongings stored with the Thompsons a year earlier. Paris, Key West, Piggott, Kansas City, Sheridan, Chicago, Key West, Paris, Spain, Paris, Switzerland, Paris, Key West: for two years, they have not lived under one roof longer than a month or two at a time. Without knowing it, they have come to their *querencia*, that part of the ring where the bull feels secure. It is not home, but it feels like it.

Ernest has come to Key West to write and fish, in that order, but somehow it does not work out as imagined. Despite her new trust fund, his mother in Oak Park is not without needs: car insurance, new gutters, and taxes; his sister, Carol, needs tuition help at Rollins College. And when, his mother wants to know, when would she be told if her oil paintings would be in the Paris Spring Salon? Did he plan to have anyone let him know? "Drat her," said Hadley, his first wife, who was left with the paintings. "Not for me and the pictures but for you and everything. Thank God you are removed from her these days."[4] Easier to say than do: his mother, he found, was always with him. Call her a bitch as he might, Grace Hall Hemingway, former voice teacher, contralto, and now self-taught painter, was a force always in his life, and he was his mother's son.

At the same time, New England painter and old friend Waldo Peirce, in Paris settling a divorce from his wife Ivy, sent his very young, maybe too young, wife-to-be, Alzira, to Key West with money (but not enough money) to await his now delayed appearance. In a village so small, her unwed pregnancy became public information as soon as she went to the local doctor. Having lent her a little money and then more money, Ernest was trying to be helpful, but if Waldo was thinking of living with his Alzira out of wedlock in Key West, Ernest had to say,

What's simple as hell in Paris is complicated as same in U.S.A. or K.K.K. . . . if you're planning to stay somewhere and have a baby K.W. is too small a place now that you . . . are known by so many local merchants. . . . Guys like you and me that live and have lived around and don't give a damn what people say about anything so long as the law aint invoked are one thing and merchants that have to live on in a town and have people say to them "so your swell friends just turned out to be a bunch of scandalous bastards" are another.[5]

The "merchants" referred to were Charles and Lorine Thompson, but the voice speaking was from Oak Park; without yet admitting it to himself, Hemingway, too, was about to become a "local merchant."

To Peirce, he claimed Key West was no longer a place to work, but it was largely because of his own invitations to friends that his writing was disrupted. Mike Strater, Max Perkins, Pat Morgan, John Herrmann and Josephine Herbst, John and Katy Dos Passos, Archibald and Ada MacLeish all came down from New York. John and Josie were there on their own initiative, but the others came at Hemingway's calling: it is never enough to be in a good place without a gang of admirers to instruct. The Over Sea Hotel, at a dollar a night, housed a steady flow of Hemingway customers, who are like his summer people at Walloon Lake, like his Paris people at Pamplona, like the winter people on Swiss ski slopes. To Charles and Lorine Thompson, trapped in Key West by the Thompson name and its attendant responsibilities—icehouse, hardware and chandlery, fish—the Hemingways are liberators who open doors to the wide world. Charles plays younger brother to Ernest while Lorine becomes Pauline's closest friend. The Hemingways need only ask, for no task is inconvenient for the Thompsons, and the Hemingways do regularly ask. In Key West, whose population has dwindled almost by half in a ten-year period and where the twelve thousand who remain are largely down on their luck, the Hemingways and their entourage are an unexpected windfall.

As usual, Hemingway does nothing by halves. While making enormous emotional demands upon those around him, he brings to them his intensity. Waldo Peirce said that Hemingway "could make a fisherman for a day out of anyone." He was "the best host and sportsman and the most generous, always giving first chance to the visiting firemen and a more than even cut of Fundador [brandy]."[6] No visitor is left untouched. Archie MacLeish, referring to Ernest's impact on his poetry, said:

> *Every time I see you . . . I get a new revelation from god about the whole business—about why it's worth while to play as well as you can play to an empty house and an old gentleman in the last row. . . . somehow you make it all right for me to go on no matter how empty they make it on my side of the street. Also, goddam it, I like being with you. . . . As you saw I am no fisherman. But I got more out of those days on the water and my clumsy efforts at trolling than I've gotten out of anything in years. I can't get that day on the Gulf Stream out of my eyes.*[7]

Having hired Burge, a local fisherman, by the month for $130 to be his guide and paid another $125 a month for Burge's fishing boat, Ernest considers any day without fishing a day wasted. Add on the cost of liquor and gasoline, of food and rent, of loans to friends and family bills, and Hemingway's monthly expenditures, the jot and tittle of which he keeps exactly, mount up. In April he spent $1,200, which was only $100 less than the average 1930 income for full-time employees.[8] Given that his total earnings for 1929 were $18,416 with another $6,000 from Pauline's trust, the Hemingways were living and spending at a level far removed from his early Paris days or his earlier days in Oak Park.[9] He was, in fact, living even more intensely the life he once admired and sometimes envied of wealthier Oak Park families. In Key West—a village of peeling paint and outrageous flowering plants—with their small child, his French maid, and their seemingly endless flow of visitors, Ernest and Pauline were conspicuous among the usual winter visitors.

When the morning breeze picked up at sunrise, clearing out the night mosquitoes, Ernest began his Key West day at his writing tablet with pencil in hand. In May he finished the ending to "Wine of Wyoming," a curious marriage tale three-quarters written two years earlier. Low-key and oblique, the story contrasts husbands and wives, America and France, past and present against the background of prohibition. The Fontans are displaced French Catholics trying to live in Wyoming as if it were France. The narrator and his wife are summer people passing through a country that looks to them like Spain. It is a story of lost amenities, displaced customs, echoing Villon's rhetorical question "Where are the snows of yesteryear?" "The summer was ending," the narrator tells us, "but the new snow had not yet come to stay on the high mountains; there was only the old sun-melted snow and the ice, and from a long way away it shone very brightly."[10] American promises were always brightest from a distance. As Hemingway writes these words, morning heat is rising in the room. Soon he will begin to sweat.

To Waldo Peirce he writes, "My simple idea of coming to Key West to write and see no one and fish when through writing appeals to no one."[11] By May 20, despite complaints about Paris intruders, despite the wonderful time-consuming run of high-leaping tarpon and a six-stitch cut on his writing hand from the Thompson punching bag, Ernest has completed seventy-four pages[12] on a book like no other he knew, a book without models or comparisons, a book in several voices, many tenses, and doubling points of view. About many things—the rearing, fighting, and demise of bulls, a history of bullfighters, an explanation of their art, a guidebook to Spain, a discussion of writers and their craft, of critics and their shortcomings, a book of landscapes with and without figures, a philosophy of life in the lap of death, a Spanish food and wine digest—it is a discursive book of huge risks which no publisher would have encouraged had the author not been Ernest Hemingway. But he is Ernest Hemingway, and it is a book of natural and unnatural history which he must write to redeem himself from his self-phrased epithet: *Professional Writer, of which there is nothing lower.* Refusing to be merely a fiction writer, he insists here and later that he is a man of letters. Eventually he will call this book *Death in the Afternoon*.

As the Hemingways made plans to escape from the tropical heat to the high country of the west, Ernest wrote Uncle Gus the benefactor, explaining what sort of a book he was writing and what he needed for reference. Gus immediately sent a shopping list to his Hudnut man in Barcelona, advising him that "Mr. Hemingway is very anxious to get the books." All he needed were subscriptions to four bullfight periodicals, bound back issues of four other periodicals, and a few crucial histories of tauromachia. The next day, worried that the mail would take too long, Uncle Gus telegraphed his Barcelona man the list of books.[13] On June 7, Ernest put Pauline, Patrick, and Henrietta on the train to Jacksonville to connect for Piggott, and a week later, he stepped onto the Havana Special returning to New York to meet his five-year-old son, John Hadley Nicanor Hemingway, arriving from France.[14]

After checking into the Brevoort Hotel off Washington Square, Ernest has four days to take care of business. At the Scribner's offices on Fifth Avenue, Hemingway convinces Max Perkins that they should reissue his 1925 book, *In Our Time*, as it was written and meant to be read. To avoid having the book banned, Boni & Liveright, the original publishers, made Ernest take out the opening story, "Up in Michigan," and forced him to make changes to "Mr. and Mrs. Elliot." If they can strike a deal with Horace Liveright about the publishing rights, Ernest will provide revised copy for those two stories and perhaps write an introduction. Despite the depressed state of publishing and stiff competition from Doubleday with its "Dollar Books," reissuing was a sound idea, for fewer than fifteen hundred copies of the book were printed earlier. Max agrees without having seen either of the two censored stories; a hotter version of *In Our Time* would be good business, keeping the Hemingway market primed for his new book, which Max hopes to publish within a year, a book he has not seen and about which Hemingway is not forthcoming. Max may think it is a novel.

Hemingway also does some quick business with Louis Cohn, book dealer and sometime publisher, who wants to compile a bibli-

1930: THE ARTIST'S REWARD

ography of Ernest's work to date. It will be a limited edition (five hundred copies) with a stiff price tag ($6). In April, Ernest said he might write an introduction for $350 "so long as I get it in cash and whenever I want it."[15] Now in June, he is having second thoughts. To become involved with limited editions or bibliographies of his own work, he tells Cohn, will jeopardize his artistic integrity, without which the game is not worth the play. He simply cannot write an introduction or sign any more books, but maybe Edmund Wilson or Allen Tate, both of whom he trusts, would write one.[16] To temper his response, he says he will provide a page of unpublished manuscript which could be reproduced.

On Saturday, June 21, the *Lafayette* arrives two days early, delivering Jinny Pfeiffer and Ernest's son, nicknamed Bumby. The next evening, father and son are once again riding the train west, getting off in Cincinnati, where Ernest picks up his Ford roadster, which friends from Key West have ferried that far, and drives on toward St. Louis and finally Piggott, Arkansas. Stopping long enough to deposit some manuscripts in the Piggott bank, play son-in-law to Paul Pfeiffer's polite interest, and share a drink with Mother Pfeiffer, the Catholic center of the family, he walks dusty roads for morning exercise before the heat rises. It has been a dry, hot, early summer; cotton bolls are puny in the green fields, but he sees and counts the coveys of quail. Complaining to MacLeish of forty consecutive hot nights with little sleep, he is eager for the cool Wyoming mountains. "It will be fine in the mountains—need like hell to work too."[17]

Two days later, after leaving baby Patrick in Piggott with his grandparents and Aunt Jinny, Ernest, Pauline, and Bumby are off for Kansas City, where they stop with Ernest's cousins long enough for Dr. Guffey to say Pauline is well recovered from her cesarean delivery. When the journalist from the *Star* finds him, Ernest claims to be working on a new novel with bullfighting as the background.[18] After Kansas City, they disappear into the great American plains of corn, then wheat, then cattle, all languid under the summer sun, finally gaining altitude with the nights cooling. Making less than fifteen miles to the gallon at thirty to forty miles an hour top speed on two-lane roads, oiled or graveled, they bounce along, eye always out for the next filling station, a decent café, a likely tourist cabin for the night. They cross a sun-blistered Nebraska and drive into Wyoming's grass and cattleland—Casper, Salt Creek, Buffalo, Sheridan—looking for a place to write. But places that worked two summers before are now too civilized with eastern dudes who are charmed to meet an author. They move farther west up through Billings and into Yellowstone Park, through that wonderland and out the northeast corner, coming finally on a dirt road into Cooke City, Montana: end of the line; the only road in or out has grass growing between dusty ruts. Sometimes a load of whiskey on muleback comes over the Beartooth Pass from Red Lodge; sometimes, given a very good reason, a truck might make it southeast to Cody on rough ranch roads. But these few log cabins, frame houses, filling station, and general store are west of the mail, west of publishers, west of gossip, west of mothers, siblings, in-laws, west of almost everything. The Cosmopolitan Hotel, weather-beaten and largely empty, remembers better days. Surrounding this smattering of buildings, the Absaroka Range rises up like a rocky green and stone dream of mountains, with granite uplifts sheltering snow in the high crevices. In four weeks, by train and by car, Hemingway has traveled five thousand miles across the American landscape, arriving finally at this remote mining outpost on the edge of Yellowstone where there is no morning paper, no rail line, and no exit after the first snows fall.

———

L-Bar-T Ranch, July 13. Follow the ranch's station wagon east from town on a faintly etched road, crossing the Wyoming line and turning south along Clarks Fork with Pilot and Index peaks over the right shoulder, and then cross the river at the second ranch. The bridge of pine planks suspended on cables anchored to each side bucks, rattles, and sways beneath the car. Just beyond a smooth stone outcropping, the lodgepole barn and corrals with mustangs at rest, farther on the ranch house cum lodge with cabins fanned out above. Like every other building on the dude ranch, their double cabin—two bedrooms, one toilet, and a cold shower—is made of pine logs notched and fitted at the corners and caulked at the seams. Banked on the small porch, a pile of split wood is ready for the potbellied stove.[19]

———

For a month they disappear into the daily routine of the ranch: early breakfast in the lodge, writing all morning for Ernest, fishing on the river after lunch, early-evening supper in the lodge with Lawrence and Olive Nordquist attending to the several paying guests, and whiskey afterward in the heavy chairs around the fireplace. Situated at 6,800 feet on the floodplain of the Clarks Fork of the Yellowstone River, the ranch is sheltered by Squaw Peak rising to ten thousand feet behind it and the Beartooth Mountains at eleven thousand feet across the river. Along the Fork, creeks enter the flow, their names speaking of earlier days: Crazy Creek, Pilot Creek, Ghost and Beartooth creeks, Blacktail, Timber, and Hoodoo creeks. Here every turn and rise has its particular name, given to it by men and women now forgotten: Sugarloaf Mountain, Cathedral Cliffs, Painter Gulch, Beartooth Butte, Dead Indian Ranch. River and valley take their name from Lewis and Clark, whose expedition first brought eastern eyes to rest on this country whose richness exceeded all expectations.

Terrain maps, filled with detail, are Hemingway's travel companions, even in this newfound country where the geodetic survey is quite recent. Names of creeks, heights of mountains, distances between ranches, the direction of roads and rivers all matter to him. It is good to know where you are, where you have been, where you are going. It is even better to have some detail of it afterward: he records mileage driven, money paid, books read, and fish caught. He does not need a compass or a map to tell him the river runs east-southeast in front of the ranch. But afterward the map will be there to confirm memory and aid creation if he is writing. Having fished one steep canyon with gravel siding impossible to climb, he can read the map of a never-fished river canyon and understand it almost as well as the first. In his new fishing log, Ernest makes detailed notes on each day's catch, baits used, numbers taken, weights, and stream conditions. Rain or shine he fishes the river, horsing in the trout, netting small trout high out of the water without bending to meet them. His form is a little disappointing. When it rains, he notes how long it takes the river to clear. On his birthday, July 21, he and Pauline release fourteen and keep eighteen cutthroat trout. The next day, Pauline's birthday, returning from the river they see a fat black bear walking down the dirt road.[20]

On a marker tree beside One-Mile Creek where it passes a few hundred yards above the Hemingways' cabin, a bear's claw marks reach higher than a man's head. In mid-August, according to Hemingway's hunting log, a local rancher needed help with a "large old male bear" who was killing cattle high up off Crandall Creek. How much help was needed may be questioned, but that was the excuse for outfitting Ernest for a bear hunt out of season. On August 17, well attended by Nordquist's cowhand, Ivan Wallace, Ernest rode the now familiar pack trail southeast along Squaw Creek to the Crandall Ranger Station. From there the North Fork trail rising into mountains narrows as it passes under Hunter's Peak and into a rugged forest of fir, whitebark pine, and spruce based on volcanic rock. The trail, becoming little more than an animal path, crosses Blacktail and Cow creeks before it drops down through switchbacks to the North Fork of Crandall's Creek. Here Ernest and the redheaded Ivan shoot the old horse they brought in for bait and leave it to "rise." That was on Sunday. By Wednesday morning, predators are feeding on the carcass; in that rare air at eight thousand feet, odors intensify and the heart pounds, but no bear shows. By Tuesday night, Ernest is back at the L-Bar-T, without a bear but still eager for the hunt. Friday morning, reoutfitted with fresh supplies, his new Springfield rifle, Zeiss field glasses, and a raincoat, he and three ranch hands set out again for the bear bait. Before they reach the ranger station, Ernest's horse bolts, lurching him through a pine thicket that lays open the left side of his face, blood dripping and the horse spooked. A bandage won't do. He needs stitches, and the closest doctor is fifty miles away in Cody. By midnight, having traveled the unspeakable dirt ranch road through countless gates in a car rented from the ranger, they are in Dr. Trueblood's office, where the veterinarian turned doctor sews up Hemingway's wound with six stitches, using a little whiskey taken internally as anesthetic. A white bandage now swaddles his jaw and the left side of his face. The resulting scar will add to his bulging forehead scar from the falling Paris skylight, the one on his finger from the Key West punching bag, and the scars on his rebuilt right knee and his right foot from the war.

Returning through the Wyoming night, they are back at the ranger station by morning. That evening at the horse bait, as the light is about to fail completely, with the brown bear in the telescopic sight of his new rifle, Ernest is letting out his breath slowly and squeezing the Springfield's trigger with an even pull, and then the bear falling in slow motion. A week later, on the same ripe bait, he kills a second bear. Ernest, camera-shy and proud, stands beside the huge black pelt stretched upon the cabin wall. Admirers stroke the glossy fur.[21] Nine years later he will remember Clarks Fork Valley with trout rising to dry flies, remember waking in the cold night with coyotes howling. "You could ride in the morning, or sit in front of the cabin, lazy in the sun, and look across the valley where the hay was cut so the meadows were cropped brown and smooth to line of quaking aspens along the river, now turning yellow in the fall." The years blend together into one year with all the good days combined: "all the hunting and all the fishing and the riding in the summer sun and the dust of the pack-train, the silent riding in the hills in the sharp cold of fall going up after the cattle on the high range, finding them wild as deer and as quiet, only bawling noisily when they were all herded together being forced along down into the lower country."[22]

Evenly spaced along the Fork are ranches similar to Nordquist's, most of which were homesteaded at 320 or 640 acres: not enough land to raise cattle and too far from the market if you did. Some raised horses, but with little profit. Others, like Nordquist, caught hold of the dude-ranch craze bringing soft-seated East Coast families west for summer vacations. By putting on a little show for the summer dudes and picking up some hunters in the fall, a man could get by. Give the guests an evening cookout on the trail, ponies tethered and campfire smoking, or a makeshift rodeo in the high meadow where bangtails buck the boys about faster than a dude's camera can pan the field.[23]

Rising up under blankets to the odor of pine smoke and frying bacon, the air cool and resinous, Pauline standing there with her hands in her hip pockets, ready for whatever, Ernest watches the wranglers get dudes saddled up for the morning run, smells horse piss in the straw. This is country without a phone or electricity where the mail comes once a week, and no one particularly cares one way or another if Ernest spends his mornings writing, afternoons fishing, evenings reading. His contemplative and his active life are jammed together so tightly that only minutes separate them. By the end of July he is talking about having his bullfight book finished before the November snows force him out. Brave self-promises on a difficult book. He takes time to write Louis Cohn, promising that as soon as his "book trunk" arrives he will send a page of manuscript for the Hemingway bibliography Cohn is putting to press. "Thank you so much for the offer of the Galsworthy Conrad," he tells Cohn, "but it is doubtless too valuable for you to give. I'll take the Scotch or Rye and let the first editions go." Then he adds, "nor heed the rumble of the distant drums."[24]

The Nordquist ranch provides the conditions in which he works best and steadily, for he prefers to write in transient places, close to the natural world. *The Sun Also Rises* was written on the road in Spain, following the bullfights; *A Farewell to Arms* was drafted under transatlantic and transcontinental circumstances. At Nordquist's, five minutes after setting down his pencil he can be on a horse, or within twenty minutes his line is in the water. He arrived at the ranch with seventy-four pages of manuscript drafted on a book without a title and with problems to solve about the new edition of *In Our Time*. A month later he tells Max Perkins he is writing six days out of seven and has forty thousand words done, roughly another fifty pages of manuscript. By early September he is on page 174 or about sixty thousand words.[25] Max wants new material added to *In Our Time*, but Ernest is uncomfortable jazzing up an old book with new stories written in a different manner. Nor does he want Max

Perkins rearranging the stories or grouping together all the vignettes which divide the stories: "Max *please believe me* that those chapters are where they belong."[26] However, his earliest story, which he was forced to cut out of the 1925 version of the book—"Up in Michigan," a brutal seduction story told from the woman's point of view—he tries to revise, but the scene with the drunken Jim Gilmore forcing himself on Liz Coates and her being left with the pain and the ignorance becomes less readable the more he fiddles with it. Finally he gives up, telling Perkins, "I know you will not publish it with the last part entire and if any of that is out there is no story." He has promised Max to have mailed the book with corrections, including the original, uncensored version of "Mr. and Mrs. Elliot" and "with or without a couple of short pieces of the same period depending on how these seem in the book between now and then."

But he cannot write the preface Max wants for the collection of short stories. "I am too busy," he said, "too disinterested, too proud or too stupid or whatever you want to call it to write one for it." Determined to resist as much of the whoring expected of "Professional Writers" as he can, Hemingway suggested Edmund Wilson for the job.[27] Looking for other material from the 1922–25 period which might honestly meld into *In Our Time*, Hemingway remembers "The Death of the Standard Oil Man," an unpublished story set during the Greco-Turkish War of 1922. But in August when his "book trunk" arrives from Piggott, the manuscript is not there. Instead he finds a story about the Greeks at Smyrna in 1922 when the Turks were about to burn that town, a story written in late 1926.[28] Its doubled narration—a reporter telling the reader what a British officer at Smyrna said—pulls the reader quickly through the page into the fiction. Ernest, who was never in Smyrna, knew reporters who saw and wrote of the Greeks breaking "the legs of the baggage and transport animals" and shoving them "off the quay into the shallow water."[29] It was a strong piece with refugees jammed on the quay and Greek mothers refusing to give up dead babies and "nice" debris floating in the water. It fit with the other stories like the Elliots trying but unable to have a baby, and the bloody cesarean operation at the

Indian camp, war sketches with the dead in the street, and Nick having to return to the States because of his pregnant wife, the punchy boxer that night by the rail line, and Nick ending up after the war not quite right on Big Two-Hearted River.

On September 3, Hemingway mailed Perkins a corrected copy of *In Our Time*, including a somewhat sanitized version of "Mr. and Mrs. Elliot" and the Symrna sketch, which he agreed to call "Introduction by the Author," which would follow the introduction he hoped Edmund Wilson would write because someone had to explain that this was an early book. His accompanying letter was a confusion of disclaimers: reissuing the book was Scribner's idea, not his, although it was a good book, but should not be called a "new" book; however, they could say it had new material, yet giving the readers an old book now would probably hurt sales of his bullfight book to follow (174 pages written). And Scribner's better check for libel, because they published this book at their own risk; he would give no guarantees against lawsuits. Sick of the interruptions caused by this reprint of *In Our Time*, he would take days to get back into the bullfight book.[30]

He was also working on an experimental story told in two voices and several parts, a story not unlike the bullfight book. The story began with a naturalist commenting, tongue in cheek, on the work of earlier observers of flora and fauna, complaining that war dead were ignored by natural historians. "Can we not hope to furnish the reader with a few rational and interesting facts about the dead?" he asked. The second paragraph, which he lifted word for word from Bishop Stanley's *A Familiar History of Birds* (1881), told of Mungo Park, on the brink of death in the African desert, finding God's fingerprints in a small moss-flower. Hemingway's naturalist asks, "Can any branch of Natural History be studied without increasing that faith, love and hope which we also, every one of us, need in our journey through the wilderness of life? Let us see what inspiration we may derive from the dead."[31]

Similar in theme to the vignette of the refugees on the Smyrna quay, which it references, but written in a different style, "A Natural

History of the Dead" was an experiment in both structure and voice. The first half developed the premise; the second half illustrated the premise with an example. The narrator, a veteran out of the last war, speaks in a sardonic voice and with the detachment of a natural historian observing the dead bodies on the Italian front of 1918. Bodies left unburied go from "white to yellow, to yellow-green, to black." Left long enough in the sun, "the flesh comes to resemble coal tar," and swells inordinately, straining at the confining uniform. Everywhere there is paper of the dead blowing in the wind. And the smell of the unburied dead, mixed with the lingering odor of mustard gas, one cannot forget.

Nothing the narrator has seen gives him much cause to rejoice in God's presence in the natural world. Soldiers die like animals, some from wounds seemingly slight but deep enough to serve. Others "die like cats: a skull broken in and iron in the brain, they lie alive two days like cats that crawl into the coal bin with the bullet in the brain and will not die until you have cut off their heads." This observation leads him to an extended illustration: a mountain field station with wounded bodies and an overworked doctor. The dead are carried into a cold-storage cave; one of the badly wounded, "whose head was broken as a flower pot may be broken" and who was presumed dead, lies in the dark, moaning, like the cat refusing to die. Under pressure of the wounded crowding the station, the doctor refuses to move the dying man out of the cave, having no way of making his suffering less nor the faintest hope of saving his life. No, he will not give him an overdose of morphine, he tells a wounded artillery officer. He has little enough to operate with now. The officer can shoot the man if he wishes. Doctor and patient trade insults until the artilleryman loses all composure. "Fuck yourself," he said. "Fuck yourself. Fuck your mother. Fuck your sister. . . ." At which point the doctor throws iodine into his eyes, disarms him, and has him restrained. Meanwhile the moaning man in the cave of the dead has become permanently quiet. "A dispute about nothing," the doctor calls it.[32]

The story was not finished on September 13, when Ernest and Pauline, preparatory to her going east with Bumby, signed new wills.

His money went to Pauline, Patrick, and John, in that order. If they were dead, the estate was payable in equal shares to his first wife, Hadley, and his sister-in-law, Jinny Pfeiffer. His Italian war medals should go first to John and then to Hadley. The will did not mention Hadley's divorce settlement—all the income from *The Sun Also Rises*—nor did it mention what he expected her to do with the war medals.[33] Two days later in Billings, Pauline and Bumby boarded the Burlington train for Chicago and from there, connections to St. Louis. It was time for her stepson to return to his mother in Paris; Henrietta, their French nursemaid, would act as his traveling companion. That same day the fall hunting season opened, and Ernest's bullfight book was 188 pages of dense manuscript.[34] In two months at the ranch, he averaged about two pages a day. Over the next forty-five days, with only one fruitless hunt in the high mountains and customary afternoons of grouse shooting to take his mind off the book, Ernest completed another hundred pages of manuscript. He was close to the end: two more chapters and the appendix, he told Max.[35] Meanwhile, his public visibility was increasing dramatically: *A Farewell to Arms* was being translated into French and German; the Lawrence Stallings stage version of the novel was about to open on Broadway; and Paramount Pictures purchased the film rights to the novel for $80,000.[36]

November 1, Route 10 outside of Park City, Montana. Gently rising and falling as it follows the north bank of the Yellowstone out of sight in the dark, the two-lane road is empty except for a Ford roadster with two bearded men in the front seat and a third in the rumble seat. Hemingway drives. Next to him sits John Dos Passos, on his way to Billings to catch the night train east. Floyd Allington from Red Cloud is hunkered down in back. A diminished bottle of bourbon is shared against the cold, as the sun sets behind them and blue shadows go black. Fresh gravel laid down the day before is not yet properly rolled or settled, and the center line is not marked. With the lights of Laurel faint over the far hill, a car approaches, its lights bright; Hemingway, his night vision marred by a weak eye, blinks and moves the Ford as far right as seems safe. Someone is speaking, but with the noise of the engine and tires on gravel, it is difficult to hear.[37]

In the Saturday-night emergency room of St. Vincent Hospital, Dorothy Buller checks in for her night shift duties to find three strangers, two in pain, one of them seriously hurt. Bob Bass is telling someone how he helped pull the big fella from the overturned Ford out on the Livingston road and gave all three a ride into Billings. The Red Lodge cowboy, with a dislocated right shoulder and a few scratches, is taped up and sedated. The larger, darkly bearded man with the broken arm is being taken to x-ray. The third man, also bearded but unhurt, his glasses unbroken, wants to know if his friend's money belt is missing. Nurse Buller assures him that no one has touched anyone's money belt.[38]

On Sunday morning in Piggott, Arkansas, Pauline receives the telegram from Dos Passos telling her that Ernest is in the hospital injured. Packing quickly and putting her own problems on hold, she leaves Piggott Monday morning, reaching Billings on the Tuesday-evening train.[39] By this time Ernest is no longer in the three-person ward where he spent his first night. When Dr. Louis Allard, an orthopedic surgeon recognized nationally for his work on polio victims, discovered that his patient was Ernest Hemingway, he immediately moved him into a private fourth-floor room; when Pauline arrives, he moves him again, across the hall to 421, so that she can stay in the adjoining room. On Thursday, Dr. Allard operates to restructure the oblique spiral fracture three inches above Ernest's right elbow. Using kangaroo tendon to bind tight his bone work, the surgeon sews up his nine-inch incision and immobilizes Hemingway for three weeks to let the fracture heal properly.

That afternoon the *Billings Gazette* announces that Sinclair Lewis has won the Nobel Prize for literature, and off-year election results are being posted across the country. Democrats are close to breaking the Republican control in both houses of Congress, and Governor Franklin Roosevelt of New York is returned to Albany by a record plurality.[40] In steady, gnawing pain from the repaired fracture, Hemingway is not particularly interested in literary or political prizes. After the fifth day, the doctor takes him off the morphine, leaving him alone with the pain and his night thoughts.[41] For three weeks unable to move for fear of ruining his writing arm, he has plenty of time to think, too much time. He has been there before, badly wounded in the Milan hospital twelve years earlier, worrying then whether he might lose his leg, and sometimes now in the night he wonders which hospital he is in this time. He is, Pauline says, "pretty nervous and depressed from the pain and worry." Once again he is sleeping fitfully by day and lying awake in the night. Not even Pauline, with her seemingly inexhaustible capacity for tending to his needs, can stay on his schedule. Tall, stately Harriet O'Day, the special nurse assigned to him, provides the small bedside radio that, along with a little prohibition whiskey from his well-stocked bar, gets him through the nights.[42]

Three days after Hemingway's operation, two new patients, Martin Costello and Alec Youck, are moved into the ward across the hall from Hemingway's room. In the Surita Café, Costello and Youck had been shot by an unknown assailant. Youck, a Russian farm worker, was hit in the thigh, but not seriously. The *Gazette* said that Costello, a Mexican beet worker, might die from the bullet that passed through his stomach. The newspaper said:

> Two men . . . were arrested . . . Thomas Hernando, restaurant cook, and Joe Aglo, who lived in a room above the restaurant. A box of cartridges was found in Aglo's room. . . . Arriving at the café, [Constable] Thomas found Youck on the floor in a rear room. At the foot of the stairs . . . Thomas found Aglo and Hernando supporting Costello who was bleeding profusely. . . . Costello . . . refused to talk of the shooting. Officers recalled that three years ago when a bullet wounded the arm of a girl with whom he was walking and tore into his coat sleeve, he also refused at that time to name the person who fired the shot. . . . Joe Diaz, operator of the Surita café and the rooms above . . . said he knew nothing about any quarrel in which Costello

Being a doctor's son, he always exaggerates his illnesses and is quick to project the worst possible scenario—traits which sometimes lead those who know him well to underestimate the seriousness of his condition. For the nurses he can always joke, but when Archie MacLeish, alarmed by the accident, flies into Billings from New York to comfort Hemingway, a hazardous two-day trip on Northwest Airlines, Ernest is surly and suspicious, accusing his friend of coming only to be present at his death. Maybe it was a joke, but Archie does not think so. The next day, he is a different Ernest, the one who would never have said such a thing and who carries on, in fact, as if he had not. A month later, MacLeish gave Max Perkins his report on Hemingway:

> He suffered very real & unrelenting pain over a long time. I went out because I know how his imagination works when his health is concerned & because I thought any normal event such as the arrival of a friend might give him some kind of a date to hold on to. When I got there the pain was largely over & the wound beginning to heal. . . . I think all his friends can do is to keep him cheerful in idleness—a hell of a job. Poor Pauline.[50]

A friend of Max Perkins who was visiting while Archie was there found Hemingway "pale and shaky although cheerful. . . . We drank a couple of bottles of Canadian beer. . . . I sent him up four mallards and some trout again."[51]

Facing what might be six months of physical therapy to rehabilitate his badly weakened arm, Hemingway finally admits to himself and MacLeish, whom he invited along all expenses paid, that he will not be able to go on an African safari in 1931. Gus Pfeiffer, his private banker, put up $25,000 of stock to underwrite Ernest's dream of African hunting, a dream he has nurtured since, as a ten-year-old, he followed in the magazines and on the movie screen the African hunting adventures of his hero Teddy Roosevelt. Now in Billings, with snow falling and Christmas decorations up in the halls, Africa is as remote as the moon. Ernest dictates a letter to Henry Strater, the

New York painter, saying his promise of a paid-up safari is still good, but they will have to put it off for a year. In letters he can joke about being an "ex-writer," but it is a hollow joke.[52]

Early on the morning of December 21, Ernest and Pauline warm themselves in the Billings railway station, waiting for the eastbound Burlington train to arrive. Late the next evening they will be in Kansas City, and the following morning in St. Louis, to be met by Pauline's father, who will drive them on to a Piggott Christmas. Outside falling snow is accumulating in empty streets as the Zephyr pulls into the station. On Christmas Eve when they arrive in Piggott, he is running a fever; weak from two months in the hospital bed, he goes back to bed in his in-laws' house, where he never felt at home, not that feeling "at home" was ever a particularly calming experience for him. He cannot write left-handed, nor can he dictate. This he tells Owen Wister in a letter dictated to Pauline, who types as he talks. As for writing about a real person, as Wister did in his Roosevelt book, it could not be done well. "You can't recreate a person," Ernest says, "you can only create a character in writing. You can record an actual person's actions and recreate them in a sense, i.e. present them through this recording but it takes great detail."[53] As a constant reader of histories and biographies, he speaks as much to himself as to Wister, and speaking, perhaps, to others to follow. His book in progress, a study of the bullfight and a good deal more, is built on details small, numerous, yet selective, and didn't he always work that way, choosing the telling detail from the welter of possibilities?

Chapter Three

1931

ON THE ROAD AGAIN

Key West, Havana, Pamplona, Kansas City

Across old and new Spain that winter and early spring, revolutionists are at work. In Nicaragua, when the capital goes down in an earthquake, out of the ruins rise up the Sandinistas once again, killing nine Americans and several native sons. To the halls of Montezuma, President Hoover sends more U.S. Marines, and to Honduras where other American citizens are caught in a revolution, he dispatches the Navy. Bombs rock the colonial heart of Havana, where newspapers close overnight, their editors no longer to be found in the cafés. The university is shut down, and a young student, jailed on charges of attempting to kill President Machado, hangs himself in his prison cell. By the end of March, the streets of Madrid are stained with the blood of students in revolt.[1]

The Hemingways return to Key West, seeking shelter, a quiet place in which to recover the use of Ernest's writing arm and

Pauline's composure. Very slowly, sometimes so slowly he does not believe in it, his arm improves, sensations returning to his fingers. Typing awkwardly with his left hand, he tells his mother-in-law that their next car will be one guaranteed to kill the driver when it goes into a ditch instead of leaving him a nuisance to everyone.[2] As for composure, Pauline's is sorely tested by too many visitors and the worst winter anyone in Key West can remember. January sets record low temperatures that keep their quarters continuously chilled. The old house on Whitehead Street, "out near the mullet seller," rents for only $25 a month, but its large, poorly insulated rooms are impossible to heat. The wettest February on Key West record is worse, crowding them and their guests too tightly together.[3]

During the six months since their last visit to Key West, the quality of life here has visibly declined. Some say that it cannot drop much lower, but that is before the best baker in town shoots himself, and someone, never named, ambushes one of the local dairy's cows to butcher a haunch of meat.[4] Elsewhere, out of sight but not far from mind, rural banks across the country close their doors, unable to refund deposits to bewildered citizens. Good times and bad always cycle, politicians say. Four million people may be out of work, but work will return. It always returns, Republicans promise. Any public relief program, according to President Hoover, is indefensible, for "federal aid for the distressed would strike at the root of government." He is certain that the Red Cross can "take care of the drought and the unemployment situation." And to prove it he gives $7,500 to the Red Cross relief fund.[5] Into the Key West harbor that January came a bounty of luxury yachts—the *Placida*, the *Arcadia*, and twenty-six others from the northeast—an addition to the economy but calling attention to the disparity between those with and those without means to make ends meet. By February, the town is on the verge of bankruptcy, unable to collect enough taxes to pay the firefighters whose intent to walk out is a serious threat to a wooden, windswept town. The firemen compromise, taking $25 and a promise of more when tax collection improves, which it does not. With a delinquent tax sale hanging over several Key West homes, fear of displacement is real. Boston,

Newport, and New York money is moving into town, changing the faces and voices on the winter streets.[6]

Some locals leave town. Some despair. But if a man has access to a boat, he can make risky money during prohibition on the Havana run, ninety miles across the water, where liquor is cheap. Sometimes, in the dark of the moon, a man simply "borrows" a boat. In February, officials from the Key West customs house pick up a "missing" boat and 263 quarts of liquor. In a town where every boat's owner is widely known, this owner is never identified.[7] Key West protects its own. The grand jury might point out that over the last four years only eighty-five prosecutions involving gambling and prohibition laws have taken place, but that does not mean that anything is going to change.[8] As frequenters of the numerous small holes in the wall ("blind pigs") that sell Cuban rum, the sheriff's men occasionally make a show of rounding up a few locals, but not enough to slow business. Federal law out of Miami once in a while comes to town, but the grapevine intelligence system usually keeps the obvious places on Duval Street well warned. When the system fails, it is Key West news:

12 ARRESTED HERE TODAY IN
RAID BY U.S. DRY OFFICERS
RAIDERS COME IN BY BOAT AND TRAIN AND
SWOOP WITHOUT WARNING ON NUMEROUS PLACES[9]

Later that month, two well-known Key Westers—Henry Hollerich and Albert Taylor—are arrested in Havana for violating quarantine and maritime laws of Cuba. They were running booze and Chinese aliens through the Bahamas and into Miami. Ever since Congress, reflecting the national fear of "the yellow horde," reduced the Asian immigrant quota to near zero, Havana's Chinatown has exported illegals this way.[10]

Early March, Key West to the Dry Tortugas. From Garrison Bight, where small boats harbor, follow the ferry route out northwest channel, bearing west and passing just above the Marquesas Keys and across the edge of the quicksand where the *Valbanera* went down. On a clear day you can see her hull in the sand. Then bear west northwest from Rebecca Shoal until the brick fort appears low and square on the horizon. Watch the markers coming up on Garden Key, because it shallows up real fast around Fort Jefferson, and any storm can shift the bottom. It's fifty miles more or less. With wind out of the east, an easy trip going out, slow coming back.

———

All that winter while his arm healed and its damaged nerve restored itself, Ernest tended to guests who arrived, overlapped, and left entertained. To their rented house[11] came relatives and friends. From New York came Mike Strater, Max Perkins, Uncle Gus, and Aunt Louise Pfeiffer:[12] Strater and Perkins came for fishing and male camaraderie; Gus to check on his investment, encourage the postponed African safari, and suggest the Hemingways buy a Key West house for which he would put up the money. From Oak Park, Ernest's mother arrived for a two-day visit, the first time he has seen her since they buried his father;[13] his nineteen-year-old sister, Carol, a scholarship student at Rollins College, came down from Winter Park, Florida. Jinny Pfeiffer came, as did John Hermann and Josie Herbst, both writers wintering that year in Key West. From the L-Bar-T came Lawrence and Olive Nordquist for a visit, and their ranch hand, Chub Weaver, who drove the now-repaired Ford down from Billings.

They all come to see Ernest, who does not disappoint them. Until the nerve in his right arm regenerates, he can neither write nor fish, but he can take the citizens out in rented boats, work the line until he has a strike, then turn the rod over to one of them.[14] But the coldest January in twenty-five years makes it "a bad winter for fishing—one norther after another—never more than 2 successive fishing days between."[15] So when the big sailfish hit the teaser skipping on the surface, he is happy to see it; when it took the bait, he asks Chub Weaver to set the hook before giving the rod to Pauline. As with so much of their increasingly famous lives, the event does not go unnoticed:

Sailfish records for the present season were climaxed Monday when
Mrs. Ernest Hemingway, wife of the noted author, captured one that
upon accurate measurement showed a length of seven feet and one
inch. Mr. and Mrs. Hemingway have spent a number of consecutive
winters in Key West. They are credited with a number of remarkable
catches.[16]

But he cannot turn over his book for someone else to reel in, the
book he has not been able to write now for five months. All that late
winter in Key West, as he instructs, arranges, and worries, the nerve
slowly comes back, the arm recovers; the book of the bulls, however,
remains dormant.

If some days he is surly, most visitors forgive him. But after what
he said to John Hermann returning from the Dry Tortugas, Josie
Herbst neither forgave Ernest nor forgot the way her husband folded
before him; she was not a woman who accepted his "lord of the
manor" domination with as much patience as the men. Nor had she
particularly enjoyed the two previous weeks making small talk with
Pauline, with whom she had little in common, and trying to be
amused by young Patrick, who was fraying her nerves. She had not
come to the moonlit island to be left alone by her husband. At thirty-
eight, Josie Herbst, nine years older than John, looks even older. In
the photograph, her pale eyes, once so attractive, are now sunken
and circled; John looks more like her son than her mate. When he,
who is quickly becoming an alcoholic, and Bra Saunders, who seldom refuses a drink, show up in a small boat from the Tortugas to
fetch ice for three hundred pounds of fish about to spoil, Josie
returns with them and later wishes she had not. Despite the four
days it has taken John and Bra to make the one-day round-trip, John,
Josie, Bra, and the ice arrive in time to save the fish but not the Hermann marriage, which crumbles under Ernest's sarcasm, mocking
John's failures. "Look, the expert seaman afraid of a little storm.
Look, the hero of Lake Michigan, stuck on a sandbar. Look, the
famous handyman, can't even get the motor repaired." John smiles
and keeps on steering the boat. That night back in Key West, when

Hemingway starts in again on John, Josie walks out of the room in tears of rage. "Hemingway follows her, making excuses. His damn arm is bothering him, he tells her."[17] As they speak, an old Paris friend's essay in *The Nation* takes Ernest to task for the eccentricity and dullness of "the Hemingway school of writing." One student in that school, Josie Herbst, will never reach her potential, he says, if she cannot outgrow the fetish of simplicity Hemingway fosters.[18] Isidor Schneider could not have anticipated how quickly his advice would seem to take effect.

A visit to the Hemingways usually makes extraordinary demands upon all involved, but some visits, like that of their L-Bar-T friends the Sidleys, take the experience right to the edge:

VISITOR NEARLY DROWNED IN THE CITY PARK POOL

CHICAGO WOMAN, DRAGGED UNCONSCIOUS FROM
WATER BY MRS. ERNEST HEMINGWAY

> *Mrs. W. P. Sidley, of Chicago, narrowly escaped drowning this forenoon while swimming in Bayview park bathing pool with Mrs. Ernest Hemingway.*
>
> *Life was thought to have been extinct when she was brought ashore. After being rushed to the Marine hospital in an ambulance where restoratives were promptly administered by Dr. Lombard . . . Mrs. Sidley revived and in a short time was able to be conveyed to the home of Mr. and Mrs. Hemingway, on North Beach, where she is resting nicely this afternoon. . . . At the time of the near-tragedy Mr. Sidley and Mr. Hemingway were out on a fishing trip, not expected to return until late today.[19]*

But neither near-deaths nor afternoons on the water can long distract Ernest from how much his mending arm bothers him, both physically and in his head. The pain of the spiral fracture is past but not forgotten; the nerve slowly regenerates, but the arm is weak, his handwriting shaky, his letters few. Worse than the memory of pain is the auto wreck's affirmation of a world that could, on whimsy, take from him his ability to write. At the completion of each book there was always that emptiness and silence when the machine inside him shut down, and the fear that he might not write another book, might have nothing left to say. In a note, he reminded himself that he had survived periods like this before, periods between books when the writing did not happen. As long as he was not dead, it would come back. Finally, like an old friend, it always came back. All it took was confidence and a good memory to weather through the hiatus, but it was scary, the waiting, and worse each time the gift left him.[20] But this time the fear is different: not his head but his body has failed him. He can neither write nor fish, neither contemplate nor participate. In the 1918 Milan hospital, behind an infectious smile, he worried that his wounded right leg might be amputated. Every day of his life, the rubber brace on his rebuilt knee reminds him of that fear.

Through visitors and winter storms, Pauline remains the self-effacing family center, paying the bills, providing meals, tending to the tedious. Sometimes autocratic, she does not mix much with local Key Westers, nor does she have projects of her own. There is no competition between them, for Ernest is her life. When they are together, she purrs; when separated, she writes long daily letters. When he wakes in the night with terrible dreams, she is there. Her reward is his writing, for the well being of which she will sacrifice almost anything. Like many fathers of his generation, Ernest takes little interest in the rearing of his son who is too young to be interesting. Pauline accepts his disinterest, paying the nanny to keep little Patrick occupied and meals cooked. Never thrilled with the hunting life, to please Ernest she has become a fair shot and a competent fisherwoman who encourages him always in his pursuits. Whatever he wants, she wants. He wants a daughter; she will try to give him one: by early February Pauline is once again pregnant. All that she lacks is a permanent home, a place to make their own.

Not until April, five months after the wreck, is he able to write Scott Fitzgerald that the paralysis is gone, the nerve returned, the arm stronger, and the writing begun again on his unfinished book,

four hundred words his daily limit.[21] That same day he writes Max
Perkins, ordering a fresh supply of books to take with him in May
when he and Pauline return to Europe: Baedeker's latest volume on
Spain and Portugal came packed beside Dashiell Hammett's *Glass
Key*, a biography of Whistler, the poems of Gerard Manley Hopkins,
and Erskine Caldwell's *American Earth*. His arm is his own again, his
mind again active and inquiring. He tells Max that he will outwrite
all the competition, of whom only Faulkner is sometimes good
enough to be taken seriously. The only true competition are the great
writers dead and time itself: brave talk from a man picking up the
pieces of a book five months cold.[22]

First he fiddles with "A Natural History of the Dead" to get the
juices flowing, and has it typed, unable to say how much is enough
with a story so strangely mixing genres—short fiction, reminiscence,
and commentary. From the mountain field station where the Italian
doctor has just thrown iodine into the officer's eyes to quiet his rage,
the view shifts back to the narrator's memory of a sergeant on burial
detail hacking gold fillings from the teeth of Austrian dead. "Now, as
I write this, I think it is perhaps enough about the dead," the narrator
says.

> There is no need to continue and write accurate observations on a dead
> friend, a dead lover or a dead parent since a writer can deal at length
> with these in fiction rather than in natural history, an ill enough paid
> branch of writing. So perhaps the inspiration from the moss flower of
> extraordinary beauty, is to be derived not from the dead themselves,
> swollen too big for their uniforms in the heat, but from the contempla-
> tion of the sergeant at work on them. Let us learn from observing the
> industrious sergeant, let us take inspiration from the sergeant's
> researches, who knows how profitable the dead may be if we live long
> enough? Who knows how much gold may be extracted from them?

It is a rough start, ragged, unfocused and eventually deleted, a warm-
up before turning to the cold meat of the bullfight book.[23]

Writing, after such a hiatus, starts with Ernest talking to himself, saying what he needs to say to begin again—an apologia for his craft, stating his principles, laying out the rules he tries to live by. A writer, he tells himself, does not need to live in the country of his fiction, for if

> *he is a writer who deals with the human heart, with the human mind and with the presence of [or] absence of the human soul then if he can make a heart break for you, or even beat, make the mind func-tion, and show you what passes for the soul then you may be sure he does not have to stay in Wessex for fear that he will lose it.*

Having vacillated between living in Spain and living in America, he now realizes that no matter what unpleasant changes are wrought on the American landscape, this is his home, the place he was born to. The new road into his Wyoming preserve may ruin the country and Key West may become another Provincetown, but "as you get older, privacy becomes internal and nothing can be spoiled from the out-side."

Unlike an honest painter who can paint numerous variations on a single theme, a writer, once he gets it absolutely correct, must never repeat himself. The writer may be a less than admirable human being, he may cheat on his wife, disappoint friends, or have "this or that ugly sexual habit," but so long as he does not "lie to or deceive the innermost self which writes," he is still an honest writer. As such, he has the right to make whatever money from whatever market is available to him. If he is lucky enough to live on his income, he faces the danger that expenses will rise to exceed that income, compelling him "to write another book for money." Which is all right "so long as he does not consciously or subconsciously change one word, sen-tence, paragraph or chapter . . . from the way he wanted to write it."[24] Having said it, he tore the pages out of the old bound galleys he was using as a note pad and got on with his real book.

———

Deeds were filed yesterday transferring ownership of the fine home at Whitehead and Olivia streets, to Ernest Hemingway,

whose summer home is his chateau near Paris, France. Mr. and
Mrs. Hemingway have spent a number of winters in Key West.
They like the climate here so well and enjoy fishing so much that
they decided to invest in a residence. The place they have
acquired is conceded to be one of the most ideally located home-
sites in the city. With but little improvement of the large lawn and
substantial building, the premises will become one of the most
beautiful spots in Key West. Sale of the place to the Hemingways
resulted in the payment of taxes amounting to $3,000 including
city and county assessment. The county's share was slightly more
than $1,000. Contract has been let by Mr. Hemingway for the
immediately necessary repairs to the property at a cost of $500.
Work on the proposition is under way today.[25]

—*Key West Citizen*, April 30, 1931

When they signed the deed on the "haunted house," as Lorine
Thompson called it, Pauline was over two months pregnant and
ready to adjust her expectations. They were not going to live in a
French chateau, as the Key West paper called their Paris apartment.
That part of their lives was finished. Nor would her husband choose
any large city as a permanent home. He needed a secluded place in
which to write, a place close to fishing or hunting grounds. She
needed conversation and access to night life, music, a little dancing.
Key West was not ideal for her, but Ernest wanted Key West, and she
wanted Ernest. It was that simple. Miami was a train ride away, and
old-world Havana's night life was only six hours by ferry. With air
travel becoming a reality, the two-day train to New York would soon
be unnecessary.

Although the pre–Civil War place was in terrible shape, she and
Lorine settled on the Whitehead Street house, for which Uncle Gus
put up $8,000 to pay off the bank and back taxes. Large enough for
their purpose, with a huge yard, a few scraggly palms, and an enormous cistern, the old coral structure needed paint, plaster, and roof
repairs. It needed a new kitchen and a second bathroom. It needed
walls removed, rooms opened, windows glazed, tiles laid. It needed

more work than any $500, as the paper reported, could buy. Pauline, accustomed to rented quarters and domestic help, had much to learn about the joys of homeowning, but they were largely postponed. Five days after signing the papers, Ernest was in Havana boarding the *Volendam* en route to Spain, where Pauline would join him at Hendaye later in May. If he needed to go to Spain to finish his book, she would go with him, remaining in Key West only long enough to have the roof patched and the wire-mesh fence contracted to be built. By May 16, boxes of Hemingway belongings were waiting for the drayman to move them into the new house, and Pauline was on the train to New York with Patrick and Henrietta; for months to come, nothing else was going to happen to the house on Whitehead Street.[26]

The day Ernest arrived in Havana, two army majors were indicted for commanding a "death squad" using wire garrotes to strangle victims. When he was seven days out of Havana on the *Volendam* bound for Spain, Monarchists in support of the abdicated King Alfonso took to the streets of Madrid. Before sunset, taxis and streetcars were on strike, two men were dead, and heads were bleeding.[27] The night before landing at Vigo, Hemingway told Waldo Peirce that he wanted to get to Madrid "before they set up the guillotine in the Plaza Mayor."[28] He arrived in Madrid to find the capital under martial law and Republican sentiment running so high that the Catholic Church, the long and avid supporter of monarchy, was in retreat. Cardinal Segura, the Primate of Spain, barely escaped across the Pyrenees en route to Rome, while at Loyola, reactionary Basques protected their beloved Jesuits.[29] It was all quite interesting to a writer looking for subject matter.

In Madrid, he settled into the Hotel Biarritz, where he could follow the street violence and the new season of corridas, beginning with Madrid's San Isidore feria, followed by weekly Thursday and Sunday cartels. On May 24, he watched his first son's namesake, Nicanor Villata, perform at the Corrida de Abono. When he wasn't at the Madrid ring, he took the train out to Aranjuez on the river to preview Domingo Ortega, highly touted by his old Pamplona friend

Juanito Quintana as "this year's revelation, and of whom it is said by those who have seen him that he is the best bullfighter born since bullfighting exists. . . . By what they say he must be a very serious thing."[30] Always there was a new revelation, a fresh savior born to restore the corrida's dignity, and always there was the disappointment, followed by more talk of the degenerate state of the art. Talk could be found in the cafés with Hemingway's new friend Sidney Franklin, who was in Madrid as a novillero, an aspiring but unfledged matador who talked a wonderful game and who gathered to his strange attraction "the ones coming to ask for work when he was fighting, the ones to borrow money, the ones for an old shirt, a suit of clothes; all bullfighters, all well known somewhere at the hour of eating, all formally polite, all out of luck."[31]

That summer, as Hemingway gathered new information and collected photographs for his book, there was plenty of blood in sandy bullrings and in the stone streets of Spain. As much as he missed Pauline, he was wise to have insisted she remain in Paris. All that summer revolution popped and simmered, angry men of all stripes waiting on the national elections. On May 27, six died in the San Sebastián streets, another twenty-five wounded when the Guardia Civil fired on striking fishermen.[32] On May 31 in the Madrid ring, the first bull hooked, catching Gitanillo in the thigh, tossing him against the barrera, where he was pinned to the wood with a horn through his back. Gitanillo took ten weeks to die slowly from meningitis.[33] The Republic took several years longer.

Since the early nineteenth century, the government of Spain had cycled through various constitutions regularly pricked by colonial wars and internal revolutions. The monarchy, the great landowners, the Catholic Church, and the military formed tenuous alliances to remain largely in power, until the 1930s. By 1931, the left side of the political spectrum included Republicans, liberals, socialists, syndicalists, communists, and anarchists; to the right were Monarchists, Carlists, fascists, Jesuits, and the military. Basques, Catalans, Galicians, and Andalusians all wanted home rule. With King Alfonso in self-exile and the military out of power, the left-leaning elected politicians tried to assure the populace that "Spanish Communism is of slight importance. . . . We are as far from Muscovite dogma as from that of the Socialist Second International. The dictatorship of the proletariat is continually mentioned. We want no dictatorship. Workers must be educated in freedom, not tyranny. . . . Political revolution has been accomplished in Spain. Next should come social revolution."[34] Nevertheless, fear of communist domination drove the peseta to new lows and kept middle-class burghers awake at night.

Throughout June, while Hemingway made brief trips to Hendaye and Paris, the Spanish political stew simmered and thickened. In midmonth, the provisional Republican government abolished the ruling system of military governors, who were told to retire. At the same time Cardinal Segura, who slipped back into the country, was again expelled, "garbed as a simple prelate, sitting stiffly beside a representative of the Department of Public Security. . . . A mob massed in front of the Paulist monastery in Guadalajara, where he spent the night 'detained,' cried 'Long Live the Republic!' and 'Death to the clergy!'" Meanwhile, Don Jaime de Bourbon, Carlist pretender to the Spanish throne, was exciting the Basque separatists of Navarra with promises of returning to Spain, where he had not been seen in twenty-five years. The Pyrenees were "full of Jaimistas and Itegralistas who would restore under the Carlist pretender a monarchy putting religion above everything."[35]

Meanwhile in Catalonia, a young aviator on the separatist ticket was making headlines:

Madrid, June 25—Spain's revolutionary flyer, Ramón Franco, who is now grooming himself as the savior of the masses, taking a flight of oratory tonight, fell off the platform at village of Lora del Rio and broke his leg.

The Major could have broken his neck and thus made the provisional government very happy. He has taken to stumping the centers of unrest like Catalonia and Andalusia where he has his little "Republican revolutionary" party and has continually outraged their finer sensibilities.

He told the masses in Barcelona that the revolution had to be
made safe for them even if they were forced to invade Parliament. . . .
Today the Government had to notify the energetic birdman . . . that it
wouldn't do for the director of the nation's aviation to fly about and
do any more dropping of electoral handbills from the air.

The next day, "the little aviator with the restless eyes, who last
December was willing to bomb Alfonso out of the palace," was dismissed as head of the nation's aviation and placed under informal
house arrest until after the elections.[36]

Two days before votes were cast, Hemingway wrote John Dos Passos that twenty-three different political parties had "steamed up" the
country, which appeared heading for a Republican landslide. Galicians, however, were on strike, refusing to vote, while Andalusia
would not "boil over" until it saw the new parliament's plan for land
reform. Navarra was enthusiastic for Don Jaime to restore the Carlist
monarchy, and Catalonia was biding its time.[37] When votes were
counted, a left-of-center coalition was in control of the Cortes, the
Spanish parliament, but it was not a total victory. Nationalist parties
with their separatist agendas controlled Navarra and Catalonia.
Diehard rightist Ramón Franco was elected in one of the Barcelona
districts, although his forces were badly defeated in Madrid and
Seville. In a Madrid hospital, the airman himself was recovering
from his accident under guard.[38] A month later Ernest wrote Max
Perkins, "Wish there were some market for what I know about present Spanish situation. Have followed it as closely as though I were
working for a paper. Damned hard to break habits."[39] Socialists, Rad-
icals, Radical Socialists, Catalonian and Basque Nationalists: all the
pieces of the political puzzle were out on the table, waiting to be
formed into the bloody picture they promised.

Fourth of July, 1931. At a London registry office, James Joyce and
Nora Barnacle, after living together for twenty-seven years, were
married. On that same day by the Swiss lake in the house for the
mentally ill, Zelda Fitzgerald was waiting for Scott's phone call

from Lausanne. At Bad Ausee, Austria, the Gerald Murphy family celebrated the day with their usual panache, pleased that Patrick's stricken lung remained under control by gas injections. At the beach of Hendaye where Ernest and Pauline had taken a small cottage, the American colony was too small to make much noise. In Berlin, Adolf Hitler was putting his shoulder to the wheel of German politics; in upstate New York, Governor Franklin Roosevelt, on crippled legs, was preparing to run for the presidency of the United States.

———

Five months pregnant, Pauline chooses to remain at the beach with Patrick and Henrietta while Hemingway takes his almost-eight-year-old son, John, to see his first bullfight in Pamplona. Juanito Quintana, their friendly hotelier, has saved them a room and secured "unsurpassable" first-row seats at the "place where the young lads with the swords place the capes."[40] When John Haldey Nicanor Hemingway saw his namesake, Nicanor Villata of the long neck, he hated him immediately. When the rowdy Pamplona crowd threw cushions at Nino de la Palma for a poor performance, the boy asked, "Can I throw mine, Papa?" It was at Pamplona during the now epic feria of 1925 that Hemingway first saw Nino de la Palma, a nineteen-year-old then hailed as the savior of the corrida. Having immortalized him as Pedro Romero in *The Sun Also Rises*, Ernest was always disappointed with Nino's performance after his first serious goring took away his valor. Nothing Ernest sees that day with his son causes him to revise his opinion: "If you see Nino de la Palma, the chances are you will see cowardice in its least attractive form."[41]

After the fights, Sidney Franklin, Ernest, and his son sit under the Iruña arcade, where they review the day's corrida, interrupted by well-wishers, old friends, and strangers. Winifred Mowrer is one of those at the table. Her reporter husband, Paul, is consentually elsewhere with Hadley Hemingway, with whom he has had an open affair for several years. Winifred has come to Pamplona with her two teenage sons as a rite of passage. They are almost of age, and she is almost ready to leave their father permanently for a different life. At

Paul's request and with some difficulty, Ernest secured them rooms at the Perla and tickets to a corrida: anything for the man who is going to marry his former wife and provide for Bumby, now sitting at the table quite comfortably with his almost stepbrothers. The next morning as she and her sons continue on their walking tour across the Pyrenees, Winifred leaves a short, pleasant note of thank you. It is all very civilized.[42] Twenty-two years will pass before Ernest returns to the feria of San Fermin.

As soon as the last corrida is complete, Ernest rejoins his manuscript and his wife, complaining immediately that his writing could not go much worse.[43] Neither could the world at large. While the Hemingways are on the beach at Hendaye, banks in Germany, Hungary, and Austria close for twenty-two days as the old Hapsburg empire staggers beneath punitive war-debt repayments. While he and Pauline follow their usual Spanish itinerary to the Valencia feria, Seville is racked with syndicalist riots and martial law. In Havana, American intervention prevents yet another attempt on the life of President Machado; on Wall Street, U.S. Steel falls to 84 when directors reduce its dividend for the first time in sixteen years. The Bank of England raises its discount rate to staunch the flow of gold out of the country, and the great steamship lines make deep cuts in their transatlantic fares.[44]

Throughout July and into August when Ernest and Pauline once more retreat to the relative coolness of Santiago de Compostela, Spain bleeds. Strikes bring Bilbao and Cordova to a standstill. Catalonia votes to become independent, but the Cortes will not allow it. Elsewhere there are more transatlantic flights and more lost airmen. More screen stars romp in even briefer bathing suits at Cannes and Antibes. Charlie Chaplin thinks of building a house at Juan-les-Pins, but by August he is racing motorboats at Biarritz. In Germany four million are out of work, and in Great Britain the cabinet resigns, its budget unbalanced. In Cuba, sixty-six die in another failed attempt to bring down President Machado. After promising otherwise, U.S. Steel cuts salaries 15 percent, dropping its stock even lower. In Oklahoma and east Texas, five thousand wells are

shut down in an effort to raise the price of crude oil, which has
fallen below fifty cents a barrel. State militias are mobilized, and
banks are closing in New York and New Jersey. President Hoover
continues to maintain that no government "dole" is required; this
crisis will pass.

While the world elsewhere churns and falters during the first
week of August, Hemingway finishes an eighty-page glossary of bullring terminology, including a running commentary on Spanish custom, a curious collection of anecdotes, and related information on
Spanish insults, shellfish, regional wines, street scams, and local
beer. When Pauline returns to Paris to be more comfortable in her
pregnancy and see to the shipment of apartment possessions, Ernest
returns to Madrid to complete work on his book. The hundred or so
photographs he has collected are being annotated, the glossary is
almost finished, the first eighteen chapters have been revised and
augmented, but the last two chapters remain as unwritten as when
he arrived in May.[45]

His return to Paris at the end of August lasts only long enough to
wind up some business with Caresse Crosby's Black Sun Press, balance his checking accounts, and prepare for the return to the States.
For Pauline, now in her seventh month of pregnancy, the charm of
Paris is waning, and three months of hotel life is enough. Their
apartment furniture, en route to Key West, includes paintings by
André Masson and Joan Miró's *The Farm*, which belongs to Hadley
but is moving to Key West.[46] In a separate shipment, they send home
their newly acquired oil painting—Juan Gris's *The Guitar Player*.
Pauline completes last-minute shopping, while Ernest makes obliga-
tory rounds. At Sylvia Beach's he buys D. H. Lawrence's novella *The
Virgin and the Gipsy* and T. E. Lawrence's *Revolt in the Desert*, which
is the very book for a man interested in violent political revolutions.[47]

The Hemingways avoid old Paris acquaintances and former
haunts, but no matter how much they keep away from Montparnasse
café life, their lives are never completely their own. A *Tribune* columnist and sketch artist catches them on the street and puts them in
the paper:

The author of The Sun Also Rises, Farewell to Arms, Men Without Women, *and many brilliant short stories of the war and other subjects, has lost none of his enthusiasm for bullfighting and boxing.*

At the hotel near the Place Saint Germain des Prés where he is stopping he talked yesterday of Sidney Franklin the Brooklyn bullfighter . . . who is going into the arena at Madrid today for the first time in several months.

"Sidney is a marvelous fighter," he said. "He is absolutely courageous and keenly intelligent. He knows what it's all about. He's better than many of those boys who grow up in the tradition. They learn to go through the motions gracefully, but they don't know how to use their heads, as Sidney does. He's a regular Christy Matthewson."

Hemingway talked for about half an hour while he was posing for a sketch, but did not mention literature or himself, except to explain that he is ten pounds overweight because his arm was broken in an automobile accident and hasn't yet sufficiently healed. This keeps him from boxing.

He also had other worries. A young man who resembles him strikingly has been masquerading around New York recently as the original Ernest, telling wild stories of his adventures in the Italian ambulance service during the War, borrowing money and bumming drinks.

This has made Hemingway wary. When he signed the sketch which was made of him there, his wife remarked that the signature was hardly legible.

"Yes, I know, I wrote it that way purposely," he replied. "This town is full of chiselers. If I put a legible signature on this drawing and The Tribune *prints it, there may be a half dozen bad checks at the bank by Monday morning. I'm taking no chances."*[48]

Ernest's doppelganger continued to appear off and on in Paris, in New York, and later in St. Louis, casually saying he was on his way to Arkansas to visit his "wife's people."[49]

Three days after his interview appeared in the Paris paper, Ernest, Pauline, and Patrick take the afternoon boat train to Havre, where, along with the director of the Boston Symphony, the director of the

Morgan bank, the Grand Duchess Maria of Russia, former Senator Guggenheim, Grant and Jane Mason, and old friend Don Stewart and his pregnant wife, they board the *Ile de France*, homeward bound. As they do so, Gerald Murphy is in Cherbourg boarding the *Europa* for New York, and Scott and Zelda Fitzgerald are disembarking in New York from the *Aquitania*.[50] That the Murphys, Fitzgeralds, and Hemingways were traveling simultaneously on separate liners, having made no attempt to group together, would have been unthinkable only a few years earlier.

Arriving finally in Kansas City to be close to Pauline's surgeon, Don Carlos Guffey, the Hemingways live first with Ernest's cousin Ruth White Lowry before moving into the Riviera Apartments when Pauline's delivery nears. On November 12, when her labor pains begin, Dr. Guffey waits twelve long hours before admitting Pauline cannot produce a natural birth.

———

Sedated and exposed on the operating table, the thirty-six-year-old white female in the ninth month of her second pregnancy is nearing the end of her childbearing years. Although her fertility will remain a potential for some time, after thirty-six the birth rate for white American women drops significantly. As the surgeon makes his lateral incision at the base of the uterus, he retraces the scar he left from her first cesarean section three years earlier. From the bloody opening he extracts a nine-pound male baby, slaps him to life, and sutures first the exposed uterus and then the mother's abdomen. (For every thousand such births, six mothers and sixty-one babies will die this year.) In the waiting room afterward the surgeon and the father congratulate each other on the successful delivery. He tells the father the twice-opened uterus will not stand the strain of another pregnancy.

———

They name their new son Gregory Hancock Hemingway: Hancock for Ernest's grandmother's family; Gregory "for any of numerous Popes, for Gregorian chant, and for Greg Clark of Toronto," he says.[51] But they cannot call him Pilar, the daughter's name they have saved since first using it as Pauline's nickname during their 1926 affair. "I want a girl very much," says he, having grown up in a house full of sisters, "but don't know how to go about it."[52] Soon he will be calling any woman younger than himself "Daughter," but there will never be a daughter.

While Pauline remains one month in Research Hospital recovering from her operation, Ernest lives alone, visiting her and working on his bullfight book. By Thanksgiving her wound is almost healed, the stitches out, and she is able to laugh again without fear of tearing something loose inside. For supper that night Ernest brings her wild ducks he shot on the Missouri River. On Thanksgiving day a year earlier, she was sitting in the chair, he lying in the Billings hospital bed. This day his writing arm is still crooked from his car wreck.

Outside, on the night streets of Kansas City, Christmas 1931 comes in chancy times. Corporate America is cutting wages, reducing inventory, limiting production; U.S. Steel falls to 59, down two hundred points over the last two years. In Manchuria, the Japanese invasion continues to move south against the hapless Chinese army. Guy Hickok predicts that in Germany, "Hitler [is] coming in, shoot up a few; then the [crown prince] will step out from behind him and restore peace and the dynasty."[53] With almost eight million Americans out of work, Ernest and Pauline have much to be thankful for: their bills are paid; their Key West home is debt-free; royalty payments from Scribner's continue; and Uncle Gus has added to Pauline's trust fund while setting $25,000 aside for a Hemingway African safari. Young Patrick is with his grandparents in Piggott in the keep of his new, enormous French nanny, Gabrielle, who was said to specialize in child care, veterinary surgery, cooking, and brewing.[54] Bumby has returned to his French boarding school; Jinny Pfeiffer is on her way to Key West, where Ernest's sister Carol will join her to install the furniture shipment from Paris for the Hemingways' arrival on Whitehead Street. After living well for several years in Europe on the strength of the dollar, Ernest and Pauline are now in the enviable position of having a little money when others have less or none. Prices are falling as businesses are sucked under. Coming through New York City on their way home from Europe, Ernest rents a safety deposit box, where he shrewdly caches several thousand dollars to hedge against the possibility of bank failures or government closures.[55]

Although Pauline's one-month hospital stay is lonesome for her and expensive for them, it gives Ernest the uninterrupted writing time he needs to bring his book of the bulls to conclusion. In the sterile furnished apartment, fortified by prescription whiskey, he finishes the penultimate chapter which began: "There are only two proper ways to kill bulls with the sword and the muleta and . . . both of them deliberately invoke a moment in which there is unavoidable goring for the man if the bull does not follow the cloth properly."[56] He might as well have written: "There are only two proper ways to finish a book like this and both of them risk unavoidable goring for the writer if the reader does not follow the story properly." For this book about the bulls and their matadors is equally a book about the writer, his writing, and the relationship of both to the reader. Writer and matador appear to be antithetical to each other: the one contemplative, the other active. But as artists, they bear metaphoric similarities. "Bull fighting," he wrote in the ninth chapter, "is the only art form in which the artist is in danger of death and in which the degree of brilliance in the performance is left to the fighter's honor."[57] The writer as artist takes similar risks, his art based on the same sense of honor, and his life as artist is equally dependent upon the response of his audience. While not literally in danger of death while writing, the author lives with the same possibility that his skills will diminish, that he will fall from the public eye, that his courage will fail. "Courage comes such a short distance; from the heart to the head."[58]

Having mastered his text as thoroughly as the matador his bull, having maneuvered it skillfully about the ring, leaving it finally stock still before the reader, he was now ready for the finish, the clean, honest ending that closes the text and opens the reader, an ending richer than anything he has ever written. It does not come easily, nor completely right the first time, but he gets it down on paper, saying what he needs to say, knowing he will cut it later where necessary. The hardest parts were always the beginning and the end, and he frequently starts too soon and just as often writes past the end. This book, for which no ending was obvious, came finally to close with the narrator admitting he is not able to get all of Spain between the covers:

> *My God, you could not get in all the bootblacks; nor all the fine girls passing; nor all the whores; nor all of us ourselves as we were then. . . . the smell of olive oil; the feel of leather; rope soled shoes; the loops of twisted garlic. . . . There ought to be . . . the chestnut woods on the high hills, the green country and the rivers, the red dust, the small shade beside the dry rivers and the white, baked clay hills; cool walking under the palms in the old city on the cliff above the sea, cool in the evening with the breeze.*[59]

The missing parts named, they were no longer missing, and the reader had the heart of Spain there at the end where it was most needed.

By the first of December, with the first draft of the book finished and Pauline still confined to the Kansas City hospital, Ernest went to Piggott for a week of quail hunting in the ruined fields of corn and peas: the hunter up early and out with the dogs, coming in after dark with his game bag warm and filled to the legal limit. When he returned to Kansas City, he began packing for their trip to Key West and answered letters. The book's last three chapters, he told Max Perkins, were so well written that the "hard times" surrounding them seemed not so hard. When his writing went well, nothing else mattered; when it did not, silly things became important. And when he was finished with a draft, he might have added, too many silly things began to matter, including other writers like Max Eastman, whose latest book, *The Literary Mind*, Ernest called "pretentious rubbish . . . cheap whoring articles . . . the fondler of the arts and unable to fornicate with them, the respectable radical—the revolutionary who never missed a meal."[60]

Earlier that day he wrote Archie MacLeish, "Believe made the god damn miracle we have to always make happen at the end happen again. Although may disillusion on it when see it in type. But if anything should happen to me it would be all right to publish it as it is."[61] In this book's conclusion, he says, "There is no security in any life that death is the end of, nor has economic security ever existed, nor is it possible."[62] At the same moment, Andrew Mellon, the richest Secretary of the Treasury in America's history, proposes a 1 percent increase in the federal income tax to offset the government's $1 billion spending deficit.[63]

———

Key West, Christmas. Plumbers in the kitchen, carpenters on the roof, the new nurse sick, the baby crying as his brother douses him with the flit can full of mosquito spray: another year ending. Winter is somewhere else; here it is as warm as early spring, southeast breezes holding steady, day and night. They sleep in the dining room until Pauline's scars can take the strain of the stairs; Ernest's throat is once more inflamed and raw, as are his nerves. On his writing table, amid the unanswered letters and various rubble of moving into Whitehead Street, is Archie MacLeish's new epic poem looking for a supporting blurb. In the living room, a typist hammers away on his manuscript. On the floor with other paper trash is the local paper, which says: "To 'Love at First Sight' for Key West, Ernest Hemingway Attributes His Coming Here."[64]

Chapter Four

———

1 9 3 2

WINNER TAKE NOTHING

─────────────────────
═════════════════════
─────────────────────

Key West, Havana, Cooke City

N O, HEMINGWAY SAYS, no, he cannot become part of any as yet unnamed cooperative magazine where writers share profits, because like all writers, he writes alone, sells alone, gets turned down alone, is remembered or forgotten alone. Maybe there were some who could work together, but not him, not with twelve dependents counting on his income. (To a stranger, like George Albee, he feels such an exaggeration is permitted.) Tough times, he insists, may be "instructive" to a writer even if he has to stand in a breadline. Sooner or later, for God, country, or belly's sake, everybody must stand in line.[1] There in Key West plenty were out of work, and those he employed worked at half speed.

In the new year, Gabrielle, the Hemingways' recently hired cook and nanny replacing Henrietta, took to her sickbed, leaving little Patrick and baby Gregory to Ernest's visiting sister Carol's care. Pauline, not fully recovered from her cesarean, tried to do her part, but ended up back in bed herself.[2] That's when Patrick ate the ant poison and began to vomit. In the middle of this chaos, as roofers roofed and plumbers plumbed, Ernest continued to revise his typescript, which he now called *Death in the Afternoon*, a title jotted down the previous summer with notes for a story he never wrote:

> *Two boys—same town—same age—play bull in streets—one killed— Saragossa incident—one becomes matador—one becomes Revolutionist—/girl/—careers—matador takes girl—corrida—final——of ring*[3]

As those notes disappear into Hemingway's welter of saved paper, Max Perkins is forwarding an agent's unsolicited offer from Hollywood:

METRO GOLDWYN MAYER HIGHLY RECEPTIVE MY SUGGESTION
TO SECURE HEMINGWAY AT HIS PRICE FOR BULL FIGHT PICTURE
TO BE WRITTEN IN HOLLYWOOD[4]

The next morning, having been up most of the night with Patrick, Ernest writes Max that he has no intention of whoring in Hollywood.[5]

All he wants to do is finish this book already three years in progress, but he cannot let it go. At the ends of chapters he inserts dialogues between a generic character called "Old Lady" and another called "Author," allowing him to speak as "I" in the chapter proper while moving the reader effortlessly from time past to present. Raising the book to another level, Hemingway takes an enormous risk: if the device fails, the book will fail with it. In Key West, as far removed from both bullring and publishing world as an author can be, he weighs the risk against the gain, but not without tongue in cheek:

> Old Lady: *Sir, I do not know.*
> Author: *Madame, neither do I and it may well be that we are talking horseshit.*

Old Lady: *That is an odd term and one I did not encounter in my youth.*

Author: *Madame, we apply the term now to describe unsoundness in an abstract conversation or, indeed, any over-metaphysical tendency in speech.*[6]

On January 14 at St. Mary's Star of the Sea, Father Dougherty baptizes the two-month-old Hemingway baby, whose name is misspelled in the parish index as Gregory Hancock Hemmingway, son of Ernest Hemmingway. That same day, Ernest wrote Archie MacLeish that the book was finished, his son properly blessed, and he a little drunk. But three weeks later, with the typescript in New York, Ernest was still fiddling with the text, adding more of the Old Lady.[7] He was also arguing with Max Perkins about serializing parts of the book. Alfred Dashiel, editor of *Scribner's Magazine*, wanted to publish a selection of his own editing, which Hemingway would not allow. Ernest was furious at Dashiel's paltry offer when *Cosmopolitan* offered $1,000 for first refusal on a story.[8]

With Gabrielle now a regular convalescent on Whitehead Street, Pauline could either nurse, nanny, and cook herself or find a replacement. It was not a real choice, for Ernest, who required a good deal of care, was always her first concern, her children second. Needing more than a nanny for their boys, she required a woman trustworthy enough to run the household when they were elsewhere, stable enough to deal with their unconventional life, and intelligent enough to be part of the family without intruding. Gabrielle was given a ticket home, and her replacement sought first in Miami and then in New York, where Pauline scoured the agencies before running an ad in the paper.

The morning of Pauline's departure, Ernest wrote Archie MacLeish that he should use Ernest's power of attorney to take some cash from Hemingway's Empire Trust safety deposit box—five hundred, a thousand, even two thousand if needed—whatever it took to get Archie and Ada to come to Key West. "I am a hoarder," Ernest said. "I made that money myself and I have as much right to keep it any damned place I please as to give it to a bank to pea away or to spend it. . . . there is 14 grand there and I want very much to put one or two in circulation . . . in answer to the President's plea." Six days earlier, President Hoover had appealed to the country to cease the hoarding of currency, which he estimated at $1.3 billion. "It is in the interest of the hoarders and it is their patriotic duty," the President declared, "to return this wealth to circulation."[9]

Hemingway put away his "small cash reserve . . . when they were planning to give us all the works last fall." Given that over two thousand banks failed in 1931, Hemingway has every reason to fear for his money. Nothing he has seen in Europe or at home gave him reason to believe deeply in government promises. President Hoover's Reconstruction Finance Corporation, designed to prevent bank failures, was only able to reduce them by a third. "If they think it will help them," he told MacLeish, "they will make the money worthless in which case we may have to spend it fast." *They* are the bankers, the money men, the government, the ones he saw turn the German mark to worthless paper almost overnight. However, as Uncle Gus taught him, times of great risk are also times of great opportunity; throughout the decade, he invests in blue-chip stocks at depressed prices. Because his hoarded money is earning no interest, he tells MacLeish that Pauline might need to "buy a few depreciated bonds" to make up for lost income.[10] Later that month when asked to move $5,000 to Hemingway's Key West account, MacLeish takes Max Perkins with him as a witness, knowing that for all Hemingway's generosity, money is serious business. "I didn't count the balance," he wrote Ernest, "but the envelope was sealed so I suppose it was all you left."[11]

By the time Pauline returned from New York with newly hired Ada Stern to care for the boys, John and Katy Dos Passos, on their way to Mexico, had stopped in Key West long enough for Dos to read and comment on *Death in the Afternoon*, always a tricky business with Ernest. While there is plenty in the book to praise, Dos has to tell Ernest that the attacks on living people are unnecessary and the philosophizing, at times, tedious. "And then later when you . . . give them the low down about writing and why you like to live in Key

West etc. I was pretty doubtful . . . it would be a damn shame to leave in any unnecessary tripe."[12] With the typescript in New York, already on its way to galleys, Ernest eliminated several of the passages that Dos Passos fingered. Gone was the discourse on the transient beauty of Spanish women, gone such passing comments as "It takes a long time to be a good whore and receiving visitors is a form of whoring." And the last chapter, the one he was so certain was the "miracle we always have to make happen at the end,"[13] he ruthlessly pared down to its solid core, leaving only the best parts about Spain.[14] "Have just finished cutting out all you objected to," he wrote Dos Passos, "and may god damn your soul to hell if it's not right. Seemed the best of the book to me."[15]

The curse was more good-natured than it sounded on paper, for Hemingway was riding a manic high not unlike the one in 1924 that produced *In Our Time*, his first book of short stories. Even at a distance Uncle Gus can sense the difference in Ernest's demeanor, a "radical and desirable change," he calls it.[16] Having gone five years while publishing only one story, Hemingway returns to that genre with skills honed, ready to push the limits of short fiction. In a six-week period tangled with intrusive carpenters, small children, and a recovering wife, he writes three new stories and brings several others to conclusion. On February 11, to *Cosmopolitan Magazine* he mailed "After the Storm," a story he heard from Bra Saunders about diving on the *Valbanera*, which sank during the 1919 hurricane in the Half Moon Shoals quicksand. None of her 488 passengers and crew survived, nor was Saunders able to retrieve any of her wine and liquor cargo. As a Miami paper told the story,

> *Greek sponge fishermen found her wreck first. She lay on her side, with the name visible from the surface. Her master apparently had been trying to guide his ship through the narrow channel between the Blue Moon and Rebecca shoals. Missing the deep water by a scant hundred yards, the Valbanera crashed on the bar.*
>
> *When she was found every port and door was closed. The spongers said they found some bodies in the ship as they searched for valuables*

*in her hold, but no bodies were ever found floating on the surface and
no wreckage from the ship came ashore. . . . Soon after the spongers
had salvaged everything they could find and moved on, the wreck was
officially found by the United States coast guard.*[17]

Hemingway's fiction, using all the reported elements of the *Valbanera* sinking, went through three drafts, each less discursive and
more focused. Without pity or fear for the dead trapped inside the
wreck, the working-class waterman tells matter-of-factly how he
failed to break the porthole through which he could see the face of a
dead woman: "Her hair was tied once close to her head and it floated
all out in the water. I could see the rings on her hands." His focus is
on her jewelry, for she is now an unimportant part of the food chain,
a meal for jewfish that feed in the wreck just as birds are feeding off
edible scraps that float to the surface. Without salvage equipment,
the narrator leaves the wreck to Greeks who blow her open with
dynamite. "First there was birds," he says, "then me, then the
Greeks, and even the birds got more out of her than I did."[18] Devoid
of sentiment, it is a story for the times: when banks fail and jobs disappear, men on the edge cannot afford fine feelings.

At the end of February, Hemingway wrote Perkins that he had
seven stories done for a collection and two more in progress. Of the
seven, two were published—"Wine of Wyoming" and "The Sea
Change"—and "After the Storm" was in press; "A Natural History of
the Dead" he was now thinking of working into *Death in the Afternoon* as counterpoint for his "Old Lady" to consider. The three other
stories were probably "God Rest You Merry, Gentlemen," "The
Mother of a Queen," and "Homage to Switzerland," disturbing tales
all. Set on Christmas day in a hospital "reception room," the first
story has two Kansas City "ambulance surgeons" telling a reporter
about a young boy whose request for castration in order to avoid sins
against purity was refused by the doctors; the boy then misper-
formed the operation on himself with a straight-edged razor. In "The
Mother of a Queen," a somewhat unreliable narrator unwittingly
exposes himself while telling about a homosexual bullfighter who

won't pay to bury his mother properly: "There's a queen for you. You can't touch them. Nothing, nothing can touch them."[19]

"Homage to Switzerland" is a triptych in which each part begins exactly the same way: a cold night at a Swiss rail station where an American man waits for the Simplon-Orient Express to arrive. The train is late. So is the hour. In the first part, Mr. Wheeler, who does not care for women, toys with the Swiss waitress, offering her money to go upstairs with him. "He had been in that station before and knew there was no upstairs to go to." In the second part, Mr. Johnson becomes slightly maudlin about his recent divorce, but talking about it "had not blunted it; it had only made him feel nasty." In the third part, Mr. Harris, whose father "shot himself, oddly enough," engages in a surreal conversation with a member of the National Geographic Society.[20]

Lesbian wife, homosexual bullfighter, castrated boy, divorce, suicide, and death by water: if a man at war with the genteel tradition wanted to make a statement to his publisher about full use of the English language, he might choose such characters and themes. Without using a single objectionable word, Hemingway opened new possibilities in American fiction, a part of the landscape which his reading audience was not quite ready to explore.

———

Dry Tortugas, March. Squalls forming out on the gulf; lightning flickers burnt orange on the horizon, too far out to hear its thunder; a thin moon is rising. At the Fort Jefferson dock, where prisoners once arrived, the fishing party is gathered. Bra Saunders has muttonfish frying; whiskey's in the glasses. Around the fire, Mike Strater with his sketch pad; Archie, Uncle Gus, and Charley Thompson listening to Ernest; behind them the old brick fort rises up in the night black on black where men once died of yellow jack. Africa is all the talk, guns and shells, boots and baggage. Should they ship all the way to Mombasa or go overland from Cairo? Gus, the safari banker, listens and grins.

———

In the wake of the Tortuga trip, Archie MacLeish wrote Ernest that hard times had canceled all his dividend payments, making the safari impossible. But it was more than money that canceled Archie out: when a grass fire broke out, Ernest found fault with the way Archie responded to it. Shifting abruptly into his sarcastic mode, Ernest would not let loose of it; on the water going back to Key West, words were said not easily forgiven. As MacLeish remembered years later, "I told him somebody ought to prick his balloon and that led to ribald observations about my not having a big enough prick. . . . That began eating at him and he went on and on and on from there." Back on Whitehead Street, the argument continued, and Archie took the next train east.[21] Back in New York, he tried to say it clearly: "The thing that troubled me always was that you seemed to be on the defensive against me and not to trust me. I know that you do not believe in trusting people but I thought I had given you about every proof a man could of the fact of my very deep and now long lasting affection and admiration for you and it puzzled me that you should be so ready to take offense at what I did."[22] Not for the first time nor for the last, offense was taken, but this was the last time Archie left himself so vulnerable to Ernest's unpredictable rage: their seven-year friendship remained intact but never quite the same.[23] As with many another Hemingway contretemps, Ernest, who quickly forgot most of the incident, was surprised that Archie took it so seriously. "Bad weather but a grand trip," he told Max Perkins. "A fine trip with good storms."[24]

Perkins was probably happy to have missed the trip after reading Ernest's lecture about the photos for the bullfight book. Max's suggestion that they use only sixteen pictures was sound economics, but he was talking to the wrong author. Ernest was furious. Had he not promised the reader that the photos would show what he could not describe in words? Had he not spent the entire, expensive summer in Spain ruining his eyes looking at negatives? What did Max think he was going to do with two hundred photos? Had he not agreed to edit them down to only a hundred? Sixteen was ridiculous. Take out the color frontispiece, the paintings in color, but not the hundred photos. Maybe he could compromise, but not sixteen, not thirty-two. Maybe sixty. Could they still sell the book at $3.50 with sixty photos?[25]

At this point in a new book's production, Max had come to expect such letters from Ernest, but this year he was sorely distracted by his promotion to Scribner's editor in chief and by his daughter Bertha's automobile accident resulting in mysterious convulsions. None of his authors was getting Max's full attention that summer of the deepening national depression. Once he had soothed Ernest by placing sixty-four pages of pictures behind the bullfight text, he tried to prepare his prize author for the possibility that Scribner's might publish Zelda's Fitzgerald's manuscript. "It was very much autobiographical," Max said, "about herself, and biographical about Scott. In fact, she even named her hero Amory Blaine. . . . This was written very recently, and I think when Zelda was ill with her breakdown, though that did not show in it in any obvious way." Scott was now involved with the revisions, raising Max's expectation that the "novel will be quite a good book when she finishes it."[26] Caught awkwardly between his two authors, whom he would never have published in the same season, Max tried to make the best of it. Two months later, *Save Me the Waltz* was under Scribner's contract for fall publication side by side with *Death in the Afternoon*.

About this same time, Hemingway's mother wrote from Oak Park, her letter beginning: "I won't bother you with any more letters after this as it will take you some time to answer the past six that I have written you."[27] It was the sort of jibe guaranteed to irritate him. Always uneasy with women who pushed their boundaries, he was never easy with Grace Hemingway, the mother with advice for all her children: "Surely we all need to be jarred out of our complacency and made to see life, only, as an opportunity for service."[28] He was sure, he said, that there was nothing personal in this advice, "but there is nothing makes it more difficult for me to write a letter than receiving one written in a noble moral tone. . . . I remember how you used to write me you would rather see me in my grave than smoking cigarettes etc. and I suppose—what is the use of writing like this? None and I won't do it. But it shows you why I don't write more."[29]

Grace Hall Hemingway, a woman born before her time, never let a man, much less a son, tell her what to do or say. One of the first women to vote in Oak Park, she was a self-reliant, ambitious, and articulate woman who loved to perform in public. When her contralto voice aged out, she taught herself to paint well enough to have Chicago shows and real sales. While most boys grow up in conflict with their fathers, Ernest's conflict was with his mother, whose every characteristic he shared without ever acknowledging the debt. After his father's suicide in 1928, Ernest chose to ignore the clinical depression of the Doctor and blame his mother for the loss. In October, responding to a review of *Death in the Afternoon*, Hemingway wrote, "There are no subjects I would not jest about if the jest were funny enough (just as, liking wing shooting, I would shoot my own mother if she went in coveys and had a good strong flight)."[30]

Havana, spring and summer. Dark painted doorways, yellow painted plaster of houses, the courtyard where the men were bowling, auto buses, trucks, men with sacks on their heads, shiny headed niggers, lottery ticket sellers . . . the land smell and the smell of the harbor, the brown water with the silver roll of the tarpon, the launches crossing, the spars of a smack sunk in the hurricane . . . the iron balconies and the iron grills, the stringy whores, the fat whores, the half niggers, the boxer training on the roof . . . the billiard room where the pilots play, the Cojo, the round tiles on the roof like poles of bamboo, the market, 100 radio police cars, 25,000 soldiers, the stool pigeons bar across from the Jefatura, view of Sloppy Joe's bar from the smooth stoned light and airy top windows.[31]

—Ernest Hemingway

On the 21st of April, after stopping by Thompson's chandlery for supplies, Ernest, his Kansas City cousin Bud White, Charles Thompson, and Joe Russell in Russell's thirty-two-foot *Anita* crossed to Havana under a full moon. Their plan for a ten-day trip was immediately forgotten as soon as Ernest hooked his first marlin: days turned into weeks, weeks into months. Wives came and left; others appeared and disappeared, all taking their turns at the heavy rods: Grant and Jane Mason, Ernest's sister Carol, Bra Saunders. Every day but a few they fished early and hard, keeping a running account: the log of the good ship *Anita*.

About the same time the *Anita's* first marlin hit the trailing bait, three Cuban university students were brought before a military tribunal for having tried six times to blow up President Machado with a dynamite-laden car. At 8:45 a.m. Pauline's marlin ran her line out three hundred yards, jumping and jumping, jerking her about for forty minutes until Ernest pulled it to gaff. Before the marlin's colors faded, the three students were sentenced to eight prison years on the Isle of Pines.[32] Chugging back into the harbor that afternoon, no one on the *Anita* noticed that the *Orizaba* had docked during their absence; they were at dinner that evening when that ship departed for New York. On board were the critic Malcom Cowley's estranged wife, Peggy, and her sometime lover and troubled poet, Hart Crane, who at noon the following day went over the fantail to his death by water.[33]

Each day began with the air foul around Arsenal Dock, the men sleeping sometimes on the *Anita*, sometimes joining the women at the Ambos Mundos, where a room with bath overlooking the harbor and the cathedral was only $2 a day.[34] Sleeping wherever but rising with the sun, they had their baits in the water before passing under Morro Castle guarding the harbor. For those two months, Ernest's intensity never lessened. His fishing partners came and left, but he continued unsated. Once, with that same intensity, he was married to trout fishing up in Michigan; then trout gave way to the corrida. Now, with *Death in the Afternoon* in galley proofs, that ten-year passion is waning. These Gulf Stream days, pursuing fish as large as his imagination, are the beginning of a new pursuit which will last him the rest of his life. Hunting, of course, was always there in the fall, but others, hunting before him when the country was new, had the best of it. The purple Gulf Stream of huge fish is the new country. It beats everything: hunting, flying, skiing, everything. He is "completely and utterly satisfied on this as sport, living, spectacle and exercise," he writes Mike Strater. For years commercial fishermen pulled in the marlin on handlines, but "we are the first to take them on rod and reel and have virgin fishing." Like the natural historian he dreamed of being as a boy, Ernest calls life in the stream "damn fine pioneering. Truly the most wonderful damned thing I have ever been on."[35]

Trolling in the stream, he sees the marlin smash his bait, take it in his bill, and run out a hundred yards or more with himself waiting, tensed to set the hook. Then long, impossible jumps, the sun glittering off a huge body completely out of the water, its weight on the line enormous, its head shaking like an angry terrier to throw the hook. Sometimes bringing him to gaff, sometimes losing him, twice to sharks who leave only the head and bill. Once, with the gaffed marlin almost pulled across the transom, another marlin "came to the boat and jumped high out of [the] water to look at what was happening to his partner . . . very strange."[36] Calm days and rough, squalls breaking over them, sun burning their backs, they fish fifty-four days out of fifty-eight, selling their catch at the dock or giving it away. For a few days in June, they were able to hire Carlos Gutiérrez, captain of the fishing schooner *Paco*, to join them in the stream. When fishing slacks, Carlos tells stories of whale sharks 120 feet long, of a shark fighting a porpoise, and of a black marlin who took 495 fathoms of line three thousand feet straight down. He claims to have seen marlin leap over his small skiff, and once landed three of the four marlin hooked at the same moment on his handline.[37]

Soon after Ernest arrived in Havana, a reporter caught up with him, hoping for some pithy quotes only to be disappointed when "it was of fishing that he talked, ignoring totally the subject of Hemingway." Ernest told him,

> The Cuban coast offers one of the best fishing grounds in the world to the fisherman who is looking for big game. Professional fishermen have brought marlin and swordfish to the local markets, which, even after they are dressed, weigh more than the world record catch, and it is this size of fish we are looking for.
>
> In three days of fishing we have caught four marlin and three sailfish, one of which was landed by Mrs. Hemingway. . . . Professional

fishermen in the harbor assure us that we would have to fish to a depth of fifty fathoms to catch them. And yet, yesterday, our teaser bait trailing behind the boat brought six of them to the surface. . . . I really shouldn't be telling this because as soon as fishermen learn the possibilities here and Havana prepares to care for fishermen, it will become famous and crowded. And when it does, we'll find some other fishing ground.[38]

They did not speak of Hemingway the author, nor did they speak of the unspeakable, the condition of martial law which ruled Cuba, criticism of which could close a paper and many a mouth. When a political prisoner "disappeared" from his cell shortly after Hemingway's arrival in Cuba, the secret police were asked to investigate. No one in Havana held his breath waiting for the unspeakable answer. On May Day, the *Havana Post* was not printed; whatever happened in the streets went unrecorded. Three weeks later, on the eve of the Republic's thirtieth anniversary, the secret police arrested sixty revolutionists from all walks of Cuban life. President Machado, surrounded in his palace by loyal forces, put extra police into the streets. Finally all official anniversary observance of the island's independence is suspended, and three hundred more Cubans are in jail. By June bombs are exploding here and there in the city while sons and daughters of prominent Cuban families are under arrest.[39] Unable to report the extent of unrest, newspapers are reduced to ambiguous statements:

Seven Spaniards and one Polaco were ordered deported by the president. Cleaning the riff raff out of Cuba in the form of these undesirables is claimed to be an excellent idea.[40]

The desperate ones do not get out so easily:

Found drowned in the harbor with his hands tied, Ignacio Iglesias, skipper of the tug Providencia, is reported by his son to have suffered from delirium of persecution for some time past.[41]

Having been a student of revolutions since his early Paris days, Ernest tells Max Perkins that the new grist he has acquired for his writing mill is not merely about fishing.[42]

On the 2nd of June, with the stream running strong to eastward and no marlin striking, Hemingway came in early to answer mail. Sending corrected galleys to Max, he said he was thinking of postponing his much-planned African safari for another year. Too much was going on, he said, too many stories to write. The galleys were revised with much eliminated; he is annotating photos by night, fishing hard by day, learning more about his quarry.[43] To MacLeish, he confirms his decision about postponing Africa: "My goddamned conscience says not to go now. Too long away the way things are going."[44] To Mike Strater, he suggests they hunt that fall in Wyoming before the country is ruined by the road being built over Beartooth Pass.[45]

"The way things were going" across America is not encouraging unless you are a writer looking for subject matter: angry veterans marching on Washington demanding their promised bonus; angry policemen searching in vain for the kidnapped Lindbergh baby. With millions out of work and the federal deficit approaching $1 billion, President Hoover insists on reducing government spending and raising taxes to balance the budget. Unemployment, he argues, is not going to diminish unless more credit is invested in private enterprise, but when he asked for a manufacturing excise tax, Congress instead raised the income tax. By early June, staggering under a $13 million deficit of its very own, U.S. Steel watches its common stock fall to 24 1/4.[46] Ernest, who was thinking of putting part of his New York cache into U.S. Steel preferred, chooses instead to buy ten shares of Guaranty Trust and $2,000 of Belgium bonds.[47]

When she isn't in Havana with her husband, Pauline writes daily letters, missing him always, but never petulant or complaining seriously, never causing him worry. Greg's new tooth and Patrick's measles are fine; the house, fine. She is fine. (Her nagging Catholic conscience never lets her forget that Ernest is hers by virtue of her having destroyed his first marriage.) On Mother's Day she sent telegrams to both their mothers. Paying bills, supervising carpenters, forwarding galley proofs, she did not wish him home until the marlin stopped running. The good wife settled down with *War and Peace*, while in the yard Jane Mason's gift of peacocks preened beneath the fig trees.[48] Pauline knew what Ernest expected and when, knew his moods and methods. It was she who balanced the bank account, paid the bills, and managed the children. While he fished through the month of May, she was planning their excursion to Wyoming: what to do with the house, the children, their clothes, the car. She did it all, giving Ernest the room to roam and to write, for she knew that his writing, which fed off his enormous energy, mattered most. He is her husband, her lover, her project, her satisfaction, and she does whatever is necessary to protect his gift and to keep herself on his mind.[49]

———

Key West, June 26. Fifteen hours coming back across the Gulf sick, running a fever, finally making the American Shoals light, returning to the house empty except for the odor of Pauline's perfume and her letter from Piggott, where she missed him, wanted him. Hurry, she said, hurry. He could not hurry the fever, and at night he woke sweating, sheets damp, the lighthouse across the street playing off the bedroom wall and the peacock screaming in the yard. Page proofs on the desk carry a running head: Hemingway's Death.

———

After leaving Patrick and Gregory with Pauline's parents in Piggott, she and Ernest return like migratory animals to the high country, living that summer and early fall once again in a log cabin at the Nordquist ranch. Their new Ford roadster, having carried them safely cross-country against the tide of displaced, road-weary Americans, rests while they ride horseback, fish, and hunt. Rising up early in the morning, he passes the cabin of Josie Merck, calling out, "Up, up, Daughter!" on his way to the lodge breakfast. While he corrects page proofs for *Death in the Afternoon*, Josie and Pauline take long walks in the woods, returning with small flowers and wild strawberries that stain their hands bloody red.[50]

In August, before invited friends arrive, Ernest finishes a story about young Nick Adams, the boy he invented in Paris, giving him many of his own experiences: summer fishing in upper Michigan, parents like his own parents, fears like his own fears. The story began abruptly with Nick and Tom, teenage road boys, walking into a small-town bar: "When he saw us come in the door the bartender looked up and then reached over and put the glass covers on the two free lunch bowls," Nick tells us. On their way out of town, with the sharp smell of tan bark in the night air and water beginning to freeze in the puddles, they stop at the railway station, where five whores, six white men, and three Indians are crowded into a hot waiting room reeking of stale smoke. As soon as they enter, they notice one of the men with a white face and white hands. Another man asks them, "Ever buggar a cook? . . . You can buggar this one." As the boys listen and watch, two of the whores, Alice and a peroxide blonde, begin to argue over which of them actually knew a once famous but now dead boxer, shot down by his own father. Nick becomes fascinated with Alice, an enormous woman with a pretty face, "but my God she was big." As the boys move toward the door, the cook asks, "Which way you boys going?" Tom tells him, "The other way from you." "What the hell kind of place is this?" Tom asked. Night visitors in a surreal world of words without action, threats unrealized, temptations unanswered: it was an enigmatic story whose center lay just beyond definition. Hemingway called the story "The Light of the World."[51]

Pauline typed the story between trout fishing and bird hunts from which they never returned empty-handed. Two days in alfalfa fields full of sage hens, they killed twenty-five birds for the Nordquist dinner table. On the second day, Ernest, pumping his 12-gauge as fast it would fire, brought down three hens and a running jackrabbit with four shots. Pauline, with her double-barreled 28-gauge, brought down three winged cripples. Both of them, having grown up among men who hunted, accept blood sport as a natural activity; what they kill, they customarily clean and eat. Pauline participates because it is Ernest's passion. Her witness at his kills gives him pleasure, and in the fields, she is his pupil just as she was at the bullrings in Spain. She loves him and what he loves as hard as she is able, but there is a part of him that goes beyond her ability to follow, a need to kill so long as birds flew or marlin rose to the bait. During that fall season, his hunting log recorded: 32 sage hens, 2 rockdogs, 1 porcupine, 2 elk, 11 rabbits, 2 bears, and 1 eagle shot on the wing.[52]

Ernest arrived at the L-Bar-T slim, dark, and confident if a little weak from his bronchial infection. Two months of heavy hauling against huge marlin built new muscular structure across his back and forearms. Turning thirty-three, he is approaching his physical and literary prime, stretching his limits. Nothing he can imagine is out of reach. Soon after arriving at the Nordquist ranch, he sent Bill Lengel, editor at *Cosmopolitan*, "Homage to Switzerland" in response to his request for a new story. "Homage" was a new form for the short story, Ernest told Lengel, three stories in one, all opening the same way.[53] Unwilling to run such an experimental story in his mass-market periodical, Lengel declined the story. Smarting from the rejection, Ernest immediately offered "Homage," "Light of the World," and "Mother of a Queen" to Perkins for *Scribner's Magazine* at a cut-rate price of $2,100 for all three. He would like them to run in three successive issues "to bitch Cosmopolitan—they have offered $1.00 a word up to 3500."[54] No need to tell Max about Lengel's rejection.

That same day he responded at his virulent best to Paul Romaine, whom Hemingway allowed, in a moment of weakness, to reprint in a limited collector's edtion an early poem. When Romaine suggested that Ernest might benefit from the current leftward swing of literature, Ernest told him that was "so much horseshit." He did not follow fashions, then or ever. The only ones disillusioned by the state of the nation were not paying attention to what was happening all through the Twenties. Left and right were equally despicable, along with limited-edition publishers, who should be shot when the revolution started. Romaine, sorry to have touched an exposed nerve, said he knew that Ernest, restrained from going left for "reasons we both understand," would stay to the political right. Ernest dismissed the reply as the "same presumptuous poppycock," refusing to state his political beliefs, which, if published, could put him in jail.[55] Having never voted, never supported a political party, and having never believed any poltician since his postwar education as a reporter in Europe, Hemingway was, if anything, a passive anarchist who wanted all government, except tribal, out of his life.

In August, possibly with a hint of malice, MacLeish sent Ernest the summer issue of *Hound & Horn*, which felt obliged to "condemn" Hemingway for defects in his imagination, sincerity, and virtuosity. "Laziness," claimed Lawrence Leighton, "confines Hemingway's attention to primitive rudimentary beings." His "sincerity and appeal exist only for the tabloid mind." Addicted to the first-person narrator, Ernest was "not playing fair." His characters did not live. "They are nervous instead of passionate." His vision and imagination were defective; his attitude toward life revealed his spiritual poverty. If only Hemingway might learn what Henry James had to teach him about the life of the mind. But it was a hopeless case. Ernest's sentimental-ity, "his desire to obtain emotion without earning it," was barely "con-cealed by his habit of saying as little as possible. If only Hemingway, who was such an influence on contemporary American writers, could write more like Raymond Radiguet, whose "qualities of mind and ways of thinking" Mr. Hemingway lacked. Radiguet's strength was his ability to use his inherited tradition. "One feels behind Radiguet," the long article said, "Mme. de Lafayette, Benjamin Constant, Proust, even Racine."[56]

Furious, Ernest promised Archie that the next time he was in New York he was "going to beat the shit out of" Lincoln Kirstein, the editor of the magazine. But he did find Leighton's arrangement of who stood behind whom sexually amusing. Possibly Radiguet, a homosexual, might stand behind the lady, but he would certainly "have felt the oth-ers behind him and well up into him, doubtless, if it would have helped him to get along."[57] Having said it to Archie, he immediately wrote a letter to the editor, calling the essay "very interesting," but taking exception to the arrangement of the French tradition:

Surely this should read "Radiguet behind Mme. de Lafayette." The rest of the sentence might stand although it would be more just to place Cocteau behind Radiguet and give Racine the benefit of the

*doubt. But perhaps Mr. Leighton has a feeling for Racine and would
not wish to deprive him of his place.*[58]

As a footnote in *Death in the Afternoon,* Hemingway included a dialogue in which the "Author" explained to the "Old Lady" that the
meaning of decadence depended largely upon who used it. For
example, he told her, Cocteau found it decadent when he discovered
that his young lover, Raymond Radiguet, was having a clandestine
affair with a woman.[59]

With five bank accounts in three states and one foreign country,
their Key West house paid for and clear, and no outstanding debts,
the Hemingways were floating easily with the depressed economy. If
book sales fell, so did the price of gasoline. If royalties were reduced,
so were transatlantic fares. The "American Earthquake," as Edmund
Wilson called it, was not threatening their lives. While the political
rhetoric of President Hoover and freshly nominated Democrat
Franklin Roosevelt heightened toward the fall election, Hemingway,
whose distaste for both parties was acute, listened to coyotes where
no radio could reach him. On his birthday (July 21), while police
were telling the Bonus Expeditionary Force to evacuate Washington,
Ernest deftly dropped his MacGinty fly onto Sealey's pool, and the
cutthroat trout rose to it as in a dream.[60]

Visitors arrived early in September. First came the tribe of Murphys: Gerald, Sara, Baoth, and his sister, Honoria; Patrick, who
seemed to be recovering from his tuberculosis, was still hospital-
ized. The two families fished and camped out, Ernest and Gerald a
little uncomfortable with each other but trying to be decent. As
Ernest told Archie, "I always get along well with Gerald and like him
when I'm with him. But the countries you love best are the ones you
miss when you are away from them."[61] Gerald, of course, complained amusingly about the food: all that beef and not a decent
chef in sight. When canned fruit salad appeared on the table with a
dollop of mayonnaise and a maraschino cherry on top, Sara laughed.
High up at the lake campsite, Ernest took their daughter in hand,
teaching Honoria how to catch a trout and how to clean it after-

ward, explaining the beauty and function of all its parts.[62] As the
Murphys were preparing to depart, Gerald explained by letter to
MacLeish that Ernest was "never difficult with the people he does
not like, the people he does not take seriously." To those who did
not matter, like Gerald himself, he was indifferent "to the point of
open inattention." Murphy also found him "more mellowed,
amenable and far more charitable and philosophical than before—
and more patient also. But the line has been drawn between the
people whom he admits to his life and those he does not. . . . He is
fast taking on the qualities which are necessary to a working
artist,—and he *is* of the race."[63]

As the Murphys left, Charles Thompson arrived to join Ernest on
a strenuous, frustrating hunt for mountain goats too wary for the
novices. When they came down from the mountains, Pauline left for
Piggott and Key West, torn as she frequently was between her duties
as mother and wife. On September 23, while Ernest was killing a
seven-point bull elk up on Timber Creek, *Death in the Afternoon* was
published in New York. Reviewer Lawrence Stallings, who adapted *A
Farewell to Arms* to the stage, caught the complexity of the book:

> *Certain books, notably ones in which authors are constrained to fol-
> low their daimon, are definitely without calculation. . . . They
> remain forever out of literary categories and become, according to the
> depth of originality in the writer, a work unto themselves. Their
> influence is not to be calculated. So it is with "Death in the After-
> noon." It is one of the great vagaries and we have not had another
> such in a long time.*[64]

The *New York Herald Tribune* review urged readers with no taste
for bullfights to read the book anyway, for it was "teeming with life,
vigorous, powerful, moving and constantly entertaining."[65] Other
reviewers, less open to experiments, were not impressed. The *New
York Times* found the subject matter too technical and the prose
style beneath Hemingway's best: "Action and conversation . . . are
his best weapons. To the degree he dilutes them with philosophy

and exposition he weakens himself."[66] *The New Yorker* called the book "suicidal" on Hemingway's part. Granville Hicks could not stand the book; at great length, Malcolm Cowley avoided the question.[67]

A week after the book's publication, with the first heavy snow already fallen, Ernest and Charles Thompson rode into the Closed Creek and Pilot Creek wilderness, where a Nordquist horse had been shot to ripen for bear bait. The two men were pushing their luck, for winter snow would soon close Cooke City and the Clarks Fork Valley until the following spring. Just before an October 7 storm dumped more snow thick on the trails and deep in the woods, Charles killed his black bear feeding on the bait. Despite the now heavy snow, Ernest would not give up. Four days later, as the light was failing, a hulking bear approached the frozen bait. Unable to see the front of his open sight against the bear's black mass, Ernest breathed out slowly, squeezing off a shot that hit the animal high on the shoulder with a solid thump. Wounded and angry, the bear thrashed off into the woods, trailing dark blood on the luminous snow. With a fresh round in his chamber and a moon rising overhead, Ernest, alone, followed the ragged tracks and blood spoor black against the snow into the thickening darkness. He could not see the bear until, separated by only twenty feet, they were on top of each other. When Ernest's quick shot struck the animal, he "bawled like a bull," collapsing dead in the snow. Leaving his kill to skin the next day, Ernest rode twenty-five cold and dark miles beneath the risen moon back to the ranch. By the next day's light, the stiffened hide fetched out at eight feet between back and front paws.[68]

Three days later, Ernest and Charles packed up to run in front of a fresh storm coming out of the west. In his last letters before departing, Hemingway said they have "killed enough meat for two guides to get married on." Early the next morning, Ernest paid the month's bill with a check for $1,620.[69] By that night, he and Charles are in Cody with the smell of snow in the air and winter setting in thickly behind them.

———

Key West: Election Day, 1932. Black-habited nuns lead school-children into the Convent of Mary Immaculate. Up Whitehead Street, searching for truants, comes Cayo Hueso, the two-wheeled ice cream seller's boat, its black funnel curved backward. In Grunt Bone Alley, a pushcart loaded with yellowtails and grunts will sell you a "bunch" for twenty-five cents. Down Duval Street, the Hard Times Drag, hauling freight in a handcart, nickels-and-dimes its way across town. Papayas, sea grapes, sapodillas, and Spanish limes are bunches of color on the sidewalk display next to Demerrit's corner market, selling "fresh fish" to customers who cannot imagine any other. In "jungle town" where colored folk live, Welter's Coronet Band is marching a funeral party to the graveyard.[70]

———

The day began with no rain falling out of a gray scudding sky, but water is standing in pools and puddles from yesterday. At the First Precinct polling station, Hemingway's neighbors cast 131 votes for Roosevelt and 32 for Hoover. Charles Thompson's brother Karl is elected county sheriff by a two-to-one margin; Norberg Thompson, the eldest and wealthiest brother, is unopposed for county commissioner. Three thousand citizens of Monroe County vote, but not Pauline, who this day is riding the train to Memphis, where her father will meet her. In Piggott both of her boys are sick with whooping cough. Ernest and his visiting first son, Bumby, are in the almost renovated and half-redecorated Key West house. If he voted, he makes no mention of it. At Taiku, China, in the province of Shansi, his uncle Willoughby Hemingway, medical missionary for thirty years, dies quietly this day from influenza.[71]

By the time Hemingway joins Pauline in Piggott, Mr. Stitt, a publicity man for Paramount Pictures, is hounding him with telegrams, wanting to set up a showing of A Farewell to Arms right there in Arkansas. Ernest, more interested in jumping coveys of quail with the dogs, Hoolie and Jack, declines the offer. When the second telegram announced

You and guests are cordially invited to the World Premiere of Farewell to Arms Strand Theatre Piggott Wednesday December Seventh (Stop) Kindly advise number seats you wish reserved regards.[72]

Ernest asked if there was something about his first answer, no thanks, that Mr. Stitt had not understood. He is absolutely uninterested in being Mr. Stitt's publicity project. Paramount purchased the film rights, but they did not purchase the book's author. Moreover, he has heard that the nurse, Catherine Barkley, was miraculously restored to life in the film version, ruining the end of the book. Would Mr. Stitt kindly stop annoying him. By December 6, the AP wire service in Little Rock spread the story that Ernest was "indignant over the traditional 'happy ending' in the screen version of his book," and would not attend the Piggott showing of the movie.[73] Mr. Stitt wired his reply:

Interpreted your first answer correctly I am sure and since I followed the advice showing of film in Piggott naturally off stop my endeavors were plainly for your reaction publicity-wise to help put picture over stop I may add if you call a woman dying in childbirth a happy ending then the picture has just that stop with all regards.[74]

Two days later, well-meaning Uncle Gus, having attended the film's New York premiere, wired Hemingway that the film was faithful to the book's conclusion and quite moving, with Gary Cooper and Helen Hayes giving excellent performances. A Mr. Stitt had called Gus, wondering how to get Ernest to see the movie, for he was anxious to have a private showing so that the author might make suggestions for improving the film. As politely as he could, Ernest explained to Gus Pfeiffer that he simply was not interested in Paramount's using him to make more money for themselves. Gus wired back that he understood Ernest's position and that he should "stick to it."[75]

The Paramount effort to use Hemingway was not an isolated incident, for increasingly his private life was becoming public domain. When he invited Max Perkins to come to Arkansas for a pre-Christmas duck hunt, Ernest also asked Max to issue a statement which, in part, said:

> Mr. Ernest Hemingway has asked his publishers to disclaim the romantic and false military and personal career imputed to him in a recent film publicity release. . . . While Mr. H. appreciates the publicity attempt to build him into a glamorous personality like Floyd Gibbons or Tom Mix's horse Tony, he deprecates it and asks the motion picture people to leave his private life alone.[76]

Such statements, of course, merely fired the public's curiosity to know more about his life, which would never again be private. The persona he created to narrate *Death in the Afternoon* would, before the decade was finished, displace the sometimes shy, frequently reserved, and always observant private man. Recognition translated into income from book sales, which allowed him the luxury of his expensive pursuits, but that same recognition came at a stiff price. Part of him understood the cost, but once he was seated firmly in that saddle there was no way to dismount short of shooting the horse.

Between telegrams to New York and afternoon quail hunts in the ruined fields of the river bottom, Hemingway was part-time nurse to Pauline, Jinny, and Bumby, who were down with the flu, a virus which always frightened Ernest. About that same time the Pfeiffer's barn, converted into a guesthouse, caught fire from an overheated woodstove. Before the blaze could be quenched, it and the firemen's water destroyed Ernest's typewriter, his boots, several of his guns, books and letters, and most of their clothes. Only his manuscripts and his cherished Woodsman pistol were rescued.[77] By December 15, Ernest was more than happy to leave the cares of the Piggott Christmas to the Pfeiffers while he headed for Memphis to meet Max Perkins's train.

Their week's hunting trip began on the coldest day of the year, the temperature in the twenties, snow and sleet turning the road into a nightmare with Ernest driving. Telephone lines were down all along the route to Watson, where they were booked into the *Walter Adams*, a houseboat on the Arkansas River with hunting guides provided. The next day was so cold that ducks were found frozen on the ponds, so cold no one who was there ever forgot it. The eerie silence is regularly broken by tree limbs crashing down in the woods, now on one side of the river, then on the other. All the while the men squint against weak sunlight glittering through iced branches, their breath hanging in the air before them. Given the number of minor crises he has recently faced, Ernest is in remarkable form, shooting well, sleeping well, waking in darkness eager to crouch in the duck blind waiting for the first flight to come into the decoys with the sun rising behind them. Sometimes drifting on the river, jump-shooting singles they scare up, sometimes hunkered down in the blind with retrievers at their feet, he and Max share the days so intensely that if they never hunt again, it does not matter. Despite cold weather and what passed for poor hunting in that part of Arkansas, Hemingway shipped fifteen ducks to Charles Thompson in Key West and another fifteen to Piggott.[78]

At Helena, Arkansas, four days before Christmas, Ernest put Max back on the train for Memphis and New York, his editor's flawed hearing unimproved by a week of shotguns blasting over frozen duck ponds and rivers. Chilling in the baggage car were Max's seven mallards and several of Ernest's. In his hand luggage, Max also took with him the typescript of a new Hemingway story so spare and oblique that nothing seemed to happen, no action, no overt conflict, little but dialogue. In a late-night Spanish bar, two waiters, one younger than the other, discuss an old man, past eighty, drunk in his customary cups, their last customer, who won't go home. Their conversation reveals that the old drunk, who has plenty of money, tried to hang himself the previous week, but was cut down by his niece. Finally the younger waiter refuses to refill the old man's cup, forcing him out into the night, "a very old man walking unsteadily but with dignity." The younger waiter goes home, leaving his older friend to turn out the lights. As he does so, he assesses his own condition and that of the world where a clean and pleasant café can be a haven against the nothingness that is everywhere. "It was a nothing he knew too well. It was all a nothing and a man was nothing too. It was only that and light was all it needed and a certain cleanness and order." To himself he mutters a parodic version of the Lord's Prayer, beginning "Our nada who art in nada, nada be thy name." He would go home to a narrow bed where he would lie awake until daylight came. "It is probably only insomnia," he tells himself. "Many must have it."[79] Ernest called the story "A Clean, Well Lighted Place," a phrase so apt that it would become a permanent part of the American vocabulary.

Many did have "it" that year of Hoovervilles cobbled together out of packing crates, loose tin, and cardboard boxes. Many had "it" in high-rise buildings with windows opening conveniently onto nothingness; others had "it" on high bridges, in lonely alleys, among strangers. That previous fall, over Wyoming whiskey, Ernest upset Charles Thompson by saying that one day, like his father, he would have to kill himself.

Pauline Hemingway just prior to departing for the African safari in 1933. (John F. Kennedy Library)

Patrick, Bumby (Jack), and Gregory summering on Cat Cay while Ernest fished for tuna.
(John F. Kennedy Library)

Financial angel to the Hemingway family, Uncle Augustus "Gus" Pfeiffer on board the
Pilar. (John F. Kennedy Library)

Sara Murphy with her three children, Baoth, Patrick, and Honoria. (John F. Kennedy Library)

Years later, all her friends are saying
"Her skin is simply exquisite—really
lovelier today than ever before"

Jane Mason as she appeared in the
1933 Ladies' Home Journal
advertisement that Hemingway
used to characterize Margot
Macomber.

Martha Gellhorn in Cuba in the late 1930s. (Toby Bruce Collection)

The Saturday Review
of LITERATURE

VOL. XIV No. 22   NEW YORK, SATURDAY, SEPTEMBER 26, 1936   TEN CENTS A COPY

Library
N. C. State College   8 26 '36

IN THIS ISSUE

BERNARD DEVOTO
A Generation Beside the Limpopo

ELMER DAVIS
Reviews "The Anatomy of Frustration" by H. G. Wells

MABEL S. ULRICH
Reviews "The Trouble I've Seen" by Martha Gellhorn

LOUIS ADAMIC
Reviews "The History of the Haymarket Affair" by Henry David

CHRISTOPHER MORLEY
Translations from the South American

MARTHA GELLHORN

"Miss Gellhorn has seen not only physical hunger and spiritual despair on the relief lines. Existing side by side with these she has seen love and courage" . . .
(See page 7)

Martha Gellhorn as Hemingway first saw her on the cover of The Saturday Review of Literature.
(Photograph by Jules Pierlow)

John Dos Passos, the "old muttonfish," in a pose that became all too accurate a description of his relationship with Hemingway. (John F. Kennedy Library)

Taken from the lighthouse across the street, Hemingway's Key West home on Whitehead Street before the brick wall and swimming pool were built. (Monroe City Library/Library of Congress)

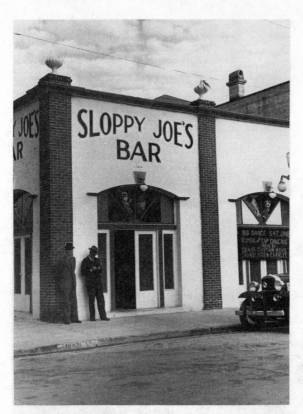

Having moved his bar from Greene Street to Duval, Josie Russell began featuring free, live music on Saturday nights. (Library of Congress)

SPECIAL'S

YELLOW TAILS POTATOES 35
TURTLE STEAK-POTATOES 40
CONCH-STEAK-POTATOES 35
JEW FISH STEAK-POTATOES 35
KING-FISH-POTATOES 35
& FRY OYSTERS-POTATOES 45
FILET STEAK-POTATOES 40
HAMBURGER STEAK-POTATO 35
HAM+CABBAGE DINNER 35

Depression-era prices in front of a Key West café. (Monroe City Library/Library of Congress)

Aerial view of Key West looking up Duval Street. To the left, Whitehead Street, the light-house across from Hemingway house visible. (Monroe City Library/Library of Congress)

Relief workers trying to identify Matecumbe hurricane victims before cremating the bodies.
(Monroe City Library/Library of Congress)

Chapter Five

1933

ONE TRIP ACROSS

Key West and Cuba

Most modest of all American writers is Ernest Hemingway whose half-dozen published books have set a new style in contemporary literature, but who, nevertheless, shuns personal publicity as an owl shuns daylight. Hemingway . . . does not even care to have any biographical material about himself made public. . . . Though hundreds of thousands of persons know his works, however, very few know anything about the man himself. With what amounts almost to a mania, he avoids personal publicity of every kind.

—*Key West Citizen,* February 11, 1933

In the first week in January, Hemingway loaded up his Ford, kissed his family goodbye, and drove over the gravel road out of Piggott, heading east. Pauline and his three sons would take the train to

Key West; he is on his way to New York, driving through Nashville and Knoxville and up over the Blue Ridge Mountains to Roanoke, Virginia. With only two weeks having passed since Max Perkins's return to the city, there is no single, compelling reason for this trip. He has a contract to sign for his as yet untitled book of short stories and some tax business with his lawyer, Maurice Speiser, all of which could be accomplished by mail. Call it road work, a trip to clear his head after too many in-laws, too many sick children. As much as he needed an orderly family life for refuge, sometimes he simply needed to be on the road again counting miles; sometimes he needed the rush of New York: take in a fight, see Strater, buy some books, have a little hotel life, which he truly enjoyed. Leaving Knoxville on Saturday, he sent Max a telegram: "Arriving Sunday morning." Passing through Marion, Virginia, without calling on Sherwood Anderson, his old mentor and no longer friend, he arrives in Roanoke, stores his car, and catches the night train into New York.[1] By the time he reaches Penn Station, skies are gray, the temperature hovering in the thirties, not quite freezing.

At his Scribner's office on Fifth Avenue, Max and a tall, gangly Thomas Wolfe are waiting when Ernest arrives. The two authors, meeting for the first time, are wary but friendly. In 1929, Wolfe's staggering first novel, *Look Homeward, Angel*, ran cheek by jowl with Hemingway's *A Farewell to Arms*. Born within a year of each other, they, along with Fitzgerald, are the headliners in Max's stable of bright young writers. For lunch, Max walks them up to Cherio's, where his customary table is waiting in the downstairs dining room, his martini on the table, and his customary order of guinea hen's breast in the offing. If he hopes, as he once said, that Hemingway's restrained style may somehow exert an influence on Wolfe's gargantuan appetite for words, the lunch is a failure. But the two writers seem to enjoy it, Hemingway talking, Wolfe listening.[2]

Later in the week, having signed copies of *Death in the Afternoon* along with his Scribner's book contract, Hemingway shopped for new phonograph records, ate lunch with acerbic Dorothy Parker, dined with Uncle Gus, visited Sara Murphy, talked safari with old

African hand Dick Cooper, bought and shipped books to Key West, and attended the Sunday-evening fights. With Gus Pfeiffer, he discussed the African trip scheduled for late December. He also found time for Sidney Franklin, the Brooklyn bullfighter he met in Spain: "He looks sort of shoddy in Spain sometimes," he said, "but by god he looked awfully good in New York. I believe he is the best story teller I've ever known." During the second week, he paid the taxidermist bill on his black bearskin rug with head attached, picked up presents for Pauline at Bergdorf Goodman, and bought a Friday-night train ticket back to Roanoke.[3] One afternoon with no Paramount publicity men hounding him, he took Josie Merck, his friend from the L-Bar-T, to see the movie version of *A Farewell to Arms*. At the end, when Gary Cooper carried the dead Helen Hayes to the hospital window and white doves fluttered past, Ernest whispered, "Josie, those are just damn sea gulls."[4]

New York was never his town, but he was sometimes its darling. Not only was *A Farewell to Arms* playing on the screen, but at the newsstands, *The Nation* carried Clifton Fadiman's essay "Ernest Hemingway: An American Byron"—claiming the author was more of a public hero than an artist.

> *Hemingway is a man born in his due time, embodying to perfection the mute longings and confused ideals of a large segment of his own and the succeeding generation. He is the unhappy warrior that many men would like to be. About him has sprung up a real contemporary hero-myth.*

Any publicity is good publicity if you are selling books, but if you are the writer of those books, it might not help to be told that you court violence, darkness, and death, that your work embodies "a kind of splendid, often very beautiful, disease of the imagination."[5] Previously, he was a talent to be nurtured, a discovery to be worn on the critic's watch fob, a young writer of promise. But this is the new territory where it is open season on his life and his art.

Between business and pleasure, he found time to have a disagreeable confrontation with young John Gardner, who presented himself as the would-be husband of Carol Hemingway, Ernest's younger sister, who was on a writing scholarship at Rollins College. Ernest was pleasant but firm: without his permission, no one married Carol, and John did not have his permission. Ernest became threatening; John stood up to him. "I was indifferent," he said later. "I really was. I didn't hold him in some kind of awe, and I was in love with Carol." Studying abroad that winter in Austria, Carol, with a mind of her own and a will equal to her brother's, was determined to marry Gardner. Ernest, behaving more like a father than a brother, became increasingly furious with the sister who looked more like him than anyone else in the family. When the young couple married in Kitzbühel on March 21, Ernest responded like a jilted lover, angry and hurt; he never let Carol back into his life and never forgave her for leaving it.[6]

Despite the Gardner confrontation, Hemingway's two weeks in New York were a flurry of reasonably pleasant encounters with old friends and new, the most important of which took place in Louis Cohn's House of Books. On Friday, January 20, he visited with Cohn to discuss a limited edition of "God Rest You Merry, Gentlemen," which Cohn was to publish in April. Quite accidentally, a Hemingway collector from Chicago was also at Cohn's to purchase a $75 copy of Hemingway's quite rare *Three Stories & Ten Poems*, three hundred copies of which Robert McAlmon once published in Paris (1923). Cohn introduced the author to his admirer Arnold Gingrich, publisher of *Apparel Arts* and soon to be publisher of a new, as yet unnamed magazine for men. Gingrich explained that back in Key West, Hemingway would find his letter asking Ernest to sign an enclosed copy of *Death in the Afternoon*.[7]

That Friday evening, Hemingway boarded the southbound Seaboard train with a one-way ticket for a lower berth, arriving early Saturday afternoon in Roanoke, where he retrieved his car. On Sunday, leaving the boys with Ada, Pauline took the night train out of Key West to be in Jacksonville when Ernest drove in that afternoon.[8]

―――

Miami, February 15. In the shirtsleeve evening, Giuseppi Zangara pushed his way forward to within fifteen feet of the open automobile. As he climbed up on the bench beside Lillian Cross to get a clear view, she saw him pull a revolver from his pocket. "He was aiming right at the President," she told reporters afterward. "I saw him. That's when I caught his arm and forced the gun up." The first bullet missed President-elect Franklin Roosevelt and struck Chicago mayor Cermak in the stomach. Four other bystanders were wounded, two shot in the head, as Zangara wildly emptied his pawnshop pistol. On March 20, thirty-two days after he pulled the trigger, Zangara went to his execution, shouting, "I'm no afraid that chair. Put me in electric chair."[9]

―――

Hemingway was interested enough in the attempted assassination to purchase the verbatim testimony of Zangara, whose "beautiful but expensive beliefs," Ernest said, demanded atonement.[10] The surface of the country, however, only rippled with the shock of Roosevelt's close encounter with death, for there were more immediate fears loose in the land. Gold coins and certificates disappeared into private places, forcing banks to close, one by one, then in pairs, in coveys, and finally they all closed, taking a "bank holiday." When Monroe County taxes went unpaid, first Key West garbage collectors, then street cleaners went hungry. A pound of flour sold for three cents, a pound of pork shoulder for nine cents. To pay workers, city governments began printing scrip. No one knew how many people were out of work, on the streets, riding the rails, standing in breadlines, or shivering under city viaducts. No one could afford to count them. Over the radio, between comedy shows laughing in the lap of despair, came the plaintive lyric "Brother, can you spare a dime?"

"Don't worry about me," Hemingway told a young man trying to become a writer, "I have a damned good time—all of the time—or nearly all." Whatever critics said about his work now did not matter. A writer's final reward came after his death: ten lines of poetry or a hundred pages of prose could make any writer immortal. Meanwhile he had the best of life now: fishing, hunting, riding, taking in all of life. As long as he was writing, he never felt "low." "Evidently," he concluded, "I only write you when I'm laid up or low because you don't want to ever worry about me being sad."[11] Now he was writing steadily, every day and well, but he was working so close to the bone that someone should have worried about him.

The usual round of visitors came, fished, drank, and departed: the rich, like young sportsman Tommy Shevlin, flew in by private plane; the less affluent, like the Jesuit priest Father Tom McGrath, arrived by bus.[12] All come to a meal equally set and leave having seen only Hemingway the host who always has an afternoon free for fishing, an evening for food and drink, a commodious man. They do not see him at his writing, nor do they read the handwritten manuscript that is piling up almost too rapidly. For reasons he neither understood nor wished to question, the long summer and fall pursuing marlin and bear refilled the well from which he drew his fiction. Between the end of January and the first of April, he finished the Billings hospital story, wrote two drafts of a disquieting war experience which he gave to his old character Nick Adams, and completed five chapters of a new novel set in Paris.

In the morning he wakes early to return to the hospital story where his fictional Mr. Frazer, the phraser with a broken writing arm, contemplates against his pain the various opiums of the people: religion and music, economics, patriotism, sex and drink and gambling, ambition and new forms of government. "What," he asks himself, "was the real, the actual, opium of the people?"

> *He knew it very well. It was gone just a little way around the corner in that well-lighted part of his mind that was there after two or more drinks in the evening; that he knew was there (it was not really there of course). What was it? He knew very well. What was it? Of course; bread was the opium of the people.*[13]

So intense are Hemingway's mornings that not even heaving against afternoon fish can take away the churning inside his head where stories keep writing themselves, summoned or not. Like Mr. Frazer, he needs at times like this a sovereign touch of gin, a few fingers of evening whiskey to take the edge off, to put his mind at rest, letting him sleep.

In the novel, which no one saw but himself, pages multiply quickly: the story of a writer who can no longer write, wants to paint but cannot paint in the cold Paris studio, where not so many years ago he, Ernest, once lived when first separated from Hadley. In one draft he called the character Philip Haines; in two others, James Allen: by whatever name, the man is a writer separated from his wife, who still loves him, while he is in love with Dorothy Rodgers, the "other woman," who has returned to the States until his divorce is final. The setting for the story Ernest knew by heart, but as his writer-cum-painter settled deeper into lonely depression, the fiction began to twist. One James Allen version begins, "For two weeks James Allen had wanted to kill a girl." In the Philip Haines version, the estranged wife, Harriet, called "Harry," is planning to remarry. When Dorothy finally returns, Philip, before driving to Havre to meet her, buys a pistol for protection on the road. As Hemingway writes about the fictional Harriet, Hadley Richardson Hemingway, eight years divorced from him, is planning to marry Paul Mowrer, a prominent journalist with whom she has maintained an open affair since Ernest divorced her and whom Hemingway's visiting son Bumby now regards as a second father. Had Pauline been reading the story in which the "other woman" so closely resembled herself, she might have worried when the writer/painter found Dorothy's letters unsatisfactory, found her refusal to return before the divorce maddening. "She'd said she would come if he asked her. Hadn't he asked her? He couldn't have asked her any plainer."[14] Before the end of February, Hemingway wrote Perkins that he was going well on a novel they had not discussed. He had four chapters written and, unlike early going in *A Farewell to Arms*, he knew how this story was going end.[15]

At the same moment, Arnold Gingrich was writing Ernest about a new quarterly magazine he was starting which would be "to the American male what *Vogue* is to the female. But it won't be the least damn bit like *Vanity Fair*. It aims to have ample hair on its chest, to say noth-ing of adequate cojones." When Gingrich decided to call the magazine *Esquire*, Ernest found plenty of fault with such an elevated title, but Gingrich held his ground. Without saying he wanted to use the Hem-ingway name to secure other writers, he asked Hemingway to con-tribute to the first issue anything he wanted to submit. "No editing whatsoever," he promised. "You write and I print." The offering price for an essay was $250, maybe more if he found he could afford it.[16] Hemingway's initial response was guarded: $250 was not worth negoti-ating, for he could get ten times that much for a story, but it was inter-esting pocket money for something less than a story. Maybe he would send something, but Gingrich should not count on it.[17]

It was not paucity of money offered that changed Hemingway's mind. By February he was picking up information that Harcourt Brace was publishing Gertrude Stein's *The Autobiography of Alice B. Toklas* and that *Atlantic Monthly* was serializing parts of the memoir that were less than flattering to Ernest. In March, he kept Gingrich on the hook, saying he might have something for the first issue.[18] In April, before he had read *Atlantic*'s first installment, he was telling Gingrich that Gertrude was "a fine woman until she went profes-sionally goofy complete lack of judgment and stoppage of all sense lesbian with the old menopause. . . . Then she got the idea that any-body who was any good must be queer, if they did not seem to be they were merely concealing it."[19] He went on to promise four "let-ters" for Gingrich's quarterly. Without telling Gingrich, he secured a platform for his own ends: if every former friend, like Stein, was going to put his private life on public display, he needed a forum to set things right. The writer who abhorred personal publicity, who would not attend the Paramount movie premiere, who would not talk about his writing with the *Havana Post*, that writer is about to enter the public arena with only the barest fictive mask between himself and his audience.

Dear Mr. Hemingway:
I would like to be a man and to write the way you do. The last

chapter of Death in the Afternoon makes me sadder than anything
I ever read. . . . it makes me remember that I can't ever live the
whole of life, that I can't have the beautiful soundness of domesticity and the rightness of three children . . . and the deep fine
delight in the color and drama of a quick, moving, unsettled life . . .
because having one would give an edge of guilt or unrightness to
the other. . . . it makes me sad because it reminds me I am a
woman and can't possibly get the savor out of life a man can—
because a woman always has the feeling that she musn't lose an
ounce of what she hates to call "womanliness."

Mary Post[20]

The way he wrote was early and often, every day when it was
going right. Sitting in bed with several sharpened pencils, he wrote
in cursive on legal-size sheets of unlined paper with a flat surface
beneath them. That morning in the bedroom on Whitehead Street,
he began a new story: "As I came into the town walking the bicycle
along the street to avoid the shell holes." Then he crossed it out, and
started over with shattered trees and dead bodies floating in the
ditch and the narrator pushing his bicycle along that Italian road.[21]
The handwriting runs for several lines smooth and parallel to the
bottom of the page before it begins to slope down from left to right
as he picks up speed only to break it off and start over.

The second draft told the whole story of the American narrator
returning to visit his old battalion along the river that he remembers
too well. Drawing on fragments discarded from "A Natural History of
the Dead" and his own still vivid war memories, Hemingway opened
this draft with a dispassionate review of a battle's aftermath left in
the fields of Fossalta, the village where he was blown up that night
fifteen years earlier.[22] Still writing in the first person, he raced
through the story, scribbling revisions between lines and up the margins. As he writes, the story splits into two parts: the narrator's shaky
return to the front Italian lines to raise troop morale by walking
about in an American uniform, and an embedded story of a "hysterical" Italian lieutenant, who first appears charging two enlisted men

with sexually perverse activity, for which he says they should be shot. The Major, who cannot afford to lose soldiers unnecessarily from his thinly defended position, sends the men back to their posts with a reprimand. That same day, when shells fall on the Italian lines, the "hysterical" lieutenant, whom we learn behaved badly during a previous attack, shoots himself through his palm, pretending it is a shrapnel wound. The Major, perfectly willing to lose a useless officer, puts him under guard to face charges later. On either side of these two incidents the narrator and Major Paravicini reminisce about early days in the war when they both faced attacks fortified with grappa laced with ether. The story ends with the narrator being sent on his way by the Major.[23]

Thematically the story is about the failure of courage, a condition with which the narrator says he has some experience, having been unable to face an attack sober. But never getting inside the narrator's head keeps the story at a distance, which no amount of piecemeal revision could fix. In the next draft, composed on the typewriter, Hemingway threw out the hysterical lieutenant, salvaged all useful details, and focused the story completely on the narrator's now clearly unstable mental state, a condition vaguely suggested in the first draft. On the first page of the new draft, he changed the point of view so that his character had a name—Nicholas Adams—and the new, offstage narrator could tell the reader what was happening in Nick's head. Keeping the same structure as the first draft, the author used two views of Nick's shell-shocked behavior, in and out of his head, to replace the two incidents with the lieutenant. What began as an unpleasant but not threatening story, told with little comment, became a complex, disturbing trip into that other country of the mind where

> some did not get down but we went up and we went back and we
> came down, we always came down, and there was Gaby Delys, oddly
> enough, with feathers on, you called me baby doll a year ago tadada
> you said that I was rather nice to know with feathers on with feathers
> off the great Gaby and my name's Harry Pilcer[24] . . . those were the

nights the river ran so much wider and stiller than it should and out-side Fossalta there was a low house painted yellow.[25]

Having known the Paris weirdness of shell-shocked, death-loving, war-wounded veterans, having observed up close the erratic behavior of Zelda Fitzgerald and Jane Mason, and having lived with his own bad dreams and night sweats, he let the words run free, writing a prose beyond his previous limits.[26] Nick, speaking in tongues about the efficacy of grasshoppers as fish bait, is a mind clearly out of control. Paravicini thinks that Nick's head wound should have been trepanned—core drilled and drained. "It's a hell of a nuisance," Nick says, "once they've had you certified as nutty. No one every has any confidence in you again." He called the story "A Way You'll Never Be."

As he was working on the second full draft, Jane Mason dropped into Key West for several days of fishing, drinking, and storytelling. In the Hemingway yard, her gift of peacocks preened in the sun, and on Duval Street that week, the Strand Theater, with unintentional irony, featured *Ladies They Talk About*.[27] As the stunning wife of the Pan-American Airlines man in charge of the Caribbean, Jane was accustomed to being talked about, partied around, photographed, and remembered. At eighteen, she married Grant Mason, a bright, athletic, moneyed Yale graduate who spurned Wall Street for the excitement of the new airline industry. Now seven years into their marriage, Jane's sometimes erratic behavior was a continuing puzzle and sometime irritant to Grant. "If only she had been at rest with herself, with her own talents," her son said years afterward.[28] Hemingway would later say that he wrote "A Way You'll Never Be" to distract a young woman who was losing her mind. Everyone took the woman to be long-legged Jane of the golden hair, the graceful young Jane of the magazine ads, but if Ernest thought she was going crazy in March of 1933, he kept it to himself, not that he wasn't keenly attuned to aberrant behavior lurking beneath smooth surfaces.

———

Censorship of all the Cuban domestic press, of all incoming papers from abroad and of all outgoing cables . . . a reign of terror

is operating under the direction of President Machado. Political
assassinations of opponents are the order of the day. Criminals let
loose from jails have been given authority to inaugurate a regime
of the bludgeon. Freedom of the press, assembly, and petition is
dead. . . . Secret police infest the island. Misery is almost universal
and the rumbles of approaching revolt are swelling.

—*Key West Citizen*, March 3, 1933

Pushing hard to finish a book of short stories for the fall season,
Hemingway wrote almost every morning that March. When Lent
began, he took his list of sins to confession and received communion
on Ascension Day, fulfilling his Easter Duty.[29] At St. Mary's Catholic
church, he was not the most regular parishioner, but he and his family attend Mass when they are in town, and he supported with modest donations the various causes of the resident Jesuits, whose order
he admires. When attending Mass, he stands at the back of the
church, never taking a pew, for his right knee, which is still braced
from his war wounding, cannot take the hard kneeling. His parish
priest, Father Dougherty, said, "Oh, yes, he never misses Sunday
Mass. . . . Easter duty? Most assuredly. Lovely wife and children, all
of them Catholics, good Catholics too."[30]

By the middle of March, most of the nation's banks are once more
open, President Roosevelt's new regime having certified them sound,
and hoarders of gold are surrendering it under threat of punishment
as the United States went off the gold standard. On March 15, the
stock market, closed for twelve days, reopened. In Germany, Chan-
cellor Adolf Hitler's government refused to buy from Jews; in the
universities Jewish professors were barred from their classrooms. In
Key West, *Mädchen in Uniform*, the talking German picture that
broke all New York movie-run records, opened at the Strand.[31]

The nation, the President said, has nothing to fear but fear itself;
Hemingway was less certain. A few days before the stock market
closed, he invested part of his Scribner's advance money in blue-chip
stocks to hedge against what he thought would be inevitable inflation.[32] Also rightfully worried about Cuban repression becoming a

threat, he asked Max Perkins to provide a letter signed by Charles Scribner on his "most impressive stationery" that might, in time of revolution, keep Ernest from being shot.[33] The resulting insurance letter said that Hemingway was "preparing for publication by us a work on the migratory fish of the Gulf Stream, their habits, and capture, with a special reference to the fishing in Cuban waters from the sporting standpoint."[34]

On Wednesday afternoon of Holy Week, Ernest, Charles Thompson, and Joe Russell on board the *Anita* waved back to their wives as they motored out of Garrison Bight, heading for Cuba. As they passed beyond the Sand Key light, a large school of porpoise were leaping from the water in front of a refinery tanker. By eight o'clock that night, with a new moon rising, they picked up the white glare of Havana on the horizon; at 1:30 a.m. on Holy Thursday, they passed under the battlements of Morro Castle and into Havana harbor. The three men slept late that morning, cleared their papers with the harbormaster, lunched at the Florida, and caught dolphins that afternoon with Grant Mason on board.[35] In the early evening of Good Friday, while the fishing party is eating supper, explosions rock Havana, marking the beginning of "Red Week," as the student ABC Revolutionary Society has threatened. All through the night, bombs detonate at fifteen-to-thirty-minute intervals, emptying the streets; by morning, troops armed with revolvers and rifles bring Holy Saturday traffic to a standstill as they stop and search anything moving. On Easter Sunday morning, church bells speak of the risen Christ, but in city jails and prison, chemists, doctors, lawyers, students, and many university faculty are in holding cells, some never to be seen again.[36]

Neither that day nor the next did the *Havana Post* speak of bombings, or of martial law, or of "La Porra," as government death squads armed with bludgeons are called. Reprisals came as swift, public applications of *ley de fuga*, the law of flight. In a residential neighborhood, two young brothers are pushed from a Secret Service car and told to run for their lives. As they flee in opposite directions, government sharpshooters posted above the street open fire. From his apartment balcony, a newspaper correspondent sees what happened to one of the students:

> The first fusillade missed the boy and he started running, shouting, "Don't shoot any more." Despite his cries for mercy, a second volley followed. The victim, hit in the head by bullets, staggered, ran some twenty feet and collapsed as a third volley poured into his body. The uniformed Negroes who had done the fatal shooting came down the side of the cliff, with rifles and revolvers in their hands, to inspect the body, after which they sauntered off, unmolested by the uniformed national police, who arrived on the scene immediately.[37]

On Easter Sunday, waiting for Uncle Gus and Karl Thompson to come over from Key West, Ernest went to Mass and then out to the Masons' house for lunch, where he stayed through supper. In his day log, he noted that he drank too much.[38]

For the newspaper, Hemingway maintained and amplified his intentions of writing a book on the marlin:

> Ernest Hemingway returned to Havana yesterday for 65 days of deep-sea fishing in adjacent waters. An avocation of long standing, fishing in the Gulf Stream will be the subject of another epic comparable to "Death in the Afternoon." . . . A deliberate study, Hemingway has assembled quantities of material on the subject which will be amplified during his stay here. At the same time he is working on another novel; and a volume of short stories will be published by Scribner's during the coming autumn. . . . As is their custom, the party is stopping at the Hotel Ambos Mundos.[39]

The week after Easter, as bombings and nightly gunfire diminished, the Hemingway party fished hard by day and did nothing to attract attention when ashore. The following Friday night, bullet-riddled bodies of four students were brought to the Havana morgue, and the American manager of a local theater, informed by police his life was in danger because of his associations, departed immediately for New Orleans.[40]

———

In the photograph a young Cuban lies face-up on the pavement. His head is turned to the left facing the camera, which is quite close. On the left cheek is an almost perfectly round, black spot, too dark to be a birthmark, perhaps either a bruise or dirt. Across the right cheek are fainter stains that seem to be the residue left after a hurried washing. Black hair, neither long nor short, cushions the head and spreads into shadow. The white shirt has been pulled down, exposing smooth shoulders. Because the mouth is slightly open, one can see small, even white teeth. The eyes are closed, as if sleeping. From the left corner of the open mouth a thin trickle of dark blood runs across the cheek, past the ear, and blends with the mass of darker hair.[41]

———

The face of Jane Mason was a study in white and gold, a face to turn any man's head, an effect in which her husband took pride. Her beauty was, in fact, a business asset for Grant Mason, who was busy extending Pan American's network of airlines throughout South America. At their home looking out on the exclusive Jaimanitas golf course, they gave parties so exhilarating that old men remembered them thirty years later. Jane and Grant were the Murphys and Fitzgeralds of the Anglo-Cuban Havana establishment: he the clubbable Yale man, she the young beauty whose wild streak added to her excitement. Tallish, big-boned, and athletic, she wanted all her life to be remembered for something more than her beautiful face, but most of her life she belonged to some man. The tombstone inscription she wrote for herself years later reads, "Talents too many, not enough of any." She was an active sportswoman and sometime daredevil, danced so well the floor cleared to watch her, at one time owned and managed a Havana art gallery, and was fluent in three languages.

That summer of 1933, while the Machado regime tottered, the Masons, like most of the Anglo-Cuban establishment, lived as if nothing were different. Their English nanny, Haitian houseman,

Chinese cook, Italian butler, German gardener, and Cuban chauffeur maintained order, managed the house and grounds, fed and cared for the family and the animal menagerie: honey bear, monkey, peacocks, flamingos, fox, parrots, Doberman, Dalmatian, and Great Dane. Cuban revolutions were, after all, not exactly a novelty: there had been dicey times before and they would come, no doubt, again, but that did not mean that their lives would be affected. When Cuban soldiers during an uprising actually threatened the Masons and American Ambassador Guggenheim, who lived next to them, Grant stood on the front porch with a megaphone telling the soldiers that he was armed with two shotguns, "and that if they dared trespass on American soil, he was going to shoot the hell out of them."[42]

Despite street killings and bombs in the night, despite rumors which exaggerated both, Jane and Grant were occasionally on board the *Anita* in search of marlin, but almost always with Pauline at hand. Later many would say that a torrid affair took place that summer between Ernest and Jane, but letters, the *Anita* log, and the *Havana Post* show that Hemingway had little time for adultery. Between April 14 and 27, while Charles Thompson and Gus Pfeiffer were both in Havana, Ernest could not risk encouraging Jane, no matter how interesting he found her. During the following two days, Pauline arrived with Bumby and Patrick, staying until May 13, when Jane and Grant left for Miami. The Masons returned to Havana on the morning of May 23; that evening, young Patrick and Ada Stern returned on the ferry from Key West to join Bumby and Ernest; the three boys and Ada became guests at the Mason's house at Jaimanitas. The following afternoon:

HAVANA WOMAN,

THREE CHILDREN

IN AUTO CRASH

Mrs. Grant Mason and

Hemingway's Sons Escape Injury

Mrs. G. Grant Mason, Jr., her 3-year-old son Tony, and John and

Patrick Hemingway, sons of Ernest Hemingway, the writer, narrowly *escaped serious injury and possible death yesterday afternoon at 4:45 p.m. near El Cano when Mrs. Mason's car left the road and plunged over a 40-foot embankment, turning over three times and landing upside down.*

Extracting themselves from the car which was almost totally wrecked, they found that except for minor bruises and scratches, all had escaped unhurt.

En route from Finca Milagras to Jaimanitas, Mrs. Mason had just passed through El Cano when she met a bus coming at high speed and pulled out of its path to the edge of the road. The shoulder of the road gave way and the car, traveling at a slow speed, slowly turned over, gathering momentum as it rolled down the embankment. Aware of the possible danger of fire from broken fuel lines, Mrs. Mason shut off the ignition as the car started to overturn. The doors of the sedan were jammed but a small opening in the window of the front door enabled them to crawl to safety. The bus for which they had turned out continued on its way with the driver and the passengers unaware of the accident. Passing motorists, employees of the Pan-American Airways, brought Mrs. Mason and the children to Havana.[43]

Years later, her son remembered Jane's Chevrolet with the yellow wire wheels slipping off the road and rolling down into an earthen amphitheater dug out for baseball games.

Patrick was on my right and Bumby was in the backseat. And I remember the car sliding, and then started to head down the hill. . . . it rolled over and over. And I remember . . . the door jammed so that Patrick held on to me and I held on to my mother . . . Bumby had put his hands on the ceiling. . . . He sort of cartwheeled inside the car down the bank.[44]

The same day the story appeared in the *Havana Post*, Grace Hemingway in Oak Park read the wire service version. She wrote to Ernest: "We are all so shocked to read in the papers this morning of your near tragedy. God is so good to have spared their lives and kept them safe and sound, apparently. I shall pray that no after effects come to

them. I just could not spare my two oldest grandsons."[45] From Key
West, where she was probably informed by phone, Pauline, still
dazed from the news, said it would take her a while to "grasp" the
accident, but Jane, who had grasped it completely, had all her sympathy.[46]

The following morning at nine-thirty, Jane appeared at the dock
with a terrible hangover, but apparently unhurt, ready to fish. As the
paper reported and the *Anita*'s log confirms, she landed two marlin,
fishing that day and the next two.[47] Afterward the story turns opaque.
Some say that Jane tried to kill herself by leaping from the low balcony of her Jaimanitas home, but the lawn and shrubs that were
then below the balcony made it an unlikely choice for a suicidal
jump. One newspaper said she was shot in the back by a revolutionary—a story quickly denied. For certain, there was the auto accident
followed by two strenuous days of fishing, followed by the newspaper story: "Mrs. G. Grant Mason, Jr., is a patient at the Anglo-American hospital undergoing treatment for shock brought on by an
automobile accident several days ago."[48]

At which point Jane's summer came to an end. She remained in
the hospital, where "treatment for shock" may have been the case, or
it may have been a polite phrase to obscure the causes. In his log-
book, Hemingway noted at least one hospital visit to Jane before
Grant sent her to New York for extended treatment:

MRS. GRANT MASON WILL SAIL TODAY
*En route to New York, Mrs. G. Grant Mason, Jr., will sail this after-
noon on the Morro Castle.*

*Mrs. Mason has been in the Anglo-American hospital recuperat-
ing from nervous shock resulting from an automobile accident several
weeks ago; and upon the advice of her Havana physician will remain
in the Doctors' hospital in New York for a few days before going to
Tuxedo Park to visit Mr. Mason's family.*

Their young son, Tony, went north three weeks ago.[49]

Three weeks later, Hemingway, thanking Archie MacLeish for visiting Jane in the New York hospital, tried to explain about her husband, Grant, who, five days after placing his wife in the Havana hospital, left for Miami to buy a new motor launch.[50] Any husband tolerated long enough became the wife's own fault, Ernest said.

> *All women married to a wrong husband are bad luck for themselves and all their friends. . . . Mr. M. is a man of great wealth and will have more[,] none ever as yet having been spent. People seem to put up longer with a rich than a poor twirp. Also people put up with each other beyond our understanding. . . . I tried to write a very short story about it by saying Every spring Mrs. M. wanted to marry someone else but in the spring of 1933 she broke her back. That's a little too simple too.[51]*

It was not until early September that Jane Mason, having spent months in a body cast, was able to write the Hemingways that in another two months she would be fitted with her "iron virgin" back support which she would have to wear for the next year. With more back treatment a possibility, she was continuing sessions with a psychoanalyst, apparently at Grant's insistence. Nothing like it, she said, for diminishing what small ego was left. Down the middle of her back was a seven-and-a-half-inch scar, and another on her leg where the bone graft was taken to repair her fractured vertebrae. She hoped to go to Europe and maybe meet the Hemingways on safari, but it seemed unlikely.[52]

———

Cabanas. In a small hotel miles from Havana, they sleep beneath mosquito netting to wake at four to the grinding of morning coffee; breakfast at six: tortilla, guava paste, soft-boiled eggs in a glass, chorizo, cider, black coffee. Sun rising on a calm bay, royal palms dark-leafed, their white trunks rising out of mist white on the water. Behind, dark mountains, and closer, green wooded hills of mahogany and cedar. The surface of the bay ripples with a rising school of small fish; an alligator slides off the bank. Flocks of white egrets and herons along the river and the water turning from

brown to blue where it meets the sea. The writer and his wife drift
through this day and another, and one other outside of time.[53]

––––––

Max was pleading with him for the book title so they could set up
the salesmen's dummy, but Ernest could not find one—not in
Baudelaire, the Bible, or in Old English poetry. *The Twelve Good Joys*
was ironic but misleading; *Strange Countries* was no better. When he
and Pauline, that first week in June, motored down the coast to
Cabanas, the missing title was on his mind as he rearranged the stories in various sequences. In unlikely places, like Thomas Browne's
Urn Burial, he is reminded of what he knew, forgot, and always
relearned: nothing lasted—neither friends nor places—they all went
under. In forty years, Browne told him, a man's gravestone is no
longer legible. Putting aside the reference books, he finds the title
within himself: *Winner Take Nothing*. Before he returns to Havana
to put Pauline on the Key West ferry, he adds a neomedieval epi-
graph of his own device:

> *Unlike all other forms of lutte or combat the conditions are that the*
> *winner shall take nothing; neither his ease, nor his pleasure, nor any*
> *notions of glory; nor, if he win far enough, shall there be any reward*
> *within himself.*[54]

As effusive as he ever got, Max Perkins said it was "a very fine title. I
wish you would tell me where that quotation came from."[55]

Max also wanted the stories as soon as possible, for the deadline
on fall publication was close. Hemingway resists. With thirteen stories being typed, he still does not have the anchor, the story at the end
that will hold the others in place. Two days after Pauline returned to
Key West, Ernest woke well before dawn and while still in bed began
writing a story about his father's suicide, a story he has tried to tell
several times, a story that is now coming out right. Often his writing
process, which he did not like to analyze for fear of "spooking" it,
worked that way: some fragment of an idea, broken off, shelved but
remembered, and then when he least expected it, the story was there

because it had been writing itself somewhere in his head.

The story about his father's suicide he first tried to tell at a distance, using a young boy discovering his father's hunting death was no accident. After ten pages, he quit it, unable to deal with the real issues: the dead father and the dominant mother. Years before Clarence Hemingway pulled the trigger that ended his life (1928), Ernest wrote "Indian Camp," in which an Indian father, unable to bear his wife's protracted labor pains, slits his own throat with a straight razor while Dr. Adams delivers the screaming woman by a primitive, jackknifed cesarean section without anesthesia. In the rowboat coming back across the lake with his father, the doctor, Nick asks, "Do many men kill themselves?" It was too prophetic to think about, the death of the father, the inquiring son, sex and death. The hunting father who kills and cures; the screaming mother, all bloody in birth: the secrets were out. What else was there to think about? Hemingway returns now to that father/son impasse: the knowledge of sex and death.

He wants to blame the father's death on the mother, his own mother, because that is easier than admitting his father's "nervousness" is like his own: highs and lows, cycling each time a little farther down that dark road he will one day call "black ass." He needs to blame his mother, whom he cannot forgive for being alive.[56] So there in Havana, he writes:

> *There is only one thing to do if a man is married to a woman with whom he has nothing in common, with whom there can be no question of justice but only a gross fact of utter selfishness and hysterical emotionalism and that is to get rid of her.*[57]

But when he said it, he knew he could not let it stand, because she will read it. No matter how much he wants to hate his mother, and he insists he does hate her, tells everyone what a horror Grace Hemingway is, but no matter, he cannot hurt her that directly. Having said it, he takes out the page and never uses it.

With idyllic Cabanas days with Pauline fresh in his mind, and with memories of his father rising up while his own son, Bumby, is with him on the boat, roles flicker in and out of focus: father, husband, son, and lover—a continuum. He is now the father, the self-named Papa, and he is still the grieving son. The story begins in a car with Nicholas Adams driving through a small, depression-era town where the traffic lights "would be gone next year when the payments on the system were not met." As the town gives way to harvested fields of corn, soybeans, and peas, Nick hunts them in his head, thinking which way the quail would fly. These fields take him back to hunting fields of his youth with his father as instructor. About hunting, the father's advice was always useful, just as it was unsound on sexual matters.

> His father had summed up the whole matter by stating that masturbation produced blindness, insanity and death, while a man who went out with prostitutes would contract hideous venereal diseases and that the thing to do was to keep your hands off of people.

This memory leads Nick to his father's suicide, which he needs to write about if he is ever to put it to rest, but it is too soon, too many people still alive. He remembers his father's face, repaired by the undertaker, a face that had been making itself for a long time. "We all betrayed," Hemingway wrote, "some more than others, in our several ways."

That reverie takes Nick back to his own sexual education with the soft and pliant young Indian girl in the summer woods of his youth. As he fondly remembers their naive and innocent coupling, the light begins to fail, and Nick's mind returns to his father, who was with him always "in thickets, on small hills, or when going through dead grass, whenever splitting wood or hauling water." The father he loved, admired, and even hated, hating enough once to draw a bead on him, holding the shotgun loaded and cocked, thinking, "I can blow him to hell. I can kill him." At this point Nick's son, silently riding beside him through this remembrance of things past, asks Nick what it was like when he was a boy hunting with the Indians. He cannot tell his son that the Indian girl "did first what no one has ever done better." The boy wants to know about his grandfather, but Nick can only say he was a fine hunter with amazing eyesight. The boy wants to discuss where the grandfather is buried, when they will visit his "tomb," and where Nick will be buried.[58]

Stories embedded inside a story: Nick and his father, sex and death, Nick and his son, past and present—it was a rich story but not the whole story. Stories never were the thing itself. Nick was never himself but someone he remembered in the mirror. He left out his mother and the way she seemed to dominate his father, left out their arguments, said nothing about his father's moodiness, erased the pain when his father's depressions left the puzzled son hurt and isolated in a house full of women. He might never be able to write the whole story.

He first called it "The Tomb of My Grandfather" before finding its final title: "Fathers and Sons." With it, his book of stories was focused as clearly as he could make it. On July 13, he mailed Perkins thirteen stories, with this anchor story to follow as soon as he had it revised. He wanted to lead off with young Nick and the whores in "The Light of the World" and end with Nick and his son driving past the darkening fields of autumn.[59]

—————

But what a book, they both agreed, would be the real story of Hemingway, not those he writes but the real story of Hemingway. . . . they both said, it is so flattering to have a pupil who takes training . . . he looks modern and he smells of the museums. But what story that of the real Hem, and one he should tell himself but alas he never will. . . . Hemingway although a sportsman was easily tired. He used to get quite worn out walking from his house to ours. . . . Ernest is very fragile, whenever he does anything sporting something breaks, his arm, his leg, his head.[60]

—Gertrude Stein

—————

Gertrude Stein got in the first blow, but he was always a counter-puncher, promising to write his own memoirs, funny and accurate, when there was nothing else to write.[61] Then in June, Max Eastman, another old friend, got inside his guard with an essay review in *The New Republic* of *Death in the Afternoon* that hurt his pride. "Romantic gushing and sentimentalizing," Eastman called Hemingway's descriptions of the bullfight, "child's fairy-story writing."

> *To drag in notions of honor and glory here . . . [is] rather sophomoric. But to pump words over it like tragedy and dramatic conflict is mere romantic nonsense. . . . It is of course a commonplace that Hemingway lacks the serene confidence that he is a full-sized man . . . [he has] a continual sense of obligation to put forth evidences of red-blooded masculinity. . . . and it has moreover begotten a veritable school of fiction-writers—a literary style, you might say, of wearing false hair on the chest.[62]*

On June 11, Ernest, having read the essay in Havana, wired Max Perkins, "Tell your friend Eastman will break his jaw."[63] Perkin's reassurances that Ernest was invulnerable to his critics did nothing to soothe his anger. "The swine aren't worth writing for. I swear to christ they're not. Every phase of the whole racket is so disgusting that it makes you feel like vomiting."[64]

Taking Eastman's jibe about being a "full-sized man" to be a question about his sexual potency, Hemingway wrote *The New Republic* a sarcastic letter, inviting Eastman to "elaborate his nostalgic speculations on my sexual incapacity. Here they would be read (aloud) with much enjoyment (our amusements are simple) and I should be glad to furnish illustrations to brighten up Mr. Eastman's prose if you consider them advisable."[65] In private he was less restrained. "I suppose it is good to see while you are alive the process that takes place after you are dead," he wrote MacLeish, "but I have so god damned much pride (and it is all I have) that I can't watch it with pleasure."[66] There was another alternative, of course: don't wait for others to write your life.

The first week in July, Pauline returned briefly to Havana to pick up Bumby, and was back in Key West packing for their African safari when the giant marlin began their annual run. On July 6, Ernest hooked and fought a huge marlin for over two hours, only to lose him while changing rods. The following day, Ernest, his back muscles sore and knotted, tied into another enormous marlin that pulled the *Anita* stern-first, while he fought the fish to a standstill. Fearing that his back and hands would give out before he brought the marlin to gaff, he promised a hundred Hail Marys, a hundred Our Fathers, and $5 to the Church.[67] It was not the record fish that he came for, but it was the biggest fish he'd ever brought across the transom.[68] On July 18, three days before his birthday, Ernest and Joe Russell called it quits for the marlin season with a total catch of fifty-four. Shortly after midnight, having been guests of honor at an Ambos Mundos farewell party, they took the *Anita* out of the harbor and set a course for Key West, ninety miles away.[69]

As soon as he got unpacked, he began writing "A Cuban Letter," for the first edition of Arnold Gingrich's *Esquire*, the quarterly which quickly became a monthly. Accompanied eventually by seventeen photos, the "Letter" took its reader from the Ambos Mundos out through the harbor and into the Gulf Stream where marlin rose to the teaser baits. The reader learned what to eat for breakfast and lunch, how to fix baits, the feeding habits of marlin, when to slack and when to strike, how to fight the fish, tire him, bring him to gaff. By the time the essay appeared in print, Ernest would be in Paris on his way to Africa, each stop becoming another "Letter." For the next two and a half years, his life was a continuing serial, reaching an expanding, largely male readership. The first edition of *Esquire* sold out its 105,000 printed copies. Two years later, it was selling half a million copies a month, reaching the largest audience ever afforded an American author.[70]

Chapter Six

1 9 3 3 – 3 4

AFRICAN GAME TRAILS

Spain and East Africa

AVING LEFT GREGORY in the care of Ada Stern, Ernest, Pauline, her sister Jinny, and his sons John and Patrick arrived in Havana on August 4, just as the lights were going out. During the three days before they sailed for Europe, the Hemingway party in the Ambos Mundos had a good view of the streets where the Machado regime was reaching its violent conclusion. After all the political maneuvering, the student ABC underground, bombs in the night, and assassination attempts on Machado, what brought down the Cuban dictator were the drivers for a local bus company striking over wages and working conditions. Slowly, other trades across the city joined the drivers, until the machine stopped. By August 4, before its typesetters joined the shutdown, the *Havana Post* ran a banner headline: GENERAL STRIKE THREAT SPREADS. The Hemingways arrived with no buses, no streetcars, no taxis running. On the docks, longshoremen and stevedores let fruit rot and freight sit. No food came into the paralyzed city. Machado bargained with the leftists, thinking they controlled the workers, but the strike was beyond anyone's control. On August 7, the Hemingways' ship—*Reina de la Pacifica*, with unloaded freight for Havana still on board—managed somehow to leave port, but not before a false rumor was in the streets that Machado had resigned. The riotous mob that poured into the Boulevard de Prado was met with gunfire from a loyal cavalry detachment; when the streets cleared, forty were dead, two hundred wounded, and the army occupied Havana under martial law.[1]

Three days out of Havana, Ernest wrote Max Perkins, furious that galley proofs for *Winner Take Nothing* had not reached him in Havana. Despite the general strike closing the post office, Hemingway held Scribner's to blame for insufficient postage. Angry over Gertrude Stein's accusations of his fragility and Eastman's slurs on his manhood, he took out his anger on Max, accusing Perkins of disloyalty to him and to *Winner Take Nothing*. His detractors, whom he called Max's friends, could not touch this new novel he was writing. Gertrude and others so eager to pronounce him finished would break, but he, Ernest, would outlast them, outwrite them, be there when the final counting was done.[2]

By the time the Hemingways docked at Santander, Spain, the Cuban government was in shambles. In the predawn darkness of August 12, President Machado, his retinue, and twenty-eight pieces of luggage were ferried out to a Pan Am seaplane waiting in the harbor by arrangement of the U.S. ambassador to fly them to safety.[3] It was the age of revolutions in Russia, Germany, Spain, South America, Cuba—some at the ballot box, some at gunpoint, and Ernest's interest in revolutions was neither lukewarm nor recent. One of his earliest sketches (1923) became a one-page story he called "The Revolutionist," and in the fall of 1927, he had begun a novel ("A New Slain Knight") about a professional revolutionist which he broke off, admitting in a note to himself that he did not yet know enough to write that story.[4] In 1934, a character in *Green Hills of Africa* would remember:

I was crouched down behind a marble-topped table while they were shooting in Havana. They came by in cars shooting at everybody they saw. I took my drink with me and I was very proud not to have spilled it or forgotten it. The children said, "Mother, can we go out in the afternoon to see the shooting?" . . . I don't want to just hear about revolutions. All we see or hear is revolutions. I'm sick of them.[5]

After disembarking at Santander on August 17, the Hemingway party made its way first to La Coruña to decompress and then by train to San Sebastián, where Hadley's telegram of greetings was waiting for them.[6] Having recently married Paul Mowrer, her longtime friend and lover, Hadley was as happy as Ernest to turn the care of Bumby and Patrick over to their old nanny, Henrietta. This arrangement left Ernest, Pauline, and Jinny free to spend two months in Spain, where their dollars were worth more than in Paris.[7] True to Ernest's prediction, President Roosevelt was devaluing the dollar in an effort to pull American industry out of the depression. On Uncle Gus's advice, Ernest did not sell the depressed Warner stock Gus had given them to finance the safari. Instead he borrowed money from Gus against the stock's future value while making nominal interest payments on the loan.

By the end of August, Ernest, Pauline, and Jinny were registered at the Hotel Biarritz in Madrid, where he was correcting the finally delivered galleys for *Winner Take Nothing*. Still worrying over story placement and titles, Hemingway changed "Give Us a Prescription, Doctor," as it was printed in *Scribner's Magazine*, back to its original title, "The Gambler, the Nun, and the Radio." Uncertain about "Fathers and Sons," he invited Max to cable him if one of the alternates he proposed sounded better. The book's dedication should be "To A. MacLeish." He also asked that a note be added as inconspicuously as possible to "A Natural History of the Dead" saying that it was being reprinted at the author's request. Perkins honored the request with a footnote probably more detailed than Hemingway had in mind.

This story was published in a rather technical book called Death in the Afternoon, *which sold, or rather was offered for sale, at $3.50. It*

is reprinted here in case any one not caring to spend that appreciable
sum for a rather technical book should care to read it.[8]

More significant changes were made at Max's urging: three
"anglo-saxon phrases" eliminated and other possibly offensive
phrases revised. When the bartender in "Light of the World" chal-
lenges Tom's attempt to sample the "free lunch," Tom no longer
replied, "Up your ass." Now it was "You know where." And in "God
Rest You Merry, Gentlemen," Doc Wilcox's advice to the sexually tor-
mented young boy—"Oh, go and jack-off"—was reduced to a blank.
In "A Natural History of the Dead," Ernest told Max he could either
leave "fuck" as "f--k" as it was printed in *Death in the Afternoon*, or
change it to "f----." Max, given that opportunity, took out the "k." In
his "small" campaign to reform the genteel tradition, Hemingway
always argued for full usage of the English language, but without his
publisher's strong support, he could not afford to lead a one-man
crusade. In Paris, Henry Miller was writing furiously on books that
would not be published in America for another twenty-five years.[9]

Hemingway completely ignored Perkin's inquiry about the new
novel Ernest said he was writing. Never mentioned again by Hemingway, the James Allen (failed writer) novel was abandoned but not
forgotten. Once centered in Madrid, with Pauline next to him and
Hadley remarried, he probably realized that the James Allen story
would deeply hurt both women, who were easily recognized as the
wife and lover in the story. Like his 1927–28 attempt to write about a
revolutionist, the Allen exercise served its purpose of keeping him
writing when he did not know what to write next. Another reason to
abandon the story was the question it raised—had James Allen made
a mistake in leaving his wife for another woman? Unresolved but not
forgotten, the issue would reappear in Hemingway's Paris memoir
begun at least fifteen years later.

With no book-length effort in mind, Hemingway turned to a number of minor projects, the sort he often agreed to do when he was at
loose ends. He wrote a tongue-in-cheek dust-jacket blurb for James
Thurber's *Life and Hard Times* which was also his first counterpunch

in the Stein-Hemingway match: "Even in the days when Thurber was writing under the name of Alice B. Toklas, we knew he had it in him if he could get it out."[10] For Sidney Franklin, who was translating a Spanish novel of the bullring for Scribner's publication, Ernest read typescript, "cutting, re-doing some of the conversation and straightening out the sentences." It was a "trashy" book, Ernest said, but with a flashy book jacket and Sidney's picture on the back it might sell well. Hemingway tried to pressure Perkins into a better royalty payment for Franklin while he himself was paying for the operation to repair Franklin's intestinal damage from a rectal goring suffered in the bullring three years earlier. Franklin, as always, was an expensive friend, both emotionally and financially, but Ernest enjoyed Sidney's theatrics and his flair for storytelling.[11]

By the end of September, the Franklin typescript was revised and the promised "Spanish Letter" for Gingrich was in the mail.[12] Loosely structured, the *Esquire* piece was a lament for the politics of the failing Republic and for unfulfilled promises of the Spanish bullring, the two issues being metaphors for each other. Bullfighting, always in decline from some previous golden age, was as depressing as the seashore, where the newly affluent "did not seem to know whether they were having any fun or not." The best matadors lacked style, killing in a monotonous manner; the worst lacked intelligence or courage or both. Like the Salamanca feria bulls who were "without force, bravery or style," the governing politicians rooting in the tax trough gave no one confidence in their performance. "People are traveling," Hemingway wrote, "who never traveled before; people go to bull fights who could not afford it before; and many people are swimming who never took a bath before." Spain's developing middle class was rubbing the charm off Hemingway's special places. An office building now stood where the old café Fornos once catered to those in the know, and the Aquarium café looked "like the last phase of Montparnasse."[13] Always more comfortable with either wealth or poverty, Hemingway, like Yeats, Pound, and Eliot, had little sympathy for the plodding middle class from whom he sprang and who were, in fact, the buying audience for his work.

Not quite as generically anti-Semitic as Pound and better than Ezra on revolutions, Hemingway tried to arrange a meeting with his early mentor, asking him to come up from Rapallo, Italy, to Paris in the fall. Ezra's replies were disoriented and ragged. He might come as far as Toulon, because Ezra was worried about the safari. If Ernest was determined to be a naturalist, Ezra approved, but if he was merely going to Africa to slaughter lions, well, that was hardly a worthy task when so much intellectual work remained to be done. "Y'orter take a little mental xercise now'n again," Pound advised. Ezra jokingly suggested that instead of butchering defenseless animals, Ernest assassinate one or two on Pound's growing list of exploitive villains, the tracking and finishing off of whom Ezra thought might appeal to Ernest's sporting interests. "Yew are getting too lazy to think," he warned, signing off as "Yr fexshunate unkl."[14]

As soon as he had finished revisions on Franklin's translation, Hemingway began a Cuban story that started: "You know how it is there early in the morning in Havana with the bums still asleep against the walls of the buildings; before even the ice wagons come by with ice for the bars?" Speaking was Harry Morgan, sometime fishing guide out of Key West, sometime rumrunner, a common man with uncommon nerve, a man down on his luck. When his insufferable fishing client leaves Morgan unpaid and broke in Havana, the story changes dramatically. Out of options, Morgan contracts with a Mr. Sing to smuggle Chinese aliens into the Florida keys. The price is $1,200; the risk is ten years in prison if caught; the scam allows Morgan to dump the illegals anywhere: Mr. Sing does not care. After picking up his passengers, Morgan cuts his risks to zero by taking the payment, breaking Mr. Sing's neck, and dumping the Chinese back in Cuba. It was a brutal, depression-era story about money: those who had it and those who needed it. Coming on the edge of Pound's needling, it was also Hemingway's first extended proletariat fiction. Jinny Pfeiffer was certain the story, which Hemingway called "One Trip Across," was true, which amused Ernest, who always insisted his best stories were the ones he made up.[15]

When Jinny and Pauline left for Paris that first week in October,

Ernest was not exactly isolated, but there were no women in his vicinity, a condition which put him alone in his night bed, where he did not sleep well. By day he was not much better. Almost immediately he began worrying that his pulse was too fast, his heart failing. Real or imagined, the condition drove him to the doctor, who assured him he would die but not from heart failure and not anytime soon.[16] Before leaving Madrid, he sprained his wrist falling on the stairs in his new hunting boots, and was back at the doctor's office for his chronic strep throat.[17] There were, of course, several good reasons for Hemingway to remain in Madrid. His new hunting boots of Spanish leather needed more fitting, and he was waiting for the final page proofs to arrive. Another good reason for being in Madrid rather than in Paris was *The Autobiography of Alice B. Toklas*, partially serialized in *Atlantic Monthly* and now in hardcover, which the Paris *Tribune* headlined as the "Season's Most Brilliant Book."[18] Gertrude Stein "was a good psychologist," as Ernest readily admitted: "She knows I don't get sore at being called any damn thing that I am, truly. But blow up like a set piece of fireworks if accused of anything I'm not. . . . It's damned intelligent malice."[19]

With equally intelligent malice, Hemingway wrote a short response which he called "The Autobiography of Alice B. Hemingway." The six-page sketch is told by the wife, Alice, but written by her husband, Ernest. "Listen," he tells his wife, who tells us he always starts with "Listen," a less than endearing characteristic. Listen, he says, no matter how excellent a critic of his stories Gertrude may be, she is already the past. No longer willing to be critical of her own work, she never corrects anything she writes. Lazy to a fault, she cannot lose because nothing is at risk. He should write about her, Alice tells Ernest, but he says no, he still likes Gertrude. But he could tell some stories about the Polish woman who lives with her, the disciplinarian who runs their life. Arriving unexpectedly one day, he once overheard things about their relationship that he will someday tell Alice, but not now. He still likes both of the women too much for that.[20]

Waiting for page proofs and with nothing left to write, Hemingway went to the bullfights with Luis Quintanilla, an artist he admired, scheduled a private estate hunt to break in his new boots, read books, and answered letters.[21] To one of his readers who thought Hemingway should write more decorously, Ernest explained:

> *I am trying to make a picture of the world as I have seen it, without comment, trying to keep my mind as open as a doctor's when he is making an examination, and am always trying to concentrate rather than elaborate. Naturally much will be unpleasant, much will be obscene and much will seem to have no moral viewpoint.*[22]

To his mother-in-law, Hemingway wrote a long letter about his hatred for Hitler's warmongering and about the dishonesty of Roosevelt's inflation of the dollar. He also cautioned her that *Winner Take Nothing* might not be as well received as his earlier books. If she (an ardent Catholic) did not like it, she should not make an effort to be polite about her response. He was afraid the stories would be distasteful to many readers.[23] His calculated frontal attack on the genteel tradition—stories of whores, homosexuals, suicide, castration, and insanity—no matter how well written were now giving him second thoughts. Torn between desire for broad audience acceptance and his need to maintain credentials as a serious artist, he may have written a book doing neither.

And every day they are apart, even when there is nothing to say, Ernest and Pauline try faithfully to write each other. Alone, he is lonely, given to moping and worse. Pauline, knowing his condition from much experience, punctually responds lovingly and anxiously, filling in with small talk. He tells her how exhausting it is to live in another language, trying to please everyone. Relating an incident in Spanish leads to his departing "consistently and utterly from the truth" for the sake of the story. The exhaustion he feels after such ordeals is the same as he felt when he was writing fiction; in fact, it is the "same damn business as writing really."[24] Underneath that observation lay the disturbing truth that Hemingway was never completely at ease with the idea of fiction. Like most of his contemporaries, he was raised to tell the truth, and punished for telling lies. Fiction, by definition, was telling a story not factually true; any story not true was a lie. The syllogism might be logically flawed, but emotionally it carried its weight. More than once Hemingway categorized his stories as those that actually happened and those he made up. When he told Pound that he was training to be a naturalist, he returned to his earliest dream of being a natural historian. He told one critic that he was going to write a book on the Gulf Stream and its migratory fish, about which he had acquired a good deal of knowledge. "Knowledge of a thing is like hours in the air in flying," he said. "I study what I'm interested in and have a damned good time doing it. Anyway it's always valuable if it's true. [The book] will be true."[25] Hemingway never stopped believing that there was a truth to tell.[26]

This moral dilemma was made worse by overly zealous Catholics wondering how Ernest could claim to be of their faith while writing such immoral fiction. He had to admit that the two parts of the equation appeared to be at odds with each other. He told one inquisitor, "I would not wish to embarrass the church with my presence. You may state . . . that Ernest Hemingway, the writer, is a man of no religion. My beliefs I cannot change but I have no right at present to practice them."[27] He sent the letter to Pauline to critique, saying the church might kick him out for writing *Winner Take Nothing*, but if he could keep Hemingway the writer separate from Hemingway the private man, he would still say his "prayers, go to mass, contribute to support and anywhere not known officially can go to confession."[28] Pauline's reply was noncommittal, saying only his letter might be shorter. On the issue of his having no right to call himself Catholic, she was silent, mentioning only that she was attending Mass once again at St. Sulpice, their former parish church.[29] If she worried about her husband's increasing paranoid fears that others were trying to ruin his writing—old friends, his publishers, the critics, the Church—Pauline kept her concern to herself.

======

Madrid, Oct. 15—Madrid will miss Ernest Hemingway, who showed himself a more knowing bullfight fan than many a native in his *Death in the Afternoon,* when he leaves next week for Paris with big plans in view. Paris is only the stepping-off place for an adventure in Africa. Mr. and Mrs. Hemingway and a friend named Thompson from Key West, Florida, will sail from Marseilles next month on the first stage of a big-game shoot. Mr. Hemingway has been staying some months in Madrid and the torrid summer heat has not prevented him from keeping busy on a new short novel.[30]

—Paris *Tribune,* October 16, 1933

By the time he reached Paris, Hemingway was long reconciled to hunting in Africa with only Pauline and Charles Thompson, but plans for the safari did not begin that way. Originally, the safari was going to be an all-male affair with Pauline waiting in Paris for the hunters' return. As another of Hemingway's attempts to reassemble the "summer people" of his youth, the expedition first included Archibald MacLeish and Mike Strater, both of whom backed out of their commitment: Archie because of money problems, Strater because of family problems. Replacements were invited, but none could accept Hemingway's invitation to a cost-free adventure. Uncle Gus, who paid for the safari, looked on the $25,000 as an investment in the book that would result from the experience.[31] Pauline's parents were not enthusiastic about her trekking in primitive Africa, but Hemingway promised them he would take good care of their daughter. Among the entourage of drivers, trackers, cooks, and hunters who were to be her close companions for sixty days, Pauline would be the only woman. Because it was important to her husband, Pauline, neither an outdoors woman nor an avid hunter, tried to match and verify his enthusiasm for the adventure; Ernest, disappointed that the men would not be with him, tried to be a considerate husband.

In the Paris-Dinard Hotel on rue Cassette,[32] Ernest and Pauline were based in their old neighborhood, close to Place St. Sulpice and St. Germain des Prés. With less than a month left before their departure for East Africa, they made lists of what remained to be done. The tailor must be paid for Ernest's safari jacket and shirts, but the buttons were wrong, the cartridge loops unsatisfactory, and the shirt sleeves too tight. They bought more film for the 4×5 Graflex and priced a telephoto lens; they found mosquito boots and sunglasses. The "Indian" needed to be paid for the tin trunks, and Pauline needed a nail brush. Money was moved from New York to Paris to pay for the necessaries, and the tin trunks filled with clothes and books. With the dollar worth 30 percent less than when they last lived in Paris, Ernest's thriftiness was continually challenged, but he did buy Pauline's Christmas present, one of those new dustproof, waterproof watches she wanted.[33]

When he arrived in Paris, Ernest found in the stack of mail the first edition of *Esquire*, leading off with his "Cuban Letter," retitled by Gingrich "Marlin Off the Morro." With full-page color cartoons of barely clothed women saying to each other, "Yeah, and then after he insulted you, what else did he do?" the magazine was a splash of then familiar names: Gilbert Seldes, author of *The Seven Lively Arts*; George Ade, writer of humorous fables; John Dos Passos; Dashiell Hammett; Erskine Caldwell; James Farrell; Gene Tunney, retired heavyweight boxing champion; Douglas Fairbanks, Jr., film star and writer. With a 10×14 format, color ads, men's fashions, and Chicago breeziness, *Esquire* was more than Hemingway expected. Along with the magazine was a long letter from publisher Gingrich, telling about his troubles with U.S. Post Office censors who would not allow Dos Passos to write "get your ass kicked," nor would they allow Gingrich to print clear photos of a burlesque stripper. They rejected a cartoon "showing nude shoulders of man leaning over dividing wall of two roofs to speak to nude girl lying face downward taking sun bath—gag line reading, 'Perhaps I'd better introduce myself.' " Gingrich also explained that he wanted to expand immediately from quarterly to monthly production; could Ernest supply twelve such letters a year at the same $250 rate? A letter a month was asking a lot from a man going on safari, miles from a post office, paying $100 a day to hunt. Maybe he could write more letters, but Gingrich would have to take them as they came. "I deliver what I promise," Ernest told Gingrich, "and you must see—what ever your need—that I can't promise now."[34] In the Paris-Dinard, Hemingway, as was his custom, rented a separate room to write the "Paris Letter" for which Gingrich had already deposited payment.[35]

The Paris of his early years was much diminished, a time and place already legend but no longer recoverable. Half the Americans who once lived in Paris had gone home; the half that remained were all too serious. That summer, Wambly Bald gave up his *Tribune* chronicle of the Left Bank, saying that Montparnasse was no longer a handkerchief to wave at friends: "It is a filthy rag one drops into the nearest garbage can." Having become the haven of dilettantes and fakes, tourists and poseurs, the Quarter had lost its charm and its heroes— the unknown painters and writers who graduated to greatness. "The world," Bald wrote, "is leveled off. Montparnasse is Main Street. . . . Even automobiles are going Picasso. The staunch army may disband. Gertrude Stein has crashed (of all things) *The Atlantic Monthly*, and her autobiography is accepted for publication by the Book-of-the-Month Club."[36] The modernist revolution was now mainstream.

Informal, discursive, and personal, Hemingway's "Paris Letter" opened with memories of Wyoming hunting, moved on to Paris, where old friends had disappeared, reminisced about French boxers from seasons past, and ended with two disparate points: a warning that there was another war coming, which America should avoid; and a closing nostalgic paragraph on Paris:

> It was a fine place to be quite young in and it is a necessary part of a man's education. We all loved it once and we lie if we say we didn't. But she is like a mistress who does not grow old and she has other lovers now.[37]

Along with praise for Hemingway's letter from Spain, Gingrich included unsolicited advice in response to Hemingway's comments on Gertrude Stein and critics in general:

> Your growing cynicism about human relationships in general is understandable . . . but I regret it just the same. You get too set in this

attitude and you can't help, before long, beginning to hurt yourself by
adding needlessly to the number of your ex-friends. . . . people who
knew you when you were fairly far down on the way up are always
prone to resent the fact that you didn't stay there. But the inevitable
outcroppings of professional jealousies are doubly unfortunate if
they're going to make you feel that the world is peopled exclusively by
bitches and their sons.[38]

Like most prophetic advice, Gingrich's perceptive remarks did little
to deflect Hemingway's anger with the critics' response to *Winner*
Take Nothing, which was published on October 27, the day after he
arrived in Paris.

Max Perkins's telegram was waiting: "First review Tribune very very
good think prospects excellent."[39] Archie MacLeish's followed soon
after: "Deeply gratefully affectionately moved magnificent book
unworthy dedicatee incommunicable sentiments."[40] In the third year
of the depression, when good books selling fewer than five thousand
copies were thought a wonder, Perkins wired on November 11, "Plenty
speak well sale eleven thousand will push till Christmas."[41] The
reviews, however, even Max found "unsatisfactory and a good many
are absolutely enraging."[42] Written as if a group project, the reviews
uniformly recognized Hemingway's impact on contemporary writing:
"He has created a fashion, almost a tradition." All acknowledged that
his distinctive and much-imitated style was a marvel: "I take for
granted that his prose always reaches certain levels of excellence, that
his art has always been deliberate." Most found one or more stories in
the collection to praise. But, and the "but" loomed large, the Twenties
were over, the postwar generation's say had been said; New York critics
wanted something different, something more compassionate in hard
times.[43] The *New York Times* review said the writing was superlative:

the dialogue is admirable; . . . [the] picture is vivid, whole; the way of
life is caught and conveyed without a hitch. . . . It is not that the life
they portray isn't worth exploring. But Hemingway has explored it
beyond its worth.[44]

Taking out his anger as usual on Max, Hemingway said that Scribner's was trying to ruin him by not advertising the book effectively, by giving up on him, by using damning quotes in what ads they ran. The critics were shits, demanding better stories than the best he had written. "God damn it there can't be better ones. . . . I'll be goddamned if I like to have to say how good my stuff is in order to give the business office confidence enough to advertise it after they have read an unfavorable review and think I'm through."[45]

There is not enough time to vent all his spleen, for with his departure for Africa upon him, Hemingway has plenty of items remaining on his checklist. Two days are spent gathering visas from the consulate offices of Egypt, Ethiopia, and Great Britain.[46] A deposit is paid on return tickets in March; trunks are packed, books selected, guns oiled, and last letters mailed. On November 22, Ernest, Pauline, and Charles Thompson (who joined them in Paris on November 15) sail out of Marseilles on the *General Metzinger* bound for Mombasa to fulfill the African dream he has nurtured from his boyhood.

––––––

Madame Bertrand de Jouvenel, the former Martha Gellhorn of St. Louis, Mo. has a first novel, *Nothing Ever Happens*, appearing shortly on London bookstands. Critics who have seen it in manuscript or proof describe the novel as sensational for its literary quality and for its subject matter. Madame Jouvenel has already started a second novel and is leaving shortly for the United States in order to gather material for it with her husband, brilliant young French journalist and economist. While Jouvenel is making a lecture tour, Madame Jouvenel will study at close range the reaction of American youth to the New Deal. Her work in progress deals with the problem presented by the moral and social disintegration of the depression generation, particularly the new poor.

—Paris *Tribune*, November 20, 1933

––––––

The *Metzinger*, lacking the amenities of a large liner, is a time traveler, chugging away from rainy Europe and into an earlier world of colonial governors, dust and flies, slow sailing dhows, and strange tongues. Ten days it takes to clear the Mediterranean and pass through Suez, where heat rises, food worsens, and the French close curtains to what small breeze blows. Finally, seventeen days out, they reach the lush green island of Mombasa with its huge-trunked baobab trees, coconut palms, white lime-washed houses, shaded verandahs, shuttered windows, palm-thatched roofs, and ebony faces. They come down the gangplank: Pauline in a white dress, gloves, and parasol; Charles in suit and tie, sweating in the heavy heat; Ernest, with white shirtsleeves rolled and wearing a wide-brimmed Stetson. "Pauline and I looked like missionaries," Thompson said, "while Ernest had the distinct look of whiskey drummer." Everywhere Indian businessmen hurry along, heads bobbing, and the rich odors of curry flow from the alleyways. At the Palace Hotel, rooms are clean, the bar is open.[47]

Next afternoon at half past four, with legs still wobbly from the sea voyage, the hunting party, paying the baggage bill, boarded the Kenya and Uganda Railway bound for Nairobi, 330 miles inland. At dusk, with coastal jungle beginning to thin, they eat a five-course supper in the new dining car, and afterward bed down in compartments with small washrooms.[48] The overnight journey, taking them from sea level to mile-high Nairobi, passes through storied country which Ernest knows well from reading, in his youth, J. H. Patterson's horrific *The Man-Eaters of Tsavo*. For most of a year, two lions so terrorized Indian and native laborers that construction of this railway came to a halt. At night these lions, slipping into boxcars where workers slept, killed and ate more than twenty-eight men before Patterson was able to shoot them. At Chicago's Field Museum of Natural History, young Hemingway stood more than once before the infamous Tsavo lions, now permanently poised on their sandstone lair, tails almost twitching. One lion crouched, ready to spring; the other stood with right foot expectantly raised.[49]

They sleep as one can to the clackity-click of rails and wake to wonder on the prairie rolling in sunlight toward distant blue mountains. Farther away than seems possible, Mount Kilimanjaro, domed with fresh-fallen snow, hovers in the western sky. Everywhere there is game: giraffe, antelope, zebra, kongoni, eland, and jackals. "Nothing I've ever read has given any idea of what this country is like," Hemingway said. Covered with fine red dust and farther from home than could be measured in miles, the Hemingway party reaches Nairobi, where most of the city seems to be waiting the once-a-day train's arrival. In midmorning heat, Ernest, Pauline, and Charles, along with heavy luggage, are transported down tree-lined Government Road to the New Stanley Hotel, which claims to be the only establishment north of Johannesburg with a bathroom attached to every bedroom.

Armed with letters of introduction, Hemingway went the next day to Tanganyika Guides to make a second payment on the safari. In his hotel room a letter from Jane Mason warned him that Dick Cooper "is afraid you may get one of those 'no-good white hunters' which abound in Africa. They promise you all the game in the kingdom and end you up with nothing but a few reels of pictures of the country."[50] The requested guide, Philip Percival, forty-nine-year-old director of the company and legendary safari man, once worked on Theodore Roosevelt's epic 1909 safari, which young Hemingway followed in magazines, and in Oak Park watched the jerky moving pictures of the Colonel's expedition on the silent screen. More than anyone else, Roosevelt, his earliest hero, was responsible for opening East Africa to Hemingway's imagination.[51] At the age of six he stood in awe beside two gigantic stuffed elephants in the Field Museum; at sixteen, he promised himself to do "exploring work" in Africa; at twenty-six, he gave his character Jake Barnes the dream of hunting in British East Africa. Now, at thirty-four, Ernest was there on Roosevelt's ground.[52] Percival, graying, understated, and very British, agreed to lead their safari, but could not go into the field until December 20.

This delay was actually a blessing, giving the group time to acclimatize, not only to the surroundings but to the altitude, which demanded more red blood cells for the thinner air. Tanganyika Guides provided hunting excursions in the Nairobi area, where Ernest and Charles shot Grant and Thompson gazelle, kongoni, and impala, which were almost at their front door. Days were no hotter than in Key West in winter, and by night they slept beneath hotel blankets. When not exploring the nearby countryside, Hemingway was in the company of two young, wealthy sportsmen, Winston Guest and Alfred Vanderbilt, introductions provided by Jane Mason. Guest, twenty-seven-year-old Ivy League lawyer with a huge inherited fortune, played world-class polo and was an avid hunter. With two large ivory tusks already taken on his license, he was in Nairobi eager for more elephant hunting. Young Alfred Vanderbilt was also in Nairobi waiting for Bror Von Blixen, Percival's partner, former husband of Karen Blixen (née Isak Dinesen) and reputedly the best white hunter in East Africa, to lead his safari. To Gingrich, Hemingway recommended Vanderbilt as a "good young kid" who knew horses and racing, spending most of his time with the fabled Vanderbilt stables, and who wanted to write for *Esquire*. "I don't know whether he can write or not but he knows racing and horses and would be the TOP in insiders for you to have writing for you."[53]

With not enough information to write his "African Letter" for Gingrich, Hemingway used the Nairobi layover to fulfill his promise of an introduction for the Montparnasse memoirs of Jimmy Charters, the Paris barman at the Dingo. Still smarting from Stein's portrait of him, he began the somewhat carelessly written introduction: "Once a woman has opened a salon it is certain she will write her memoirs." No matter how useful one might be to the salon keeper, once no longer valuable, he was certain to be slandered by her.

> *The memoir writer will usually prove that a lady's brain may still be between her thighs—but let us not make jokes about thighs—and will treat you in her memoirs as any girl around the Dôme or the Sélect would; imputing this to you, denying you that.*

In the last paragraph he finally got around to Charters, whose memoirs Ernest took to be another sign of western civilization's decline. He wished Jimmy luck, but also wished the book were not about "Montparnasse because that is a dismal place."[54] He mailed the handwritten draft to a Paris friend, who typed it, making minor corrections before sending it on to Charters.[55]

While waiting for Philip Percival to arrange their safari, the hunters were not without local distractions to pass the time. Nairobi was a small town halfway between pioneer squalor and urban sophistication. Wild and sometimes dangerous animals were as close as the edge of town and often closer. At the Indian bazaar all manner of exotic objects were for sale: snow leopard and fox furs, dik-dik skins, drums, stools, spears and shields, a "beautiful walking-cane made of one piece white rhino horn, gold mounted in London."[56] At the New Stanley bar, the talk was about a murder trial being argued in the Nairobi courthouse and across much of the colony. Henry Tarlton, whose native name meant "The Man Who Was Never Wrong," had his Caucasian skull smashed by a heavy blade. Doomed by witnesses and strong circumstantial evidence, the accused African native had "horrified the whole country," raising dark fears and prompting letters to the editor:

> Deep distress is felt amongst the old settlers in the district at the death
> of Henry Tarlton. . . . strong action needs to be taken to protect the
> white settlers and their womenfolk from the truculent attitude of the
> native, which, if unchecked, may culminate in an attack.

Meanwhile, Y. A. Hunter of Nairobi was quietly appealing the eighteen-month suspension of his driver's license for his reckless driving which killed a native. Having paid the fifty-pound fine, Hunter argued that temporarily being unable to drive was an undue hardship.[57]

On December 20, after delays about trucks and supplies and much midmorning beer-drinking, the Hemingway safari departed from Percival's farm, making straight for the Tanganyika border, riding easily across rolling plains and bush country green from recent rains. Game abounded, but they did not shoot that day or the next, which took them to the customs shed at Namanga. While the men passed guns through inspection and stamping, Pauline sat partly shaded in the noonday sun watching a bare-breasted Masai woman flirting with a tall black man—shiny and shapely she found them. With her khaki trousers and bush jacket, her small close-cropped head dwarfed by a wide-brimmed hat, only her orange-and-yellow neck scarf distinguished Pauline from the men around her. As she watched, the Masai man picked up the woman and carried her into a hut, from which laughter and wrestling noises were heard.

From Namanga on through Arusha, stopping over at a hotel with a swimming pool, trucks and hunters stepped off finally into the great Rift Valley, moving north toward the Masai game reserve in the Ngorongoro Crater. With heat waves rippling the plain, Pauline watched Ernest humiliate himself all of one morning in pursuit of a Grant's gazelle. Firing repeatedly low and away, stubbornly refusing to make corrections, he missed and missed again. They chased in the car, stalked on foot, but never got the prize head. After five or six shots at a smaller Grant, he wounded and finally killed it. Percival told him that everyone's shot was a bit off when first out. Pauline, detached, observing, making notes, infrequently shooting, did not much care for hunting by car: too hot, too dusty. As she watched, her nail polish faded in the sun.

Getting laden trucks up the wet, slippery dirt road to the crater rim took most of the morning before Christmas, leaving Pauline alone staring out into the mist of the huge, flat, green caldera beneath her, where famous lions were said to roam. When the men came up after pushing and cursing the trucks, Ernest asked her to go somewhere else, for he was having an attack of diarrhea. He didn't want to go into the three-foot grass because there might be snakes. That afternoon they took one car down into the crater, where she and Ernest saw their first lioness, driving to within fifty feet of her. After killing two zebra for bait and driving back toward the lioness, Percival, Pauline, and Ernest were stunned by an explosion beside Ernest's head. His rifle, strapped to the car top and supposedly uncocked, had fallen to the ground beside his door and unexplainably fired. Visibly shaken, Pauline's first thought was that Ernest had been killed.

The day after Christmas, wearing her new wristwatch, Pauline got her first clear view of the Serengeti Plain, full of game moving in all directions. Here their day's pattern became more regular, taking on the rhythm of their quarry: early breakfast of tea and whatever; morning hunts ending when the heat became oppressive; in the shade a cold lunch from the chop box; back to the hunt in late afternoon; returning to whiskey, a sit-bath, more whiskey, and dinner in pajamas. Antelope, guinea fowl, and potatoes became their daily fare, quickly leaving Pauline and Charles constipated from too much meat and not enough water. Constipation, however, was not Ernest's problem. No sooner had they begun the safari than his attacks of diarrhea became more and more frequent. What began as a joke quickly became a nuisance that passed into real concern. While Ernest took doses of chlorine salts administered by Percival, Charles and Pauline complained of piles. Either way, riding over bumpy terrain on stiff seats became more and more painful for the Key Westers. Between internal difficulties, heat and dust, biting flies, disturbing night noises, and her certain knowledge that she was not brave regarding wild animals larger than herself and far more deadly, Pauline's enthusiasm for the safari was hard pressed to match Ernest's.

On the morning of December 29, Pauline took her first shot at a lion and missed. As she noted in her journal, her "characteristic" shooting was always a little low, a little high, a bit to the left or right. Always splendid shots, according to Percival, but always leaving her disappointed. Ernest, shooting his relatively light Springfield .30-06, flattened the lion with a single shot, followed by another shot for safety. Word went out from her guide M'Cola to the truckers, cooks, and bearers that Mama had killed her lion, which resulted in much shouting and dancing. Chagrined and wishing that she had killed the lion, Pauline distributed traditional shillings all round. Later the day turned hot, dusty, and disappointing, with the plain stretching out endlessly and no camp where camp was supposed to be and driving on for more than two hours to find it finally with tents up in proper sequence and whiskey waiting for them.

The last day of the year went out to a chorus of missed shots and curses. The morning began with Ernest missing a roan antelope, followed by three missed shots at a leopard. Later he wounded a cheetah, which everyone tracked up and over the hill for more than a sweaty hour without finding him. That afternoon Charles fired six or seven shots at an impala, finally bringing him down. Next morning, the first of the new year, Pauline, worn out from hiking in the brush, stayed in camp while Ernest was out redeeming his sorry shooting of the previous day. Before noon he had killed a warthog and a cheetah, and then he and Charles killed three buffalo, which Pauline had to see. So they sent Ben Fourie, the mechanic and driver, an hour back to camp to haul her to the killing ground, where she admired the dead buffs with ticks still crawling on them. Too much heat, too much dust, too much male talk; Poor Old Mama, as they were now calling Pauline, had reached her limits. Gloom descended upon her, and down she went into it, taking supper that night in bed alone. Making strenuous demands upon her in the field, the men, who apparently did not understand either her disappointments or her fears, frequently added to Pauline's melancholy. A long way from St. Louis, she was trying, almost desperately at times, to be the outdoors wife Ernest so wanted her to be, but at heart's core she was addicted to city pleasures and convenience.

Three days later, approaching by car a mated pair of lions on a slight hill, the group was surprised when the two predators came toward the vehicle, the lion to one side, his mate to the other. To Pauline's rising anxiety, the men agreed that she should shoot the male lion, which had grown huge in her eyes by the time they got her out of the car. As she took aim, Percival said, "For Christ sake don't shoot the lioness!" She looked up, wondering if she could be shooting the lioness, which, of course, was on the opposite side of car. As she resighted down the rifle barrel, she could hear Charles struggling to get out of the car. Afraid the lions would spook, she hurried her shot, apparently missing. The lions quickly disappeared into a dry streambed thick with brush. No amount of beating about the edges of the donga could bring them back in sight. Pauline returned to camp in silent despair. Ernest, she noted later, had remained inside the car, unable to save her if the lion charged.

Changing camps every two or three days, the hunting party shot its way further into the Serengeti, living off the land and taking trophies. By January 8, Ernest and Charles had killed their lion, buffalo, cheetah, and leopard, leaving only the rhino to complete the five truly dangerous animals. With Percival as their guide and mediator, Pauline as their audience, and several natives as appreciative chorus, an increasing rivalry was beginning to create tensions between the two men. Ernest was by nature competitive to a sometimes unpleasant degree; Charles, the less talkative of the two, was the invited guest who had no intention of being the designated loser in this passage of arms. For amusement the two men kept track of the hyenas they shot at every opportunity.

Adding to the tension was a growing awareness that Ernest's quickly multiplying diarrhea attacks were actually dysentery. By January 11, he was taking chlorine salts continuously, but his evening drinking undermined any good the medicine might have done. By January 13, he was too weak to stay out in the field and too uncomfortable sitting in the car. On the evening of the fourteenth, driving back to camp over a punishing road, Ernest, in terrible pain, was clearly in need of medical attention. Percival sent Ben careening over bush roads 115 miles to Lake Victoria, the closest telegraph station, to arrange for an airplane to fly Hemingway to the Arusha hospital, which was three days away by car. All the next day, Hemingway remained in bed, moving to the campfire only in the evening for a bowl of mashed potatoes. Through that night of wind and rain, awakened by biting bugs and her own anxiety, Pauline tosses about while Ernest sleeps through the commotion. When Ben returns the morning of the 15th, they learn the plane will arrive at two that afternoon. All morning and afternoon, they wait in camp, listening for the motor, but no plane appears. Hemingway spends the day reading magazines, apparently feeling better for the rest and for two days of not drinking. Somehow a radio message comes through: no plane today; plane tomorrow. The next morning at ten, the small silver plane lands in the road, loads a smiling Hemingway aboard, and takes off for Arusha at the foot of Mount Kilimanjaro and the government doctor.

———

Your amebic dysentery correspondent is in bed, fully injected with emetine, having flown four hundred miles to Nairobi via Arusha from where the outfit is camped on the Serenea river on the far side of the Serengeti plain. Cause of the flight, a. d. Cause of a. d. unknown. Symptoms of a. d. run from weakly insidious through spectacular to phenomenal. I believe the record is held by a Mr. McDonald with 232 movements in the twenty-four hours although many old a. d. men claim the McDonald record was never properly audited.[58]

—Ernest Hemingway, "a.d. in Africa: A Tanganyika Letter"

———

Unbeknownst to Pauline and Percival, Ernest landed at Arusha and then continued on to Nairobi, where he registered at the New Stanley Hotel. There a Dr. Anderson treated him with regular injections of emetine, whose efficacy was most apparent in Hemingway's bar bill, which rose from four shillings for mineral water his first night to sixty-four shillings and fifty pence four nights later, when he apparently was well enough to entertain guests at dinner.[59] He used the days in bed to arrange an end-of-safari fishing trip on the coast, to write his promised "African Letter" for *Esquire*, and to answer mail.

The day after he arrived in Nairobi, he was writing Max from his hotel bed, thanking him for royalty and sales statements (over thirteen thousand *Winner Take Nothing*s sold), telling about the pleasures of amebic dysentery ("Feels as if you were trying to give birth to a child"), recounting the game bagged, and bitching about the state of public letters. His present unpopularity, which he insisted on despite healthy sales, was to be expected, for a writer's stock always rose and fell with current fads like "this present damned YMCA economic hurrah business." Having once belonged to the YMCA in his Oak Park youth, he often used it as a shorthand way of demeaning trendy salvationists, which was his view of Roosevelt's attempts to revive the nation's economy. He assured Perkins that when the economic slump passed, he, Ernest, would be better than ever, having remained a writer while others followed the ideological trend to the left. But he could not expect the public to believe in him when his own publisher appeared to have given up on him. This now familiar accusation followed every book he published with Scribner's. No matter what the sales, there would have been more if only his publisher had pushed harder, taken out more ads, done more to promote the book.[60]

While Hemingway recovered, the safari degenerated badly. The morning after his departure, Pauline and Charles poured shot after shot in the direction of an antelope they stalked relentlessly for what seemed like hours before killing him. By the next day, Percival was running a fever as he led the trucks back up to the top of the Ngorongoro Crater, where Pauline and Charles hunted to no great end while Percival remained in camp. On January 20, Pauline and Percival drove, hot and dusty, into Arusha to surprise Ernest, but only surprising themselves when they learned he was actually in Nairobi. Telegrams were sent, but not knowing whether his client was fit for more hunting and feeling somewhat sick himself, Percival repaired to the hotel bar alone. On Sunday morning, Arusha church bells ringing, Pauline thought of going to Mass, but without stockings or proper shoes, she could not face her religious duty in trousers.

After spending an awkward Sunday with Percival, whose drinking did not relieve his gloom, Pauline was delighted on Monday when an apparently cured Ernest, smiling, weak, and handsome, stepped off the small plane on the Arusha landing strip. The three of them spent another day in town, waiting for truck parts, drinking at Luigi's bar, the men telling war stories. By January 24, they were back in the field, camped on the Mosquito River, ready to begin the final month of the safari in pursuit of rhino and kudu.

Waking in the dark, still weak and thinking maybe not to go out, but after breakfast with the light beginning to break, it all looked better. Sitting on the hill with M'Cola, Pauline, and Percival, the day heating up as the beaters circle behind the hill, when here comes the rhino, breaking cover fast, heading for the river. "Not awfully good," says Percival, "but we'll shoot him." Three shots at an impossible distance and one snort from the rhino before he's out of sight. Every one running now with Droopy Lids tracking, finding blood, and then we could hear heavy breathing and then nothing but the birds. The rhino down in the grass, dead, with everyone gathered about for the photograph, one of the trackers touching the horn for luck.

―――

Unfortunately the safari has become a matter of measurements: Ernest's rhino carries a seventeen-inch horn, and Charles's rhino, killed two days later, sports a twenty-three-inch horn. Nothing can change these numbers, not even the magnificence of Ernest's remarkable shot. For good reason, therefore, Percival keeps the two men separated as much as possible during the day, sending Charles off with Ben, the mechanic, and his own trackers while he stands watch over Ernest and Pauline. Much better that way. But there is always the evening rendezvous with whiskey by the fire, where every shot is rehashed. Charles's trophy heads, somewhat larger than Ernest's, out of sight but never out of mind, color all their conversations.

With rhinos taken, the safari spends two days at Dick Cooper's place near Babiti within view of Lake Manyara's miles of pink and rose flamingoes. There they shoot ducks for the supper table, sleep in real beds, bathe in comfort, and rest for the final push. With less than two weeks remaining before the rains make the dirt roads of the Serengeti impassable, the men turn to the last animal on their list: the greater kudu. Day after day, they rise early to breakfast in the dark, returning weary and late from the bush empty handed. On February 9, they drive all day and part of the next to fresh country around Kijungu where the antelope is said to abound. Lured on by tracks, they hunt in blinds by the salt lick, but no kudu appears. With the men getting testy, Pauline waits with Percival in the camp rather than spending the day in the field with Ernest. On February

11, Charles brings in the first kudu with grotesquely twisted thirty-eight-inch horns; the next morning before dawn, Pauline wakes to see a sad-looking Ernest preparing to leave for the salt lick. Only five days are left for the hunt.

This day's hunt is spoiled by the clanking truck of a short, round little German, who remembered from the mid-Twenties reading the poet Hemingway in a German magazine. Four years later Herr Kortischoner wrote Hemingway, reminding him that he was the man

> *you found one day with a broken down motor car, who was a reader of the* Querschnitt. . . . *You pulled this man out of his awkward situation; he spent two days in your camp at Kijungu, where he met Mrs. Hemingway who kept a diary in which you may find his name.*[61]

On Valentine's Day, Percival sends one truck off with a tow rope to pull Kortischoner and his truck over a hundred miles into Handeni. Meanwhile, Ernest finds one salt lick under water from the now falling rains, another spoiled by native hunters. Back in camp, Pauline feels as despondent as the cows mooing outside her tent. Should have stayed in bed longer, she tells herself.

No kudu that day nor the next, but rain is now falling regularly, slicking the surface of the dirt roads. In another week or less, dirt will be mud, and trucks will be unable to get the safari to the coast. Philip Percival, against best judgment, pushes his luck to satisfy his clients. On February 16, Ernest and his tracker take food and mattress by car into a far salt lick in order to be on the killing ground at first light and all next day if necessary. The morning he leaves, Charles and Ben, who have, for two days, been on their own at another likely spot, kill an enormous kudu. When Percival moves their camp to Kibaya, there are the horns, lovely, long, dark, and spiraling. Sad that Ernest has apparently not gotten his kudu and none too glad about Charles's getting one, Pauline goes to bed early. Thirty minutes later, she awakens groggy to shouting and banging. Dashing out in pajamas, she sees Ernest there in the car lights with natives singing and Percival clapping him on his shoulder. Then she sees the

horns, two pairs of lovely kudu horns and a sable for good measure.
The next morning in a group photo, Ben, Charles, Philip, and Ernest
kneel, smiling, each holding vertical a set of horns on a still-bloody
skull: three kudu and Ernest holding his sable. Ben looks pleased,
Philip relieved; Ernest grins. Charles, his face covered by one of the
horns, seems to be looking somewhere else. Measurements are
taken: the horns of Charles's kudu extend fifty-seven inches; Ernest's
measure fifty-one and a quarter. The safari is finished.

———

Of the antelope family, they killed four Thompson gazelle, eight
Grant, seven wildebeest, seven impala, two klipspringers, four
roan, two bushbucks, three reedbucks, two oryx, four topi, two
waterbuck, one eland, and three kudu. Of dangerous game, they
killed their licensed limit: four lions, three cheetahs, four buffalo,
two leopards, and two rhinos. They also killed one serval cat, two
warthogs, thirteen zebra, and one cobra. Animals wounded but
never found included two cheetahs, two warthogs, one eland, one
buffalo, and one dik-dik. For amusement forty-one hyenas were
also killed. There may have been more but these are the recorded
kills.[62]

———

Chapter Seven

1934

PURSUIT REMEMBERED

Key West, Havana, and Key West

ON THE AFTERNOON of April 11, as Hemingway stepped off the Havana Special from New York, a Key West jazz band hired for the occasion struck up a raucous march and a throng of greeters surrounded him: Pauline and five-year-old Patrick, Ada MacLeish, John and Katy Dos Passos, Charles and Lorine Thompson, and other assorted well-wishers.[1] In his luggage is a copy of Scott Fitzgerald's recently published novel, *Tender Is the Night*, for whose heroine Sara Murphy, standing beside him, was one of the models. Two weeks later, when Ernest wrote Gerald Murphy, thanking and repaying him for the train ticket, he said that Scott's book was not much good. "There's been too bloody much flashy writing," he said. "There is almost no true writing and people do not like to read it."[2] As he wrote that sentence, on his shelf there were twenty-three rare volumes on African hunting, recently purchased in Paris, background and reference books for his next work, a story which was to be as true as he could make it to his African experience. When Hemingway's interest focused on new material or a new genre, he first read broadly and deep to find what not to write.[3]

Hemingway also brought with him from New York a catalog from the Wheeler Shipyard advertising a thirty-eight-foot Playmate cabin cruiser which, with some modification, could become the fishing boat he dreamed about but could no longer afford, having sloughed off too much of the $7,000 he'd saved to buy it. Arnold Gingrich, seeing a chance to keep Hemingway's name on his magazine's masthead, offered him a $3,000 advance against twelve future *Esquire* "letters." Hemingway quickly agreed, promising that Pauline would pay off the debt should he die before fulfilling it, but adding that the debt would be canceled if the magazine went under.[4] Six days later Hemingway signed and mailed a contract for the boat with a $3,000 down payment to Eugene Wheeler, specifying several modifications:

> *more gas tanks for longer cruising*
> *transom lowered twelve inches for pulling in big fish*
> *a live fish well*
> *a second deck chair*
> *an auxiliary motor independent of the main engine*

The hull was to be painted pirate black, and on its stern in white letters the name should read *Pilar* of Key West.[5] During their 1926–27 affair, "Pilar" was Pauline's code name, and more recently the name they saved for the daughter they now knew they would never have.

Hemingway quickly arranged with Max Perkins to borrow another $2,500 from Scribner's to pay off the *Pilar* when it arrived in Miami. This loan would become part of an advance when Hemingway delivered his next book, a plan for which was forming in his mind. Taking an earlier advance, he rushed *Winner Take Nothing*, a mistake he said he would not make this time. (Somehow a 4 percent loan was not the same as an advance.) Talking to himself more than to Perkins, he said that

> *my idea of a career is never to write a phony line, never fake, never cheat, never be sucked in by the y.m.c.a. movements of the moment, and to give them as much literature in a book as any son of a bitch has ever gotten into the same number of words. But that isn't enough. If you want to make a living out of it you have to, in addition every so often, without faking, cheating or deviating from the above give them something they understand and that has a story.*[6]

And his idea of how to write was to get up every morning, go to the spare room over the garage, sit down to the table, and put penciled words about Africa onto bond paper. At the start, there was no plan, only the joy of recreating the zebra shoot on the hot, dusty plain, and the flamingos turning the lake all pink at one end. Like many simple things, it was difficult work: much detail to be left out; scaffolding to come down when the story stood on its own. Sometimes he was only saying things that he had to see on paper before removing them. On his return from Africa through Paris, he used up part of his safari experience in two more *Esquire* letters, one on lion hunting, the second on other dangerous game. He intended to write at least two more: one on rhino hunting, one on kudu and sable.[7] But as soon as he was back in Key West, reading in the old safari books, he told Gingrich that there would be no more African letters for *Esquire*.[8] By May Day, he was already twenty good pages into a story of the kudu hunt, not knowing how long it would be and not really caring. It was to be as true a story as anything remembered can be true.[9]

While he was living mornings in Africa and afternoons on the water, other, less local Americans were reading his story "One Trip Across" in the April *Cosmopolitan*, and the April *Esquire* featured his "a.d. in Africa: A Tanganyika Letter." Many of these same readers were amused by *Vanity Fair*'s full-page spread of the Ernest Hemingway paper doll. Centered on the page was a caricature of Ernest as Neanderthal wearing a leopard skin and holding in one hand a club and in the other a dead rabbit. Four cutouts framed him: the Lost Generation Hemingway seated at a sidewalk café table covered with wine bottles; the Isaac Walton Hemingway in the rowboat *Anita* loaded with six marlin; the Unknown Soldier Hemingway in uniform and on crutches; and the Toreador Hemingway in a suit of lights holding a bull's head in one hand.[10]

While most of Hemingway's generation were moving into their midlife course with their notoriety behind them, he was just hitting his stride. (Scott Fitzgerald, once the darling of *The Smart Set*, was no longer a madcap youth driving cars into public fountains; the once lovely Zelda, her mouth hardened and her blue eyes more vacant, was spending quiet evenings in the sanitarium.) Almost thirty-five years old, Ernest Hemingway was a newsworthy figure whose every public act was grist for the media; his broad shoulders, and his round, mustached face with its pronounced widow's peak becoming as widely recognized as some movie stars. Where once his fiction drew attention to his active life, now that life drew attention to his writing. His sportsman's adventures also drew the attention of natural historians. On his way back from safari, Hemingway answered the Philadelphia Academy of Natural Science's questions about game fish in Cuban waters—classifications, life histories, food, and migrations. Hemingway said he would be happy to cooperate with the director, Charles Cadwalader, for "it would be very interesting to have a complete collection of these fish and determine scientifically which are truly different species and which are merely sexual and age variations of the same fish." His own theories, he said, were "too extensive to put in a letter."[11] After Hemingway stopped for an afternoon in Philadelphia on his train trip back to Key West, Cadwalader and Henry Fowler were eager to join Ernest in Havana for the summer marlin run.[12]

Back in Key West with his "extensive" marlin theories fresh in mind, he wrote his seventh *Esquire* letter, in which he raised questions of the sort that interest natural historians. Why won't a mako shark eat a hooked marlin when other sharks will? What is the purpose of the sailfish's sail? Why do marlin always travel against the current? Why do the great fishing years in California and Cuba coincide? Could the white, the striped, and the black marlin be variations of the same fish? He admitted that he would fish marlin "even if it were of no scientific value at all and you can't expect anyone to subsidize anything that anybody has a swell time out of. As a matter of fact I suppose we are lucky to be able to fish for them without being put in jail. This time next year they may have gotten out a law against it." (There should have been a law against editor Gingrich's having the letter illustrated with a woodcut of Hemingway fishing with one hand and swigging from a liquor bottle with the other. Protruding over the stern of the *Pilar* are sixteen bottles of liquor, one of which is being guzzled by a marlin in the water.)[13]

Three days after Ernest arrived in Key West, E. B. White's poetic jibe about Hemingway the African hunter appeared in *The New Yorker*. Taking off on a newspaper story in which Hemingway was quoted as having shot only lions who were utter strangers to him, White advised "friends" to "cling to Ernest Hemingway"

> *Who writes by night and hunts by day,*
> *Whose books with gore are fairly ruddy*
> *But not with gore of pal or buddy,*
> *And who, in time of darkest danger,*
> *Will only dominate a stranger.*[14]

Old and former friends like Sherwood Anderson who read these lines must have winced, knowing that strangers were, in fact, frequently better treated than themselves. At that moment, Ernest was assuring Sara Murphy by mail that he had stopped treating John Dos Passos so meanly.[15]

Having been in Key West only one month out of the past twelve, Hemingway was returning to a visibly diminished island where three out of every four citizens now qualified for government relief, where property taxes were not paid for lack of cash, and where trash uncollected by unpaid workers was piling up. Under President Roosevelt's Federal Emergency Relief Act (FERA), a few hundred men were employed clearing land for an airport and building a saltwater aquarium to attract tourists, but most of the have-nots were living off fish and small cash handouts from the government supplemented by free flour, beef, butter, and vegetables delivered on an irregular schedule. With the Army and Navy bases closed, even bars and prostitutes were short of customers. Before the summer was out, every New York train was met by a welcoming band working for FERA, hoping to lure Havana-bound tourists into stopping over in Key West.[16] This was the summer that the midwest drought finally turned west Texas and places north into a hopeless dust bowl; the summer of garish bank robbers, made famous by the media, going down in bloody shoot-outs: Pretty Boy Floyd, Bonnie Parker and Clyde Barrow, John Dillinger; a summer of riots, strikes, and discontent.

————

His "method" is dictated by his own physique, his raw masculinity, and the type of experience he constantly seeks in life. The success of his works is to be attributed to their possession of qualities not usually found in "literary" writing. . . . The legend of Hemingway is modern-Byronic. It is made up of tales of drinking, bull-fighting, carnal experiences in the war, rough talk and bad manners, and then wine and more wine. . . . People who have had only a glimpse of him are forever bragging about his athletic prowess and his shocking manners. It is easy to attribute to him all of the experiences that are in his books, for he has penetrated perfectly and even sympathetically all of the most abandoned types of human beings. . . . his weakness as an author is the eternal sameness of his material and of his method.[17]

—Lawrence Conrad, August 1934

————

The morning before he and John Dos Passos took the P&O ferry to Havana for May Day, Ernest was writing Max Perkins about Fitzgerald's *Tender Is the Night*, eight years in the making. Angry with Scott for arbitrarily mixing characters—first the heroine is Sara Murphy, then Zelda, then back to Sara—and for not understanding the emotional complication of Gerald Murphy but only his exterior,

Ernest complained that despite Scott's beautiful prose style, he still could not consistently think straight. Loaded with talent, always readable, Scott never grew up, never learned his trade, was "never a man." All that Hemingway said about Fitzgerald's use of prototypes others once said about his own practice in *The Sun Also Rises*. He was lecturing to himself as much as to Perkins: "Using actual stuff is the most difficult writing in the world to have good. Making it up is the easiest and the best. But you have to know what things are about before you start and you have to have confidence."[18] There was no way for Max to know that Hemingway was describing his own concerns about the African story he was writing—a story about which he said little to anyone.

Late on May Day when Hemingway and Dos Passos arrived in Havana, the shooting was over and the wounded counted. That morning, as 25,000 workers, labor leaders, communist agitators, and spectators gathered in a park, police confiscated banners considered slanderous to the American ambassador and Colonel Fulgencio Batista, who was the military power behind the post-Machado government. With intimidating Cuban army planes stunting noisily overhead, the crowd began its procession through the streets toward Cristal Stadium. Then snipers opened fire from rooftops, panicking the marchers, who disappeared into side streets never to regroup. Only eleven were wounded; no one died. Afterward the working class claimed the government was responsible for the shootings; the government argued that communists pulled the triggers so they could blame the government. The snipers were never caught.[19]

The two authors went to Havana for fresh observations of revolution in action, for the abdication of Machado did not bring peace to the troubled island only one president away from the Batista dictatorship. Havana did not disappoint them. On May 2, transportation workers shut down the city for an hour in protest over the snipers. The next day, when high school students gathered in front of the Havana Institute to protest the May Day shootings, soldiers sent to suppress the affair opened fire with rifles, killing one student and wounding six others. A government investigation, as usual, was said to be under way, which meant nothing would come of the outrage.[20] A more personal reason for Hemingway's visit was to secure a preferred docking site for his new fishing boat, which he intended to bring over in July for the marlin season. (Hemingway and the Masons seem to have viewed revolutions as a spectator sport, no more threatening than a summer baseball league.) It took him four days to get six different required signatures on the required forms.[21]

Hemingway returned from Havana just in time to help bury Father Dougherty, the parish priest who had baptized Gregory, and to ride the train to Miami to take command of the *Pilar* on delivery. Bra Saunders, who knew boats, motors, and the protected Hawk's Channel route back to Key West, accompanied Ernest; in Miami they picked up the Wheeler shipyard representative, who motored back with them on the *Pilar*'s shakedown cruise, making sure everything worked properly. At the Key West Navy submarine base, which was being opened to visiting yachts, a welcoming party met them at the dock: Pauline, children, and household staff; the Thompsons; Arnold Samuelson, a young would-be writer Hemingway was feeding; and Ernest's nineteen-year-old brother, Leicester, and his shipmate Al Dudeck, who had sailed their tiny, homemade *Hawkshaw* from Mobile into Key West on their way to Venezuela. As if this were not entourage enough for a man trying to write, Ernest, over the next month, entertained Archie MacLeish and Archie's father-in-law, followed by Father MacGrath, a Jesuit fisherman out of Miami, who hooked an Atlantic record sailfish that Ernest landed.[22]

Waiting for Hemingway in the stack of letters was Scott Fitzgerald's plaintive question "Did you like the book?"[23] It took him two weeks to send an answer, beginning: "I liked it and I didn't like it." It wasn't Scott's use of the Murphys that he disliked, it was the liberties he took with them that resulted not in real characters but "faked case histories." Sara and Gerald were characters ready-made for a novel, but first you had to understand them, you had to see and listen. Scott saw them clearly enough, but he had stopped listening. Being a "rummy" married to a crazy woman bent on destroying his work was a hell of a handicap, but one that Scott might overcome if he would only write honestly. He signed the letter, "Always your friend, Ernest."[24] With that out of his system, he wrote Perkins that *Tender Is the Night*, aside from its essential weakness, was much better than he first said it was.

———

At the Thompson fish company that May, when they opened the shark to remove its hide, they found a slipper with bones from a human leg and foot. Eight days later, a mirage of Havana hovered in the evening sky over Key West: hundreds could see the Morro Castle, the Hotel Plaza, and the crowded Prado with pedestrians walking along it. Four days later a strange animal, something like an alligator, was seen swimming in the Key West harbor, and the keeper of the Fowey Rocks lighthouse caught an even stranger sea animal eight feet long with three rows of teeth and curious pale green stripes. That these oddities were signs few doubted, but as to what they meant, even fewer could agree.[25]

———

On the Fourth of July, citizens of Key West celebrated as if their property were not at risk for unpaid taxes. Opening with a morning parade, the day expanded with races—on foot, horseback, in boats under power and under sail—a bathing beauty contest, and fish fries that culminated with a jitney dance and fireworks in the dark. That night, those with a little money continued dancing to a small combo at the Cuban Club. Around midnight, as the last dance began to the strains of "Good Night, Sweetheart," the typesetters at the *Key West Citizen* were preparing a banner headline:

KEY WEST NOW UNDER STATE CONTROL
PASSES INTO HANDS OF FERA
IN REHABILITATION PROGRAM
STATE ADMINISTRATOR JULIUS F. STONE ACCEPTS
GOVERNOR SHOLTZ'S INVITATION TO TAKE
CHARGE OF AFFAIRS IN EMERGENCY OPERATIONS[26]

Not every townsman was thrilled with this unprecedented move by the federal government, but alternatives were limited: either move most of the population off the island or rehabilitate Key West into a tourist attraction. Food handouts and piecemeal FERA projects were reducing islanders to the status of beggars while barely keeping their families from starvation. Within ten days, beautification of the island began. On government money, piled-up garbage and trash were collected for burning, and free flowering plants were distributed to every household. In an appreciative gesture, the city council immediately renamed Main Boulevard as Roosevelt Boulevard.[27]

If cities have phases to their extended lives, one of Key West's was over, another begun, but Hemingway was not there to watch the transformation. On July 18, leaving his wife and three sons (Pauline had gone to New York, picked up Bumby, and returned) in Key West, he signed clearance papers, oath of manifest, and shipping articles to pilot the *Pilar* to Havana. He listed himself as master, Charles Lunn of the P&O Steamship Line as seaman, and Arnold Samuelson, who knew nothing of engines, as engineer.[28] Stowed in lockers and under the deck were thirty-two cases of canned vegetables, fruit, soups, chili, tamales, pork and beans, coffee, and sardines, a gallon of vinegar, three quarts of mustard: enough supplies to feed them for months. Along with motion-picture and Graflex film, anchor and line, thirty-five gallons of motor oil, and a half-dozen bottles of Sani-flush was a copy of Zane Grey's *Tales of Swordfish and Tuna* and 201 pages of Hemingway's handwritten manuscript of what had started to be an African story and was now neither a novel nor exactly a safari narrative but something else.[29]

With Lunn aboard to give navigational advice on the *Pilar's* maiden voyage to Cuba, the ninety-mile trip went smoothly enough until, within sight of Havana, the cooling pump failed, overheating the main engine. Using the four-cylinder auxiliary engine for emergency power and bucking the current, Ernest and company spent two hours covering the last three miles into port, an inauspicious start to their summer expedition.[30] Clearing customs and health inspection the following morning, the *Pilar* was allowed to put into the San Francisco docks within spitting distance of Ernest's favored

Ambos Mundos Hotel, its crew free to go ashore. Lunn was given his certificate of discharge in time to catch the return ferry and was replaced as planned by Carlos Gutiérrez, dedicated Cuban friend and experienced fisherman, who signed on as seaman (age fifty-two) and found a man who could rebuild the water pump. On the Friday evening, after meeting Pauline at the P&O ferry slip, Ernest registered at the Ambos Mundos, where they would celebrate his thirty-fifth birthday the next day and her thirty-ninth the day after.

On Saturday morning, the *Havana Post*, with its usual inaccuracies, made their presence public:

> So quietly and unheralded, however, did Mr. Hemingway make his return to Havana this year that only a few were aware of his presence yesterday morning when he put in for the clearance papers on his piping new motor yacht Pilar, in which he entered Havana Bay Thursday night. . . . Designed by Mr. Hemingway, the trim 38-foot yacht . . . is named after his daughter. . . . Mrs. Hemingway, prominent American sportswoman and a well known writer in her own name, arrived in Havana last night on the P&O liner Florida to join her husband. . . . Mr. Hemingway recently returned . . . from an African expedition which rivaled the most thrilling jungle adventures of the late "Teddy" Roosevelt.[31]

Three days later Pauline returned to Key West, Grant Mason came back from Miami, Havana phones went dead during a brief operators' strike, and the natural historians from Philadelphia joined the *Pilar* to gather specimens for their collection.[32]

With Charles Cadwalader and ichthyologist Henry Fowler aboard along with Samuelson, Carlos, Juan the cook, and a steady stream of guests, Ernest was kept busy being host, instructor, captain, owner, and principal fisherman on a new boat. In wicker deck chairs offering no substantial help against large fish, the men butted thick rods into the crotch cups of leather harnesses that left their back muscles knotted and sore after an afternoon's excursion. Doing that every day for a month, two months, three months, back muscles begin to harden and swell, calf muscles to bulge, shoulders to fill out. Fishing without Josie Russell at the helm was a learning situation for Hemingway, for Russell knew from years of experience when and how to maneuver the boat to the angler's advantage. On Hemingway's new fishing team, Carlos manned the gaff and Juan took the wheel; every command was in Spanish. As Ernest wrote for *Esquire*:

> *In Spanish you cannot tell a man just to put her ahead. You have to tell him to put her ahead for the love of God and his mother or he does not believe in the existence of an emergency. When you want her thrown out, the clutch, that is, you must say throw her out, disengage her, remove her from functioning, for the love of God such stupidness, throw her out.*[33]

For almost three weeks no amount of Spanish cursing or English vernacular produced anything like a sizable "needle fish," as Carlos called the marlin. The big fish were someplace else.

That first month in Havana, between frustrated fishing and too many guests, Ernest wrote almost nothing on his African book. Five days after the Philadelphians arrived, Sidney Franklin, his sister, and her husband came in on the largess of a local public relations group trying to promote live bullfights in Cuba. With his usual flair, Franklin drew attention to himself and his sometime profession through newspaper interviews, public lectures, and a radio talk show, all of which resulted in a month's worth of letters to the editor pro and con on the ritual killing of bulls. When he was not being interviewed, Sidney spent time on or around the *Pilar* just as marlin began to feed on the surface.[34]

———

On the Havana dock encompassed by young Cubans in white shirts, an enormous blue marlin hangs from the hoist head down, mouth open, spear almost touching the wet concrete. Ernest, in moccasins, white trousers, and work shirt, one hand resting on a fin, the other holding a fishing rod. Between Ernest and the marlin's head, Carlos crouches; behind him, Cadwalader is framed in the open space between Ernest and the fish. To the left of the marlin and behind its full dorsal fin, Juan, in an undershirt, is framed by the hoisting ropes. And there beside Juan is Sidney Franklin in a buttoned suit, tie, and black *boina*, standing with his hands clasped at his crotch, looking oddly formal and vaguely out of place.[35]

———

Between July 20 and August 25, Pauline came four times to Cuba, leaving her children in Key West, far from the Havana polio epidemic, not to mention the virulent outbreak of malaria. In the first week of August, forty cases of polio were reported in Havana; seven children died. All that month, confusion and anomalies were the rule. In the harbor, a man-eating shark took down a young swimmer and then another before being caught and beaten to death by fishermen. On August 7, Pauline and her cousin Ward Pfeiffer Meriner were met at the dock by Sidney and Ernest, who after supper entertained them and other guests on board the *Pilar*. That same day, the government announced the capture of three Americans, including soldier of fortune and veteran of earlier Cuban revolutions Arthur Hoffman. With the arrests a rumor spread that a large arms shipment had come ashore close to Havana.[36] Bombs continued to explode in the sultry night, "wrecking the home of a high government official, slightly injuring his son, and damaging buildings within a radius of four blocks."[37] Conspirators, regularly arrested, disappeared into ancient prisons. Briefly striking workers just as regularly brought the streetcars, the telephones, or the postal service to a standstill.

If all of these excitements and intrusions were not enough to disrupt Hemingway's vulnerable writing schedule, worrying about his younger brother kept the African story on hold. On August 14, Leicester Hemingway and the *Hawkshaw*, forty-eight hours out of Key West, were overdue in Havana. Ernest, keeping a composed face for the press, said he wasn't worried. That was on Tuesday. When the top-heavy home-built sailboat that could not point up into the wind had not made port by Thursday morning, Ernest put the *Pilar* out to sea, half fishing while scanning the horizon. As the light was failing that evening, he found Leicester and his new sailing companion, Bob Kilo, twelve miles off the coast without a hope of reaching port that night. Tying on to the *Pilar*, the young sailors were towed without ceremony into the harbor in time for supper.[38]

Because Hemingway was now fishing both mornings and afternoons until the squalls break, he returns to port too tired to write. A month after arriving in Havana, he has added less than three thousand words to his manuscript, but he knows where it is going and how to get it there.[39] Working from memory, photographs, and his own notes, he began with only a ragged notion for a good story—the kudu hunt. What is developing is the story of a hunt, a meditation on writing, a semifictional autobiography, and a discourse on aesthetics. Like so many modernists—Joyce, Pound, Stein, Yeats—Hemingway is consciously creating a handbook for his readers, explaining how to read his texts. He is also creating a prose more complicated than any of his earlier writing, a prose that stops time, twists time, escapes outside of time. If Einstein could imagine more dimensions than three, just maybe a writer can work through the fourth dimension of time and into a timeless fifth dimension: a continuous present tense both *now* and *then*, *here* and *elsewhere* simultaneously.

Using the last month of the safari as his narrative line, Hemingway is able to flash back to earlier episodes without having to retell everything. The story began close to the end when the little Austrian in his noisy truck ruined the day and the kudu hunt looked hopeless. Then it moved the reader back "to the time of Droopy, after I had come back from being ill in Nairobi and we had gone on a foot safari to hunt rhino in the forest" (p. 46). "I" was a character who looked and spoke as Ernest spoke, but was a creation, both better and worse than his creator. This semifictional "other," this man in his mind's mirror, made wonderful shots on running animals at great distances (true) but, unlike the hunter in Pauline's journal, never missed so badly, never left wounded animals unfound in the field. This man living in the manuscript was recovering from "being ill," but without the graphic details Ernest described in the *Esquire* letter on dysentery. Quite deliberately, Hemingway was creating an exaggerated man with all faults exposed, a man afraid of snakes, a sometimes cruel man who bragged excessively, a man like himself who was always teaching someone, a lecturer, an authority on literature ("it all started with *Huck Finn*"). This mirrored man's wife was ever supportive, never bored or depressed; Charles Thompson's avatar, "Karl" in the book, was almost invisible except when he brought down trophies larger, better, more splendid than Ernest's. The competition between his two male hunters, which Hemingway was using to teach his created self and his readers a lesson, was exaggerated. What emerges is and is not the safari of record, for the very act of storytelling inevitably transforms what is remembered.

Writing once more on the run or back in Key West, jamming it all in—smells and sounds remembered, daydreaming at the noon break, whiskey talk at day's end—this writing is a joy unlike any pure fiction. Stopping at midday on the rhino hunt to read in Tolstoy's *Sevastopol* leads him back to riding his bicycle down rain-slick Boulevard Sevastopol in Paris, and now remembering that early apartment above the sawmill (*its parenthetical sounds and smells italicized*), and eventually taking him into the Luxembourg Gardens past Flaubert's bust. This dreamy stream of consciousness takes him finally and appropriately back to Joyce, who patented the process and whose fiction is for Hemingway a sovereign measuring stick.

"All I wanted to do now was get back to Africa," he wrote. "We had not left it, yet when I would wake in the night I would lie, listening, homesick for it already" (p.72). Revising this passage, he worried that the reader might miss the point. Loving the country, he explained, gave a happiness that was like being with a woman, postcoital, spent but recovering and wanting more:

> *You can never have it all and yet what there is, now, you can have, and you want more and more, to have, and be, and live in, to possess now again for always, for that long, sudden-ended always; making time stand still, sometimes so very still that afterwards you wait to hear it move, and it is slow in starting.* (p. 72)

That was how he broke time apart until the reader is inside and outside of it all at once, but never getting too removed from the hunt.

During the night of September 4, more than a dozen bombs
exploded in Havana and surrounding towns. The next morning,
Hemingway put Arnold Samuelson and Carlos Gutiérrez to work
scraping and varnishing the *Pilar* while he returned to Key West during the dark of the moon, waiting for Carlos to send word that big fall
marlin are again feeding on the surface.[40] In Key West, young Patrick
fawns upon him, hungry for attention; Pauline he finds transformed,
her hair turning blond for the second time. It was the year of the
blonde: Mae West's and Jean Harlow's platinum screen images are
being imitated by housewives across America. Ernest, for whom
blond hair was an erotic adventure, could not have been more
pleased to be home.[41]

For eight working days in Key West, he lived in the Africa of memory while penciled manuscript piled up on the table: twenty-two
pages one day, thirty the next, then another twenty.[42] It was a book
with no name, only a working title, *The Highlands of Africa*. (The title
almost always came last.) All that remained to tell was the trekking
down dusty roads, fruitless waiting, tempers strained during the last
days of the kudu hunt. And always there was counterpointing discussion, Ernest saying that if he ever wrote about Africa "it will just be
landscape painting until I know something about it" (p. 193). So
simple to say, but time melted and bent: the writer writing about an
African hunt in which his narrator, a writer like himself, says he is
not ready to write about this African hunt.

Trying to reach a prose beyond his earlier work, Hemingway uses
the hunt, the quarry, and the hunter as metaphors for his trade.
Hunter and writer are both professionals whose ground rules are
stringent, whose conduct at parallel activities is meticulous, whose
expectations for performance are high. The hunter pursues the
lovely kudu, the promise of whose impossible spiraling horns makes
the hunt valid. The writer is equally driven to write a book beyond
anything he has done before, and in doing so exhausts an experience
he can never again write. The greatest joy is in the pursuit of both

kudu and book; the successful hunt puts one trophy on the wall, the other on the bookshelf. Leaving out most of the safari's killing and using the kudu hunt as a guise, Hemingway is writing a book about writing a book.

On September 14, in response to an urgent message from Carlos, he returned to Cuba only to find the giant marlin already come and gone.[43] He fished another month, but it was all over this season. He has not boated the thousand-pound marlin of his dreams, but at the Ambos Mundos, he is finishing his manuscript. During the rest of September and into October, writing beautifully clean pages that need little revision, he doubles the length of the manuscript. By October 3, he tells Max Perkins that he has fifty thousand words written "on this long thing," and three new projects: a collection of all his previously published stories; a collection of the *Esquire* letters; and a novel, the content of which he does not specify.[44] Perkins's immediate response must have worried Hemingway a good deal. Thinking that Ernest referred to the book at hand, Max replied that the novel was wonderful news. "I'd felt morally certain," he said, "you were doing a novel, but not quite, because when you were here you spoke of having written a great deal on a narrative and of thinking you might reduce it to a story. . . . You do a novel and we will strain every muscle for it. . . . For God's sake don't get to be too much of a naturalist or you won't have time to write."[45]

In late September, Pauline spent ten days in Havana, her hair having reached what Ernest called "the fine South American white gold color."[46] Two days after she took the ferry back to Key West, Ernest towed three enormous sharks into the harbor to distribute at the dock, where a crowd, expecting his customary free marlin, had gathered.[47] First the marlin left, and then he sliced his finger open on a bait, producing a swollen hand that acted like blood poisoning, and then the rains began, ending everything but the writing in which the African rains threatened the hunt. The only excitement on the Gulf Stream was a rare pod of whales that appeared one afternoon. Before using the experience for *Esquire*, he wrote Charles Cadwalader:

I harpooned one using over fifty fathoms of line . . . but the harpoon
pulled out. Had all the life belts tied on one end and were going to let
the line go over if we had to. . . . I thought by working on him with
the Mannlicher whenever he came up we could kill him. We had a
very exciting time. When I struck the whale the spout of another one
along side went all over us.[48]

The next day, John and Katy Dos Passos arrived in Havana, Dos
sick and Katy distraught over the recent death of her father. From
Hollywood, Dos had a Paramount paycheck for working on the Mar-
lene Dietrich film *The Devil Is a Woman*, and a bad taste in his mouth
from the experience.[49] Accustomed to being upstaged by Hemingway,
he was not surprised by his interview in the Sunday *Post*:

John Dos Passos, eminent American liberal organizer and writer, is
extremely interested in Cuban political developments, but has not
had time thus far to study the situation. . . . Ernest Hemingway was a
visitor in the room of Mr. Dos Passos during the interview. . . . has
been in Havana more than three months . . . disclosed that he has
succeeded in landing at least 12 of the giant fish this year.[50]

The day after revolutionaries bungled an assassination attempt on
the U.S. ambassador, Hemingway put away his fishing gear for the
season. With fall storms regularly churning the Gulf and the
prospect of more "northers" on the way, it was time to give up on the
marlin. On October 26, at five in the morning, he and Arnold
Samuelson motored the *Pilar* past the Morro Castle and headed
back toward Key West to finish his African book. In his suitcase he
packed a copy of the *Havana Post* with stories on twenty-four
accused terrorists being freed from the Havana jail and a local man
arrested for having two rifles and ammunition. Navigating by compass and adjusting for the current, Hemingway, on his first unaided
trip across, raised Sand Key nine hours and forty minutes after clearing Havana. The long summer was over.[51]

Another good reason for Ernest's return was the family's diminished Key West checking account, for which he, like his father before him, required a strict accounting of all expenditures except his own. Pauline managed their local bills, took care of wages for their hired help, balanced the books, and felt guilty when funds ran low. On the first of October, after moving $200 from their New York City account to Key West, Pauline sent Ernest a detailed accounting of expenditures ($306) so he would not think she was "throwing money away." Not included were groceries, for which she usually signed and paid for only when the total became significant; nor was her monthly deposit to Ina Hepburn's savings account for washing included. ("You look just like a devil standing out there," Ernest told Ina as she boiled clothes in a blackened backyard kettle.) Nor did the $306 include wages to their cook (Isobel), their "house boy" (Lewis and/or Nathaniel), or their gardener (Jimmy). One hundred dollars of the total went to Ada Stern as salary and expense money for keeping Gregory, who had been with Ada in Syracuse, New York, all summer and into the fall.[52]

When Isobel left cooking in the Hemingway kitchen, her friend Miriam Williams replaced her. Years later Miriam recalled that she was hired despite her inexperience: "Between Miss Pauline and Ada Stern, the housekeeper, I learned, but I'll admit the first year was rough. They were good to me and very patient. After that I could cook almost anything. I learned how to tend bar, too." Miriam learned to prepare Hemingway's favorite dishes: baked fish, black beans laced with salt pork, garlic, and onions, with either broccoli with hollandaise sauce or string beans. In the formal dining room, dress was casual and the wines French. On weeknights Ernest and Pauline were in bed by ten o'clock, but on weekends after dinner they would go downtown to drink and dance. Every morning at seven-thirty, Miriam took two full trays upstairs to the Hemingways, who always breakfasted in bed. "There was some kind of happiness over there [in the Hemingway house]," Ina remembered. "You never seen anything like it. . . . Some people didn't think Mr. Hemingway dressed very nice, but when he did get dressed up, it was something grand."[53]

Like most white Americans of their generation, when speaking to other whites Ernest and Pauline could refer to their black household staff as "niggers" while trusting them with the well-being of their children and the safekeeping of their possessions and treating them as part of the family, albeit less privileged. In the same way, Ernest and Pauline were both generically anti-Semitic while having close Jewish friends. Ernest, for example, could genuinely embrace Sidney Franklin while saying that he might move his children to Africa rather than have them grow up "in this F.E.R.A. Jew administered phony of a town."[54] This contradictory behavior was not peculiar to the Hemingways; it was deeply embedded in the American grain. In Key West, as in most of America, anyone born white between the end of the last century and several decades later grew up in a society so prevalently racist that the racism was invisible to the dominant class. In fact, most white Americans from this period would have been offended to be called racist. Yet in Key West, African-Americans sent their children to a "colored" school, swam at the "colored" beach, picnicked in Nelson English park for the "colored" where "colored" bands gave concerts. At the Dixie Theater, they could see motion pictures never advertised in the paper; when one of them died, the *Citizen's* headline always read "Colored Man to Be Buried." As Teddy Roosevelt, hunting through East Africa, exclaimed time and again, "This could be a white man's country," as if the black Masai and Wanderobo natives were inconsequential.

———

Here in Key West we have a national rehabilitation project running everything. I am dragged by the house-renting clerk before the Rehabilitator in Chief to see if I will do, that is to say, measure up to his idea of what the new citizenry must look as if it thought, felt and acted on under God and the President in Washington. The Rehabilitator is a rich young man in shorts with hairy legs named Stone. . . . The town has been nationalized to rescue it from its own speculative excesses. The personal interest of Roosevelt in his second coming has been invoked and both mayor and governor have abdicated. . . . It is tropical all right but it is rather unsanitary and shabby. It has a million dollars worth of concrete sidewalks with no houses on them. It has three races not very well kept apart by race-prejudice, Cubans, Negroes and Whites.[55]

—Robert Frost, 1934

Ernest returned to a Key West transforming itself into something new and strange. Under the demagogic eye of FERA-man Julius Stone, the island outpost, without ever taking a vote, was becoming by default a government tourist attraction. His hairline receding, his mustache clipped, Stone ruled the island. "With a scratch of my pen I started this work in Key West," he said, "and with a scratch of my pen I can stop it—just like that!" (But he could not keep the old-time "conchs" from laughing at his hairy legs: what sort of grown man would walk about publicly in his underwear?) Vacant lots of trash disappeared; houses were painted, flower gardens planted, a Garden Club in full stride. Onetime fishermen were employed to round up stray dogs and cats for extermination. Two hundred homes, whose owners six months earlier could not pay property taxes, were being refurbished with FERA loans to be paid back from vacationers' rents. On Rest Beach, thatched-hut cabanas were being constructed. Even bars and nightclubs were getting a paint job on government loans. A mattress factory was under way, and coconut palms were being planted along the main thoroughfares. Between the island and Miami, an FERA-subsidized airline was scheduled to fly in tourists. Up on Matecumbe Key, an advance team was building camps to house the World War veterans being sent there to construct bridges for the overseas highway.[56]

Hemingway was appalled. His wire fence could not keep tourists from staring at his house on Whitehead Street, and nothing could keep them out of Josie Russell's bar. In his African book, when Percival asks what is happening in America, Ernest replies: "Damned if I know! Some sort of Y.M.C.A. show." Later he adds, "Starry eyed bastards spending money that somebody will have to pay. Everybody in our town quit work to go on relief. Fishermen all turned carpenters. Reverse of the Bible."[57] Actually, there was no work to quit, no market for fish, no money for food, but that is easy to ignore if the self-reliant strenuous life is your moral guide and your diminished bank account is in no real danger of failing, not with money in Paris and New York accounts, money coming in from Pauline's trust, gift money from Uncle Gus, advance money from Scribner's. There was always money somewhere, or if things got too tight, he could write for the magazines. *Cosmopolitan* was begging for a story.

On November 3, when Ada Stern returned from Syracuse with Gregory in time for his third birthday, their younger son saw Ernest and Pauline almost as strangers; in the previous year and half while almost exclusively in the care of Ada, Gregory saw his parents only in passing, leaving him understandably confused. Patrick said later he always knew Pauline was his mother, and Ada, whom he hated for her terrible cooking, a mean woman who could roast in hell. Jack, as Bumby grew up to become, was old enough (ten) to deal with Ada: he abetted her secret drinking with supplies from Ernest's liquor cabinet. But Gregory, delivered at three months into Ada's care, had no defense against the woman who used his fear of being unloved to control him.[58] In Pauline's letters to her frequently absent husband, Patrick's deeds and sayings appear over and over; Gregory, or "Gigi" as they called him, is largely missing.

Ernest, so eager to be called "Papa" by adults older than himself, was never comfortable with his own children until they were old enough to fish and hunt. Then he was their instructor, showing them the way water changes color over the reef, teaching them to clean their kill, instructing them on the importance of terrain. He loved his sons, but having grown up with a father who could not express his emotions, Hemingway was not good at communicating this love when they were small, nor did he let them interfere with either of his two driving interests: the outdoor life and writing. As they grew old enough to accompany him in the hunting fields and on the *Pilar* fishing, their bonding improved, except for Gregory, who remembers still his overpowering tendency to seasickness the moment the *Pilar* left the harbor.[59] All three of his sons needed desperately to please Ernest, a need not easily fulfilled.

Neither his children nor tourist traffic generated by the rejuvenat-
ing island distracted Hemingway that mild fall as he pushed the
African book to its conclusion, trying to bring all the elements
together: killing the kudu, pursuing beauty, the writer writing, memories and projections. M'Cola asking for beer from the African chop
box and brown beer remembered "sitting at the wood tables under
the wisteria vine" with Chink Dorman-Smith twelve years earlier and
Alsatian beer at Lipps in Paris: all remembered in the Key West heat,
which was not in the story but was leaving sweat stains on the paper.
Freely associating *then* and *now* produced amazing time warps: time
past always shifting, sometimes Paris, sometimes earlier in the hunt;
time present equally fluid, sometimes at the African salt lick, sometimes removed without saying where, the narrator making judgments
and connections.

On African roads, escaping the drought and locust plague along
the coast, African natives trudge past the safari truck; unmentioned
are the towering west Texas dust storms freshly embedded in the
American mind through newsreels. From associations stated and
silent, the narrator tells us that "the earth gets tired of being
exploited." The promise of America, fulfilled for earlier generations,
is no longer real:

> Our people went to America because that was the place to go then. It
> had been a good country and we made a bloody mess of it and I would
> go somewhere else as we had always gone. (p. 285)

Whether he is referring to the streets of Key West or the American
dust bowl, the narrator's conviction that the American dream is a
dream gone by spoke to the gnawing fears of a country now entering
the fifth year of the depression.

Hemingway's increasing need to pontificate, which even tolerant
friends began to question, led to excesses in the manuscript, some of
which Hemingway eliminated, some he retained. As Katy Dos Passos, who had known Hemingway since he was a twelve-year-old at
Walloon Lake, told the Murphys:

Did I tell you Ernest was translated when seen in Havana? Remember how irascible and truculent he was before. Now he's just a big cage of canaries . . . He was sweet, but had a tendency to be an Oracle I thought and needs some best pal and severe critic to tear off those long white whiskers which he is wearing.[60]

On November 10, Perkins, who still had no idea what Ernest was writing, said that if Hemingway's novel was ready for publication, they should put "The First Fifty-seven" collection of stories on hold.[61] Four days later, Hemingway began telling Max and other correspondents that the new book was finished (492 pages of holograph), and that he was starting another story. "Might as well take advantage of a belle epoque while I'm in one."[62] Max convinced himself it was the novel begun before Hemingway went to Africa. Because Ernest never told Max any details about the abandoned Philip Haines/James Allen chapters, the assumption was understandable.[63]

On November 20 at the Pierre Matisse Gallery in New York, Hemingway helped his Spanish friend Luis Quitanilla with the opening of his first American show. Impressed with Quintanilla's Goyaesque etchings and his radical politics, Hemingway arranged for the show, fronted money to pull the etchings, and contributed, along with Dos Passos, a statement for the catalog. He was now asking his New York friends to support the opening because Quintanilla was in a Madrid jail, charged with "being a member of the revolutionary committee" fomenting a riot against government policy. Hemingway asked Perkins to put the Scribner's publicity department to work on the show, perhaps pulling the two introductory pieces he and Dos Passos wrote into some sort of press release. What Max and *Time* magazine found in the catalog was good copy but not about the etchings. Hemingway wrote:

Now this may possibly be a good time to suggest that a small tax be levied on the use of the word revolution, the proceeds to be given to the defense of, say, such people as Luis Quintanilla, by all those who write the word and never have shot or been shot at; who never have

stored arms nor filled a bomb, never have discovered arms nor had a
bomb burst among them; who have never gone hungry in a general
strike, nor have manned streetcars when the tracks are dynamited;
who never have sought cover in a street trying to get their heads
behind a gutter.[64]

Having seen most of it, he wrote as the insider angry with those who
had not borne actual witness to violence.

Riding a manic high, when words came easily and nothing touched
him, Hemingway put aside the African story long enough to rip off an
Esquire letter making fun of Gilbert Seldes, Alexander Wollcott, and
William Saroyan, all of whom appeared in the magazine:

Now a lot of us weren't as bright as you, Mr. Saroyan, see I'm giving
you a break. You're bright. So don't get sore. But you're not that
bright. You don't know what you're up against. You've only got one
new trick, and that is that you're an Armenian.[65]

Having called New York writers "angleworms in a bottle, trying to
derive knowledge and nourishment from their own contact and from
the bottle," Hemingway was gratuitously baiting much of the literary
establishment, alienating potential reviewers of his next book.[66]

With the *Esquire* letter in the mail to Gingrich, Ernest tried to
explain for the first time to Max Perkins about the African book,
which, starting as a story, grew into something like "Big Two-Hearted
River," his long, controlled land- and mindscape with fisherman from
1924, only better. It had the landscape painting in it, "but a hell of a
lot happens in this one and there is plenty of dialogue and action. . . .
plenty of excitement. . . . I've written it absolutely true—*absolutely*
no faking or cheating." He tried to say it three times, but words did
not explain the book, which he knew Max expected to be a novel and
which he insisted was "the best thing I've written—True narrative
that is exciting and still is literature is very rare." Worried over Max's
possible disappointment and Scribner's risk of having put up a loan
against this book, Ernest suggested publishing it as a long story to

lead off a collection of all his stories. They could even let this African book wait, publish the stories and the essays, and then he might do an Oak Park novel, except his mother and his father's brother were still alive.[67] By this point in the letter, Max was thoroughly confused about what it was Hemingway had written. So was Ernest, for the book, which he was still calling *The Highlands of Africa*, defied generic categories. In his cautiously understated reply, Max said that these were tough questions raised by Ernest which required careful thought.[68]

After working through the possibilities, and discussing it with Charles Scribner himself, Max said they should publish the long story as a freestanding book, without appendages, for readers resented padded books, and added stories would distract the reviewers. Putting it as a lead story to "The First Fifty-seven" would make too large a book for the market, and the new story would not get the reviewers' full attention. "I see that you regard this as a story, not a novel," Max wrote, still not understanding what Ernest was telling him, "but that makes no difference." If Hemingway could only modify the title to *In the Highlands of Africa*, implying that something happened there. Otherwise people might think this was merely a travel book.[69]

Hemingway chewed on Max's advice while he worked on revisions, inserting sections, chopping out others, all the while dealing with winter visitors. Unexpectedly, Alfred Vanderbilt and Dick Cooper flew in one day and out the next in the Vanderbilt amphibian. *Esquire* editor Arnold Gingrich, at Hemingway's invitation and lured by the scent of the new book, flew in on the FERA airline, fished with Ernest and Dos Passos, and flew out two days later.[70] Working steadily every morning, Hemingway wrote Perkins that he could "beat the present title," but first there was a Piggott Christmas to attend.[71] Leaving Gregory (three) behind with Ada Stern in Key West, Pauline departed by train for Miami while Ernest and Patrick (six) followed in the car, picking her up and driving north to Memphis and into Piggott two days before Christmas.[72]

Chapter Eight

1 9 3 5

HEAVY WEATHER

Key West, Bimini, and Matecumbe

DURING THE SIXTH year of the economic nightmare, thieves begin breaking into Key West homes where
a few years earlier no one had anything worth stealing.
Nevertheless, the Key West city council remains optimistic. Having
made Duval Street a "Great White Way" with streetlights which
they could only afford to turn on for weekends, they now order two
electric traffic lights to control the anticipated tourist traffic. They
also put out a handbill on good driving manners which include not
stopping the car in the middle of the street to speak with friends. In
the Navy harbor, expensive wintering yachts now dock with some
regularity—*Placida, Sylvia II, Minoco, Alva, Azara, Kallisto, Mari-
posa*—bringing new money to town. Each day, more vacationers are
renting winter quarters in Key West. Winter guests staying at the
Casa Marina are catching toothy barracuda, which, to the amusement of the locals, they are having mounted for their northern

homes. Three new clubs open with live music and featured enter-
tainment on weekends. For the three to four to five hundred week-
enders coming in by train, car, and plane, Key West provides band
concerts, parades, flower shows, semiprofessional boxing matches
in the high school gym, the town's first art gallery for WPA artists,
and a saltwater aquarium. Where once the Dry Tortugas were available only to dedicated fishermen in seaworthy boats, now for $10
anyone can fly round-trip to see Fort Jefferson, leaving at 11:00
a.m., returning at 2:30 p.m. The government men, pleased with
their progress in Key West, are thinking of turning the Tortugas into
a tourist attraction.[1]

Not everyone, however, is prospering. By the time the Hemingway
family returned from their Piggott Christmas, rowdy war veterans
were creating problems. Sent in by the WPA to construct bridges
linking all the Keys with a continuous highway, many of the vets are
displaced and disgruntled "bonus marchers" run out of Washington
by the U.S. Army. Eight hundred and seventy-five of them are
housed in hurriedly constructed camps, men carrying war memories
and bad debts, men without women and without much hope,
reassembled with others of their kind. Before Christmas, Sheriff Karl
Thompson (brother of Charles) sent deputies to Lower Matecumbe
to preserve order and reduce the sale of bootleg liquor. In Key West,
citizens complain that vets on liberty arrive drunk, get drunker, and
make a public nuisance right there in the front yard.[2]

On the last day of February, Key West's Battery E of the Florida
National Guard is mobilized and sent up to Matecumbe to quell a
strike already three days in progress. Despite rumors of violence, the
Guard found the strikers playing baseball or sitting around swapping
stories. The strike was

> brought about by a number of agitators, or camp lawyers, who were
> undesirables. . . . the disturbers were men who had stressed a demand
> for improved sanitary conditions, the reinstatement of certain com-
> mittee members who had been rejected from the camp and . . . a scale
> of wages for skilled labor equal to that being paid civilian workers.[3]

A week after the strike began, a vet stepped up on a Duval Street front porch, took off all his clothes, and began telling a gathering crowd how bad things were on Matecumbe. Police soon took him off to jail to sober up.[4]

When the National Guard came home, a regular patrol of Key West auxiliary deputies remained stationed on the island to maintain order. On March 21, two vets were brought into Key West in irons, arrested for "interfering with an officer." Three weeks later they brought in two more, one behaving "strangely," the other with his wrists slit in a botched suicide. The quickly convened lunacy commission, which found both men insane and dangerous, exported them to a veterans' hospital in Tennessee.[5] And on any Key West Saturday night in the Silver Slipper or Sloppy Joe's, drunken vets not yet annoying enough to be arrested or crazy enough to be exported curse, carouse, and brawl, leaving the floor slippery with spilled beer and blood.

———

Don't be surprised when you see the town—There's been changes. The New Dealers are here . . . and Key West is now a Greenwich Village Nightmare—They have stirred up all the old art trash and phony uplifters that sank to the bottom after the war, and they're painting murals on the café walls, and weaving baskets, and cutting down plants and trees, and renting all the homes (with Washington money) and arranging sight-seeing tours, and building apartments for tourists so they can observe the poor Hemingways. They even wrote to Jed Harris' sister that she would have an apartment "with a view of Ernest Hemingway," and all the dreary international smart-alecs are turning up as they always do about six years later, "discovering" the place, . . . you can't stir out of your house without being run over by a little Jewish woman on a bicycle. . . . The little Jewish women are always either circling around the Hemingway house or else taking their book reviews to the post office. It's a paradise of incompetents, all floating around in a rich culture of humanitarian graft. . . . There is even a band of fake Cubans with velvet pants and red sashes that meets the train every

day and the sky is full of aeroplanes and the speakeasies are
jammed with drunk and cynical newspaper men. They are putting
in Tea Rooms painted in black and orange . . . and those fearful
cork candlesticks and fishnets.[6]

—Katy Dos Passos, January 1935

While Ernest revised his African book and fed it to his typist,
Pauline worked feverishly on the house, preparing for the usual spate
of winter guests, invited and otherwise; young Patrick, avoiding
adults as much as possible, went about singing softly to himself a
song he'd learned from a Victrola record sent by the Murphys:[7]

> *Cellophane, Mr. Cellophane*
> *Ought to be my name.*
> *You walk right past me,*
> *Look right through me,*
> *And never know I'm there.*

Every morning Ernest secluded himself, sometimes in the bedroom,
sometimes above the garage, changing, inserting, moving words
about and reliving Africa. In Gregory's earliest memory of his father,
Ernest looms enormous on the second-floor porch glaring down at
him in the yard below, where he is beating on tin pans. Ernest shouts
at him: "Will you please be quiet! I'm trying to write."[8]

On January 16, Ernest wires Scribner's that he is delighted that
Max Perkins and his wife, Louise, are coming to Key West. He wants
Max to read the manuscript, rough as it is, hoping that *Scribner's
Magazine* will serialize it as it did *A Farewell to Arms*. Timing is deli-
cate: if the serial runs six or seven monthly issues, to publish the book
version in the fall they will have to begin in April, May at the latest.
Four days before Max arrived, Burt MacBride, an associate editor
from *Cosmopolitan*, registered at the Casa Marina, carrying a personal
letter to Ernest from editor in chief Harry Burton. The word on the
New York street says that Hemingway has a new novel finished;
maybe this time he will give *Cosmopolitan* the first look for a serial.[9]

MacBride gave the African book a quick read, made enough notes to talk to Burton, and put Hemingway on hold for two days until a decision is made in New York. As Perkins arrives in Key West on the Havana Special, MacBride is leaving on the flight to Miami, where he wrote Hemingway that Burton was not going to agree to a four-part serial of nonfiction, sight unseen. "Due consideration" was required. He had to think of his audience: would this African book appeal to them? A Hemingway novel was a sure thing, but Burton would not take MacBride's word on nonfiction, which he "to be quite frank" could not recommend anyway, despite thinking it "a swell performance. . . . Better luck next time."[10]

For eight days, Max and Louise Perkins stay at Casa Marina, fishing afternoons on the *Pilar*, and dining at Whitehead Street more than once. Max also spends several days reading what he thought was going to be a novel, while Ernest, suffering from a recurrence of amebic dysentery, manfully plays host between doses of emetine and castor oil. At the Key West dock next to two suspended swordfish, Max stands, almost smiling, with his ever-present hat oddly in hand, his tie tightened against his collar, his striped suit double-buttoned. Erl Roman, editor of the "Rod and Reel" section of the *Miami Herald*, stands to the right, more causally dressed in working pants and a windbreaker. On Max's left, Ernest grins broadly, hair blowing in the wind, wearing an open collar, buttoned sport coat, white pants, and bedroom slippers.[11]

Before the Perkinses leave for New York, Max tells Ernest the book, for which there is no generic term, is wonderful and *Scribner's Magazine* might serialize it for maybe $5,000, which was more hesitant than Ernest needed to hear just then. Two days later, Max wired:

> *All keen about idea of serial but as arrangements depend on number of issues will need to study manuscript stop send as soon as you can stop writing all about it tomorrow stop grateful to you and Pauline for fine time.*[12]

Without waiting for further explanations, Hemingway immediately wrote Arnold Gingrich, trying to interest *Esquire* in the serial version. *Cosmopolitan*, he said, offered him big money but asked him to reduce the text by almost half, which was not possible (nor was it true, but this was business). At the very least he needed a minimum of $10,000 for the serial; less than that would not help. As soon as Max returned the typescript, he would send it to Gingrich on spec.[13]

When word came from Perkins that the *Scribner's Magazine* offer was $4,500 for the serial, Ernest was furious, reminding Max how loyal he had been to Scribner's. Were they offering so little because they wanted him to turn it down? "We do not intend there shall be any hard feeling about price," Max had written. What was that supposed to mean? Hemingway's response was an old story that Perkins knew by heart. Negotiating between Ernest's demands and Scribner's accountants, Max raised the offer to $5,000, which Hemingway reluctantly accepted.[14] With the first installment scheduled for May, there was little time to waste. Having decided not to use his photographs in the magazine or in the book version, Hemingway immediately sent moving pictures and safari photographs for the illustrator, Edward Shenton, to use for models, but he insisted there be no illustrations of dead animals. Hemingway's brittle moodiness, which kept family and visitors tense, was made worse by his touch of dysentery and the effects of emetine taken to cure it.[15]

About that same time Sara Murphy, arriving without Gerald, rejoined John and Katy Dos Passos to share a Key West house, frequent the Hemingways, and spend occasional afternoons on the *Pilar*. From New York, Gerald sent breezy news along with new Fats Waller phonograph records for Ernest to enjoy. Patrick Murphy (fourteen), still fighting the tuberculosis contracted seven years earlier, was under constant care at Saranac Lake; Baoth Murphy (fifteen) was recovering from measles at his Massachusetts boarding school. On February 20, Gerald's telegram said Baoth was "mending," and that Sara should "get some rest." The next day Baoth's measles became a double mastoid infection, rushing Sara northward in the night to a connection with the plane to Boston.[16] What followed were days and nights of dull horror, one operation after another with hourly telegrams carrying bad news south to Key West:

Blood transfusion tomorrow morning to combat toxemia and replenish depleted condition stop holding his own we are hopeful stop feel your prayers much love.[17]

Two days and two transfusions later, Baoth Murphy, fifteen years old, died from meningitis with Gerald beside him and Sara, bending over him, pleading, "Breathe, Baoth, please breathe."[18] Ernest tried to say it several ways, none of them worth a damn, but still saying it: "Very few people ever really are alive and those that are never die; no matter if they are gone. No one you love is ever dead."[19]

————

The house at present occupied by your correspondent is listed as number eighteen in a compilation of the forty-eight things for a tourist to see in Key West. So there will be no difficulty in a tourist finding it or any other of the sights of the city, a map has been prepared by the local F.E.R.A. authorities to be presented to each arriving visitor. Your correspondent is a modest retiring chap with no desire to compete with the Sponge Lofts (number 13 of the sights), the Turtle Crawl (number 3 on the map), the Ice Factory (number 4), the Tropical Open Air Aquarium containing the 627 pound jewfish (number 9), or the Monroe County Courthouse (number 14). . . . Yet there your correspondent is at number 18 between Johnson's Tropical Grove (number 17) and Lighthouse and Aviaries (number 19). This is all very flattering to the easily bloated ego of your correspondent but very hard on production.[20]

—Ernest Hemingway, April 1935

————

Once painter and fisherman Mike Strater arrived in Key West, Hemingway was ready to leave for Bimini, where Mike swore there were tuna larger than Ernest's imagination, not to mention marlin well over a thousand pounds. With Dos Passos and Charles Thompson rounding out his latest version of "summer people," Hemingway planned to take the *Pilar* twenty miles out in the Gulf Stream by day, letting the current carry them up the Florida coast, fishing as they went. At night they would pull inside the coastal barrier reef to anchor safely in Hawks Channel. By the second night they would reach the Carysfort light, and from there next morning steer east-northeast into the Atlantic toward Gun Cay and Bimini. The fishing team included Albert "Bread" Pinder, who knew engines and something of navigation. "Saca Ham" Adams was signed on to cook for the group. On Sunday morning, April 7, having loaded aboard navigation charts, two months' worth of canned goods, extra water, rods, reels, and plenty of line, the Mannlicher rifle, and Hemingway's favorite .22 Colt Woodsman, the six men waved goodbye to the women at the dock and headed out toward blue water.[21]

That evening they returned to the dock, Ernest nauseous from having accidentally shot himself with the Woodsman. While Pinder was gaffing Ernest's shark and Ernest was standing by with his pistol to finish him off and Dos Passos was trying to film the event, the shark twisted, the wooden gaff snapped, the pistol fired, and two holes appeared in Ernest's left calf. "I'll be a sorry son of a bitch," Hemingway said. "I'm shot." The soft-nosed lead bullet had ricocheted off a brass railing, splattering as it did so, one small piece entering below Ernest's kneecap, a larger piece farther down, and tiny fragments smaller than birdshot elsewhere. Back in Key West, Dr. Warren "removed the fragments, probed, had an X-ray made, decided not to remove the large piece of bullet which was about three or four inches into the calf."[22] A week later, the crew and the fishing team without Dos Passos put to sea once more, reaching Bimini on Tuesday evening, April 16.

Lying south from Grand Bahama Island and northwest of Andros, and forty-five miles east of Miami, the Biminis are a cluster of small green-and-white islands, only three of which, North and South Bimini and Cat Cay, are inhabited. On North Bimini, barely seven miles long and less than five hundred yards wide, two tiny villages exist; on South Bimini, a sheltered harbor for fishing boats, four hundred souls, several bars, and Mrs. Duncombe's boardinghouse, The Compleat Angler, with ten rooms and decent food. During prohibition, two liquor barges anchored in the harbor ready to fill the steady orders from Miami bootleggers. Now a pilot boat out of Miami, captained by George Kreidt, freights in supplies every Tuesday, and Pan American seaplane service brings in passengers and mail to nearby Cat Cay on Mondays and Fridays. Without phone service, the only direct communication is by telegraph: Ernest Hemingway, Bimini, BWI. On protected beaches there are shells and pristine white sand; above high tide line, windblown royal palms. The Gulf Stream passes so near the shore that one could not harbor closer to it.[23]

When the Dos Passoses came over to visit for a week in May, they found "a wharf and some native shacks under the coconut palms and a store that had some kind of barroom attached where we drank rum in the evenings . . . and a couple of sun-eaten bungalows screened against the sand-flies up on the dunes." With miles of shallow, clear water between and among lightly wooded, uninhabited islets, day sailing could not be better.[24] Katy called Bimini "a crazy mixture of luxury, indigence, good liquor, bad food, heat, flies, land apathy and sea magnificence, social snoot, money, sport, big fish, big fishermen, and competitive passion."[25] In the evening with the rum flowing, Nattie Saunders would be singing his homemade songs with Ernest listening and remembering long afterwards:

> Oh, they got John in jail
> No one to stand John bail
> Oh let's go see Uncle Sonny
> Ask if he got any English money
> English money can stand John's bail
> English money can take him out of jail.[26]

Over on Cat Cay, where the Pan Am plane splashed down, the very rich were building a private development the way the rich always do: find the place, import a lifestyle theretofore unknown, and leave it when the flavor is gone.

Bimini was not Cat Cay. Bimini was barefoot country where a man did not have to shave unless he wanted to, did not have to do anything. "It's like the end of the world," Ernest said, his kind of place where rules were local and negotiable.[27] Visitors came, fished, and left: Charles Thompson, the Dos Passoses, Bror and Eva Von Blixen, even Uncle Gus. In May, Pauline was back and forth, without children, staying with Mrs. Duncombe while the men slept on the *Pilar*. It was, Hemingway wrote MacLeish, the best summer he could remember: clear water in the harbor, huge tuna in the stream, and good whiskey afterward. A man need not change clothes for a month if he starts the morning by diving into the harbor in lieu of a bath, and in the evenings the gentry tell fishing stories and drink.[28] Sometimes they drink too much, like the evening when Joe Knapp called Ernest a phony, fat slob and then had to back it up; three bare-fisted left hooks and a looping right put Mr. Knapp flat on the wooden dock, and Ernest not even breathing hard, his first real brawl in a long time. Nattie Saunders, who sees it all, is soon singing:

> *Mister Knapp look at him and try to mock*
> *And from the blow*
> *Mister Knapp couldn't talk*
> *At first Mist Knapp thought*
> *He had his bills in stalk*
> *And when Mister Ernest Hemingway walked*
> *The dock rocked*
> *Mister Knapp couldn't laugh*
> *Mister Ernest Hemingway grinned*
> *Put him to sleep*
> *With a knob on the chin.*[29]

It was not like Havana; Ernest's companions in Bimini were the very rich, men who liked to wager on the day's fishing, men like Tommy Shevlin, Mike Lerner, who had a grand house on Cat Cay, and Bill Leeds, whose huge yacht, *Moana*, was too large for the harbor.[30] In Oak Park, where Hemingway grew up comfortably among families wealthy enough to hunt big game, he was always on the outside looking in at a lifestyle that part of him admired and wanted for his own. Now in Key West he owned a house as fine as those in Oak Park and with more servants. But there was also a part of him that despised the very rich as a class, for they had, in Oak Park, made him much aware that he was outside, and he never forgave them. Without being terribly rational about it, Hemingway could despise the class but not the representative, just as he was raised to be anti-Semitic but was great friends with Mike Lerner, whose house he sometimes used.[31]

Warm, starry nights; hot, sun-drenched days: Bimini in summer was a fisherman's dream and an editor's nightmare if the fisherman was Ernest Hemingway with a serialized book in production. There were more isolated places than Bimini in the western hemisphere, but Max Perkins was not going to mention them to Ernest for fear he might go there next time they had a book to produce. With only three chances a week to get magazine and book proofs into Bimini and out again, trusting the U.S. mail to convey them to the pilot boat captain or to the seaplane pilot who had to remember to take the proofs to the island, and then trust that the process would work twice in a row to get them back in time to meet deadlines—all of these worries put an edge of anxiety on Max Perkins's summer of 1935.

Somehow it worked. Swahili words get corrected by Bror Von Blixen, who mislays sections but not permanently; the illustrations by Shenton are completed and approved; magazine installments appear as advertised; lost corrected proofs arrive in the nick of time.[32] By July 9, Max can almost rest easy: the fifth magazine installment is still between here and there, but they are setting book proofs. Some corrections made for the magazine probably don't get into the book; some of the book doesn't appear in the magazine. Hemingway seldom compared manuscript to typescript, typescript to galley proofs, magazine proofs with book proofs. Mistakes happen. Given the circumstances, the author, and the times, there should have been more.

Through all that summer, a tension runs beneath and between Hemingway's letters: after disappointing sales of *Death in the Afternoon* and *Winner Take Nothing*, he is certain *Green Hills* will turn everything around. From the beginning, he establishes ground rules: no photographs, he makes his own word pictures; keep the price at $2.50; never advertise it as a novel or a travel book.[33] May, June, July—the installments in *Scribner's Magazine* appear, giving potential book reviewers plenty of time to pick their shots, for Hemingway's running remarks about the worthless writers and critics of the new-found American left were guaranteed to offend. For a writer desperately wanting his work to be well received, Hemingway was almost daring the reviewers to trash *Green Hills*. To Perkins, Ernest insists that Von Blixen and Charles Curtis, both of whom know Africa, are wildly enthusiastic; if Scribner's will only do a decent advertising job, they should sell twenty thousand, enough to repay his $3,500 loan/advance money and put another $2,500 in the bank. Added to the $5,000 serial payment, he would be ahead of his expenses. It is a good story, he says again and again, a true, straight autobiography, taking people places they would never be able to go on their own.[34] Max, having prepared salient points for the salesmen on the road, promised that advertising would be good and persistent. "There's one thing I shall not worry about," he wrote Ernest, "and that is your giving up writing for sport. I do not believe you would give up sport for writing, either, although I'll bet you would that first if it came to a show down." Then, almost as non sequitur, he added, "You must finish a novel though before long."[35]

As usual, there are offensive *words* to discuss, words like "condom." Floating prominently in Hemingway's longest ever metaphor for the relationship of the temporary to the timeless, the condom was crucial to a passage he could not cut. Remembering how Havana garbage scows dump their traffic into the Gulf Stream and how bits and pieces—palm fronds, corks, bottles, light bulbs, condoms, a corset, dead dogs and cats—surface for pickers to pluck out with their long poles:

> and the palm fronds of our victories, the worn light bulbs of our discoveries and the empty condoms of our great loves float with no significance against one single, lasting thing—the stream.[36]

There were other words, he told Max, that he might employ—used rubber, safety, French letter—but "condom" was the "most dignified" word for this "very serious passage."[37] Max, so sensitive about some words that he could not bring himself to say them, balked: "I think we shall have to go against you on that word." It was one of the finest passages Ernest or anyone else ever wrote, but fanatics sought the least excuse to attack an author's work.[38]

By the end of July, with the last magazine page proofs in the mails to Bimini, Max was waiting on Hemingway's decision about chapter titles before laying out the book itself. At the same time Ernest was writing Max about his bare-fisted boxing matches on the Bimini docks: four fights, four knockouts. Island life was so good he wanted to stay, but could not leave the *Pilar* so exposed during the hurricane season. Book galleys 25 through 36 arrived, were being read, and would be flying to the mainland the next day. No chapter titles would be used because that was too much like a novel, but he was making divisions, calling them "Part One, Part Two, Part Three," each with a subtitle: "Pursuit and Conversation—Pursuit Remembered—Pursuit as Happiness."[39]

On his birthday, July 21, Hemingway caught his biggest marlin of any season (540 pounds), but no one was interested in the meat. Unwanted marlin was never a problem in Havana, where locals waited at the dock for Ernest to photograph his catch and then give it away. Killing the large fish only for the pleasure of it bothered Ernest, whose original but futile plan was to salt the meat down in wooden kegs for future consumption. "Killing fish for no useful purpose, or allowing their meat to waste wantonly, should be an offense punishable by law," he wrote for *Esquire*. "But those who should make the law should also provide a means of disposing of the fish." *Should* upon *should*, he tried to ease his conscience: there was no law; he was not responsible.[40]

———

Sunday, midmorning on Matecumbe Key, some vets washing clothes, writing letters home, others with hangovers exploding in the heat, trying to remember where they hid their postal savings books. Crossing the bridge where Snake Creek cuts through Windly's Key, an unscheduled train, filled with National Guardsmen, is trailing smoke, bound for Key West. As she hits the Matecumbe straightaway, Munn Norwood opens the throttle, blows the whistle twice. Up ahead he sees a man walking toward him on the right-of-way. Munn blows the whistle again, pulls the bell cord, and the man still walking. Four hundred feet away, doing sixty, Munn watches, unbelieving, as Fred Griset, veteran of the Argonne, quite deliberately steps into the middle of the track, faces the train, and raises his right hand. What is left of Fred's body is found in the bar ditch, his brains splattered across the front of the engine, a piece of his skull on the drawhead.[41]

In mid-August, Ernest and his crew motored twenty-six hours back to Key West, where he planned to stay only long enough to answer mail and write an *Esquire* letter before leaving for Havana. However, the *Pilar*, burning too much oil, needs to have her piston rings replaced. First the rings don't arrive from Detroit, then the local mechanic goes on vacation, putting Havana on hold until another season.[42] It was probably all to the good, for tropical storms are beginning to flare up in the Caribbean. On August 20, an advisory warns of a tropical disturbance moving toward the Bermudas. But with no better tracking information than wireless reports from Atlantic shipping and island stations, hurricane landfalls are seldom predictable. On Whitehead Street, Hemingway studies his hurricane charts showing the patterns of September storms past. That Saturday of Labor Day weekend, just as the circus is arriving in Key West, the paper says the storm is east of Bermuda, heading for the Florida keys, but not yet at hurricane force.[43] Forty-eight hours later, in middle of the night, the veterans' camps on upper and lower Matecumbe Key disappear when a fifteen-to-twenty-foot storm surge sweeps across the low island.

First reports and rumors say the vets were evacuated on a train sent down from Miami. It is almost true. On Monday afternoon, at 4:24 p.m., when someone remembers that hundreds of vets are exposed on the keys, a train is dispatched with Jim Gamble at the throttle. Three hours later, passing through Tavernier, over Windly's Key, and heading for Matecumbe, he stops at the Islamorada station to pick up stragglers when

> *suddenly the entire train blew away . . . six coaches, two baggage cars and three box cars. . . . Every car in the train was turned on its side. There were quite a number of people in the coaches and the water came up in the coaches. In some of the cars it nearly drowned the people there. All of the people succeeded in getting out, . . . [the] depot and the commissary of the Florida emergency relief administration all blew to pieces suddenly and blew around over the engine and the coaches.*

On Windly's Key, women, children, and forty men, half of them vets, have taken shelter against rising water in the hospital when they see the relief train pass. Forming a human chain in now waist-deep water, they try to make their way two hundred feet to the slightly elevated Snake Creek rail crossing, hoping to board the train on its return. No sooner are they out into the raging night than the hospital disintegrates, disappearing behind them. Only three make it to the crossing, where they climb a tree as water covers the rail line.[44] In Key West, Ernest Hemingway watches the barometer at his bedside fall to 29.55; at midnight he bulls his way on foot through driving wind and rain to keep watch over the *Pilar's* moorings until morning.[45]

On Lower Matecumbe Key, which is so narrow a man can almost throw a rock across it, hundreds of veterans wait in ragged groups around the rail line. A train is coming, they are told. As the wind howls, tents blow away, wooden buildings implode in the dark. There is no place to hide when the storm surge rises, no high ground. Next morning, when the sun is full up, Fred Johnson flies his single-engine plane low over the island to report: "Matecumbe is flat. Nothing is left standing in all that . . . [fifteen-mile] section except one building at Tavernier." Of the relief train, only the engine is on the track; some of the boxcars are four hundred feet from the right-of-way. It looks like thirty miles of track are washed out, steel rails warped and twisted.[46] On Windly's Key, the three survivors in the tree climb down, exhausted and alone. On the bank of Snake Creek, a body is turning green in the early-morning sunlight. At the north end of Islamorada, all that remains of Camp No. 1 is four smashed houses blown far off their foundations. The other twenty buildings have either disappeared or become debris. On the lee side of the key, bodies are beginning to bloat in the mangrove thickets.[47]

After a reeling night of heavy winds, Key West wakes Tuesday morning relatively unscathed: trees and limbs are twisted and torn, some roofs damaged, but no casualties. All that day, high winds and rough sea prevent anyone from going north; the ferry schedule is canceled. With all telephone and telegraph lines to the mainland down, nothing but static-ridden radio news comes in. One rumor says Tavernier has been destroyed by a tidal wave, killing seventy-five persons, but no one wants to believe it, hoping that the train evacuated the vets. By Wednesday morning, food, water, medical supplies, and a portable transmitter from Key West are being assembled at the ferry slip on No Name Key, where relief parties board Coast Guard and Navy cutters, a lighthouse tender, and a geodetic survey vessel bound for Lower Matecumbe, forty-five miles up the lee side of the keys. No one is prepared for what is found there:

> Matecumbe Hotel at Upper Matecumbe was in ruins. . . . The Caribbee colony . . . was completely swept to sea. Where the No. 5 Veterans camp had been on Lower Matecumbe Key, the territory was leveled almost to the ground, only chewed off stumps of palms and pines showed sparsely. There was no sign of the camp.[48]

Offshore the sea is calm, almost smooth in the light breeze; across the landscape, blue bedsteads are splattered like a rash. Where woods once stood, there are blasted stumps leveled as if by an artillery barrage. Here, there, in the mangroves, in ditches, some in blue dungarees, some stripped naked by the water, lie battered, bruised, and twisted bodies. Of the three camps, nothing remains alive but seventy veterans who clung in the howling dark to a tank car filled with water. The odor of several hundred other veterans, beginning to rot in the blazing sun, fills the air.[49]

On Thursday morning, more than two days after the disaster, Monroe County Sheriff Karl Thompson, who now realizes the enormity of the problem, assembles two hundred volunteers, including Ernest Hemingway, to attend to the dead on Lower Matecumbe. All that day, Key West boats go back and forth between No Name Key and Matecumbe. Equipped with axes, machetes, rubber gloves, and gas masks, the men face the stench and horror of bodies so ripened in the sun that some burst open when lifted. The living periodically stop lifting, remove the gas mask, and vomit in the sand. Where possible, the vets are named by their pay disks, but many go unidentified as bodies accumulate, some buried where they are found, some cremated in piles like cordwood. Some dead vets, once run out of Washington for bonus marching, are now dropped stinking into wood coffins for burial in Arlington Cemetery. At Camp No. 5 only eight out of 187 are left alive; two sun-swollen women are found stripped naked by the storm and deposited in a tree, as in some Goya etching. All along the keys, in shallow bays, on sandbars, in mangrove thickets, the sickly aroma of the dead arises. By Saturday, September 7, over six hundred bodies are accounted for; another four hundred remain missing. Two months later, eight civilians and three vets are cremated on the north end of Matecumbe.[50] After that they stop looking.

The Key West that complained about drunken vets pissing in residents' yards, that arrested them for vagrants but took their money, that Key West now mourned with public ceremonies and newspaper poems for the dead, twice dead, whose spirit went first, killed by those who forgot their sacrifice, and then

> *The storm killed them,*
> *And scattered their broken bodies.*
> *How could we know*
> *(We were so sure!)*

They were "worthless drunken bums"?
Weep twice for them,
Those Vets who've gone
At last to find their rest.[51]

When *New Masses*, the left-wing magazine that was home to political rebels of the Thirties, asked Hemingway to write a dispatch covering Matecumbe, he was of several minds about it. First, he was busy correcting the last set of book galleys for *Green Hills of Africa*, and *New Masses* was not his sort of venue. Neither left nor right, but opposed to government of any sort, he trusted working-class people, but not those who would lead them to the barricades and not the masses en masse; he befriended the rich on a selective basis but not as a class, nor did he trust demagogues, left or right, whose names were put up on street signs and monuments. (Huey Long was dying from an assassin's bullet in Baton Rouge and Key West was contemplating a statue of Franklin Roosevelt.) Closer to home, Hemingway had no use for *New Masses*' book reviews denigrating his work for political reasons. But his anger got the better of his judgment: what he had seen on Matecumbe he thought he could never use in his fiction. It was too gruesome and too important. So he wrote a piece he titled "Panic," which *New Masses*, without consulting him, retitled and printed a week later.[52]

———

You found them everywhere and in the sun all of them were beginning to be too big for their blue jeans and jackets that they could never fill when they were on the bum and hungry. I'd known a lot of them at Josie Grunt's place and around the town when they would come in for payday, and some of them were punch drunk and some of them were smart; some had been on the bum since the Argonne almost and some had lost their jobs the year before last Christmas; some had wives and some couldn't remember; some were good guys, and others put their pay checks into the Postal Savings and then came over to cadge drinks when better men were drunk; some liked to fight and others liked to walk around the town; and they were all what you get after a war. But who sent them there to die?[53]

———

Having already spent too much of Scribner's advance money to go to Cuba or Wyoming for the fall, Ernest was at loose ends, looking for some way to celebrate the completion of *Green Hills*. Page proofs were corrected, including his reference to Gertrude Stein as "some bitch he's tried to help get published." What would be better, he asked Max: "Fat bitch? Lousy bitch? Old bitch? Lesbian bitch? What is the modifying adjective that would improve it?" Having gotten that out of his system, he changed the word to "female." ("That will make her angrier than bitch.")[54]

That was when Gingrich asked him to report on the Joe Louis–Max Baer heavyweight championship fight scheduled to take place just one month before Hemingway's African book would be published. Never having been in New York when one of his books was released and certain that *Green Hills* was going to be a critical success, Hemingway decided to spend a couple of months visiting East Coast friends while taking full pleasure in his accomplishment. It seemed like a good idea, but Max Baer probably thought the Louis fight was a good idea until he actually stepped into the ring.

From Ernest's vantage point, it was not a pretty fight, as young Louis took his opponent apart in three rounds and put him to sleep in the fourth. Outclassed, outhit, outboxed, the more experienced Max Baer looked like a frightened amateur who should never have been in the same ring with the fighter they were calling "Dark Lightning." It was, Hemingway wrote, "the most disgusting public spectacle, outside of a hanging, that your correspondent has ever witnessed. What made it disgusting was fear." A natural and protective reaction, fear was not an unknown experience for Hemingway, but not something he expected to pay $25 to witness. Having described the fight and its peripherals, he closed his *Esquire* letter with a contemplation of Joe Louis' future: someday an older, heavier, balding Louis would take a beating from a younger fighter, but Hemingway was willing to bet that anytime Louis lost in the next fifteen years, his opponent would have to get up off the canvas to beat him. Max Baer "does not get off the floor with any such projects in mind," he said.[55]

The boxer, the writer, the matador: age eventually diminishes their skills, judgment, and timing. Eventually the best of them are crushed if not defeated by age and death. Professionals trapped in a holding action they cannot win was ever Ernest's interest from his Paris days forward. Unwilling to relinquish self-reliance, yet knowing how the story must conclude if followed far enough, Hemingway always sees the end of the road. If one loves this world, there are no happy endings. Most readers saw only the masculine world he described so clearly; those who understood what he was saying were not always happy to be reminded of their vulnerability.

As Ernest and Pauline watched the boxing match, across the country a hundred thousand *Esquire* readers were absorbing his "Notes on the Next War," written on Bimini amid whiskey talk of wealthy men who battened on war. Hemingway advised his readers:

> *Not this August nor this September; you have this year to do in what you like. Not next August nor next September; that is still too soon; they are still too prosperous from the way things pick up when armament factories start at near capacity. . . . But the year after that or the year after they fight.*

It would be a European war which America, having no European friends, should avoid. The only country worth dying for was one's own. Sooner or later, Hitler would have his war, but "of the hell broth that is brewing in Europe we have no need to drink. . . . We were fools to be sucked in once on a European war and we should never be sucked in again."[56] Because he went to the wars, studied and wrote about them, did not mean that he was their lover: a point never well understood by his readers.

Between the Louis–Baer fight and the release date of *Green Hills*, Ernest and Pauline visited with her relatives at Uncle Gus's "Homestead" in Connecticut and with Sara Murphy at upstate Saranac

Lake, drinking by the fireplace, listening to "Begin the Beguine." ("Shall we beguine?" asks Sara.) By October 17, the Hemingways return to New York, perhaps not wanting to be at Saranac for the fifteenth birthday of Patrick Murphy, who is slowly losing his fight with tuberculosis.[57] On Friday, October 25, Ernest opened the *New York Times* to read John Chamberlain's review, which began: "Ernest Hemingway went to Africa to shoot the bounding kudu and the ungainly rhinoceros and to reply to his critics." *Green Hills* was, he said quite accurately, "the most literary hunting trip on record."

Chamberlain, like many New York reviewers to follow, could not stand the narrator's lecturing nor his skewering critics and other writers. The writing, Chamberlain admitted, had its moments, but many of them were spoiled by characters all speaking in Hemingway's pidgin English. Chamberlain doubted Hemingway's prefatory statement that he was attempting "to write an absolutely true book to see whether the shape of a country and the pattern of a month's action can, if truly presented, compete with a work of the imagination." Could people really speak this way, and would they keep asking the narrator to lecture them? Five months later in the English edition, Hemingway omitted this statement, substituting a letter to the book's white hunter, asking him not to take offense at the dialogue put into the mouth of Pop. "Remember you weren't written of as Pop. It was all this fictional character."[58]

Many reviewers disagreed with what they took to be Hemingway's personal views on life and letters while admiring his landscape painting and narrative. That was not enough for Ernest. Bernard DeVoto found long parts of the book dull, but enjoyed the humor and clowning, thought Hemingway's self-exposé delightful. Charles Poore, in the Sunday *Times*, recognized the experiment of the writing, but it wasn't a novel. Reviewers wanted a novel. Van Doren in the Sunday *Herald Tribune* saw it was structured like a novel complete with Hemingway characters; he also saw that many had misjudged Hemingway: beneath what appeared tough and hard-boiled was "a very sensitive man, subtle and articulate beneath his swaggering surfaces." Clifton Fadiman never got past the bleeding animals, as if that were the whole of the book, but *Time* magazine thought the best parts were "Hemingway's comments on politics, revolution, literature and man's fate." Never had Hemingway's reviews been so disparate: he had written a book of several parts, any one of which was offensive to someone. No one saw clearly what he was trying for in his multidimensional prose, but if he did it well enough, no one on first reading should have noticed.[59] On balance, these reviews would have delighted many a Thirties writer, but not Hemingway. To seek unqualified praise from the very critics his book professed to despise was, he now saw, a game he was bound to lose. No one, it seemed, wanted natural history from a novelist whose last novel was published six years ago.

———

My Dear Mr. Hemingway,

What do you do, when it is like milk in the breasts? And will not come. And you want it to come, or else how is the baby going to get it? And it hurts not coming. Then, you are not sure it is there except you know it must be there. You feel that it is there, if it would only start. And you look around for remedies to make it come. You will try anything to get it started, no matter how foolish you know what you are doing is. And it hurts and hurts and is on your mind and you can't think of anything else. But you don't know what to do. You never know, so far. You just wait for it to come. Not really knowing if it is there. But believing it is. What do you do, when you do this?
Sincerely,
Rose Blucher[60]

———

Ernest and Pauline returned to Key West too late to help their friend J. B. Sullivan, who was running unsuccessfully for the town council. "Sully" needed twenty-six more votes, so two votes more would not have mattered, even if the Hemingways had paid their poll tax and were registered to vote, which they were not.[61] As politically astute as Ernest was, he was equally uninvolved, asking only for the absolute minimum of government. A writer, he insisted, should never be bound to any government, should always be on the outside, critical and wary, for government was never his friend.[62] He was much more interested in revolution itself than in the government established by a successful revolution.

Smarting from wounds inflicted by the critics, he reentered Key West unnoticed and morose. Early-winter weather, one norther after another, kept the *Pilar* in port and himself anxious with no outlet for his anger but his pen. He began writing long responses to critical letters from both friends and strangers, a sure sign that he was at loose ends. To one friend, he said he would like to take a tommy gun into a couple of New York establishments and wipe out some of the critics along with himself; to a stranger, he said he sometimes felt like "climbing into the stands when somebody gets snotty" but his hide was tough enough to take "chickenshit" attacks without flinching.[63] To Fitzgerald's less than enthusiastic critique of *Green Hills*, Ernest replied that he was happy to see Scott was no better at recognizing good work than he ever was. "You are like a brilliant mathematician who loves mathematics truly," he said, "and always gets the wrong answers to the problems."[64] The next day he wrote Dos Passos about Fitzgerald's "supercilious" letter telling him how bad *Green Hills* was. It was a good book, Ernest insisted, a book killed by the critics. What was the point in writing if no one could tell a good book when he read it?[65] That same day he wrote Perkins that *Green Hills* failed for three reasons: (1) the price of $2.75 was too high; (2) he had "without even thinking about it" managed to insult the reviewers; and (3) Scribner's had not pushed hard enough with advertising.[66] The faults with his publisher were the same ones he used to explain the failure of *Death in the Afternoon*. Max replied that he might have warned Ernest about attacking New York critics, "but I did not think you wanted it, and I do not believe you have heeded it for an instant. Nor do I think you should have."[67] Max, ever careful, always had it both ways.

When a Mr. Harris questioned the value of Hemingway's *Esquire* "letters," Ernest responded with a three-page, single-spaced apologia, defending some, explaining others. The *Esquire* pieces might have kept him from writing stories as Mr. Harris suggested, but he was now "trying an experiment" with four short stories; if *Esquire* writing interfered, he would "cut out" the letters, which is what Pauline was advising him.[68] In the writing room, his notebook said:

> *Finish Happy Ending*
> *Write hurricane short story*
> *Write story of boat broken down in Gulf*
> *Story of revolution in Cuba*[69]

The Matecumbe hurricane story he never wrote as fiction; the boat broken down in the Gulf would appear later in the Harry Morgan saga. The Cuban revolution was longer than a story, maybe many stories that fit together, a scheme that was forming in his head but not yet on paper. There was also an unmentioned but unfinished story about a young Madrid waiter, full of illusions, who bleeds to death from a severed artery. Much concerned with death—the dead on Matecumbe; Baoth Murphy dead, Patrick Murphy dying—the question raised in the manuscript was "When is death a misfortune?" In March, trying to comfort Sara Murphy on the death of Baoth, he said that by dying young, the young boy was spared the disillusionment of discovering "what sort of place the world is."[70]

First, he finished the second Harry Morgan story—"White Man, Black Man, Alphabet Man"—which he sent to *Esquire* in lieu of his December letter, in effect giving away what he might have sold elsewhere: "a really expensive present," he told Gingrich.[71] The working title referred to rumrunner Harry, his black crewman, Wesley, and a government official with one of the new agencies, FERA, WPA, CCC, take your pick. It was a story of self-reliance, of friends helping each other outside the law, defying the powers transforming Key West into a respectable tourist attraction.[72] *Esquire*, not allowed to say that a person was "kicked in the ass," had no trouble printing this story's numerous references to Wesley as "the nigger."

As the year was closing, Hemingway offered by letter to take Fitzgerald on a tour of Havana, where revolutionaries were now financing their cause through kidnapping and bank robberies. He was writing a story about this next revolution; Fitz could find some material in Havana as well. If nothing else, he could heavily insure himself and Ernest would arrange to have him killed: "All you'll have to do is not put your hands up quick enough and some nigger son of a bitch will shoot you and your family will be provided for and you won't have to write any more." It was supposed to be a joke, but the joke of a mind gnawing on its own dilemma: what to write when his best had not been good enough. In six years he had published three books so rich that general readers had no taste for them. He took his readers into the new country, but they did not enjoy the trip. The day before Christmas, reassessing his writing life, he decided to take his name off the masthead of *Esquire* as a contributing editor. *Green Hills*, he explained to a Mr. Green, was worth the effort if only for learning to write about terrain, a skill which would pay off if he could ever write a "big novel." "But I have worked hard enough," he said, "to be entitled to live my life for a while because you are dead so damn soon."[73] On the last day of the year, critiquing stories sent to him by a novice, Hemingway's advice was good for both of them: "Write what you know about."[74]

Chapter Nine

1936

BOXING THE COMPASS

Key West, Havana, Bimini, Wyoming, Key West

ENTERING THE SEVENTH year of a depression without precedent, Key West was more isolated than ever. When local boatmen were arrested for running illegal Turks and Armenians into the Keys from Havana for $200 a head, Key West understood why "conchs" took the risks, but not why aliens wanted to come. Pan American seaplanes were flying tourists in from Miami once and sometimes twice a day; freighters brought passengers from Tampa and Havana on a regular basis, but the storm-ravaged railroad was not being repaired; remains of the highway, still showing a fifty-mile water gap at the end of Matecumbe, were ripped, torn, and washed out in places. Almost a year after the hurricane swamped bridges, wrecked ferries, and destroyed the rail line to Key West, state and federal congressmen were still debating what to do about the situation. While one Washington committee wondered why the weather bureau could not track something so large as a hurricane, another discussed a $10,000 memorial to the dead veterans whose names were already past remembering. Key West men without money, watching luxury yachts arriving in the submarine basin, could neither grin nor well bear it. Men working on relief whistled and catcalled at tourists, who complained that a woman wearing shorts should "be able to step out of her car . . . without being made the center of attraction and comment by a group of laborers whose race and blood range from Caucasian to negroid."[1]

Behind the wire fence on Whitehead Street, where a gaudy peacock preened by day and screamed in the night, Hemingway is in a period of reassessment, melancholy and morose, waking in the dark to write in his upstairs room until dawn. In private he is moody, quick-tempered, difficult to please. In public with strangers and visiting guests he remains ever the smiling host, keeping glasses filled, hooks baited, and his eye on the water. Invited and otherwise, winter guests arrive: Dick Cooper and Seward Webb; Burris Jenkins, cartoonist with the *New York American*; Ursula Jepson, his married sister, with her daughter, Gayle; Harry Sylvester, New York writer, and his new bride; film actress Nancy Carroll with writer Quentin Reynolds; Russell Akins of *Fortune* magazine; Tommy Shevlin; Waldo Pierce with wife, three children, and nanny.

Still smarting from reviews that wanted him to be more concerned with the working class, Hemingway speaks with increasing frequency about his future death. To a Russian critic, he says he hates "the shit that will be written about me and my stuff after I am dead."[2] To Pauline's mother he writes that laurels did not come to the living: "So I am going to work for success after I am dead."[3] While caught up in fears that he can no longer write, he tells Sara Murphy that he is "going to blow my lousy head off."[4] The last time he was so preoccupied with his demise was during his separation from his then lover, Pauline, while waiting for his divorce from his first wife, Hadley. Here is no separation, no other woman offstage, but the restless, distracted condition is real enough. In his writing room, two short stories are taking shape. One is about a possibly accidental shooting death on safari in which a bitchy woman, who looks a lot like Jane Mason, kills her husband, who looks a lot like Grant Mason, with a rifle bullet through the back of his head. In the second story, a bitchy writer, dying of gangrene on the Serengeti Plain, harasses with sarcasm his faithful wife, who sounds a lot like Pauline.[5]

Adding to Hemingway's uneasy melancholy is the February *Esquire*, which carried his story "The Tradesman's Return," and the first part of Scott Fitzgerald's personal essay "The Crack-up." Writing lyrically, if somewhat vaguely, about "cracking like an old plate," Fitzgerald repented of being "a mediocre caretaker" of his own talent, and one who let himself "be snubbed by people" with no more ability or character than himself. He was through with caring about others, he said, for he was no longer able to stand the sight of former acquaintances, particularly writers. For moral support he had only childhood dreams of heroic deeds on fields of sport or war.[6] When Ernest read Scott's essay, he could joke about it even though he was, presumably, one of the writers no longer to be tolerated. "Once a fellow writer always a fellow writer," Ernest writes Dos Passos, telling him that Perkins "says he [Scott] has many imaginary diseases along with, I imagine, some very real liver trouble."[7]

In letters, Hemingway diagnosed his own insomnia and depression as the effects of not exercising while writing too hard. The experience, he said, is instructive, making him more tolerant of his father's suicide.[8] But this newfound tolerance does not carry over to immediate family, who walk softly during these touchy weeks, realizing that Ernest is explosive. When his sister, Ursula, came in one evening in tears over Wallace Stevens's disparaging remarks about Ernest, he raged out into the rain to settle the matter as he had in Bimini. In the dark, wet street by lamplight, he confronted Stevens, a large man, a little drunk, a little belligerent, twenty years Hemingway's senior. In the following flurry, Hemingway popped Stevens several times before pausing to take off his own spectacles. Then Stevens got in a solid right to Ernest's jaw before Hemingway put the poet down on the wet pavement, ending the fight. The following evening Stevens, who tended to drink too much on his Key West vacations, came to Whitehead Street to apologize to Ursula and to Ernest, but could not use his damaged right hand.[9] Promising to tell no one of their fight, Ernest was soon writing the details to Sara Murphy, excusing himself from his vow on the grounds that Sara will not tell anyone else. He told Dos Passos to get the story from Harry Sylvester, which would not violate the promise: "As I say am a perfectly safe man to tell any dirt to as it goes in one ear and out my mouth."[10] His exhilaration, however, was short-lived.

When the second part of Fitzgerald's essay, "Pasting It Together," appeared, Hemingway was depressed and appalled. Not only was Scott wallowing in self-pitying rhetoric, but he was also referring to Hemingway by implication if not by name. "I saw honest men through moods of suicidal gloom," Fitzgerald wrote, "some of them gave up and died; others adjusted themselves and went on to a larger success than mine." Ernest must have seen allusions to his own "suicidal gloom" during his 1926 divorce, after which he wrote Scott that he was "all through with the general bumping off phase."[11] Fitzgerald went on to refer to a contemporary "artistic conscience," whose "infectious style" he was barely able to avoid imitating.[12] Hemingway, who did not want to be remembered as Fitzgerald's artistic conscience, wrote Max Perkins that he "felt awful about Scott," whose public whining he took as the act of a coward. "It is a terrible thing for him to love youth so much that he jumped straight from youth to senility without going through manhood. But it's so damn easy to criticize our friends and I shouldn't write this. I wish we could help him."[13] Honest work is the only treatment Hemingway can recommend.

In April of 1936, shortly after reading Fitzgerald's third installment in *Esquire*, Ernest finished his story of the dying writer in disrepair, "The Snows of Kilimanjaro," in which Harry berates himself for the same kinds of failure that haunt Fitzgerald: squandering talent which never creates the fiction of which it was capable. While waiting on the African veldt for a rescue plane to arrive, Harry remembers stories he was saving to write and now never would, each interlarded story told as a fragment. The result is a collection of unwritten short stories inside of a short story about a writer who failed his talent by not writing these very stories. One of Harry's memories is of "poor Scott Fitzgerald and his romantic awe" of the very rich:

> . . . how he had started a story once that began "The very rich are dif-
> ferent from you and me." And how some one had said to Scott, "Yes,
> they have more money." But that was not humorous to Scott. He
> thought they were a very glamorous race and when he found they
> weren't it wrecked him just as much as any other thing that wrecked
> him.[14]

When Scott found himself so skewered in the August 1936 *Esquire*, he asked Ernest to "lay off" him in print; not wanting "friends praying aloud" over his corpse, he asked Ernest to take him out of the story when it was reprinted.[15]

Despite Ernest's complaints about insomnia and melancholy, he was writing well, "using his hurt," as he called it. Developed in tandem with "The Snows of Kilimanjaro," the safari story about the wife shooting her husband, begun in November of 1934, was gradually reaching its final form. As was his habit when finishing a story, he made a list of sixteen possible titles, many of which might have worried Pauline had she seen them:

> A Marriage Has Been Arranged
> The End of a Marriage
> Marriage is a Dangerous Game
> A Marriage Has Been Terminated
> Marriage is a Bond
> Through Darkest Marriage[16]

While Ernest was making last revisions to the story, which he finally called "The Short Happy Life of Francis Macomber," Grant and Jane Mason, prototypes for the fictional Francis and Margot Macomber, motor their *Pelican II* into the Key West yacht basin for a few days' visit.[17] While the Masons dine at the Hemingway table, out in the writing room sits the manuscript describing Margot as "an extremely handsome and well-kept woman" who "five years before, commanded five thousand dollars as the price of endorsing, with photographs, a beauty product which she had never used." In Ernest's clipping file is a three-year-old face-cream ad from *Ladies' Home Journal* in which Mrs. George Grant Mason's stunning photograph appeared purporting to have said, "I could enthuse indefinitely over the creams I use. I do believe they take care of your skin more effectively than any others."[18]

When not writing in the early mornings or fishing in the afternoons, Ernest works out with Harry Sylvester, a visiting New York writer and former Notre Dame boxer. Over at the Navy Field Arena, the two writers are training young Emory Blackwell, reputedly the best light-heavyweight on the island, for a bout with Baby Ray Atwell. On March 19, more than six hundred people, many of whom have side bets riding on the fight, pay money to enter the arena. The evening began, as most matches did in Key West, with a battle royal in which five skinny black kids in ill-fitting trunks bashed each other simultaneously about the ring until only one lad was left standing: "a fair exhibition," the paper called it. The main event was "short and sweet." In the second round, with Hemingway and Sylvester in his corner shouting instructions, Blackwell began connecting with heavy blows, counterpunching Atwell, who left himself open every time he threw his right. In the third round, Blackwell staggered Atwell with a right, jabbed him into a neutral corner, and knocked him out with a right hand to his unprotected stomach. Ernest and Harry help carry the defeated boxer back to his corner, where he does not regain consciousness for almost ten minutes. In the semifinals, the two writers take turns refereeing a six-round match between Bobby Waugh and Kid Pelican. "At the end of the fight," the newspaper reports, "Mr. Hemingway raised the hand of Bobby Waugh as the winner." In his next letter to Max Perkins, Hemingway says, having "made quite a lot of money gambling," he is not yet asking for more advance money.[19]

———

Hemingway's home is a block or two back from the water and occupies a city square. Smothered in huge palms, it is more than 100 years old, of Spanish Colonial type with two-story porches on all sides. The ceilings are fifteen feet high and the floors are of oak plank and Spanish tiles. . . . At strategic points on the walls various heads of animals shot by the Hemingways on their African safari have been strikingly mounted. . . . Hemingway writes from early morning until lunch and refuses to be disturbed. His studio is on the second floor of an outbuilding which once served as slave quarters. He reaches it by a bridge swung from the second floor balcony. A large square room lined with bookcases to the ceiling, it contains no furniture except a flat top desk and a chair. The floors are strewn with skins of lions and tigers [sic] shot in Africa. . . . At the moment he is working on a novel dealing with the contemporary scene.[20]

—*Kansas City Star*, June 2, 1936

———

By mid-April, Hemingway was run down with the flu, emotionally uneven, overly sensitive to criticism, and, at 208 pounds, overweight, a sign of his lassitude. Defending himself in letters to friends and strangers, he resented being told he was selling out his talent (having just finished a story about a writer who felt guilty about selling out his talent). To whom and for what? he wanted to know. Money from his first two novels went to his former wife and his mother's trust fund. "Am probably the only living son of a bitch who is universally believed to have sold out and who did not sell out nor get any dough for it," he protested to Gingrich. The "chickenshit communists," who wanted him to write about labor strife, ought to know that his books were selling well in Russia. Defensively, he told one critic that he wanted to write three more novels, a book on the Gulf Stream, and a "study in the mechanics of revolution."[21] To Perkins, he complained about ideologists like Malcolm Cowley, "as dull as cold tallow and as permanent." The New York bunch, who wanted to destroy him, could not tell "literature from shit," and he would never again "notice them, mention them, pay any attention to them, nor read them. Nor will I kiss their asses, make friends with them, nor truckle to them." From now on he was working by and for himself and the judgment of the future.[22]

Clearly distressed and out of joint, he knew it was time to get out of town: too many visitors, too many distractions, too much food. On April 23, the *Key West Citizen* reported, with its usual inaccuracies:

> *Ernest Hemingway is planning a trip to Cuba soon. Then he is going to Africa [sic] again for fishing and hunting. That chap has done a lot for Key West, entertains every personage that comes to town, has had most of the important newspaper and magazine men here as his guests, and writes a Key West Letter and other articles advertising this locality.*

The next day, Pauline and Gregory took the steamer north to Tampa en route to Piggott to give her parents a dose of their youngest grandson, leaving Patrick with Ada. The following evening, Sunday, the *Pilar* left for a night crossing to Havana with Ernest at the wheel, Josie Russell in charge of the engine, and Jane Mason along for the ride home.[23]

Not having been in Havana since October of 1934, Ernest returned to a city changed, its power structure shifted: new names on doors and mastheads. Many Havana reporters had taken up less dangerous trades or moved on. The *Havana Post*, having forgotten how to spell his name, could not remember exactly what Ernest had once done to become famous:

> *Ernest Hemmingway . . . got in yesterday from Key West. . . . years ago he obtained the winning prize among thousands of competitors of $56,000 for a striking title to a picture, Farewell to Arms. . . . Greetings are also to be made extensive to Mrs. George Grant Mason . . . a guest on the Pilar on the trip from Key West to Havana.[24]*

There were more clubs, more Americans, more bars, movies, gossip, gambling, and soldiers. The military, controlled by former sergeant

Fulgencio Batista, kept their violence out of the papers, but in dark alleys and on country roads, revolutionists still died, if not so publicly as in the old days; bombs still exploded, but no one officially heard them. Tourists—playing the horses, betting on the jai alai, overpaying the whores—were not to be disturbed.

On May 4, at Ernest's invitation, Sara Murphy and John and Katy Dos Passos flew into Havana's harbor on the Pan Am seaplane from Miami for an eight-day visit; two days out of the next six on the *Pilar* they catch marlin, the bill of one becoming a letter opener for bedridden Patrick Murphy. With Sara, whom Hemingway admires and whose affection he values, Ernest is the considerate host, wanting her Havana experience to be perfect. After a hard night's drinking, she gave him "bromoseltzer and whiskey sours" for breakfast, and he took her up the coast to his favorite cove, where the party lunched on an untouched beach. In the cool of the evening at the Ambos Mundos café, Sara delighted in musicians who played "No Hubo Barrera en El Mundo" at their table, and in the morning when the *Pilar* left the harbor in the wake of the odoriferous garbage scow, she assured Ernest that their late start was not his fault. On Saturday night before his visitors flew back to Miami, Ernest accompanied them out to the Masons' expensive home in the wealthy Jamanitas enclave for a dressy dinner party. "What wonderful places you live in," Sara told Ernest later, "and what a good life you have made for yourself and Pauline, and what a lot of people you have made love you dearly!" The following Monday, Jane Mason, Sara, Dos, and Katy boarded the morning Pan Am flight for Miami, where two days later Sara, in her ever-present pearls, met Pauline, who was en route to join Ernest in Havana.[25] Pauline "went on to the Havana plane looking like a delicious, and rather wicked little piece of brown toast," Sara wrote Ernest, "and the opinion was unanimous that she, & her hair, had *never* looked better & that she is a divine woman."[26]

Having been den mother to many writers, painters, and musicians of the "lost generation," Sara Murphy was nobody's fool when it came to reading between the lines of a letter or a face. If her praise of Pauline seemed a little thick, it may have been that she sensed that something was changing in the Hemingways' life. In fact, Ernest's dark moods were becoming more erratic and unpredictable. As one friend remembered, "There were days when he was absolutely a malevolent bastard, full of self-loathing. But the awfulness would leave him after a couple of hours. Generally, before he lost that black mood someone caught hell for it."[27] Even his trusted, aging mate Carlos Gutiérrez was not exempt from Hemingway's sarcasm. Deeply unhappy with his writing career, angry with critics, and under pressure to produce a successful novel to redeem himself, Hemingway was not made less bitter by Dos Passos's spending his time in Havana correcting galleys for his new novel, *The Big Money*. Ernest's genetic inheritance of cyclical depression and insidious paranoia that led to his father's suicide was surfacing in his own life, most obviously in disturbing mood shifts.

Pauline, whose antennae were as finely tuned as Sara's, must have recognized that Ernest's moodiness was similar to his behavior in 1926–27 when he was caught between herself as lover and Hadley as wife. This time the only other woman in sight was Jane Mason, whom Pauline at one time likely saw as a threat, but no longer. She and Ernest, both of whom enjoy Jane's company, recognized her as a woman dangerous to herself and those around her. Like Zelda Fitzgerald before she was confined to sanitariums, Jane is too intense, walks too close to the edge. Her stunning beauty, with which Pauline never thought of competing, gives Jane no protective cover from the eyes of men. More than one of the Hemingways' friends thought Ernest was having an affair with Grant's lovely wife, but Pauline knew them both too well to be overly worried. When Ernest had an affair, it did not take a private detective to discover the evidence. Yet this angry and sometimes self-destructive moodiness of his, striking out at people closest to him, herself included, is very like the dying writer in his recently finished short story: "I'm crazy as a coot," he tells his wife, "and being as cruel to you as I can be." Harry Walden, watching his leg rot on the African plain, hates himself for abusing his talent, for betraying himself, for dulling his perceptions with alcohol, for letting his rich wife provide him with too many

comforts. Harry is not Ernest Hemingway; Pauline is not that ficti-
tious wife. Nevertheless, she can not deny the piece of their life
there in text, nor does she know what to do about it except wait it
out, keep her nest attractive, and remind Ernest of their joint
resources. When she returned to Key West after her ten-day visit,
she wired Ernest that the chandelier they admired in Havana would
be perfect for their bedroom.[28]

Intending to return to Key West the day Pauline left, Hemingway
instead spent five days at the Ambos Mundos, waiting for heavy
weather to clear. On May 23, Pauline warned him by telegram that
strong winds were blowing steadily over the Keys. Ferryboat cap-
tains, sticking to their daily schedule, confirmed high seas and dangerous winds. Finally on May 27 at 11:00 p.m., believing the worst
to have passed, Ernest and the *Pilar* clear port, making the night voyage alone under scudding clouds. At the same time the S.S. *Florida*,
en route between Key West and Havana, found herself, without
warning, wallowing in huge seas that crashed over the bow, ripping
out her port railing and twisting steel support stanchions. Three
hours out of Havana, the first big wave, unseen in the dark, hit the
Pilar from the starboard side, forcing Ernest to turn upwind, steering
northeast, forty-five degrees off course up the Florida Straits. All that
dark night, he hangs on the wheel as the *Pilar* goes up, up, and over
rolling walls of water, catching the full blast of gale-force winds at
the top before crashing down into the next trough. Seams creak, and
the bilge pump strains to stay ahead of salt water in the hold.

With the night storm demanding Ernest's every resource, there is
no time to check the engine oil or the packing on the pumps. During
that long night, the engine block cracks, but Ernest does not know it.
Every time he hears the intake pump sucking air at the top of a wave
as the *Pilar*'s bow noses over into the trough, his heart skips a beat.
In the gray dawn that takes forever to appear, he can finally see enormous waves dwarfing his tiny fishing boat, and fear returns. Unsure
of his position and steering by guess on a quivering compass needle,
Hemingway turns the *Pilar* ninety degrees back to the northwest,
barely heading her up before the wave that would have swamped her

catches the stern and pushes her ahead. For the next three hours, he travels with the wind, riding up and down the black slopes like a roller coaster. At 8:00 a.m., he turns the bow as far into the north as possible, and at eleven-thirty "coming out of a blind squall had Sand Key dead ahead." This trip across, taking Ernest as close to death by water as he has ever been, has lasted almost fourteen hours, pushing him and the *Pilar* to their limits. He wrote Archie MacLeish, that he had a "recurrence of the old difficulty of keeping voice sounding normal. It scared you somewhere between your ankles and your balls. My balls felt very small. When the Capt. of the Cuba heard we'd left to cross that night he told Sully they'd have to give us up."[29]

He is very bitter about the critics, and very bold in asserting his independence of them, so bitter and so bold that one detects signs of a bad conscience. . . . Would Hemingway write better books if he wrote on different themes? "Who Murdered the Vets?" suggests he would. . . . I should like to have Hemingway write a novel about a strike, to use an obvious example, not because a strike is the only thing worth writing about, but because it would do something to Hemingway. If he would just let himself look squarely at the contemporary American scene, he would be bound to grow. I am not talking about his becoming a Communist, though that would be good for the revolutionary movement and better for him. I am merely suggesting that his concern with the margins of life is a dangerous business. In six years Hemingway has not produced a book even remotely worthy of his talents.[30]

—Granville Hicks, November 1936

Everyone knew exactly what he should be writing, and was quick to tell him so. Harvard wanted him to write a check for its 300th Anniversary Fund.[31] Max Perkins was desperate for a novel. *Cosmopolitan* wanted short stories like the ones he'd written ten years earlier, only without offensive words. Ezra Pound, despairing, he claimed, of interesting Ernest in serious subjects, wanted him, for unclear reasons, to write an *Esquire* piece on *The Life and Letters of*

Walter Hines Page.[32] Abner Green pleaded with Hemingway to take up the cause of political refugees who were being denied asylum in United States. Hemingway eventually agreed to lend his name to that cause, and his tactical compass led him to the heart of the issue: find a legal way to get them into the country. "Otherwise you are simply going to publicize an endless series of deportations which is O.K. if anybody wants martyrs but God damned unpractical as tactics."[33]

In the face of these various well-meaning suggestions, Ernest instead wrote out an order list for the Bimini pilot boat: 2 tins of candy, 1 caviar, maple syrup, vegetables, fruit, 2 dozen lemons, a dozen tomatoes, dill pickles, 2 jars of goose paste, walnuts, pecans, barbecue sauce, crackers, cookies, jelly, tripe, mustard, a jar of pickled onions, and a tinned ox tongue.[34] No sooner was he back from Cuba than he and Pauline, with Patrick, Greg, and Bumby in tow, moved into Mike Lerner's spacious summer home at Cat Cay in early June for a month's fishing. Bimini itself was still recovering from the same hurricane that had destroyed Matecumbe a year earlier. The small rental cabins had lost their thatched roofs, coconut palms were stripped, shrubs devastated. Among the five hundred blacks and the handful of whites who lived through the storm, typhoid and malaria were commonplace.[35] None of which deterred the rich and the dedicated when large tuna began their summer run: Tommy Shevlin, Kip Farrington, Dick Cooper, and Jane Mason were there to compete as members of teams and as individual boats. Very much with them was Ernest. When Arnold Gingrich flew in for a consultation on "The Snows of Kilimanjaro," Ernest remarked, "You and I are the only peasants here."[36]

All that June, Pauline, her sister Jinny, the three boys, and Ada Stern lived on Cat Cay in the lovely home above the beach, collecting shells, swimming in the shallows, and occasionally accompanying Ernest on the *Pilar*. Bumby, now Jack (twelve), kept four birds flying loose in his room; Patrick (eight) set fire to the house, resulting in expensive smoke damage; and Gregory (five) refused to swim out over his head. In the cool of the evening by the Bimini dock, with the children in bed, Pauline and Ernest gather with the wealthy sportsmen to talk of tuna tactics and the fall presidential election. The Barbados rum is heady, night breezes fair, and Fats Waller, singing on the phonograph, insists he is not misbehaving, saving all his love for someone.[37]

I'd heard so many tales in Bimini of his going around knocking people down, that I half-expected him to announce in a loud voice that he never accepted introductions to female novelists. Instead, a most lovable, nervous and sensitive person took my hand in a big gentle paw and remarked that he was a great admirer of my work. . . . the day before I left he battled six hours and fifty minutes with a 514 pound tuna, and when his Pilar came into harbor at 9:30 at night, the whole population turned out to see his fish and hear his story. There was such a mob on the rotten dock that a post gave way, and his Cuban mate was precipitated into Bimini Bay, coming to the surface with a profanity that was intelligible even to one who speaks no Spanish. . . . As the Pilar made fast, Hemingway came swimming up from below-decks, gloriously drunk, roaring, "Where's the son of a bitch who said it was easy?" The last anyone saw of him that night, he was standing alone on the dock where his giant tuna hung from the stays—using it for a punching bag.[38]
　　　　　　　　—Marjorie Kinnan Rawlings, June 1936

Hemingway went to Bimini intending his next publication to be a complete edition of his short stories, followed by a novel, but Arnold Gingrich's visit to Bimini changed that plan. As Ernest explained later to Max Perkins, the novel would come first, the collected stories to follow; the Harry Morgan stories would become part of the Key West–Havana novel, which contrasted the two settings, including all Ernest now knew about revolution and its effects on its constituents. Back in 1923 when he first wrote about a revolutionist, he stayed outside the sketch, barely knowing enough to get it right with the young kid riding the train into Swiss exile. Two years later he tried a story about Spaniards plotting to overthrow the monarchy from a Paris café, but broke it off before completing the first page. In

1928, he wrote twenty or more chapters about a soldier of fortune taking his young son to Europe for his first revolution. That novel never got to the war zone before he gave it up, admitting he needed more data, more experience, to tell the story.[39] About this planned novel, he told Max, "I got the last stuff I needed for it on my last trip across." He spared Max the details: the friend whose ankles were broken, his testicles smashed, gas poured over him and set aflame.[40]

He explained to his editor that the themes of this newly conceived novel were "the decline of the individual" and his "re-emergence as Key West goes down around him" and "a hell of a lot more."[41] His private notes were rough, hurried, and contradictory, not an outline but a working through of ideas. There were three themes running sometimes in parallel, sometimes, in counterpoint, reinforcing each other. The first was local: the rise and fall of Harry Morgan in tandem with the decline of Key West into penury and its resultant destruction by government bureaucracy. The second theme would contrast the two islands—Cuba and Key West—both tropic, both aquatic, both Hispanic and Anglo but with their power structures reversed. The third theme was the overview pulling the two stories together: the dream of what might have been in the new world, the promise of Eden so quickly destroyed by greed and politics. He would include the lost dream, the death of the Cuban revolution that began so idealistically, and the rise of oppressing army control. Inside this plan, there were to be other parallels and contrasts of characters and events, enrichments and further complications. He would give his readers the Matecumbe vets in their darkest night going under as the hurricane's surge swept across the island, give them the revolutionists in the same storm running dynamite out of Key West and into Cuba, and give them finally the betrayal that brought everything together: the bridge that had to be blown, the Key West and Cuban revolutionists betrayed but not defeated, and it all going down to failure. It was an ambitious, complicated plan, a *War and Peace* in miniature.[42]

On July 16, with the barometer falling, Ernest and his son Bumby left Bimini on the *Pilar* to return to Key West. While the two Hemingways sailed from one island to the other, in the Canary Islands, General Francisco Franco sailed from his virtual exile on Tenerife toward the island of Las Palmas, where he immediately declared martial law. With coordinated right-wing uprisings in Morocco and Andalusia, the fratricidal Spanish war was beginning, which would make ephemeral Hemingway's outlined novel. On July 18, Ernest apologized to his mother for having missed writing her on her birthday, professing to have had neither calendar on Bimini, nor her address, nor any way of getting a letter off the island. As he prevaricated, Madrid radio was assuring the Spanish public that no one on the mainland was part of the Moroccan plot, which would soon be crushed.[43]

On his thirty-seventh birthday, Ernest wrote Gingrich that he was unable to cut the remarks in the Macomber story about not shooting lions from the car. He missed Gingrich, he said, and missed Jinny, who was still on Bimini. In fact, the only people he really cared about were Pauline, Jinny, and his kids. Katy had changed Dos Passos, "shifted his compass a little." Ernest was about to leave Key West for the L-Bar-T ranch, where he planned to work on the novel just as the two of them had discussed on Bimini. Four days later he wrote Lawrence Nordquist to expect himself, Pauline, Bumby, and Patrick in about two weeks: "Am sending some express out, my book trunk with manuscript of a book I'm writing in it." The following day, by seaplane, Pauline, Gregory, and Ada Stern flew to Miami, where nanny and child boarded the next train north to Ada's home in Syracuse for the rest of the summer and fall. Leaving Key West on the same day by car, Ernest, Bumby, Patrick, and a chance acquaintance, English professor Harry Burns, met Pauline that night in Miami just as a hurricane out of the Bahamas was making its way up the Florida coast, delaying them three days waiting for Jinny to fly in from Bimini. By the time the group arrived at the Hotel Monteleone in New Orleans for a hard week's partying, Harry Burns, now nicknamed "Professor McWalsey," was on his way to becoming a prototype in Ernest's incipient novel. As he warned in *Death in the Afternoon*, "It is always a mistake to know an author well."[44]

———

The kudu was a good 470 meters away. I grabbed up my
Mannlicher, muttering to the Laconic Limey, "Thoreau is lousy—
Willa Cather is a bum—Josephine Johnson is an illiterate brat." I
threw down the Mannlicher and grabbed up my Sharp's. The n.g.
with his usual native-guide surliness said, "N'bo?" which meant,
"Why, in the name of the crocodile god, don't you try a Thompson
submachine gun—that's the only wagon you can hit that kudu
with now!" . . . By now the kudu was 516 meters away. I aimed
pretty carefully. "You're a swell woodchuck killer!" jeered the L.L. I
went on aiming. It was swell. I felt fine. The o.l. shouted, "It's certainly swell! I feel fine! You're a swell shot!" And maybe I was, for
the kudu, hit in the belly, was crawling, his guts dragging, while he
made a foolish noise like a woman dying in agony.[45]

—Sinclair Lewis, October 1936

———

All that late summer and early fall, Ernest and Pauline lived in the
Sidley cabin, where river music from Clarks Fork of the Yellowstone
played in the background. Close to the L-Bar-T lodge for social comfort when needed but distant enough to avoid Lawrence Nordquist's
other paying guests, they have the best of the dude ranch. Until mid-
September, when his Chicago Latin School called him home to
Hadley, young Jack was with them, riding and fishing, Patrick trailing
in his wake. Chub Weaver returned to the ranch on Ernest's payroll
($75/month) as cook, factotum, and outdoor instructor for the
young. Ernest also paid a crewman ($60/month) to keep the *Pilar* in
shape, and Ada Stern ($100/ month) to care for Gregory in Syra-
cuse.[46]

In September, after fishing hard with Ernest at Bimini, young
Tommy Shevlin and his wife, Lorraine, joined the Hemingways at
the ranch. About Hemingway, Shevlin later said:

*He was a complex, very difficult man with a tremendous zest for life,
and when he did anything he did it absolutely up to the hilt, no half
measures. . . . Although I greatly admired him, I was always on guard*

because of his hair-trigger temper. . . . He was self-confident about
everything in the field and in fishing. But he was terribly shy if he
had to go out to dinner. . . . He had a terrific sense of humor, but he
hated jokes on himself. . . . At times he was very much a bully, mostly
when he was drinking, although I never told him so.[47]

About Shevlin, Ernest said he was "a nice kid, but he can't shoot. He
has known so many big game hunters he became a big game hunter
without ever burning the necessary cartridges."[48]

Hemingway, however, came to the ranch neither for the hunting
nor the fishing but to finish his novel. During the first two weeks he
wrote almost every day, adding eighteen thousand words to the manuscript, finishing the section where Cuban revolutionaries rob the Key
West bank. Over the next month, interrupted by a three-day antelope
hunt and one high-country fishing excursion, he wrote another
twenty thousand words.[49] Writing in almost discreet sections, he was
telling the story of Harry Morgan's fall from economic grace in the
Key West depression; counterpointing Harry's principles of self-
reliance with the self-indulgent lives of the very rich yachtsmen in the
Key West harbor, Hemingway was writing a natural historian's view of
the species. The rich were spoiled rich, lazy rich, but not oppressive,
merely careless; the poor were hardy poor, blunt and basic, but far
from noble. In between the two classes were a college professor and a
writer, each with his own point of view. The several story lines inter-
sected and diverged, commenting on each other as they did, and
coming back together in the aftermath of a bank robbery.

Among the many characters were more than a few drawn from
local Key Westers and Hemingway's visiting friends. Jane Mason was
blatantly portrayed among the idle rich as the collector of interesting
men, Helene Bradley: a tall, blonde, lovely, small-breasted woman
with her shining hair drawn back and her cocktail gown trailing
behind, hips moving as she walked, gracious, vital and lovely. She is
said to collect writers, painters, and big-game hunters as sexual trophies. "The big slob," as Hemingway refers to his own persona, is said
to be the only best-selling author who was never in Helene's bed.[50]

Joe Russell, fishing friend and owner of Sloppy Joe's, was in the story running Freddy's Bar, and George Brooks, a prominent Key West lawyer, was pinned on the page like some interesting specimen as "Bee-lips," the middleman who helps the Cubans stage the bank holdup. Harry Burns became MacWalsey, a genial, hard-drinking academic who ends up by default with the wife of Richard Gordon, proletariat author of *The Ruling Classes*, *Brief Mastery*, and *The Cult of Violence*. Taking a page of the poet Yeats, Ernest has Gordon, bicycling past the Hemingway house on Whitehead street, say to himself that the overweight writer who lives there has betrayed his promise, letting down a whole generation of young writers who once admired him. After that one great novel, nothing followed. All he was writing now was tripe for *Esquire* when there were plenty of stories in Key West bars about the drunken vets and the poor fishermen, but in six years, the "slob" had not written a thing about them. Probably he was too drunk to write.[51] While Gordon, in his Joycean consciousness, thinks these thoughts he passes the heavy-set author on the street without recognizing him, a moment at once ironic and satiric, but eventually deleted.

In his first draft, even Hemingway's old friends John and Katy Dos Passos are skewered. Nameless but recognizable, Katy is characterized as a "charming" woman with one defect: "She likes to steal as much as a monkey does." Her husband is said to live off loans given him by rich friends while he attacks the very rich in his fiction: "In a year he'll borrow about what the average writer makes." Earlier he repaid his debts, "and was really incorruptible." Now he no longer feels obliged to pay the debts.[52] The words, vicious and unnecessary, vent some of the anger boiling up in Hemingway, anger over critics and publishers, anger with himself, unfocused anger that is as liable to strike old friends as enemies. There was also professional jealousy in Ernest's caricature: the August reviews of Dos Passos's *The Big Money* were wonderful. They said that Dos was "the most incisive and direct of American satirists." To find his equal the reader must look to *War and Peace* or Joyce's *Ulysses*.[53]

The fictive Tommy Bradley, Helene's strangely permissive husband, who sounds like Hemingway but looks more like Waldo Peirce, spices the novel with extraneous literary gossip about the demise of writers. Speaking of Harry Crosby's suicide, Bradley says rather callously that Crosby was a crazy, terrible writer who should have killed himself sooner. Another suicide, the homosexual Hart Crane, had a talent for picking the wrong sailors, who regularly beat him up. Having already received the request not to use Scott Fitzgerald's name in his fiction, Hemingway lets Bradley say that Fitzgerald, who lacked good sense but was all charm and talent without brains, had gone straight from youth into senility without passing through manhood.[54]

August, September, October, he wrote steadily in the Sidley cabin, wasting no time with *Esquire* letters and very little with correspondence. The exception was fellow Scribner author Marjorie Rawlings, whom he had met briefly on Bimini. Inviting him to stop at her Cross Creek farm on his drive to or from Key West, she said she was stunned by the artistry of "The Snows of Kilimanjaro," a story sure to last. Quite shrewdly she suggested that he has "taken some sort of hurdle" in his own mind—"being done with something that was bothering you—being ready to be free." His sports writing she thought "gorgeous," but those who most enjoyed it were, in her mind, not his true audience. She wanted to know if there was conflict within himself "between the sportsman and the artist."[55] The day her letter arrived, Hemingway answered it, something he rarely did when immersed in his fiction. He agreed that most sports fishermen were a dull lot, old-maidish men who never excelled at baseball and who now reeled in fish by using mechanical advantages. As for the active life of sportsman versus the contemplative life of writer, he could not choose one over the other. Without the fishing and hunting, he "would probably go nuts."[56]

In that same letter he said, "Lately, I have felt I was going to die in a short time . . . so I have been haveing more fun maybe than I deserve." For a thirty-seven-year-old man at the height of his physical and mental powers, Hemingway was inordinately drawn to the contemplation of his own demise. A few days earlier, he had writ-

ten Pauline's mother that the Pfeiffer bloodline was what his children needed "to try to breed some of the suicide streak" out of
them.[57] Tommy Shevlin, remembering that fall at the ranch, said,
"It's extraordinary the number of times he mentioned suicide."[58] Six
weeks after his letter to Rawlings, he told MacLeish, "Me I like life
very much. So much it will be a big disgust when have to shoot
myself."[59]

A world away, General Franco's rebel army was consolidating
early gains as it moved toward the capital of Madrid. On September
26, Hemingway wrote Perkins that he wanted to finish the book in
time to reach Spain before the fighting ended, pledging to revise the
novel when he returned. Seeing such a trip as a real threat to his
prize author's life, Perkins hoped that Madrid would fall and the war
end before Ernest got there.[60] On October 27, after writing a
$1,934.73 check to pay their bill at the L-Bar-T, Ernest, Pauline,
and Patrick packed up for the drive back to Piggott and Key West.
Ernest's trophies included three grizzly-bear hides, two prize elk
heads, and 352 pages of typed and handwritten manuscript of his
still untitled novel.[61]

The Hemingways did not vote that November when Roosevelt
swept Arkansas and forty-five other states, but they stopped off at
Piggott long enough to discuss the President they and the Pfeiffers
despised for his socialist tendencies. Ernest was son-in-law-polite,
and Pauline made arrangements with Ada Stern, still in Syracuse, to
return with Gregory to Key West on November 12. When Ernest and
Patrick left Piggott with their newly hired driver, young Toby Bruce,
at the wheel, Pauline remained at the Pfeiffer home for a few more
days before going first to her St. Louis dentist and then on to New
York City. After three months in the high country of male camaraderie, she was ready to spend a couple of weeks in New York visiting Jinny, shopping for Christmas, and seeing some theater. While
she is watching John Gielgud's performance of *Hamlet*, dining with
the MacLeishes, and visiting with Jane Mason, Ernest is in Key
West showing a reporter where he was going to build his trophy room
and Key West's first swimming pool.[62]

He has become the legendary Hemingway. He appears to have turned into a composite of all those photographs he has been sending for years: sunburned from snows, on skis; in fishing get-up, burned dark from the hot Caribbean; the handsome, stalwart hunter crouched smiling over the carcass of some dead beast. Such a man could not have written Hemingway's early books. . . . It is hard not to wonder whether he has not, hunting, brought down an even greater victim.[63]

—John Peale Bishop, November 1936

By the time Hemingway reached Key West, the first international brigade was arriving to stop Franco's troops at the gates of Madrid. Men he knew, men like Hadley's journalist husband, Paul Mowrer, were already in Spain and back again, reporting the war. In the Key West paper, Spain's turmoil barely rippled the water, but in the New York paper that came in the mail, Ernest followed the war closely as he rushed to finish his novel. Having waited until he knew enough to write the stories of Cuban military revolution and American social revolution, he may have waited too long. American attention was turning back to Europe, where armed violence was taking on new dimensions.

Spain had to wait until he brought this complex novel to conclusion, which he once thought he understood but now was not so certain. Using multiple voices, jump cuts from place to place, and differing views of high life and low, he was trying to write beyond his previous limits, pushing the edge of possibility. Lives were crossing in his fictional Key West streets like those in Joyce's *Ulysses*. The very rich on their harbored yachts, the vets smashing each other mindlessly at Freddy's Bar, the Cuban revolutionaries dead, and Harry Morgan redeemed but dying from stomach wounds: these several strands required "the old miracle you always have to finish with," as Hemingway wrote Gingrich.

The "miracle" Hemingway had in mind for his fiction was going to take wealthy Tommy Bradley into Cuba with a load of dynamite to blow up a crucial bridge. Before leaving Key West the previous July, Ernest asked his journalist friend in Havana, Dick Armstrong, to collect newspaper or eyewitness accounts of specific events that he might use as source material for the Cuban theme. He planned to alternate revolutionary violence and Batista atrocities with Key West chapters, leading to Bradley's conversion to the revolution's cause.[64] Unable to find back issues of the newspapers Hemingway requested, Armstrong sent thirteen typed pages of information on the splintered revolutionary groups—CONC, Joven Cuba, various communist cells—and specific details on places and events: the floor plan of the police station at Monserrate and Empedrado; the killing of Antonio Mesa and his three sons; the retaliation by *deconocidos*; the curious death of Octavio Seigle.[65] By early October, with the necessary ending half clear in his head, Hemingway was planning to return to Havana to finish the novel: "There is some stuff I would like to see again. Some places seen at night [I] would like to see in daytime and viceaversa."[66] Given the length of his manuscript, he must have realized he could not encompass as much of the Cuban revolution as he once planned, not without another six months of writing.

When Pauline flew into the Key West seaplane basin on November 29, Ernest, having worked hard on the novel for three solid weeks, was ready to cross to Havana. Harry Morgan, after killing the fictional Cuban bank robbers, was gut-shot and dying in the Key West hospital; the rich and idle yachtsmen were pinned on the page; and Tommy Bradley and Richard Gordon were en route to Cuba with the explosives. As a Cuban voice explained, it was crucial to blow the bridges across the Almendares river to delay government troops from counterattacking. If the bridges were blown, a very few revolutionists could hold up the troops for a long time. But without the dynamite, there was no way to take out the bridges, and their attack would be hopeless.[67] In the remainder of this "Interlude in Cuba," as he titled it, Hemingway used up most of the information Dick Armstrong had provided. Now he needed more site information on the bridges and a way to make the operation fail.

On December 6, Dick Armstrong and Sidney Franklin met Ernest at the P&O ferry dock; nine days later, without giving any details, he wrote Perkins that he had all he needed to finish the book. On December 15, he returned to Key West, having spent over $400, including a $50 loan to Franklin and another $50 to the Friends of Spanish Democracy's ambulance fund. The siege of Madrid, complete with artillery shelling and regular bombings, was putting a daily casualty count in the Havana paper, but not in Key West.[68] The war in Spain, where Loyalists (to the elected leftist government) were said to be killing Catholic priests and Franco's troops were killing the wounded in their hospital beds, that war was making everything more difficult for writing the book and for maintaining Hemingway's Catholic marriage. Trying to keep an apolitical stance, he was caught emotionally between Franco's fascist rebels, supported by the Catholic Church, and the leftist reform government, which included anarchists, syndicalists, socialists, and communists.

His young friend Harry Sylvester, having listened too closely to their sometimes drunken Key West conversations, had recently written a long apologia for Hemingway in the very Catholic *Commonweal* magazine. Repeating some tall tales about Hemingway's courage in the Great European War, Sylvester defended Hemingway as a once and now returned member of the Church. Sylvester speculated that Hemingway's war experience of having drunken troops under his command rape village women with the blessing of his commanding officers—not true—may have caused him to doubt God's existence, but his faith had been restored:

> One hears by word of mouth that Hemingway has become a Catholic. This is inaccurate: Hemingway has returned to the Roman Catholic Church, in which he was baptized some years ago. . . . although Hemingway has come . . . to accept again the spiritual body of the Church, he is still distrustful of at least part of the corporal body of the Church. He goes to Mass every Sunday. . . . He is of the Church, but not dedicated to it. He is dedicated to nothing but his family and his art. He will never be dedicated to the Church in the same way that Communist writers are dedicated to Communism. But

someday he may write the first great Catholic novel in the English language.[69]

As soon as Hemingway returned to Key West, he asked Sylvester to stop talking about him as a "Catholic writer" or the Church would throw him out. "When I write," he said, "I try to have no politics nor any religion nor any friends nor any enemies but to be as impersonal as a Wasserman Test. Of course nobody ever is." As for Spain, he was trying to reserve judgment until he got there, but he could never support fascists trying to "exterminate the Spanish working class" even if "the government had killed every priest in Spain."[70] Such a position was going to be difficult to defend to Hemingway's Catholic wife or to his mother-in-law in Piggott, where the priest came once a month to say Mass in the tiny, private Pfeiffer chapel.

———

Pauline seemed sharp-edged, too eager, brown and desperate. Her confessionals, her rosaries, that kept her head up during the bad years (so that she amazed everyone with her poise) do not after all fill the major gap in her life and give it a frittering quality that does not flatter. She should have a cause, beyond Saks Fifth Avenue, and a philosophy, instead of a religion.[71]

—Dawn Powell, 1942

———

Some say that when the mother, the brother, and the tall, lovely daughter walked into Sloppy Joe's in late December, Skinner, the bartender, and every other open male eye watched with admiration as the daughter crossed the room to where Ernest was sitting at the bar. Others remember she wore a black dress that did nice things for her legs and that her blond hair was a wonder. That's what they say about Martha Gellhorn's entrance into Hemingway's life. They say that she had Ernest on her mind when she walked in the door, that he drank with her through the afternoon and into the evening, missing his supper and telling Pauline to meet them at Pena's Garden of Roses club. They say that when she left the city, Ernest, unable to get her out of his mind, followed her the next day to Miami.

Certainly Martha was there, and she certainly was beautiful. That much is as true as a photograph can document. But the last five days of December when many who were not there remember all of this to have happened, Ernest and Pauline were in Miami, and when Martha left Key West, Ernest was already booked for his trip through Miami to New York.[72] So maybe Ernest was not as overwhelmed by her long legs as the bartender remembers, and maybe Martha was not bent on destroying his marriage from the moment she walked in the bar. Intentional or not on her part, stunned stupid or not on his, it did not matter. The effect was the same, only it took longer than the barroom memories rightly recall.

The Pilar *cutting a wake with teasers in the water and lines baited.* (John F. Kennedy Library)

Hemingway's Cuban mate, Carlos Guitiérrez, rigging fishing lines on board the Pilar. (John F. Kennedy Library)

The abandoned Fort Jefferson in the Dry Tortugas where Hemingway's fishing parties were more than once storm-bound. (Monroe City Library/Library of Congress)

Hemingway and his Cuban mate displaying a twelve-foot marlin on the Bimini dock.
(John F. Kennedy Library)

Hemingway, with his recently acquired Thompson submachine gun, taking aim at sharks off Bimini. (John F. Kennedy Library)

Outside the main lodge at the L-Bar-T Ranch, darkly bearded Hemingway displays his elk trophies with his black bear skin stretched out on the wall behind him.
(John F. Kennedy Library)

Left to right, Ben, Charles Thompson (obscured), Philip Percival, and Ernest Hemingway at the end of the kudu hunt: "great, curling, sweeping horns, brown as walnut meats."—from Green Hills of Africa (John F. Kennedy Library)

His characteristic glasses in hand, Ernest resting at the Percival home waiting for the safari to begin. (Collection of Wright Langley)

Serengeti Plain, Pauline's lion that she almost shot: "No I didn't. Don't lie to me. Just let me enjoy my triumph."— from Green Hills of Africa. (Collection of Wright Langley)

"We rolled the rhino into a sort of kneeling position and cut away the grass to take some pictures."— from Green Hills of Africa. (John F. Kennedy Library)

Nattily dressed, bullfighter Sidney Franklin and Ernest Hemingway on the Paris *en route to the Spanish Civil War.* (John F. Kennedy Library)

From the half-destroyed observation post they called the "Old Homestead," Ernest on location with the filming of The Spanish Earth. (John F. Kennedy Library)

Hemingway showing a Republican infantry man how to unjam his rifle during the Spanish Civil War. (John F. Kennedy Library)

Spanish Civil War photos from Hemingway's collection. Woman in the middle is dead; man on left is a heartbeat from death; the man on the right watches the executioner put a hood on the hanged woman. (John F. Kennedy Library)

Chapter Ten

1937 – 38

A STRICKEN FIELD

Spain, Bimini, Key West, Havana

W HATEVER HAPPENED THAT afternoon in Sloppy Joe's, Martha Gellhorn remained in Key West for several days after her mother and brother departed, for she was flattered that Ernest took an interest in her. However, Martha was not a star-struck novice from the midwest looking for tutelage. Since 1929, after walking away from Bryn Mawr in her senior year without graduating, she had been writing professionally, first for *The New Republic*, then six months for the *Albany Times Union*, before leaving for Europe and a variety of writing jobs, including Paris *Vogue*. In 1934 she published her first novel, *What Mad Pursuit*, with epigraphs from the two contradictory writers she most admired: Ernest Hemingway and Thomas Wolfe. Two months before she arrived in Key West, Martha's second book, *The Trouble I've Seen*, with a preface by H. G. Wells, put her on the cover of *The Saturday Review of Literature*. Martha fashioned stories based on field inter-

256

views with destitute Americans gathered for the WPA that moved the President's wife, Eleanor Roosevelt, to do a public reading from the collection in New York and to recommend the book to readers of her newspaper column.[1] Unlike either of Ernest's wives, Martha was a professional, a dedicated writer. Years later she would say: "When I was young I believed in the perfectibility of man and in progress, and I thought of journalism as a guiding light."[2] As unlikely as it seems, Martha, Pauline, and Ernest's first wife, Hadley Richardson, were all well-educated St. Louis women from prominent families. Martha's recently widowed mother, Edna Gellhorn, helped found the League of Women Voters, and had recently given an invited lecture at the meeting of the American Academy of Political and Social Science. Martha was her mother's daughter, born, it would seem, with a need to help others, particularly the victims of war.

That Ernest was attracted to Martha from the moment he saw her was never in question. That Pauline was aware of his interest was equally obvious; she was accustomed to tolerating women, more beautiful than she, attracted to her husband. That Martha, a twenty-eight-year-old writer savoring her first national recognition, found Ernest, at thirty-seven and ten years famous, "an odd bird, very love-able and full of fire and a marvelous story teller"[3] was almost predictable; many women did. But Martha Gellhorn was not desperate to have a man in her life. She had done that once, married some say to a French writer, Bertrand de Jouvenel; if not married, certainly she was with Jouvenel for four years in Europe, long enough to know what she did and did not need from a man. What Martha needed was a cause of her own, one untouched by her mother. Unlike Pauline, whose sympathy for the working class was *noblesse oblige*, Martha was a born political activist whose social conscience, with its acute sense of right and wrong, fair and foul, was both her shield and her weakness. She came to Key West already interested in the Loyalist Spanish government and its fight against Franco's Nationalist rebels. She left Key West on Saturday, January 9, determined to go to Spain. She also left interested in the Harry Morgan story, which Ernest allowed her to read in Key West, and in his anecdotes about various revolutions in Cuba. After reading one of Martha's stories, Ernest gave her advice about her writing: don't overthink it; get it on paper and have the courage to throw it away if it stinks. A writer, he told her, must push her limits, risking failure in the privacy of her workroom.[4]

The night Martha left town, Rudy and his Swing Band at Sloppy Joe's was playing rumbas, and Georgie Brooks, the diminutive lawyer and master of ceremonies, sang "Love in Bloom." The next afternoon, Ernest boarded the Pan Am seaplane for Miami, where he suppered that evening with Martha and Tom Heeney, the heavyweight boxer.[5] Two days later, Hemingway arrived at Penn Station for a whirlwind New York visit with Max Perkins (promising the novel by June), with the American Friends of the Spanish Democracy (promising to chair the committee to buy Loyalist ambulances), with the Murphys at Saranac Lake (making bearskin promises to young Patrick, dying), with Harry Burton at *Cosmopolitan* (trying without luck to sell a piece of the novel), with Prudencio de Pereda (rewriting narrative for a documentary film, *Spain in Flames*), and with John Wheeler (signing on as a North American News Alliance journalist). For $500 per cabled dispatch and $1,000 per mailed feature story, Ernest was going to report on the Spanish war for NANA's numerous clients.[6] Like his *Esquire* articles, his prominently bylined NANA dispatches, thirty over the next seventeen months, would keep his name in front of the nation's readers.

In Key West, Pauline was writing Ernest newsy letters about an evening at Sloppy Joe's, a morning tennis match, a pheasant meal with the Thompsons, cute things Gregory was saying.[7] In St. Louis, Martha was writing Eleanor Roosevelt that she was eager to get to Spain, which appeared to be the beginning of the next European war that would make everyone's life less important.[8] While she was reading Martha's letter, Mrs. Roosevelt's husband was preparing his second inaugural address, in which he said, "The test of our prosperity is not whether we add more to the abundance of those who have much, it is whether we provide enough for those who have too little."[9] Martha Gellhorn's passionate concern for the welfare of those with too little and those oppressed was sincere and idealistic; in Ernest Hemingway, whose love of Spain was equally passionate, she thought she had found a fellow writer as dedicated as she to the sad plight of others. Martha could not have been more mistaken.

———

Pauline always tried to be very tolerant of Ernest and any of the girls that sort of made a play for him, or that he seemed entranced with. I don't think he fell in love with other women. He was nice and maybe a lot of women thought he was giving them more attention than what there was; his was in a kidding way. . . . There was no question about it: you could see she [Martha] was making a play for him. Pauline tried to ignore it.[10]

—Lorine Thompson

———

On January 24, Pauline flew to Miami to meet her husband's train and to motor with him on the *Pilar* back to Key West.[11] Accompanied by Sidney Franklin, who was ready to go anywhere at Hemingway's expense, Ernest was home only long enough to pack his bags and answer mail. The hardest to write was the letter to the Murphys when Patrick (seventeen), ghostly white and tired, finally died from tuberculosis.[12] Equally difficult to write, perhaps, was the letter to Pauline's parents, thanking them for Christmas money and explaining that he was supporting the Loyalist government in Spain's civil war because it represented the working class and not absentee landlords or fascist mercenaries, a conflict in which he had previously never shown much interest. Without mentioning to his Catholic in-laws the Church's support of Franco-led rebels, or the killing of Catholic priests by Loyalists, he said his goal was antiwar journalism to keep America out of the European war to follow. On his desk lay the formation papers of Contemporary Historians, a group formed in New York by MacLeish, Ernest, Dos Passos, and Lillian Hellman to support a documentary of the Spanish war to be filmed by Joris Ivens, a Dutch filmmaker.[13]

In the margin of his letter to the Pfeiffers, Ernest added a note whose past tense seemed almost elegiac: "I'm very grateful to you both for providing Pauline who's made me happier than I've ever been before."[14] A day earlier in St. Louis, Martha Gellhorn was writing Ernest that she hoped they were "on the same ark when the real deluge begins."[15] Given the gap between Pauline's semiautocratic and deeply Catholic sensibilities and Martha's footloose idealism, Hemingway's now nagging social conscience was leading him into difficult waters. Pauline, having made her husband her life's work, tended him as carefully as her garden, writing the checks, arranging the house, managing the hired help, and raising their children. Almost forty-two, she was not interested in boarding any ark in a deluge, but she would have followed Ernest anywhere he would permit, war-ripped Spain not being one of those places he allowed. Within a month, Pauline, angry with herself for not going to Europe with him, was writing Max Perkins from what she referred to as "The Widow's Peak." "I am told," she said, "that when I was a very young baby I could be left alone on a chair and would never fall off. I seem to be still on it." To take her mind off Ernest and to keep his on her, Pauline began planning a trip to Mexico City with Key West friends.[16]

Pauline Hemingway came to the door wearing slacks, with her black hair brushed back in a boy's haircut. She was built like a boy and wore no makeup. Her face was tanned from being out in the sun and there was nothing you could see she had been doing to make herself beautiful except keeping her weight down. . . . like a boy, never sitting around, always on the move.[17]

—Arnold Samuelson

Martha Gellhorn, not yet twenty-nine, was not a tender of men, nor did she require much attendance. Whereas Pauline, who by her own admonition traveled badly, was often seasick on liners or fishing boats, Martha traveled easily, gladly, and often. She was, in this trait, almost too much like Ernest. Never willing to suborn herself or her writing for anyone, she might enjoy being on the same ark with Ernest, provided both arrived with their independence intact and with their own life vests. Many would say she followed him to Spain, but Martha never saw it that way. In her last letter to him before he left Key West, she asked him to leave word in Paris for her and to give her love to Pauline. "Please don't disappear," she said. "Are we or are we not members of the same union?" Using one of his high school nicknames with more familiarity than one might expect from a recent acquaintance, she told him, "Hemingstein, I am very fond of you."[18]

By March 10, registered at the Paris Hotel Dinard with Sidney Franklin and poet Evan Shipman in tow, Hemingway was at work gathering a correspondent's visa to Spain, securing diplomatic safe-passage letters, provisioning his two unlikely volunteers, and filing his first NANA dispatch. He also rendezvoused with Joris Ivens at the Deux Magots to discuss the documentary film.[19] From a Republican official, Hemingway carried a safe-conduct letter saying that he was "staunchly loyal" to the elected Spanish government and "was not much interested in politics."[20] This was also Ivens's initial take on Hemingway, who would be with him in Spain, where not being interested in politics could be mortally dangerous. But Hemingway's avowed disinterest was no indication of his political knowledge of how revolutions worked, a subject he had studied for over fifteen years, in books and out of books, and sometimes in Havana dry-mouthed and up very close. Ivens later said that he "set the task to make Hemingway understand the anti-fascist cause. I felt he would be an asset to our cause because he wrote such good articles."[21] Hemingway required little or no indoctrination to despise fascism, for which he harbored no illusions, but Ivens's cause was the communist one. Although Hemingway would never be a communist any more than he would support any political party, his support for the leftist Republican government of Spain was the strongest political statement of his life thus far. It was also a step further away from the politics of his Pfeiffer in-laws and their daughter, his wife, Pauline.

On Sunday, March 14, Hemingway visited with his old friend the soldier of fortune Charles Sweeny, before catching the night train to Toulouse. Two days later, when Ernest was boarding the Air France flight from Toulouse to Valencia, the provisional capital of Republican Spain, Martha was in New York, her credentials as a *Collier's* correspondent and a liner ticket to France in hand, but no word from Ernest about how to get to Spain. Nor had he left any messages for her in Paris, no directions, no encouragement. Being a resourceful woman with several years of European experience, Martha gathered the necessary documents, took the train south to the Andorran-Spanish border, and made her way on foot across the frontier, carrying in her knapsack all a woman needed to go to a war. In Valencia, Martha quite accidentally ended up in the same government car with Sidney Franklin driving to Madrid, where they found Ernest at supper in the Hotel Gran Via. "I knew you'd get here, daughter," he said, "because I fixed it up so you could." When Martha finished correcting him, it was clear that this was a self-sufficient woman.[22]

For better or worse, Ernest and Martha were together in Madrid on the edge of a war more cruel and more politically complicated than historians would ever sort out. The forces of the elected government called Republicans or Loyalists were a rare collection of regular army troops, newly trained civilians, five volunteer international brigades composed of men from all over Europe and America, most of whom spoke no Spanish, and a cadre of Russian professionals, political commissars, and field tacticians. Within this loosely organized amalgamate were Stalinists, Trotskyites, anarchists, syndicalists, and three varieties of socialists who never felt obliged to agree with each other on the course of politics or the war. Because France, England, and America, refusing to support the leftist Spanish government, would not allow arms sales to the Republic, the government turned to Russia for aid. Franco's Nationalist army of Spaniards and Algerian mercenaries, supplemented with Irish, Italian, and German "volunteer" brigades, was aligned with Hitler and Mussolini, whose fascist governments used the war to field-test their new weapons systems. Franco's Spanish support was politically divided among monarchists, fascists (Falangists), Agrarian Republicans, and Popular Agrarians. Seething within these political divisions were the separatist movements of Cataluna, Navarra, and Galicia.

By the time one counts the several trade unions, youth organizations, and the full spectrum of political agendas, over forty political factions divided Spain. For whatever happened, on or off the battlefield, during the three-year bloodletting, there were always two versions and frequently more.[23]

That 1937 early spring in cold Madrid, where they lived at the Hotel Florida, Ernest and Martha fed off the emotional rush of public violence and private romance. Madrid, having repulsed at its very gates the bloody Nationalist attack, was under steady siege from Franco's artillery and bombers. "Cold, enormous, and pitch black," Martha remembered her entrance into the city, which "was a battlefield, waiting in the dark. There was certainly fear in that feeling, and courage. It made you walk carefully and listen hard and it lifted the heart."[24] For freeing the human spirit from the tedium of responsibility, there is, ironically, nothing quite like war. As Josephine Herbst said, remembering Spain: "The unknown is dear to us, and, contrary to opinion, security is not the heart's true desire."[25] When the possibility of death is no farther away than the next incoming artillery round, past and future tenses are diminished, and *now* is as *always* as life can be. Under these conditions and despite Martha's resentment of Hemingway's need for paternalistic control, their relationship, tentatively begun, rapidly became a full-blown love affair.

———

There was never a secret about Hemingway living with Martha Gellhorn at the Florida Hotel. . . . Hemingway had a room on the sixth floor. . . . The seventh and eighth floors had been destroyed by shell fire. My wife and I lived on the fifth floor. When the hotel was shelled our great fun, Helen and I, was to stand at the foot of the stairway to see who was running out of what room with what woman. I don't need to tell you who came out of Hemingway's room.[26]

—George Seldes

———

Somehow Evan Shipman moved a load of canned food, bought in Paris and paid for by Hemingway, to Madrid, where it supplemented their restaurant fare, badly reduced in quality by the war.²⁷ Evan himself was now a volunteer infantryman being sketchily trained at Albacete on his way to the George Washington Battalion.²⁸ Sidney Franklin, who lived at Hemingway's expense in the adjoining hotel room, scavenged the markets for secondhand bullfight apparel at a bargain, always keeping his eye out for edibles, a ham here, a sausage there. Ernest, equally resourceful, was never without whiskey for his oversized canteen or the occasional wild hare for supper. Nor was he without friends and admirers. Because he always had good maps, inside information, and outrageous stories, his rooms in the Florida were frequented by an assorted cadre of journalists and writers: Herb Matthews (*New York Times*), Virginia Cowles (Hearst papers), Sefton Delmer (*London Daily Express*), Henry Buckley (*Daily Telegraph*), George Seldes (*New York Post*), John Dos Passos, Josephine Herbst, Joris Ivens.

Most of the Madrid journalists were sympathetic to the Republican cause, seeing Franco's fascist rebellion as the first act in the drama Hitler and Mussolini were preparing for Europe. Living in a city bombarded, their hotel rooms within walking distance of the front lines, these writers became an informal brotherhood for whom this war was the initiation. Twenty years after the Battle of the Somme, there was finally a cause in which to believe, a battleground upon which to decide the future. Matthews would later write: "In those years we lived our best, and what has come after and what there is to come can never carry us to those heights again. . . . We left our hearts there."²⁹

Much of the world, however, saw the war as Russia's effort to export its communist revolution, a twenty-year fear of western conservatives. In their endless "Red scare," corporate powers never met a fascist they could not support if he would only promise them to keep communism at bay. Propaganda machinery supplied lurid stories of "Red" atrocities, real and imaginary: brutal executions of priests and nuns, churches burned with parishioners inside, night vigilantes terrorizing the streets, young girls forced into whoredom, spies and counterspies, horror and counterhorror. What the world believed of

Spain increasingly came from movie theater news that favored the fascist side of the war. Contemporary Historians, founded by MacLeish and company, was producing the Ivens film as a counterweight to the mainstream newsreels. Hemingway, who invested considerable time and money in the venture, was regularly on location with Joris, carrying equipment, scoping terrain, observing and listening. Because Ivens's political contacts allowed his small film crew access to the war zone, Hemingway was, during his first month in Spain, absorbing more timely experience than most of the journalists. On the Guadalajara front, he walked the battlefield with the field commander, reviewing tactics and observing dead Italian volunteers left behind by retreating Nationalists. That evening, March 22, in his fourth NANA dispatch he wrote:

> *Over the battlefield on the heights above Brihuega were scattered letters, papers, haversacks, mess kits, entrenching tools and everywhere the dead. Hot weather makes all dead look alike, but these Italian dead lay with waxy grey faces in the cold rain looking very small and pitiful. They did not look like men, but where a shell burst caught three, like curiously broken toys. One doll had lost its feet and lay with no expression on its waxy stubbled face. Another doll had lost half of its head. The third doll was simply broken as a bar of chocolate breaks in your pocket.*[30]

While he was writing this dispatch in his hotel room, another artillery round crashed into the abandoned top floors of the Florida.

Ten days later, Ernest was with Ivens filming a tank and infantry attack at Morata outside of Madrid, and on April 9 the crew was forced out of its filming position by incoming shells at the very edge of the city.[31] Not since the night of July 8, 1918, when an Austrian trench mortar shell left him badly wounded on the Italian river, had he been this close to war. Then on April 26, while Ernest and Martha were touring the Republican front lines in the Guadarrama Mountains, miles away on the Basque coast Junker bombers piloted by the German Condor Legion killed or wounded a third of Guer-

nica's population while destroying much of the village. Neither the
first nor the last time civilians were indiscriminately bombed in this
war, Guernica would be the most remembered. Hemingway, who
tried to report only what he observed firsthand, never wrote about
Guernica, but on April 30, returning to Madrid he found the city

> late at night with the air still full of heavy granite dust and high
> explosive smoke, the sidewalks scattered by new round jagged holes
> with blood trails leading into half the doorways you passed.[32]

After twenty consecutive days of Nationalist shelling, three thousand
madrileños were wounded, 312 dead.

Sometimes with him on dangerous film locations, in the mountains, and always in Madrid, was the tallish blond woman who
looked like an angel to men in the trenches. Young, attractive, and
congenial, with a sense of humor, from the moment she arrived in
Madrid, Martha Gellhorn was very much with Hemingway. That is
how most of the journalists remembered her: an intelligent woman
who was not actually a journalist and who required much teaching.
Less attractive women remembered Martha's always fresh appearance, her Saks Fifth Avenue slacks, and her access to Hemingway's
largess. No one seems to have remembered that she had written
WPA essays, a novel, and a collection of short stories. She may never
have been to a war, but she was as professional a writer as anyone in
Madrid. If her credentials from Collier's were a favor, given with no
expectation that she would actually write for the magazine, the editor had no trouble printing her several essays from Spain. Less interested than Ernest in battlefield details and military strategy, Martha
focused on the effects of war on the wounded, the women, and the
villages, and on Madrid:

> Women are standing in line, as they do all over Madrid, quiet
> women, dressed usually in black, with market baskets on their arms,
> waiting to buy food. A shell falls across the square. They turn their
> heads to look, and move a little closer to the house, but no one leaves

her place in line. . . . An old woman, with a shawl over her shoulders,
holding a terrified thin little boy by the hand, runs out into the
square. . . . She is in the middle of the square when the next one falls.
A small piece of twisted steel, hot and very sharp, sprays off from the
shell; it takes the little boy by the throat. The old woman stands there,
holding the hand of the dead child, looking at him stupidly, not say-
ing anything.[33]

Having long admired and selectively employed Hemingway's style
before she ever met him, Martha was later said to be his creation,
which she resented as deeply as Ernest resented its being said that
he was Gertrude Stein's creation.

After two months of reporting the Spanish war for NANA, Ernest
returned to Paris, where café life in St. Germain seemed totally
unreal and absurd after the broken streets of Madrid. On May 11,
the *Tribune* announced that Ernest Hemingway and Stephen
Spender would give a public reading the following evening at Sylvia
Beach's Shakespeare and Company bookshop, Spender from his
poems, Hemingway from his unpublished novel. Reservations were
recommended.[34] That next evening, Ernest slipped into Sylvia's
place, gave her a hug, claimed he'd never read in public and would
not again, sat down at the small table with the pages of his Harry
Morgan manuscript, and said, "I don't know whether I can do this."
But he did, slowly at first, and in a slightly flat tone, but when he
reached the third chapter

his voice had lost the monotonous pitch, his mouth and half-moon
mustache twitched even more. He began to put expression into the
clean, terse phrases. . . . The picture of him which must have been
taken some twelve years ago, when he was twenty-seven and very
handsome, could be seen on the wall behind. He continued on about
Mr. Sing and the twelve Chinks.

When he stopped at the end of the fourth chapter and the
applause died down, James Joyce, "who had been sitting in the back

of the room got up and walked out," not waiting for Spender's reading.[35] Early the next morning, Ernest boarded the boat train to the coast, where the *Normandie* sailed that afternoon with his name at the head of the published passenger list.[36]

———

Morata was crowded and full of excitement. Several brigades have their headquarters there in the houses which remain standing. Besides the brigades there are a certain number of typhus germs in the neighborhood. Nearby is the front, and a little while ago there were plenty of Rebel airplanes flying over and dropping bombs very accurately. It is not a healthy place, and as a village it is no longer attractive to look at. Flies swarmed over the soldiers and camions in the main square. We asked about the road to the first-aid station: Was it safe? Well, who could say? It had been shelled off and on all morning, probably by mistake. The only way to know about it was to try.[37]

—Martha Gellhorn

———

When Pauline received Ernest's telegram that he is arriving in New York on May 18, she has been back from Mexico City almost a month. Every other day she wrote him wistful, chatty letters, feeding anxiously off his telegrams and rare responses. She wrote about money paid out and paid in, about children growing and friends drinking. They were lonely letters, trying to make jokes but sounding to herself dull and flat.[38] Probably she has not yet heard about the importance of Martha in her husband's life, but soon enough she will hear it from Katy Dos Passos, or Sara Murphy, or Josie Herbst, for too many people only one or two removes from Pauline also know about the affair. Around the perimeter of the Key West house, Pauline has Toby Bruce, chauffeur and handyman, building a brick wall to keep strangers out, or perhaps to keep family in.

What Pauline hoped for was an Ernest come home sated with the Spanish war and eager to return to Bimini for summer marlin, to Wyoming for fall hunting. But Pauline did not know how war can make once treasured routines seem ephemeral and dull. Having lived

with artillery rounds exploding in the Madrid streets, awakened to rifle
fire only two thousand yards away, and having heard machine-gun bul-
lets pinging off the armor plating of his transport in the Guadarrama
Mountains, Ernest has difficulty putting Spain away for the company
of the rich on Bimini.[39] Overweight from too much alcohol and too little exercise, Ernest returned to Pauline overcommitted and strangely
discontent: little things that once pleased him are now uninteresting.
Early morning of May 26, Ernest takes the *Pilar* out of Key West with
Toby Bruce and Josie Russell's wife on board bound for Bimini, where
Pauline, Ada, and the boys join them by plane via Miami.[40]

In New York, Joris Ivens is sweating out the final cuts of *The
Spanish Earth*, for which Ernest promised to create narration to
match the scenes. Martha, having returned separately from Ernest to
New York, is arranging with Eleanor Roosevelt for a White House
screening of the finished film sometime in July.[41] In their rented
house on Cat Cay, Ernest revises the thematic statement for the
Spanish film, worries over a speech he agreed to make at the Second
American Writers Conference, and struggles with final revisions to
his Key West–Havana novel, tentatively titled *To Have and Have Not*.
Gone is most of the Cuban revolution along with clear references to
John Dos Passos and Donald Ogden Stewart; on Arnold Gingrich's
advice, Hemingway removed from Helene Bradley's character many
of Jane Mason's more obvious characteristics. The once-planned
Matecumbe hurricane section was never written, and literary gossip
about Scott Fitzgerald, Harry Crosby, and Hart Crane is taken out.
Also excised is a fictional account of finding his father's dead body,
his head blown in and blood soaking the bed covers.[42] An entire
chapter with Tommy Bradley and Richard Gordon trying to transport
dynamite to the Cuban rebels is deleted, along with the details of
how Harry Morgan lost his arm. Reshuffling the remains, inserting
new bridges between disparate parts, Hemingway does his best to
counterpoint the "haves" (the very rich and the supercilious writers)
and "have nots" (working poor and displaced vets). With the typist's
version completed, he reads it over one final time, and then inserts
eight new pages culminating with Harry Morgan's dying words:

*"One man alone ain't got. No man alone now." He stopped. "No matter
how a man* alone *ain't got no bloody fucking chance."*

*He shut his eyes. It had taken him a long time to get it out and it
had taken him all of his life to learn it.*[43]

Leaving Pauline with their children in rented quarters on Cat Cay,
where screens were oiled to keep flies away, Ernest on June 4 flew
out of Bimini to attend the American Writers Congress on a puddle-
jumper flight with several stops, arriving in Newark barely in time for
him to reach Carnegie Hall at 10:00 p.m. to see an excerpt from *The
Spanish Earth* and to make his promised speech. When Hemingway
rose to the podium, he was greeted by thunderous applause from the
3,500 who jammed the hall for this, his first public political statement in defense of his craft. In hard, terse tones, he told them that
no true writer could live with fascism, for

*Fascism is a lie told by bullies. . . . it is condemned to literary sterility.
When it is past, it will have no history except the bloody history of
murder that is well known. . . . It is very dangerous to write the truth
in war, and the truth is also very dangerous to come by. . . . But there
is now and there will be from now on for a long time, war for any
writer to go to who wants to study it. It looks as though we are in for
many years of undeclared wars.*[44]

Writers on the stage with Ernest remembered him as nervous,
perspiring, and overweight, reading awkwardly from a loosely organized speech. The writer Dawn Powell, who knew most of the speak-
ers, including Hemingway, was able to view the evening through
comic glasses: "about ten thirty all the foreign correspondents
marched on each one with his private blonde led by Ernest and Miss
Gellhorn, who had been thru hell in Spain and came shivering on in
a silver fox chin-up." (How could she know the fur was a gift from
the Abraham Lincoln Brigade?) Dawn liked Ernest's speech, which
she said summed up "that war was pretty nice and a lot better than
sitting around a hot hall and writers ought to all go to war and get

killed and if they didn't they were a big sissy. Then he went over to the Stork Club, followed by a pack of foxes."[45] From young writer and friend Prudencio de Pereda's view from the balcony, Ernest appeared sleek and happy. "Yes, there was some awkwardness—both vocal and physical—but he faced and beat them both. . . . it was the speech of the meeting. The audience had come for Ernest; he was there for them. He lapped up the warm acceptance."[46] No matter where they were sitting, however, Hemingway's message was clear. Neutral, middle ground was no longer viable, no longer on the map; those who would not choose would be branded sympathetic to the cause they most resembled. Hemingway, after years of insisting upon his political disinterest, was now publicly committed to antifascism, if not to communism itself.

Two days later while flying back to Bimini, Hemingway worried about the Harry Morgan book as discussed with Max. One option which Max did not like was taking out the vets and the very rich, leaving only a shortened version of the Morgan stories as a novella followed by "The Snows of Kilimanjaro," "The Capital of the World," and "The Short Happy Life of Francis Macomber." Ernest now suggested giving the reader even more for his money, something new, a "living omnibus" of his writing: Harry Morgan, the three stories, "Who Murdered the Vets," several news dispatches reedited and revised if necessary, and his Carnegie Hall speech. For titles, he suggested *The Various Arms* or *Return to the Wars*. Promising a typescript by July 5, he confirmed that he was returning to Spain for the fall. Should anything happen to him, Scribner's could recoup its advance money with his collected short stories. When he returned, he promised, "I will write you a real novel. I wish I had the time to write it now. But after this fall will be better. I'll have the end of summer, fall and winter then in it. Have winter, spring and early summer now." Max, who seldom told Ernest no, was unenthused about mixing genres into an "omnibus."[47]

For ten Bimini days in June, Hemingway fished little and wrote late, trying to patch together the Morgan novel, finish the narrative for Ivens's film, and caption Spanish war photographs for a *Life* magazine special. On June 20, leaving Pauline angry, worried about his health and his behavior, he returned again to New York, this time for the Orson Welles recording of the narrative for *The Spanish Earth*. No sooner had he left than Pauline wrote him from Cat Cay to absolve his promise to return in four days and to encourage him to let the Morgan book rest before making any more revisions. For years his best critical reader, Pauline says the writing is wonderful, the substance perfect; it is the "form" that needs some thought. The next day, she again urges Ernest not to hurry home, closing with a curious admonition: Ernest should remember that tragedy comes from within, not from without, and he also should remember her without him "within limits." Martha Gellhorn is never mentioned, nor would she be, but in New York the affair is now a loosely kept secret.[48] If Pauline does not know about Martha, it is because she does not want to know.

When Ernest returned to Bimini, there is barely enough time to prepare for the July 8 White House screening of *The Spanish Earth*. He leaves again on July 6 and flies to New York, rendezvousing with Martha and flying with her and Joris Ivens south to Washington on July 8. As the three guests sit down to eat that evening with the President, Mrs. Roosevelt, and Harry Hopkins, the U.S. Navy in the western Pacific is about to give up the search for another of Eleanor's friends, the missing Amelia Earhart. While they are eating "rainwater soup followed by rubber squab, a nice wilted salad and a cake some admirer had sent in, an enthusiastic but unskilled admirer,"[49] Pauline was writing to Sara Murphy in Paris that she is leaving in two days to join Ernest when he and Joris take the film to Hollywood on a fundraising effort for the Republican cause. Ernest, she said, was returning to Spain in August.[50] At the White House, dressed in his formal dinner clothes and sweltering in the heat, Ernest noted Mrs. Roosevelt's unexpected height and deafness and the President's restricting paralysis. The visitors are all three delighted that both hosts want the film to be an even stronger statement for Loyalist Spain's condition. The following Sunday, July 11, Martha responded for the group, thanking Mrs. Roosevelt for her hospitality and apologizing for being so distracted during the evening, worrying about her two prodigies. The film, she promised, would be improved; the Orson Welles narration, which all found too theatrical, would be replaced at Ernest's expense.[51]

Afterwards when it is all over, you have a picture. You see it on the screen; you hear the noises and the music; and your own voice, that you've never heard before, comes back to you saying things you'd scribbled in the dark in the projection room or on pieces of paper in a hot hotel bedroom. But what you see in motion on the screen is not what you remember. . . . you remember how cold it was; how early you got up in the morning; how you were always so tired you could go to sleep at any time; how hard it was to get gasoline; and how we were always hungry. . . . Nothing of that shows on the screen except the cold when you can see the men's breath in the air.[52]

—Ernest Hemingway

In Spain, Republican losses, including three of Hemingway's friends, mounted over the summer of 1937, and in America, personal losses were also mounting. Hemingway's behavior with old friends was erratic, combative, sometimes intolerable. Before he returned to the Spanish war in mid-August, his relationship with Archie MacLeish was once again strained, this time over the production of the Joris film, and his relationship with John Dos Passos was ruined beyond repair.

During the previous spring in Spain, Dos Passos sought in vain to find out what had happened to José Robles, his friend and translator of his books. Hemingway urged Dos to give up his inquiry because he would bring suspicion down on all of them. Josephine Herbst, having learned from a ministry source that Robles had been executed, told Hemingway, who finally confirmed what Dos Passos had heard rumored: his friend had been executed for treason. It was not Hemingway's information that so irritated Dos Passos, but the manner of his imparting it: too knowing, too officious, too ready to accept

Robles as a traitor to the Republic. Dos Passos also had no stomach for Hemingway's ability to accept whatever the leftist factions did as necessary for the war effort. When Ernest warned John that he should not write about the Robles affair, Dos said he would only write the truth about Spain when he knew what that was. Five months later in New York, there was an acrimonious evening in the Murphy penthouse apartment, Hemingway's sarcasm clouding the air and Dos Passos walking out.[53]

In December 1937, Dos Passos published in *Common Sense* an essay, "The Communist Party and the War Spirit: A Letter to a Friend Who Is Probably a Party Member," written to former friends whose too ready acceptance of Stalinist methods in Spain Dos Passos could not accept. In March 1938, Hemingway sent Dos Passos one of his most scathing letters, accusing him of attacking for money those he once supported, of not having his facts straight, of not being able to tell the difference between a Russian and a Pole, and of not telling the truth. Ernest suggested that if Dos ever made any real money, he might repay some of the several loans made to him over the years. "Always happy with the good old friends," he said. "Got them that will knife you in the back for a dime. Regular price two for a quarter. Two for a quarter, hell. Honest Jack Dos Possos'll knife you three times in the back for fifteen cents."[54] After all the Paris nights and Key West days, after Havana and Pamplona together, after all the shared meals and friendships, it was over between these two, leaving them only their future journalism and fictions to denigrate each other.

By August 10, 1937, Hemingway is back in New York with Martha Gellhorn, preparing to return to Spain. Pauline, once again convinced that Spain is too dangerous for her to accompany Ernest, prepares in Key West to take nine-year-old Patrick and teenager Jack Hemingway to a Mexican bull ranch with Sidney Franklin as guide and dubious father figure. Gregory, approaching his sixth birthday, is going once again to Syracuse with his surrogate mother, Ada Stern.

Other than his growing need for Martha and the difficulties inherent in a duplicitous life, there is no pressing reason for Hemingway to return to Spain. With *To Have and Have Not* already galley-proofed and set for October 15 publication as a novel, and Scribner's ready to talk about his collected short stories, he does not need the NANA money, and his marriage is already severely stressed. He writes explaining the situation to his mother-in-law, who suggested rather pointedly that he might spend more time looking after his sons. He tells her in twisted syntax that he "promised them I would be back and while we cannot keep all our promises I do not see how not to keep that one. I would not be able to teach my boys much if I did." Mary Pfeiffer's charge that his extended absences were hard on Greg and Pat led him into an even more awkward defense:

> After the first two weeks in Madrid had an impersonal feeling of haveing no wife, no children, no house, no boat, nothing. The only way to function. But now have been home just long enough to lose it all; to value all the things again; and now go back knowing I have to put them all away again. So don't point out how much harder it is on them because have a little imagination too.[55]

Mary Pfeiffer, already worried about her daughter's marriage, is not reassured by Ernest's nostalgia for a life without responsibilities, nor with his fractured logic. She is also picking up mixed signals from her daughter, Jinny, who knows more gossip about Ernest's extramarital life than any sister-in-law should know.

High-strung and emotionally erratic, Ernest is in New York long enough to provoke a silly fight in Perkins's office with Max Eastman, whose jaw Hemingway once promised to break after Eastman's review of *Death in the Afternoon* seemed to question Ernest's virility. Hemingway, stirring up that old disagreement, exposes his hairy chest before blows are exchanged. Gossips pick up the fracas, then newspapers and finally magazines until it reaches mock-epic stature.[56] As *The New Yorker* finally put it,

> There was no very good way of telling who won the fight in the Scrib-ner office because one man said one thing and the other man said something different and the one man who wasn't in the fight [Perkins]

*hadn't much to say about it perhaps because he wasn't a writer himself
and therefore not especially interested in the dramatic life.*[57]

On August 14, Ernest left on the *Champlain* for Cherbourg,
reaching Paris on the 21st. Martha, traveling for propriety's sake on
the *Normandie*, arrived a day later in Havre, joining him on the 23rd
in Paris at the Hotel Foyot, where Ernest was reading page proofs for
Jonathan Cape's British edition of *To Have and Have Not*,[58] and
replenishing his various accounts at the Guaranty Trust: $3,000 into
a new dollar account; one hundred pounds from Cape; and thirteen
thousand francs into another account. Complaining of what he diag-
noses as liver problems and insomnia, he also visited Dr. Robert Wallach, who advised him to stop eating eggs and rich sauces, to cut his
drinking by half, to take two doses of Drainochol, morning and night,
to improve his liver functions and one Belladenal Sandoz tablet at
night to help him sleep.[59]

If Hemingway reduced his drinking that fall in Spain, none of his
fellow journalists noted it, nor did they remember ever refusing a
swig from his battered silver flask that seemed miraculously to refill
itself. Not that there was much to celebrate if you leaned left in this
messy war, for the summer was one disaster after another for the
Republican government. After the fall of Bilbao and the Basque
provinces to Franco's forces in early July, the Republic was internally
torn by communist purges of splinter groups in Spain and by whole-
sale Stalinist purges of the Russian military at home. Many of the
best Russian field tacticians, on loan to the Republic, were called
back to Moscow, never to reappear. In midsummer, Republican
forces began an offensive to take the pressure off Madrid; the attack
drove a wedge into rebel lines at Brunete but with terrible losses and
stopping short of its objective. Meanwhile Franco's force overran the
defenses of Santander, taking the port and encircling large numbers
of its Basque defenders, who were forced to surrender. Rebel armies
now controlled the entire Atlantic coast and the middle of Spain; if
they could drive a corridor through to the Mediterranean coast, they
would be able to split what remained of the Republic in two.

‗‗‗

Now we learned to know the wounded, the various ways of broken flesh, the limbs sliced off clean and left whole on the ground, or blown into a red pulp stuck with white fragments of bone and still hanging by throbbing veins to living bodies. We saw bared flesh splashed with a crimson wash mixed from the wound-spoutings of half a dozen men; we saw jerking limb-stumps with the blood gushing from them bright and sparkling in the sunshine; we learned the shape and color of spilled entrails palpitating amongst rags of torn underwear; we learned the faces of men dying and not knowing it, greenish, livid, with impersonal, gaping mouths.[60]

—John Sommerfield, 1937

‗‗‗

En route to Madrid, Ernest and Martha stopped first in Valencia, where they traveled out by car to survey the aftermath of the Republican offensive along the Aragon front, talking to the brigades who fought the bloody battles at Quinto and Belchite. Hemingway's dispatch, filled with precise details and close analysis, included a brief reference to Robert Merriman, who,

> a former California history professor and now chief of staff of the 15th brigades, was a leader in the final assault [on Belchite]. Unshaven, his face smoke blackened, his men tell how he bombed his way forward, wounded six times slightly by hand-grenade splinters in the hands and face, but refusing to have his wounds dressed until the cathedral was taken.[61]

Having the luxury of sending in typed stories rather than foreshortened cables or telephone reports like Ernest, Martha's version of this same encounter with Merriman was more detailed. Dusty, tall, shy, and a little stiff, Merriman explained the offensive to them,

> drawing the plan of it on the dirt of the floor, going over every point carefully as if it were his freshman class in economics back in California. Forty kilometers march . . . Quinto encircled . . . Belchite sur-

rounded . . . then the fighting in the town itself, from house to house,
cutting through the walls and bombing their way forward with hand
grenades . . . rushing the cathedral where rebel machine gunners held
out to the last . . . the dead piled eight feet deep in the streets. . . . "The
boys did well," Merriman said.[62]

Using details from the briefing without attributing them, Hemingway carefully studied Merriman, who would not survive the war but
whose presence would be recognized in Ernest's next novel.

From Valencia, Hemingway and Gellhorn continued on to
Madrid, returning to the war zone old hands at the game. Their
rooms on the second floor of the Hotel Florida[63] were amply stocked
with basics—corned beef, cheese, coffee, soups, tamales, and
chocolate bars brought with them from Paris—and with extraordinary tinned treats sent in by Sara Murphy: *poulet rôti, confit d'oie,*
jambon, saumon, boeuf aux haricots, tripe à la mode de Caen, and 3
Kraft Welsh rabbit.[64] For two and a half months in Madrid there was
sufficient food but little to report. Between September 23 and
December 19, Hemingway filed only two NANA dispatches, one of
which NANA variously headlined as "Madrid Front Is Quiet" and
"Life Goes On in Madrid."[65] Pauline heard from him barely at all—
occasional cables, a few letters. Increasingly it would seem that his
inviolable promise to return to the war was made more to Martha
than to any Loyalist cause. On October 15, when the New York critics began to dissect *To Have and Have Not,* Hemingway was happily
writing in Madrid with a sign on his hotel door—Working, Do Not
Disturb—which became the working title of his play in progress.[66]

Since writing a parody and a farce in his Oak Park high school
days, Hemingway, like many novelists of his generation, always
wanted to write a play.[67] His manuscript trunk in Key West held several outlines, fragments, and opening scenes for plays which never
matured.[68] Now in Madrid, living through the siege of the city and
having picked up various stories about Falangist spies, some caught
and executed, he began a play about a counterspy, Philip Rawlings,
and his tall, blonde lover, Dorothy Bridges. Rawlings appears to oth-

ers as a comic, brawling man who drinks too much. Nothing serious, as the Spanish might say. Posing as a journalist to cover his dangerous shadow life, he spends his nights in counterespionage trapping Madrid's fifth columnists. A modern Scarlet Pimpernel, Rawlings is the product of Hemingway's lifelong fascination with spies, revolutionists, and guerrilla warfare. In recent years, he has read, for example, everything he can find about T. E. Lawrence (of Arabia)—his two books on the desert war, his published letters, and several biographies.[69]

With Martha in the room adjoining his own (113/114) and the fictional Dorothy Bridges sleeping in the room adjoining Philip's (109/110), the drama was developing on two levels—public and private. He was not Philip Rawlings, counterspy living some wonderfully dangerous life, and Martha was not Dorothy. In fact, the real action of the drama needed no Dorothy. She was there because between the lines Hemingway was using the play to work out his own sexual dilemma. In a discarded fragment, he wrote that Dorothy caused Philip's problem by wanting to marry him. Had she remained a contented mistress, Philip could return all the more loving and tender to his wife for having been unfaithful to her. Of course Dorothy had not intended to marry him, and was quite distressed when she found that she was fated to do so.[70] In the introduction for the published version, Hemingway said that if the play "has a moral it is that people who work for certain organizations have very little time for home life. There is a girl in it named Dorothy but her name might also have been Nostalgia."[71] How else explain to Pauline the beautiful blonde in Rawlings's life when Philip looked so much like Ernest? But what was Martha to make of her pale shadow, who was so compliant, dependent, and ornamental? How to explain Rawlings's analysis of Dorothy's character: "Granted she's lazy and spoiled, and rather stupid, and enormously on the make. Still she's very beautiful, very friendly, and very charming and rather innocent—and quite brave."[72]

Wanting it both ways and neither, wanting a mistress and a wife, wanting a home but not wanting to be home, Ernest wanted both women, both worlds, in much the same way that he once kidded

Scott Fitzgerald about his, Ernest's, idea of heaven, which would be having

> *two lovely houses in the town; one where I would have my wife and children and be monogamous and love them truly and well and the other where I would have my nine beautiful mistresses on 9 different floors . . . there would be a fine church like in Pamplona where I could go and be confessed on the way from one house to the other.*[73]

Now, in the hotel room, the occasional incoming round rocking the Florida, Hemingway's counterspy completes his dangerous mission, resulting in the arrests of hundreds of fifth columnists. Exposed as a counterspy by the arrests, Philip Rawlings must transfer out of Madrid for the good of the "cause." "We're in for fifty years of undeclared wars," he says prophetically, "and I've signed up for the duration." Dorothy, still without a clue to his late-night life, begs him to go with her to St. Tropez or St. Moritz. Philip tells her she must follow the soft life on her own. "Where I go now I go alone," he says, "or with others who go there for the same reason."[74]

With the curtain coming down on *The Fifth Column*, as the play was eventually titled, Hemingway's painted portrait was appearing on the cover of *Time* magazine, which ran a lengthy retrospective of his life and work while reviewing *To Have and Have Not*. Warning its readers that this novel, with twelve gory killings, "all the four-letter words extant," as well as scenes of copulation and masturbation, would offend the "strait-laced," *Time* called Harry Morgan the author's "most thoroughly consistent, deeply understandable character." Following a long synopsis of the novel, the review concluded that those who had written Hemingway off as a has-been were premature, for this novel reaffirmed his place in the front rank of American writers.[75]

Other reviews were divided among those who could not stand a proletarian Hemingway at any price, those who were offended by Morgan's "no fucking good," those who loved the action, the many who boggled over the fragmented telling of the story, and those who loved the politics. Sinclair Lewis begged the writer, "Please quit sav-

ing Spain and start saving Ernest Hemingway." *The Nation* percep-
tively saw the novel as "a transition to the kind of book that Hemingway will write in the future." Malcolm Cowley, who blew hot and
cold over Ernest's work, now believed him "just beginning a new
career." *New Masses* hailed Hemingway's "increasing awareness of
the economic system and the social order it dominates." Impressed
or distressed by *To Have and Have Not*, no reviewer ignored it. Riding
the wave, the book was reprinted twice in October and once in
November, selling 38,000 copies in five months, a depression-era
best-seller.[76]

———

Paris burned with a million lights last night—in the cafés of its
boulevards, on the altars of its churches, in the eyes of its excited
children. . . . If anybody got to sleep before dawn, he must have
been someone far out in the suburbs, well away from the nightclub districts, away from the chimes bells of the churches, the
bedlam of shouts and songs from the bistros and brasserieres. It
was a Paris Christmas Eve.[77]

—Eric Sevareid, 1937

———

On December 20, two Atlantic liners passing in the night—
Pauline inbound for France on the *Europa*, Martha homeward bound
on the *Normandie*—bring the distressed wife to Paris and return the
lonesome lover to America while Ernest remains in Spain.[78] On
December 21, Pauline's boat train arrives in Paris during a snowstorm that blankets the city for Christmas; at Teruel, Spain, where a
five-day blizzard has left troops frozen in their slit trenches, her husband watches Loyalists attack through the snow, taking the city:

*All day long we moved forward with the steady merciless advance the
Government troops were making. Up the hillsides, across the railway,
capturing the tunnel, all up and over the Mansueto, down the road
around the bend from kilometer two and finally up the last slopes to
the town whose seven church steeples and neatly geometrical houses
showed sharp against the setting sun.*

When he wires the story from Barcelona, Hemingway asks his NANA editor to "cable my wife now Paris waiting me Christmas there correspondents credentials . . . enabling her procure visa pro-join me here Christmas rush."[79]

In November, Katy Dos Passos said that Pauline "seemed worried about Ernest, and no wonder—she was very cute and nervy, I thought—but couldn't sleep."[80] By the time Pauline was sitting alone in the Paris Hotel Elysée Park, mistakenly certain Ernest was Christ-masing with Martha, "nervy" was no longer an apt description. "Angry" and "hurt" were closer to the mark. When Ernest finally arrived in Paris, frazzled from days of exposure to near-zero cold in the taking of Teruel, Pauline exploded. Bill Bird, an old Paris friend from the earliest days, called at their expensive Right Bank hotel, to find them as dark and gloomy as the Paris weather.[81]

Ernest and Pauline remained in Paris for twelve days into the new year, quietly meeting a few friends, arranging for foreign translations of *To Have and Have Not*, buying books, and tending to Ernest's list of physical complaints. He returned to Dr. Wallach, who prescribed more homeopathic medicines for insomnia and liver problems.[82] On January 12, they left France and crossed the channel to Southhamp-ton, where they picked up the *Gripsholm* on its way to New York. There were more convenient liners leaving from French ports, but the *Gripsholm* offered a single advantage: before reaching New York, it stopped in Nassau. Earlier, Pauline had suggested that Ernest come back through Cuba to avoid New York publicity. Now, with their relationship in conflict, neither wanted to answer reporters' questions.[83] Their storm-tossed Atlantic crossing triggered Pauline's usual seasickness, temporarily taking her mind off marital problems. When the *Gripsholm* arrived in Nassau, the couple disembarked and caught the Pan Am flight to Miami, where Pauline flew on to Key West and Ernest picked up the *Pilar*, arriving at No Name Key the evening of January 28. Pauline met him with their car, taking him home to Key West, where he had been less than three weeks out of the previous thirteen months.[84]

On edge and ill-humored, Ernest found it difficult to be enthusiastic about the brick wall around their property or the excavations for the newly begun swimming pool he once wanted. Part of him was with Martha, another part brooding over the Spanish war, in which Teruel was lost, retaken, and lost again. Domesticity, with its confusion of unanswered mail, competing children, squalling peacocks, and local gentry, was small beer after the shelling of Madrid and the fierce slopes of Teruel. In a black mood with his paranoia rising, Ernest was like a decommissioned combat veteran still possessive of the war, angry with NANA for cutting his dispatches short, and furious with the *New York Times* for crediting Matthews as the only journalist in Teruel. Still brooding over the way the *Times* had reported his fight with Max Eastman and "completely sabotaged" his journalism, he railed against critics ganging up against *To Have and Have Not*. For the Key West reporter, he put on a different, slightly false face:

> *Expressing concern at the local criticism of his latest novel, "To Have and Have Not," Mr. Hemingway regretted that this is so and said, "I am delighted to be back in Key West. It is my home and where my family is. My best friends are here. No one has more admiration for the town, and appreciation of its people, their friendliness, the fine life and wonderful fishing here than I have."*[85]

That same day he wrote his former wife, Hadley, he did not give "a good goddamn" about anything, but was not suicidal. Someone else would have to shoot him.[86]

While he was writing Hadley, Martha Gellhorn, on a national speaking tour, was telling Hemingway's mother and other members of Oak Park's Nineteenth Century Club about the history of the Spanish war, its effects on civilians, and the need for all to oppose fascism:

> *With a short black dress setting off her taffy-colored hair hanging childishly about her face in a long bob, Miss Gellhorn looked sixteen but spoke in a luscious, deep, free flowing voice with words of maturity and an emphasis of authority.*[87]

Ernest read the newspaper account sent to him by his mother, who noted in the margin how happy she was to meet Martha: "She knows Ursula [one of his sisters] and you."[88] His mother could not see him there on the shaded side porch, reading the newspaper account and remembering the softness of that taffy hair, nor could she know how very well he did know Martha.

Chapter Eleven

1938 – 39

A PIECE OF THE CONTINENT

Paris, Barcelona, Madrid, Key West, Havana

T HE SEASON'S SHIFT is so mild on the island, winter blooming so lovely, Key Westers hardly notice the early changes of spring. On Whitehead Street, however, where the surface of the southernmost swimming pool in North America shimmers in the sun, a pair of pet raccoons, three pairs of peacocks and hens, two small boys, five employees, and a hurt wife are aware that the house has changed, its moody master sometimes wretched, frequently indifferent. In the coral basement, once dug out to provide building blocks for the old house, two French racing bicycles are rusting in the tropical climate. Their india-rubber tires, flattened from disuse, are melting into the stone floor. On these same bikes Ernest and Pauline, honeymooners at Grau-du-Roi, once traveled the dirt roads of the French Camargue, once pedaled together on Paris streets. To reach the racks of wine, Ernest must now step carefully past the bikes in the dimly lit cellar.[1]

Across the Atlantic, on the bare hills and plains of Spain, spring comes much later, but the war has never stopped; outsupplied, the Republic entered the third year of battle with its ravaged brigades short of men, its air force in disrepair. On February 21, Teruel was retaken for the last time by Franco's forces. Two weeks later his offensive in Aragon began the push to the Mediterranean to split what was left of the Republic in two. Lightly opposed Italian planes from the Balearic Islands were regularly dropping bombs on the civilians of Barcelona. On March 29, Hemingway and Martha return to Paris en route to Spain. That morning, he telephones the American ambassador, Claude Bowers, concerning the need for an evacuation plan for Americans in Spain should the Republican government suddenly collapse. He and Edgar Mowrer (Paul's brother on the *Chicago News*) are raising money for emergency medical help in Marseilles for those too badly wounded to move further, but the United States must be ready to send ships into Spanish ports to evacuate American medical teams and wounded who, if captured by Franco's troops, will be executed. The ambassador thinks enough of their concern to forward the plan to Washington.[2]

Two days later, at Gare d'Orsay in Paris, war correspondents Hemingway, Vincent Sheean, and young Jim Lardner (humorist Ring Lardner's son) await the night train for Perpignan on the Spanish border. Martha Gellhorn may or may not be with them, for in the memoirs of various reporters she sometimes disappears out of deference to Hemingway's marriage. On Sheean's train she is not there in the compartment with the men sharing whiskey from Ernest's silver flask. Nor does Sheean remember her sitting beside Hemingway during the Barcelona showing of *The Spanish Earth* when the "film was stopped in the middle by an air raid and we sat in the theater for about an hour until the alarm ended."[3] But in Martha's letter to Eleanor Roosevelt, dated Barcelona, April 24, she has been in the city as long as Sheean and Hemingway, has covered the Loyalist retreat in the first week of April, and tells of seeing *The Spanish Earth* again. (Martha says they were five minutes into the movie when the air raid siren sounded.) When Nationalist forces broke through the Republican defenses to reach the sea, Hemingway and Sheean are with Herb Matthews in his recollection, but Martha is invisible. Yet how clearly she is able to describe to Mrs. Roosevelt the twelve black German bombers followed by the same silver Italian planes bombing Tortosa that Matthews describes along the same road Hemingway speaks of in his April 5 dispatch datelined Tortosa.[4] Male memory or good manners not withstanding, Martha is there with Hemingway all that April and May when he appends to his cable dispatches love to his family in Key West.

Later, trying to clarify what happened in Spain, Martha said,

> *There was plenty wrong with Hemingway but nothing wrong with his honest commitment to the Republic of Spain and nothing wrong with his admiration and care for men in the Brigades and in the Spanish Divisions and nothing wrong with his respect for the Spanish people. He proved it by his actions.*[5]

His coolness under fire, his humor and generosity, and his skills at living in another country make him a boon companion in the fields of war and at the bar afterward. That they are lovers is not as important to Martha as that they are friends. That she respects his writing is clear from the start; that he is possessive of her is equally clear to all who saw them together in Spain; that she, a woman who insisted on her independence, allowed that possessiveness is part of an old story: Ernest got what he wanted.[6] That he was not as idealistic about the needs of mankind as she, or as dismayed at the stupidity of politicians, or as committed to social justice, was not so obvious in those early days of commitment to a single cause.

Hemingway's third trip to the Spanish war was a less happy relationship with his employer, North American News Alliance. No sooner were he and Martha in the field with Herb Matthews and young photographer Robert Capa than NANA requested that he separate himself from *New York Times* correspondent Matthews so their stories would not overlap. Hemingway was furious. A Jesuit plot, he called it, certain that Catholics at the *Times* resented his pro-Nationalist point of view. In mid-April, NANA wired him "suggesting future stories emphasize color rather than straight reporting." A few days later they asked him to "restrict cables to vitally important developments until further notice."[7] Having taken risks beyond those expected of a correspondent, exposing himself to artillery, rifle fire, and strafing, Ernest was understandably piqued, for he had given the news agency what it asked for: stories at once personal and timely, accurate and detailed, stories that take the reader onto the killing ground. Six weeks later, back in Key West and settling accounts with NANA, Hemingway told John Wheeler, his NANA employer, "My stuff on Spain has been consistently accurate. . . . I gave full accounts of government disasters and criticized their weaknesses in [the] same measure I reported their success."[8]

Hemingway vented his anger in a series of essays for Arnold Gingrich's new magazine, *Ken*, which allowed him to be more openly political than Wheeler would allow. On April 7, the first issue of *Ken* appeared with Hemingway's essay "The Time Now, The Place Spain." Writing for what he still considered paltry pay ($200 per essay), Hemingway was personal and direct, telling his reader a truth that was becoming obvious to many journalists: the world's democracies must defeat the fascists in Spain or eventually fight Hitler and Mussolini across Europe. U.S. State Department bureaucrats and British Foreign Office diplomats with their neutrality nonsense and appeasement policies would have much to answer for when the main feature began.[9]

Pear trees were candelabraed along the grey walls where picks had opened holes for snipers. Trenches angled through kitchen gardens full of peas, beans, cauliflower and cabbage. Poppies were bright in the green wheat between the almond trees, and the bare grey white hills of Madrid seemed far away. Then a soldier peering through the wall fired twice and you saw his cheek punched back from the kick of the long-stocked ugly Mauser. . . . Through a gap in the wall you saw with the field glasses the cone-shaped muzzle of a light machine gun looking at you through a little break in the garden fence less than a hundred yards away.[10]

—Ernest Hemingway, April 29, 1938

When Ernest and Martha came out of Spain on May 16, the war zones had stabilized, and he was still predicting that Franco's fascist rebellion would be defeated by the Republic. The lovers lingered several spring days in Paris before Ernest took the *Normandie* back to New York.[11] On May 31, Pauline was waiting at the Key West airport when Ernest's flight from Miami landed, bringing him back for the third time from Spain unscathed. Angry with her husband for his continuing affair with Martha, but not wanting to begin their reunion with an argument, she brought Patrick, Gregory, and Toby Bruce with her, hoping for a quiet homecoming.

Five minutes after he lands, Hemingway's Ford convertible with its smashed fender is centered in the intersection of Simonton and United streets; WPA worker Samuel Smart's jalopy, having been knocked across the intersection into the curb, has turned over and skidded another ten feet. Hemingway and Smart are standing toe to toe in middle of the street shouting at each other. Toby is measuring the skid marks when police officer John Nelson arrives. Unable to settle the argument, Nelson arrests both men and takes them to Police Court, where Judge Caro hears the evidence.

Facing a judge for the first time since a teenage game law violation up in Michigan, Ernest is concerned enough to have his lawyer Georgie Brooks, so roundly satirized as the shyster Bee-lips in *To Have and Have Not*, in court with him, hugely enjoying Ernest's discomfort.

Young Patrick Hemingway, Hemingway's son, testified and said his dad was going 15 miles an hour. How did he know that? He looked at the speedometer. Attorney George Brooks tried to make the child realize that the testimony was important and began with "You go to Sunday School, don't you?" but Mr. Hemingway stepped in with "No, No!"

Unable to fix blame, Judge Caro finally dismisses the case as being too minor to prosecute either way. Smart, glaring at Hemingway, demands damages, over which Caro says Police Court has no jurisdiction. Hemingway snaps, "I will not pay damages. I'll counter suit any suit he brings up. I was struck." The next day while being interviewed about the Spanish war, Hemingway says, with humorous exaggeration:

> It's much more dangerous to be in Key West and have an old jalopy without brakes crash into you than it is to be under heavy fire from airplane bombs, artillery fire, and machine guns, as I was 24 hours a day.[12]

Two weeks later, Hemingway purchases a new eight-cylinder Buick convertible. After ten years of Fords, he is moving up to a heavier car.[13]

Neither the accident nor Ernest's reaction to it is particularly amusing to Pauline, whose tolerance for her husband's explosive behavior is wearing thin. In Key West, because Ernest was so frequently someplace else, their friends—J. B. Sullivan, the Thompsons, the Cates—when forced to choose in the Hemingway marital arguments, support Pauline, who is now ready to take Jinny's advice: be tough. To the new friends of Pauline's who are strangers to Ernest, there is no question that he is acting like a son of a bitch. This time back from Spain, Ernest's only loyal support comes from Josie Russell. At home, he and Pauline snipe at each other over little irritations, and he retreats to his writing room, where a story set in war-torn Madrid is taking shape. Begun in Paris before his return, "The Denunciation" is a story of friendship and betrayal in Loyalist Madrid: the writer-narrator Henry Emmunds tells of assisting a Chicote's bar waiter in "denouncing" an old friend turned fascist to government security. Following as it did hard on the heels of Hemingway's own denunciation of John Dos Passos in a *Ken* essay, "Treachery in Aragon," the story is ambivalent.

From the old days before the war, both Emmunds and the waiter know Luis Delgado, a fascist who has inexplicably shown his face at

Chicote's bar where he is most likely to be recognized and arrested. Emmunds only supplies security's phone number to the waiter, who makes the call. Delgado, having taken a foolish and unnecessary risk, is arrested and will be shot. The waiter feels guilty for denouncing an old client of Chicote's. The writer, who says he does not want the fascist aviator to die thinking a Chicote waiter betrayed him, asks his friend Pepe at security to tell Delgado that he, Emmunds, made the phone call. In Key West, where old friends are speaking to Ernest in guarded tones and where he is something of a stranger in his own house, "The Denunciation" cuts several ways at once. Dos Passos's friend Robles was denounced and shot by Loyalist security; Ernest has denounced Dos Passos for betraying the Loyalist cause; and Jinny Pfeiffer is denouncing him to Pauline for betraying their marriage. Even at Sloppy Joe's, old customers are looking at Ernest in a different way, for a number of them were recognizable characters in *To Have and Have Not.*[14]

In the summer heat of Key West, with a thousand tourists a week streaming in from Miami over the newly completed highway bridges, Hemingway isolates himself in his writing room, which now has a window air conditioner. Edgy and unpredictable, in public and on paper he is abrasive. He wants to write an exposé of the *New York Times* Catholic bias which he feels ruined and restricted his NANA dispatches.[15] He argues in long, redundant letters with Max Perkins about the fall publication of his collected short stories. (He wants "Up in Michigan" included; Max wants the story's sexuality toned down. He wants *The Fifth Column* to lead off the collection; Max has serious doubts.)[16] Then the question of who owes whom how much for *The Spanish Earth* puts him into a seething rage. Quick to misunderstand and take offense, Hemingway thinks that Archie MacLeish is somehow cheating him out of money spent on the film; detailing his expenses in long letters, some of which are never mailed, he warns Archie:

You can make me out something better than average vile when I am not around. But when I am around Mac you will keep your long

*Scotch mouth shut and if you want another nice friendly suggestion:
try to keep your nose clean too about other people's affairs.*[17]

Almost deliberately, he seems bent on alienating his friends and his family. What once gave him pleasure, like fishing on the *Pilar*, has temporarily lost its appeal. When not writing, he turns to the Blue Goose arena, where he referees semiprofessional boxing matches and spends afternoons training Mario Perez for his next local fight. Mario, who was knocked down nine times in his last fight, needs all the help he can get. Hemingway, the paper reports, was once an amateur boxing champion, a new twist to the fictive life he sometimes creates in humorous moments, sometimes defensively when depressed. That the foremost male writer in America needs to retail such fictions says nothing good about the state of his mind.[18]

On Whitehead Street, tension sits at the table like some uninvited guest, refusing to leave. Arguments, over anything but Martha, are daily fare, and the evening meal a battleground. Once he finishes arranging stories for a collection to be called *The Fifth Column and the First Forty-nine Stories*, Ernest pulls out of Key West with Josie Russell to fish in Cuba while avoiding the throng gathering to celebrate the formal opening of the Overseas Highway. Pauline, keeping up public appearances, plans a costume party at the Havana-Madrid club, only to have Ernest return early, angry, refusing to go to the party. The argument heats up when he cannot find the key to his locked writing room. Charles and Lorine Thompson arrived at the house as the argument peaked. "He was like a crazy man," Lorine said later. "Waving the pistol around. I didn't know what he was going to do." Suddenly, while Pauline reasons with him, he fires the pistol at the ceiling, then shoots the lock off his writing-room door, slamming it behind him. Pauline and the Thompsons send Ada with the children to the Thompson house for the night while they go on to the party. Later in the evening, Ernest appears at the club and gets in a brawl with a drunken guest, ruining Pauline's evening, not to speak of humiliating her in public.[19]

Beneath the surly surface of their clearly cratering marriage is always, unspoken, Ernest's affair with Martha, about which most of his friends are by now aware and unsupportive. On July 22, an unsigned wire from Europe arrives in Key West:

> *Arrive Cherbourg twenty-eight auto Aquitania April first Colliers okay if anything ever stops our working together then future nix.*[20]

Half-coded by Martha from England, where she was on assignment for *Collier's* after doing a feature on the plight of the Czechs, it was a dangerous telegram to send to Whitehead Street: she was taking the *Aquitania* to New York; her *Collier's* feature on besieged Madrid, "City at War," was "okay"; and if anything came between herself and Ernest, "then future nix."

Despite the public and private arguments of the summer, Pauline refused to give up on her marriage. Shortly after their birthdays (she forty-three, he thirty-nine), she made her to-do list for another cross-country drive to the L-Bar-T ranch in Wyoming: pack "Papa's western gear," two rifles, three shotguns, one pistol, and four different sizes of ammunition; have the new Buick road-checked; fix the cork for the water jug.[21] They got no farther than West Palm Beach when Gregory, who is going once again to Syracuse with Ada for the summer, accidentally scratched the pupil of Ernest's eye, forcing a stop in the George Washington Hotel.[22] Two days later, wearing an eye patch and dark glasses, Ernest and family are back on the road, his attitude unimproved by the incident. Patrick, too young to understand but old enough to remember, listens in the backseat as his parents argue and pick at each other across the country.[23] They arrive at the L-Bar-T with rain falling steadily, which keeps them cabin-bound for the next week.

They came to the ranch planning to remain through the fall hunting season, but the world intrudes. By August 18, Ernest, at NANA's request, is planning to leave Pauline at the L-Bar-T to make her own way to New York while he goes to France, where it appears that Hitler is about to start the next great war. By the inexplicable chemistry that can temporarily smooth out a troubled marriage, Pauline agrees to his leaving. He promises that he won't engage in combat; she is excited about spending two months in a New York apartment waiting for his return. Explaining his behavior to his mother-in-law, he says that he could not have run his life any worse than he has, admits to being intolerant, righteous, and many times ruthless and cruel; he needs the Catholic Church's discipline, but has not been able to accept it when the Church supports Franco. Without speaking of his marital difficulties, he tells Mary Pfeiffer that Toby Bruce will pick up Pauline and the boys, driving them back to Piggott.[24] He tells neither his wife nor his mother-in-law that he plans to dedicate his collection of stories to Herbert Matthews and Martha Gellhorn.[25]

———

August 14, Paris. Martha is back from Corsica, where she went for writing peace (but there was no peace, only a man drowning on the beach). Sitting at the writing desk in her small rented room, she tells Mrs. Roosevelt how strangely cool she finds Paris in August, the waiters kinder, the trees so lovely in the Bois de Boulogne. On the dead-end street not far from the Arc de Triomphe, she spends quiet summer days working on her fiction. Along the French border, the German army's summer games pump up rumors of a war to begin before the end of September. Should Hitler, who is mad enough to do it, bomb Paris, she tells Eleanor, then mankind deserves to be doomed. Hemingway's name is unspoken, for now that they are separated lovers, she must be circumspect.[26]

———

On August 31, the *Normandie* leaves New York with Ernest on board, he having sent Pauline two wires with the promise of a thirteen-page letter and Evelyn Waugh's new book, *Scoop*. At the Nordquist ranch, Pauline writes long letters filled with the boys catching trout, the wounded baby owl eating mice, and her missing him deeply. After being berated by Ernest in front of Key West guests, humiliated by him at her costume party, and arguing with him cross-country, she is now writing him loving letters. Whatever was agreed upon between them, Pauline says she is serene about their future together. By September 6, Ernest is in Paris, rejoined with Martha, and Pauline, packing up for the trip to Piggott, writes him not to worry about her. She misses him but is confident their future together will work out just fine. Whatever he told her in his long letter leaves Pauline reassured. From Piggott she speaks of sending him a "golden key" to her New York apartment, certain that he is returning quite soon. Three weeks later, Pauline, Patrick, Gregory, and Ada are all in New York ready to move into an apartment at East 50th Street on a two-month lease; Ernest is in Paris, with and without Martha, who makes an extended trip along the Italian and Spanish borders for another *Collier's* feature. Ernest has finished a new short story and is beginning a novel, which was the supposed point of the trip as far as Pauline is willing to believe. She hopes that it is going well.[27]

His writing is the only thing going well. In Spain in late September the international brigades, their ranks now composed largely of Spaniards, were withdrawn from the front lines. In New York on October 14, Scribner's published 5,350 copies of *The Fifth Column and the First Forty-nine Stories* with Hemingway's short preface, but the reviewers concentrated their attention on the play, which few found interesting. *Saturday Review* was excited about the collection, but the *New York Times* thought it monotonous, and *The Nation* said *The Fifth Column* was "almost as bad" as *To Have and Have Not*, "by far the worse book" Hemingway had written. Even *Time* magazine called the play "ragged and confused." *New Masses* predictably praised Hemingway's newly developed social conscience; Malcolm Cowley, riding the fence, said Philip was interesting but Dorothy Bridges was another "Junior Leaguer" who prevented the play from becoming a tragedy: "If Philip hadn't left her for the Spanish people, he might have traded her for a flask of Chanel No. 5 and still have had the best of it."[28] Two weeks after the book was published, Hemingway was complaining once more about reviewers "ganging up" on him and threatening his livelihood, and bitching to Max Perkins that Scribner's was not countering the reviews with large ads. He said that Pauline could not see a copy of the book in the Scribner's Book Store window on publication day. The complaints were his customary ones, but the tone was mild, even jocular, for when he was writing well, little else mattered, not even the sickening "conflicting obligations" which he said, without naming them, were in great supply.[29]

Growing up surrounded by four sisters, Ernest enjoyed the presence of many women, preferably admiring ones, who not infrequently created "conflicting obligations." He liked nothing better than having Sara Murphy, Katy Dos Passos, and Jinny Pfeiffer all hovering around his house in Key West. There was about him a sexual magnetism which his first wife to-be, Hadley Richardson, recognized, asking, "You don't have lots and lots of infatuations do you? What could I do if you did? Course if you do I guess you can't help it."[30] What he could not help was his Jekyll and Hyde alternation between needing a wife and feeling restricted by that wife. He wanted a home, but could not remain there long without it chafing him. He loved his children, but was seldom with them. He wrote better on the run, living in monastic hotel rooms, than he did in the Key West house. In September he arrived in Paris half believing that his marriage to Pauline was permanent; on November 24, he arrived back in New York half believing that he could possess both women. He should have known better.

By early December, when Ernest and Pauline return to Key West, the arguments resume, lasting through Christmas. While Ernest keeps much to himself, revising new short stories and missing the excitement of Martha, Pauline still refuses to give up on their marriage. She remembers how he used sarcasm, tears, and melancholy to drive Hadley away when he was having an affair with her. Now, twelve years later with her role reversed, she sees it all happening again. They drink too much these days and share too little, but she is Mrs. Hemingway still. On Christmas Day, his mother writes, thanking him for a generous check and also for his letter, the first she has received in almost three years. Perhaps suspecting that something is wrong with her oldest son, she mentions the possibility of visiting Key West in February.[31] No sooner are Christmas gifts put away than Ernest flies to New York, to work on revisions to *The Fifth Column* for its possible stage production; from St. Louis, where she has spent Christmas with her mother, Martha returns to New York on January 14. The next morning she reads about Ernest in the New York tabloids:

> HEMINGWAY BY K.O. IN BIG NIGHT CLUB CARD
>
> *Ernest Hemingway, who has hair on his chest, two attorneys and two society brokers gave the night club sector one of its busiest fight sessions in weeks early yesterday.*
>
> *Hemingway was accosted in the Stork Club by a man who insisted on rubbing his hand over the writer's face while muttering, "Tough, eh?"*
>
> *Quintin Reynolds, magazine writer, advised Hemingway to "give him a poke, but don't hit him too hard."*
>
> *The author of "Death in the Afternoon" arose and clipped the unwelcome visitor on the chin. When he was lifted off the floor he gave his name as Edward Chapman, a lawyer. Hemingway previously proved his claim to a hairy chest in a scrap with Max Eastman in the fall of 1937.*[32]

Two days later, Walter Winchell in his syndicated "On Broadway" column, deflated the story:

> *A Former Chicago reporter . . . and several working newspapermen were at the next table to Hemingway's when Eddie Chapman (Hemingway's alleged victim) fell from his chair from too much woofle-water. The next day the front pages related how Hemingway and Chapman "went to it." . . . the former Chicago reporter, when he encountered us that sundown, [said,] "so these night club fights aren't framed, eh?" . . . Bill Corum, in the same group when the phony battle took place, also exposed the inside yesterday in the Journal-American column. . . . It just didn't happen.*[33]

Real or imagined, the story added to Hemingway's growing public legend, which he once cultivated but was now firmly rooted and flourishing with a life of its own.

When Jack Hemingway came into the city from his Hudson river boarding school to see *The Spanish Earth,* he was surprised to find on his father's arm an incredibly lovely woman with a fur coat and a flair for obscenities.[34] After ten days laboring with theater people by day and being with Martha by night, Ernest flew out of New York in a snowstorm on January 24, arriving back in Key West barely in time to greet Pauline's Uncle Gus and Aunt Louise, who are concerned about their niece's marriage, in which they have so much invested.

Pauline continues to invite old friends, like Sara Murphy, down to share the winter sunshine as if nothing were wrong between herself and Ernest, but Sara can read between the lines. Thanking Sara for her gift of Gregory's sailboat, which lives in their swimming pool, Pauline says the boat in the pool is a metaphor for a man's life: everything goes smoothly, when without warning it changes direction, runs up the side of the pool trying to get out to a larger body of water, then settles back into its familiar pool to begin the pattern over again. In the next paragraph she says that Ernest is home from New York, contented and relaxed.[35] From this distance one cannot tell if Pauline is simply keeping up appearances or if she actually believes Ernest to be settling in.

On February 5, he writes a late Christmas thank-you letter to Mary Pfeiffer, complaining about New York "Jews" ruining his play ("It should be called the 4.95 Column marked down from 5 now") and politicians letting the Republican cause in Spain go down in defeat. Patrick was confirmed in the Catholic Church; Pauline is fine, never looking better. (He does not say that Martha is vacationing with her mother a hundred miles due north at Naples, Florida.)[36] Two days later, Grace Hemingway drove herself into town, registering at the Casa Marina, Key West's most expensive hotel, at her son's expense. For six days, Ernest is on his best behavior, solicitous of Pauline, the good father all round, which probably does not fool Grace, who keeps her own counsel. On February 15, the day after Grace leaves for Oak Park, Ernest steps on the P&O ferry to Havana; his second marriage is all but finished, but it will take the principals some time yet to admit it.[37]

He arrived in Havana with five new stories finished, four set in the Spanish war, one set in Havana. They were some of the best stories he had written, he said, but that's what he usually said. He had two more planned, one using his experience at Teruel and another, which had been on his mind for some time, about fishing:

> . . . the old commercial fisherman who fought the swordfish all alone in his skiff for 4 days and four nights and the sharks finally eating it after he had it alongside and could not get it into the boat. . . . Everything he does and everything he thinks in all that long fight with the boat out of sight of all the other boats all alone on the sea. It's a great story if I can get it right.[38]

In Havana, he collects his mail from Pauline and Max Perkins at the Ambos Mundos desk, but he is registered at the Sevilla-Biltmore. As he explains two months later, the only way to find peace to write is to "tell everybody you live in one hotel and live in another. When they locate you, move to the country."[39]

From Key West, Pauline writes perfunctory letters, refusing to beg, getting in her points, but not closing the door: the boys have been to the dentist; the male coon is sick, perhaps dying; visitors are there and others on the way. Referring to revisions New York is asking for Ernest's play, Pauline says that when younger she might have "taken a stand about love," but she has found she knows nothing about it. The letter closes with her hoping that he has everything he wants. Yet she can invite Sara Murphy to come visit in April when Ernest would be home and life would be "VERY nice."[40] Meanwhile Ernest is stocking his Sevilla-Biltmore room with a twelve-pound ham and four pounds of various cured sausages, recreating the Madrid larder for a writer who does not want to stop for lunch.[41] At his desk sits his beat-up typewriter and two stacks of paper, the smaller of which holds pages covered in his typing: inconsistent double spaces between words and consistent spaces between the end of the sentence and the punctuation.

The typed first page begins:

We lay on the brown ,pine -needled floor of the forest and the wind blew in the tops of the pine trees . The mountain side sloped gently where we lay but below it was steep and we could see the dark of the oiled road winding through the pass . There was a stream along the side of the road and far down the pass I could see a mill beside the stream and the falling water of the dam white in the summer sunlight.[42]

By the time he reached the third page, he went back with a pencil to revise every "we" and the single "I" to "he," deciding almost from the start to write this story in the detached third person.

The man lying on the pine-needle floor is a Loyalist saboteur, Robert Jordan, who, like Robert Merriman, is a college professor, not at Berkeley but Montana. In his heavy backpack he carries sticks of dynamite to blow up a strategic bridge during a Republican attack in the Guadarrama mountains. The time is three days at the end of May of 1937, three days when Hemingway was in New York City. It is all there on the map, the road winding down along the river, the stone bridge across, thick pines above, even the cave where the guerrilla band was hiding. He has been there in his imagination, but he was not there when the actual La Granja attack failed. Because the stone bridge is too sturdy for his story, Ernest changes it to steel girders, ones that carefully placed dynamite can bring down. This is the same bridge he eliminated from *To Have and Have Not*, the boatload of dynamite here reduced to what Jordan can carry on his back. Jordan himself owes much to Ernest's reading, particularly *Revolt in the Desert*, T. E. Lawrence's autobiographical study in guerrilla warfare. Like the real Lawrence, the fictional Jordan has earlier specialized in blowing up trains.

After five weeks alone in the Havana hotel, Hemingway returned to Key West to be there when his son Jack came down for his Easter vacation, which coincided with arrival of several visitors: Ben Gallagher (a Paris hunting friend), Sara Murphy with daughter Honoria, and Jinny Pfeiffer. Reporting to Perkins that the first two chapters of the novel were in draft with heavy revisions, he gave elaborate explanations why he was going back to Havana to finish the book: wonderful place to work; no telephone to bother him; no intrusions; no matter what personal problems he had, writing was more important. He was ridiculously happy as he always was when the writing went well. His weight, another indicator of his mental state, was below two hundred pounds, another good sign. It was, he told Max, a story he did not think he was ready to write, but once he started it went along beautifully.[43] Perkins was finally to get the novel for which he had waited so patiently these last ten years. On April 5, Hemingway motored the *Pilar* out into the Gulf and returned to Havana.

When, at Ernest's invitation, Martha joined him in April at the Hotel Sevilla-Biltmore, she was not impressed with his messy room: the Hotel Florida while artillery rounds fell on Madrid was one thing, but cramped quarters in peacetime Havana were not acceptable. Although working on her own novel, she immediately began searching for a rentable house. On the outskirts of Havana in the village of San Francisco de Paula, she was shown a run-down estate called La Vigía, "The Lookout," perched on a low hill, its fifteen acres of grounds overgrown with tropical green and its swimming-pool water equally green. While Ernest wrote mornings in the hotel and fished in the afternoon, Martha hired with her own money carpenters, painters, two gardeners, and a cook to make La Vigía livable.[44] By May 17, she and Ernest were living quietly on her hilltop[45] where she wrote slowly on her novel and managed the house, for which Ernest was now sharing expenses.

In Martha's novel, Mary Douglas contemplates what marriage with her lover John might be like:

What difference would it make . . . marriage is for living in one place, and tennis with the neighbors on Sunday afternoon. We aren't like that, we'll never be settled. Maybe marriage is also for absence.[46]

———

Perhaps no American talent has so publicly developed as Hemingway's: more than any writer of our time he has been under glass, watched, checked up on, predicted, suspected, warned. One part of his audience took from him new styles of writing, of love-making, of very being . . . another section of his audience responded negatively, pointing out that the texture of Hemingway's work was made up of cruelty, religion, anti-intellectualism, even of basic fascism, and looked upon him as the proponent of evil. Neither part of such an audience could fail to make its impression upon a writer. The knowledge that he had set a fashion and become a legend may have been gratifying but surely burdensome and depressing, and it must have offered no small temptation.[47]

—Lionel Trilling, 1939

In Key West, Pauline is packing for a trip to New York with Jinny; Ada will bring the children up if she finds a suitable place to rent. Pauline's letters continue to arrive at his Ambos Mundos mailing address, and Ernest continues to write others as if nothing were changed, but from the moment he moves into Martha's country place, his marriage with Pauline is finished. At the end of May he tells his mother that Pauline and his children are "fine." In a birthday letter to Patrick, he speaks of Martha's houseman, Reeves, as if the man worked for him. In July when Pauline abruptly leaves with friends on an extended European trip, her first in their marriage without him, she tells him that other than his few unsound ideas, there is no one like him, and he is certain to figure out what is best for them. Writing as if there were no Martha in his life, Pauline signs the letter with love and luck. Ernest writes of Pauline's spur-of-the-moment trip to his mother-in-law as if it were nothing unusual. It will be "jolly," "fine," and "great fun" for Pauline.[48] Out of sight in Cuba, where it is easy to keep up appearances, he and the world are at the end of one period and the start of another.

The Great Depression is coming to a close, as is the twenty-year grace period since the Treaty of Versailles ended the Great European War. Ernest entered the decade a young writer on the wave of a bestseller; he is going out of the decade as the best-known male writer in America, but without the momumental book for which he was

reaching. In Key West the FERA plan has succeeded in turning fishermen into local color for tourists to photograph, and Sloppy Joe's
now features live music every night of the week. The Overseas Highway is bringing in a steady stream of middle-class Americans to displace the wealthy yachtsmen. Even if Martha Gellhorn had not
appeared in his life, Ernest would have soon left Key West to its
gaudy future, just as he always moved on.

In choosing Martha, he is leaving behind the burden of house and
family, the intrusive friends whom he, of course, invited but complained about, and the burden of money. Life is much simpler with
only the *Pilar*, his fishing gear, his typewriter, and his faithful editor,
Max Perkins. No more Spain, no more ferias at Pamplona for seventeen years. No more Bimini with his crew wearing white uniforms
and the *Pilar's* name across their chests. One last trip to the L-Bar-T
ranch before it is packed away, photographs in a box. No more safaris
paid for by Gus. For the first time since 1920, there is not a woman's
trust fund to help pay for his traveling life. (To ease the transition,
Hollywood replaces Pfeiffer money by paying handsomely for the *To
Have and Have Not* film rights.) Also for the first time in his adult life,
he is living with a woman younger than himself: his Red Cross nurse
during the war and Hadley Richardson were both eight years his
senior; Pauline was four years older; Martha is nine years younger.

Changing women means changing habits and habitats. When he
left Hadley, he and Pauline moved from Montparnasse to St. Germain des Prés, changing cafés just as the great tourist throngs
descended on the Dôme and the Sélect looking for characters out of
The Sun Also Rises. He is leaving Key West behind just as the next
generation of tourists arrives looking for characters out of *To Have and
Have Not*. In Paris his affair with Martha moved Hemingway, for the
first time, to the other side of the Seine: the Left Bank is abandoned,
too many ghosts, too many cafés where he once sat with other wives.
He is also leaving behind Joe Russell, Charles and Lorine Thompson,
the Murphys, Mike Strater, Waldo Peirce, Bra Saunders, the
MacLeishes, and John and Katy Dos Passos. With some he will stay
in loose touch, but none of them will again play a significant part in

his life. All whom he touched remember him, not always kindly or accurately, but more vividly than many closer friends. Archie MacLeish once said that Ernest sucked the air out of a room as he entered it. Now turning forty, his hair thinning, his beard grayed, he remains the center of any circle in which he lights. His weight is no longer so easily managed, his metabolism no longer able to handle heavy drinking so handily, but he still retains his magic, his humor, his intensity for life that exhausted so many who tried to burn at his level.

Whatever the costs of this expensive decade, Hemingway is now the consummate writer, having mastered through steady work in a variety of genres a full repertoire of skills, voices, and structures. Finally he is ready to bring all his talent to bear on this book at hand, whose action is exactly realized and whose time is perfectly now. All that summer and fall of 1939, he writes the story of the dynamiter, the girl, and the band of partisans on a hopeless mission in a world turned inside out by civil war. Finally he can write of his revolution-ist, the one he did not know enough about in 1928 nor in 1936, the one he has studied, invented, lived with these ten years and more in his head and in abandoned manuscripts. Now he knows the country and the people, in peace and war, knows the taste of fear in the high country when planes fly overhead, the smell of cordite in the morn-ing, the way men die under bombardment and how their bodies twist against the earth. He knows so much that he can leave out every-thing but these few men, two women, and a steel bridge that must be destroyed, even if the attack is betrayed, because beyond all poli-tics, a man finally must do his duty, just as a writer must write.

To create his characters, he needed all those Spanish days of *Death in the Afternoon*, studying the bullring and the faces surround-ing it. He needed the African book to learn about moving people through terrain. He needed all those experiments with structure before he could write this story which has within it several other sto-ries, each in a separate voice. He needed his affair with Martha before he could write of his fictional Maria. He needed the strength and purpose of Pauline to create the older woman, Pilar, whose name once belonged to her. He needed to watch the Italian bombers on the Tortosa road before he could describe the bombing of the lonely hilltop. This is any war, every man, a simple story as old as history. Before this book is finished, Poland is ravaged by the Nazi blitzkrieg; by the time it has a title—*For Whom the Bell Tolls*—Denmark and Holland are reeling under invasion, and death bells are tolling once again for the western world.

CHRONOLOGY

1929

May 5   Hemingways have returned to Europe.

July 6   Ernest, Uncle Gus, and Jinny Pfeiffer at Pamplona; Pauline in Paris.

July   Ernest and Pauline in Valencia and Santiago de Compostela.

Sept. 27   *A Farewell to Arms* published in New York.

Oct. 24   Stock market crash in New York.

Dec. 20   Hemingways, Fitzgeralds, Dos Passos join Murphys in Switzerland.

Dec. 31   Hemingways return to Paris.

1930

Jan. 9   Hemingways sail for United States. Arrive in Key West on February 2.

March 15   Max Perkins visits in Key West. Hemingway begins *Death in the Afternoon*.

April   John and Katy Dos Passos, Archie and Ada MacLeish visit in Key West.

July 13   Hemingways and children arrive at L-Bar-T ranch in Wyoming.

Nov. 1   In auto wreck near Billings, Montana, Hemingway's right arm severely fractured.

Dec. 21   Hemingway released from Billings hospital. He and Pauline go to Piggott for Christmas.

1931

Jan. 3   Hemingways return to Key West.

April 29   Hemingways buy Key West house; Pauline two months pregnant.

May   Pauline and Patrick go to Paris; Ernest to Spain.

June 26   Ernest and Pauline are in Madrid.

July 6   Ernest, Bumby, and Sidney Franklin in Pamplona.

July–Aug.   Hemingways are in Valencia, Santiago de Compostela, Madrid.

Sept. 23   Hemingways sail for New York.

Oct. 14   Hemingways are in Kansas City.

Nov. 12   Gregory Hemingway delivered by cesarean section.

Dec. 19   Hemingways and two children are back in Key West.

1932

Jan.   Hemingway finishes *Death in the Afternoon*.

March   Hemingway writes "After the Storm."

April 20   Hemingway in Havana for two months of fishing.

July 12   Ernest and Pauline arrive at Nordquist L-Bar-T ranch.

August   Ernest writes "The Light of the World."

Sept. 23   *Death in the Afternoon* published in New York.

Oct. 16   Pauline leaves for Piggott; Ernest for Key West.

Nov. 15   "Fathers and Sons" begun.

Dec.   Hemingways in Piggott from Thanksgiving through Christmas. Hemingway finishes "A Clean Well-Lighted Place."

1933

Jan. 8–20   Hemingway in New York. Meets Tom Wolfe and Arnold Gingrich.

Feb–April   Hemingway in Key West, finishes four stories.

April 13   Hemingway is back in Havana for two months of marlin fishing.

May 24   Jane Mason wrecks car with Hemingway children inside.

July 3   Hemingway's first wife, Hadley Richardson, marries Paul Mowrer in London.

August   First issue of *Esquire* features Hemingway's "Marlin Off the Morro: A Cuban Letter."

Aug. 7   Hemingways sail from Havana for Spain. Arrive Santander, August 17. Ernest remains in Spain until October 20.

Oct. 27   Hemingway in Paris when *Winner Take Nothing* is published in New York. He finishes "One Trip Across."

Nov. 22   Ernest, Pauline, and Charles Thompson sail from Marseilles to go on their African safari.

Dec. 20   Hemingway party departs Nairobi on two-month safari.

1934

Jan. 16   Ill with amebic dysentery, Hemingway is flown to Nairobi for treatment; rejoins safari January 21.

Feb. 28   Hemingways depart Africa, stop at Haifa, then return to Paris.

March 27   Hemingways sail for New York. Arrive April 3.

April 12   Hemingways back in Key West.

May 11   Hemingway brings his new fishing boat, *Pilar*, to Key West. Begins *Green Hills of Africa*.

July 18   Hemingway takes the *Pilar* to Havana. Returns October 26.

Nov. 16   Draft of *Green Hills of Africa* finished.

Dec. 19   Hemingways leave Key West for Christmas in Piggott.

1935

Jan.–March   Hemingway writes in Key West.

April 7   Hemingway accidentally shoots himself in the leg.

April 14 Hemingway takes *Pilar* to Bimini for tuna fishing.

May First serial installment of *Green Hills* printed in *Scribner's Magazine*.

Aug. 15 Hemingway returns to Key West.

Sept. 2 Hurricane drowns hundreds of veterans on Matecumbe Key.

Sept. 17 *New Masses* prints Hemingway's "Who Murdered the Vets?"

Sept. 24 Hemingway is in New York for the Joe Louis–Max Baer heavyweight championship fight; remains in the East for the next month.

Oct. 25 *Green Hills* is published in New York. Hemingways return to Key West.

1936

Feb. Hemingway in a fist fight with Wallace Stevens.

April Hemingway finishes drafts of "The Snows of Kilimanjaro" and "The Short Happy Life of Francis Macomber."

April 27 Hemingway on the *Pilar* arrives in Havana.

May 27 Hemingway returns to Key West.

June 4 Hemingways leave for Bimini.

July 16 Hemingway leaves Bimini for Key West. Spanish Civil War begins.

July 27 Hemingways leave Key West for Piggott and Nordquist ranch in Wyoming.

Oct. 27 Hemingways leave for Key West with Hemingway having written 352 pages of *To Have and Have Not*.

Dec. Hemingway meets Martha Gellhorn in Key West.

1937

Jan. 10 Hemingway leaves Key West for New York.

Jan. 25 Hemingway returns to Key West.

Feb. 17 Hemingway is back in New York.

Feb. 27   Hemingway sails for France as war correspondent for North American News Alliance.

March 10   Hemingway is in Paris.

March 16   Hemingway flies to Valencia, Spain, then on to Madrid by car; soon joined there by Martha Gellhorn.

April   While reporting on the war, Hemingway works with Joris Ivens filming *The Spanish Earth*.

April 26   Guernica destroyed by Nationalist bombs.

May 9   Hemingway returns to Paris.

May 12   Hemingway reads from *To Have and Have Not* manuscript at Sylvia Beach's bookshop. Next day sails for New York.

May 26   Hemingways leave for Bimini.

June 4   Hemingway flies to New York to address the American Writers Conference. Returns to Bimini two days later.

June 20   Hemingway does a quick round trip to New York to complete *The Spanish Earth*. *To Have and Have Not* is finished.

July 6   Hemingway leaves Bimini for New York.

July 8   Hemingway, Gellhorn, and Ivens are dinner guests at the White House for Roosevelt's viewing of *The Spanish Earth*.

July 10   Ernest, Pauline, and Ivens leave for Hollywood to raise funds for Loyalist cause in Spain.

July 21   Hemingway back in Bimini reading proof on *To Have and Have Not*.

Aug. 3   Hemingway leaves Bimini for Key West.

Aug. 10   Hemingway is in New York.

Aug. 11   Max Eastman scuffle in Perkins's office.

Aug. 14   Hemingway sails from New York for France.

Sept. 6   Hemingway departs Paris with Gellhorn for Madrid.

Oct. 15   *To Have and Have Not* published in New York. Hemingway working on *The Fifth Column*.

Dec. 28   Ernest joins Pauline in Paris.

1938

Jan. 12   Hemingways sail for Nassau, Havana, and Key West.

Jan. 29   Hemingways are in Key West.

March 19   Hemingway leaves from New York for France.

March 31   Ernest and Martha leave Paris for Spain.

May 16   Ernest and Martha return to Paris.

May 30   Hemingway arrives in New York and on to Key West.

June 22   Hemingway flies to New York for the Louis–Schmeling heavyweight fight.

Aug. 4   Hemingways leave Key West for L-Bar-T ranch.

Aug. 31   Hemingway sails for France where he meets Martha. They remain there all of September and October.

Oct. 22   *The Fifth Column and the First 49 Stories* is published in New York.

Nov. 24   Pauline is in New York when Ernest returns from France.

Dec. 5   Hemingways return to Key West.

1939

Jan.   Early in January Hemingway returns to New York and Martha. His play, *The Fifth Column*, is in production.

Jan. 24   Hemingway flies back to Key West.

Feb. 8   Hemingway's mother visits for six days.

Feb. 15   Hemingway takes ferry to Havana. Begins *For Whom the Bell Tolls*.

March 14   Hemingway returns to Key West with two chapters written.

April 5   Hemingway takes *Pilar* back to Havana. Meets Martha.

May   Martha rents Finca Vigia outside Havana. Ernest moves in with her.

* Many of the specific dates above are corrections to my earlier *Hemingway: An Annotated Chronology*.

ACKNOWLEDGMENTS

For permission to quote from texts, letters, and unpublished materials, I am grateful to Charles Scribner's Sons, now part of Simon & Schuster; *The Hemingway Review*; the Hemingway literary estate; and the Hemingway Foundation.

For reasons too numerous to count, I acknowledge and wish to thank Maurie and Marcia Neville, Megan Desnoyers, Steve Plotkin, John and Marsha Goin, Dave Meeker, Sarah Means Smith and Verna Chester, Dick Davison, Turner's Revenge, David LeDuc, Robert Trogdon, Amy Vondrak, Jeff Stoner, Lisa Ann Acosta, ENG-491 honors class, Anthony Mason, Patrick and Gregory Hemingway, Carlos Baker, the true scholars who gather in the back room of the Monroe County Library, Wright Langley, Louise at Hurtgenwald, Stoney and Sparrow in the high country, Jerry in Paris, reporters at the *Billings Gazette*, old friends from the Supper Club, Marty Peterson, continuous support from the members of the Hemingway Society, Tom Riker, Amy Cherry, Miriam Altshuler, Ted Johnson, Bill Henderson, North Carolina State University, its D. H. Hill Library and Interlibrary Loan staff, Princeton University Library, John F. Kennedy Library, University of Tulsa Library, the Library of Congress, University of Delaware Library. And to remember Paul Smith, who died before he could correct all the mistakes in this book. And to thank my wife, who in thirty years of questing has never questioned the goal. To thank my mother, Teresa Donnici Reynolds (1910–1995), who took us home to Kansas City and who died as this book was borning. To thank my father, Raymond Douglas Reynolds (1909–1991), who taught me to read maps and rocks. To thank them both for bearing a child in the 1930s. To thank all others from that Great Depression whom I found remembered in odd angles of this hutment we call our culture, waiting for me when I needed them.

NOTES

The following abbreviations are used throughout the notes.

NEWSPAPERS

Citizen	*Key West Citizen*
Gazette	*Billings Gazette*
Post	*Havana Post*
Tribune	Paris edition of the *New York Herald Tribune*

PEOPLE

Dos Passos	John Dos Passos
EH	Ernest Hemingway
FSF	F. Scott Fitzgerald
Gellhorn	Martha Gellhorn
Gingrich	Arnold Gingrich
Hickok	Guy Hickok
MacLeish	Archibald MacLeish
Perkins	Maxwell Perkins
PH	Pauline Hemingway
Pound	Ezra Pound

LIBRARIES

FDR	Franklin D. Roosevelt Library, Hyde Park
JFK	John F. Kennedy Library, Boston

Lilly	Lilly Library, University of Indiana
LOC	Library of Congress
MCL	Monroe County Library, Key West
PUL	Princeton University Library
Stanford	Stanford University Library
Tulsa	University of Tulsa Library
UCal	Bancroft Library, University of California, Berkeley
UDel	University of Delaware
UTex	Humanities Research Center, University of Texas
UVa	Alderman Library, University of Virginia

HEMINGWAY BOOKS

By-Line	*By-Line: Ernest Hemingway*, ed., William White (Scribner's, 1967)
DIA	Ernest Hemingway, *Death in the Afternoon* (Scribner's, 1932)
GHOA	Ernest Hemingway, *Green Hills of Africa* (Scribner's, 1936)
SAR	Ernest Hemingway, *The Sun Also Rises* (Scribner's, 1926)
SL	*Ernest Hemingway: Selected Letters*, ed. Carlos Baker (Scribner's, 1981)
THHN	Ernest Hemingway, *To Have and Have Not* (Scribner's, 1937)
WTN	Ernest Hemingway, *Winner Take Nothing* (Scribner's, 1933)

OTHER BOOKS

Baker	Carlos Baker, *Ernest Hemingway: A Life Story* (Scribner's, 1969)
Berg	Scott Berg, *Max Perkins* (E. P. Dutton, 1978)
Carr	Virginia Spencer Carr, *Dos Passos: A Life* (Doubleday, 1984)

Donaldson
: Scott Donaldson, *Archibald MacLeish: An American Life* (Houghton Mifflin, 1992)

Donnelly
: Honoria Murphy Donnelly, *Sara & Gerald: Villa America and After* (Times Books, 1982)

First War
: Michael Reynolds, *Hemingway's First War* (Princeton U. P., 1976)

Hanneman
: Audre Hanneman, *Ernest Hemingway: A Comprehensive Bibliography* (Princeton U. P., 1967)

Homecoming
: Michael Reynolds, *Hemingway: The American Homecoming* (Blackwell, 1992)

Kert
: Bernice Kert, *The Hemingway Women* (Norton, 1983)

Library
: James Brasch and Joseph Sigman, *Hemingway's Library* (Garland, 1981)

Lost Generation
: Linda Miller, *Letters from the Lost Generation* (Rutgers U. P., 1991)

Ludington
: Townsend Ludington, *John Dos Passos* (E. P. Dutton, 1980)

McLendon
: James McLendon, *Papa: Hemingway in Key West*, rev. ed. (Key West: Langley Press, 1990)

Mellow
: James Mellow, *A Life Without Consequences*. (Houghton Mifflin, 1992)

Meyers
: Jeffrey Meyers, *Hemingway*. (Harcourt Brace, 1985)

Papa
: Gregory Hemingway, *Papa* (Houghton Mifflin, 1976)

Paris Years
: Michael Reynolds, *Hemingway: The Paris Years* (Blackwell, 1989)

Paul Smith
: Paul Smith, *A Reader's Guide to the Short Stories of Ernest Hemingway* (G. K. Hall, 1989)

Reading
: Michael Reynolds, *Hemingway's Reading* (Princeton U. P., 1981)

Reception
: *Ernest Hemingway: The Critical Reception*, ed. Robert O. Stephens (Burt Franklin & Co., 1977)

Rollyson
: Carl Rollyson, *Nothing Ever Happens to the Brave* (St. Martin's Press, 1990)

Samuelson
: Arnold Samuelson, *With Hemingway: A Year in Key West and Cuba* (Random House, 1984)

Thomas
: Hugh Thomas, *The Spanish Civil War* (Harper, 1961)

True Gen   Denis Brian, *The True Gen* (Grove Press, 1988)

Young Hemingway   Michael Reynolds, *The Young Hemingway* (Blackwell, 1986)

CHAPTER 1: 1929

1. O. O. McIntyre, "Drop In Again, Ernest," *Kansas City Times*, March 9, 1929.
2. PH–EH, May 1 and 3, 1929, JFK.
3. Perkins–EH, telegram, April 4, 1929, JFK.
4. EH–Perkins, undated, c. April 1929, PUL. A characteristic exaggeration: Ernest and Pauline were never evicted from an apartment because of FSF.
5. See *First War*, pp. 20–66, and *Homecoming*, pp. 167–217.
6. See Alan Price, "I'm Not an Old Fogey and You're Not a Young Ass: Owen Wister and Ernest Hemingway," *Hemingway Review*, 9 (Fall 1989), 82–90, for a detailed analysis of this relationship.
7. Owen Wister–Perkins, May 6, 1929, PUL.
8. Perkins–Owen Wister, May 17, 1929, PUL.
9. FSF–EH, May 17, 1929, JFK.
10. EH–Robert Bridges, May 18, 1929, PUL.
11. Perkins–EH, May 24, 1929, PUL.
12. FSF–Zelda Fitzgerald, Summer (?) 1930, *Correspondence of FSF*, ed. M. J. Bruccoli and M. M. Duggan (Random House, 1980), pp. 240–1.
13. Zelda Fitzgerald–FSF, early fall 1930, *Correspondence of FSF*, p. 248.
14. FSF–EH, June 1929, JFK.
15. Typescript of *A Farewell to Arms*, JFK.
16. EH–Perkins, June 23, 1929, JFK. This letter is dated in *Selected Letters* as June 24; internal evidence (Mass and the steeplechase at Auteuil) says otherwise.
17. Item 845, Hemingway Collection, JFK.
18. Janet Flanner–EH, [June 18, 1929], JFK.
19. Nino Frank–EH, June 19, 1929, JFK.
20. H. G. Leech–EH, June 28, 1929, JFK.
21. George Antheil–EH, July 1, 1929, JFK.
22. Victor Llona–EH, Aug. 6 and 10, 1929, JFK.
23. Paul Johnson–EH, Aug. 31, 1929, JFK.

24. Paul Reynolds–Perkins, August 12, 1929, JFK.

25. Paul Reynolds–EH, Aug. 30, 1929. JFK.

26. MacLeish–EH, mailed June 24, 1929, JFK.

27. Scribner's clipping file, once in the Scribner's offices, now probably at PUL.

28. *Tribune*, Monday, June 24, 1929. Mary Hickok was not in Pamplona. Pat Morgan was.

29. *Tribune*, June 25, 1929; reprinted "Proclamation," *in transition; A Paris Anthology* (London: Phillips & Company Books, 1990), p. 19.

30. "Hemingway Gives Up Old Life with Literary Success," *New York Evening Post*, Nov. 18, 1929, p. 6.

31. *Tribune*, June 28 and 29, 1929. Total government receipts for fiscal 1928–29 were $3,998,694,187. In 1995 dollars, this figure would be roughly $28 billion.

32. "What with Drinking Wine and Dancing for 11 Days, Spain's Fiestas Tire One," *Brooklyn Daily Eagle*, July 29, 1929.

33. *El Pensamiento Navarro*, July 7–10, 1929; *100 Años de Carteles de las Fiestas y Ferias de San Fermin* (1882–1981) (Pamplona: Caja de Ahorros de Navarra, 1982), [np], 1929 feria.

34. "Crowds Revel in Fire, Wine and Chaos," *Brooklyn Daily Eagle*, July 22, 1929.

35. Ben Ray Redmond, "Spokesman for a Generation," *Spur*, 44 (Dec. 1, 1929), 77.

36. "Young Matador Risks His Life," *Brooklyn Daily Eagle*, July 25, 1929.

37. Hickok–EH, July 23, 1929, first read in a private collection, copy now at JFK.

38. EH–Louis Cohn, July 29, [1930], Cohn Collection, UDel.

39. See *Imaxe de Compostela*, ed. José Luis Cabo Villaverde and Pablo Coasta Bujan (Santiago: Publicacions do Coag, [nd]).

40. EH–Waldo Peirce, Aug. 29, 1929, copy at JFK.

41. PH–EH, c. July 7, 1929, JFK: "Do you want me to bring any of these stories you started."

42. EH–Perkins, June 7, 1929, *SL*, p. 297.

43. EH Journal, Aug. 12, [no year], internal evidence dates it 1929; JFK.

44. *Tribune*, Aug. 5, 1929, "2 Die, 20 Hurt in Nuremberg Hitlerite Riot."

45. *Tribune*, Aug. 10, 1929, "Flossie, Who Barred No Bars, Has Gone." See Hemingway's MS statement about her in *Paris Years*, p. 229.

46. *Tribune*, Aug. 11, 1929.

47. EH–Waldo Peirce, Aug. 29, 1929, copy at JFK.

48. See *Paris Years*, 230–1, 252, and Hemingway's "The Summer People," published posthumously in *The Nick Adams Stories* (Scribner's 1972).

49. "Or the morning we had come in the gates of Paris and seen Salcede torn apart by the horses at the Place de Greves." *GHOA*, p. 108. I am indebted to my thesis advisee Robert Trogdon for this connection.

50. Hemingway Journal, Aug. 13, [no year], letters mentioned from Victor Llona and Owen Wister date it as 1929, JFK. Sixty-five centavos was worth roughly ten cents at the exchange rate of 6.75 pesetas to the dollar.

51. EH–Dos Passos, Sept. 4, 1929, *SL*, p. 303; EH–Perkins, Oct. 31, 1929, *SL*, p. 311.

52. EH–Perkins, April 15, 1925, *SL*, p. 156.

53. EH–Perkins, [c. Aug. 1929], from Santiago de Compostela, PUL.

54. For any reading reference that does not appear in a footnote, see *Reading*.

55. During the previous spring, Fitzgerald and Hemingway discussed the possibilities of using a medieval setting for their fiction. Soon afterward, at Sylvia Beach's lending library, Ernest borrowed Coulton's *Life in the Middle Ages* and Villehardouin's *Chronicles of Crusaders*, and he apparently bought a copy of Haye's *Ancient and Medieval History* published that year. See *Reading*. He also owned a copy of Lecky's *History of European Morals Augustus to Charlemagne* (1869), which he took to Cuba with him in 1940.

56. "Neo-Thomist Poem," first published in Ezra Pound's journal, *The Exile*, Spring 1927. Hemingway's footnote explains: "The title Neo-Thomist refers to temporary embracing of church by literary gents."

57. See *First War* and *Young Hemingway*.

58. "The Earnest Liberal's Lament," *Der Querschnitt*, Autumn 1924, reprinted in *88 Poems*, p. 52.

59. EH–Mary Pfeiffer, Aug. 12, 1929, Carlos Baker Collection, PUL.

60. "Market Still on Its Upward Move," *Tribune*, Aug., 26, 1929.

61. *Tribune*, Sept. 2, 1929. Hemingway may well have read this story in a Madrid paper which would have been available in Palencia.

62. W. K. Klingaman, *1929: The Year of the Great Crash* (New York: Harper & Row, 1989), pp. 234–5.

63. "Swan Song of the Little Review," *Tribune*, Sept. 1, 1929.
64. Paul Nelson–EH, Dec. 30, 1929, JFK.
65. EH–Perkins, Sept. 7 and 9, 1929, first read in Scribner's offices, now at PUL.
66. FSF–EH, Aug. 23, 1929, JFK; EH–FSF, Sept. 4, 1929, *SL*, p. 305.
67. EH–FSF, Sept. 13, 1929, *SL*, p. 306.
68. Harry Crosby–EH, Oct. 3, 1929; *Tribune*, Oct. 6 and 7, 1929.
69. EH–Perkins, Oct. 4, 1929, JFK. The novel was priced at $2.50.
70. Perkins–EH, Oct. 15, 1929, first read at Scribner's offices, now at PUL.
71. Perkins–EH, Oct. 15, 1929, JFK.
72. Fanny Butcher, "Here Is Genius," Oct. 20, 1929, reprinted from *Chicago Tribune*, Sept. 28, 1929.
73. Henry Hazlitt, "Take Hemingway."
74. "Not Yet Demobilized," *New York Herald Tribune Books*, Oct. 6, 1929.
75. Agnes Smith, "Mr. Hemingway Does It Again," *New Yorker*, Oct. 12, 1929, p. 120; Henry Seidel Canby, "Story of the Brave," *Saturday Review of Literature*, Oct. 12, 1929, pp. 231–2; Clifton P. Fadiman, "A Fine American Novel," *Nation*, Oct. 30, 1929, pp. 497–8.
76. Fanny Butcher, "Here Is Genius," *Tribune*, Oct. 20, 1929.
77. Linda Simon, *The Biography of Alice B. Toklas* (Garden City: Doubleday, 1977), p. 122.
78. EH–FSF, c. Oct. 22 or 29, 1929, *SL*, pp. 308–9; other evidence establishes the date as Oct. 22.
79. Allen Tate–Carlos Baker, April 19, 1963, Baker Collection, PUL.
80. Seward Collins–EH, Oct. 3, 1929, JFK. By this time eight to ten days usually moved a letter from New York to Paris.
81. See *Gertrude Stein: A Composite Portrait*, ed. Linda Simon (New York: Avon, 1974); *The Biography of Alice B. Toklas*; *Perpetual Motif: The Art of Man Ray* (Washington: National Museum of American Art, 1988); James Mellow, *Charmed Circle* (Praeger, 1974), photos.
82. Allen Tate–Carlos Baker, April 19, 1963, Baker Collection, PUL; and Allen Tate, "Random Thoughts on the 1920s," *Minnesota Review*, Fall 1960, pp. 46–56.
83. Ibid.
84. EH–FSF, Oct. 24, 1929, *SL*, pp. 309–11.
85. *Tribune*, Oct. 25, 1929.
86. *Tribune*, Oct. 26, 1929.

87. *Tribune*, Oct. 27–30, 1929; Klingaman, *1929: The Year of the Great Crash*, pp. 270–86; *SL*, p. 311.

88. Flectheim was the publisher of *Der Querschnitt*, which promoted modernist painters at his several galleries. There are two bills for *Monument in Arbeit* at the JFK: one dated Nov. 15, 1929, and signed by Flechtheim is for 1,600 marks; the second, dated Nov. 18, from Galerie Simon for 30,000 francs. The total of the two is approximately $1,500, or the average annual income for the American workingman in 1929. Thanks to Jenny Agner, Klee specialist presently at Brown University, for helping with the provenance. In Mary Hemingway's will this picture was left to Gregory Hemingway.

89. EH–Perkins, Nov. 10, 1929, JFK.

90. Reprinted edition, *The Education of a French Model* (New York: Boar's Head Books, 1950), pp. 10–11.

91. See Paul Smith, pp. 223–4. In fact, on any points about the short fiction, see Paul Smith.

92. Dorothy Parker–Robert Benchley, [Nov. 7, 1929], in *Lost Generation*, pp.47–53. Donnelly, pp. 48–54.

93. Sara Murphy–FSF, April 3, 1936, *Lost Generation*, p. 161.

94. MacLeish–Henrietta Crosby, Dec. 12, 1929, *Letters of Archibald MacLeish*, pp. 231–2.

CHAPTER 2: 1930

1. *New York Times*: *La Bourdannais*, with stops at Vigo and Halifax, arrived several days late in New York at noon on Jan. 25.

2. Scribner's Hemingway author file #9, first read at Scribner's offices, now at PUL.

3. *Post*, Feb. 1, 1930: *La Bourdannais* arrived yesterday. EH–Waldo Peirce, Feb. 7, 1930, copy at JFK.

4. Grace Hemingway–EH, Feb. 6 and 24, March 9, 1930, JFK; Hadley Hemingway–EH, March 10, 1930, JFK.

5. Waldo Peirce–EH, March 17, 28, and 29, 1930, JFK; EH–Waldo Peirce, May 9, 1930, JFK.

6. "The Fishing Life of Ernest Hemingway," *The Fisherman*, Jan. 1958, p. 85.

NOTES

7. MacLeish–EH, [April 1930], JFK.
8. EH–Waldo Peirce, May 9, 1930, JFK; *Historical Statistics of the United States*, Bicentennial Edition (1975), p. 164.
9. Royalty statement attached to Perkins–EH, March 4, 1930, JFK. In 1995 dollars, his 1929 income translates to almost $160,000. In 1929, a one-way transatlantic liner ticket might cost $85–135, a new automobile $600–1,000. In 1930 a five-bedroom furnished house in Havana during the winter season rented for $350 a month.
10. *WTN*, p. 121. See *Homecoming*, pp. 197–8, and Paul Smith, pp. 217–22.
11. EH–Waldo Peirce, [c. April 6, 1930], copy at JFK.
12. EH–Henry Strater, May 20, 1930, *SL*, p. 322.
13. A. G. Pfeiffer–A. M. Teixidor, June 3 and 4, 1930, JFK; "Must have" books were *Tauromachia Completa* (1836), *Gran Diccionario Tauromaco* (1896 edition), *La Tauromachia de Rafael Guerra*, and *Doctrinal Tauromaco de Antonio Fernandez de Heredia* (1904). "Needed if found" books were *Los Novillos* (1892) and *Los Toros en Madrid* (1892). The one-year subscriptions were to: *El Clarin, Toreros y Toros, El Eco Taurino*, and *La Fiesta Brava*. The bound back issues were of *Sol y Sombra* or *La Lidia* (1917–29), *El Clarin* (1925–29), and *Zig-Zag* (1923–25).
14. *Citizen*, June 14, 1930.
15. EH–Louis Henry Cohn, April 23, [1930], Cohn Collection, UDel.
16. EH–Louis Henry Cohn, June 24, [1930], Cohn Collection, UDel.
17. EH–MacLeish, June 30, 1930, *SL*, pp. 325–6; EH–Louis Cohn, c. Sept. 3, 1930, Cohn Collection, UDel.
18. "Visit by Ernest Hemingway," *Kansas City Star*, July 6, 1930, p. 3.
19. Onsite research and Ralph Glidden, *Exploring the Yellowstone High Country* (Cooke City, 1982). Much of what others have written of this area will not match a 1:60,000 terrain map.
20. Hemingway Fishing Log, 1930–34, JFK; Eaton film, DPS 28:c, JFK.
21. EH Hunting Log, 1930–34, JFK. Kills dated Aug. 23 and 30; Baker, 212–3; Absaroka-Beartooth Mountains 15×30 minute quadrangle map (Rock Mountain Surveys: Billings, Mont., 1987) 1:67,000. EH–Louis Cohn, c. Sept. 3, 1930, Cohn Collection, UDel. See EH–Henry Strater, c. June 20, 1930, *SL*, p. 324, for information on the rifle. See also Eaton film, JFK.

22. "The Clark's Fork Valley, Wyoming" first published in *Vogue*, Feb. 1939, reprinted in *By-Line*, pp. 298–300.

23. Eaton film, JFK.

24. EH–Louis Cohn, July 29, 1930, Cohn Collection, UDel.

25. EH–Perkins, Aug. 12, 1930, *SL*, pp. 326–8; EH–Henry Strater, c. Sept. 10, 1930, *SL*, pp. 328–9.

26. EH–Perkins, July 24, 1930, PUL.

27. EH–Perkins, Aug. 12, 1930; EH–Louis Cohn, [Sept. 3, 1930], Cohn Collection, UDel. See also Paul Smith.

28. EH–Louis Cohn, [Sept. 2, 1930], Cohn Collection, UDel; Paul Smith, "The Bloody Typewriter and the Burning Snakes," in *Hemingway: Essays of Reassessment*, ed. Frank Scafella (New York: Oxford U.P., 1991), pp.81–3.

29. *DIA*, typescript, p. 1, JFK.

30. EH–Perkins, Sept. 3, 1930, PUL. One attempt to revise "Mr. and Mrs. Elliot" became the verso of MS p. 189 of *DIA*, UTex.

31. Edward Stanley, *A Familiar History of Birds* (London: Longmans, Green, 1881), pp. 1–2; Ernest Hemingway, "A Natural History of the Dead," *WTN*, pp. 97–8.

32. "A Natural History of the Dead," pp. 97–106.

33. Patrick Hemingway Collection, PUL.

34. EH–William Horne, Sept. 12, 1930, Baker Collection, PUL.

35. EH–Perkins, Oct. 28, 1930, PUL.

36. Assignments of Copyrights, vol. 786, pp. 97–110, LOC. Contract is dated Sept. 17, 1930, and signed for Hemingway by Matthew G. Herold, attorney in fact. Hemingway's share was $24,000.

37. "Noted Novelist Is Injured in Auto Accident," *Gazette*, Nov. 2, 1930. Carlos Baker interview with Floyd Allington, July 20, 1964, PUL.

38. Mary Pickett, "Hemingway in St. Vincent: The Booze Also Rises," *Gazette*, April 8, 1983, 2-D/6, interview with Dorothy Buller and Bernardette Martin; "Noted Novelist Is Injured in Auto Accident," *Gazette*, Nov. 2, 1930.

39. Baker, p. 217; *Gazette*, November 5, 1930.

40. "Hemingway in St. Vincent;" Baker, p. 217. Kangaroo tendon, which was packaged in hermetically sealed glass tubes, was one of several binding materials in medical use in 1930. *New York Times*, Nov. 6, 1930.

41. EH–MacLeish, c. Nov. 22, 1930, *SL*, p. 330.

42. "Hemingway in St. Vincent." See also Pauline's appended note to the Hemingway letter she typed to Waldo Peirce, c. Nov. 28, 1930, copy at JFK and in Baker, p. 217.

43. "Two Wounded in Mystery Shooting," *Gazette*, Nov. 10, 1930, pp. 1, 2; "Sunday Fracas Still a Mystery," Nov. 13, 1930. Billings was and remains a center for processing sugar beets.

44. EH–MacLeish, Nov. 22, 1930, Baker, p. 218; EH–Perkins, Nov. 24, 1930, PUL.

45. "Hemingway at St. Vincent." In 1943, Florence Cloonan died in Denver from a heart attack.

46. See *Reading*.

47. *New York Times*, Nov.–Dec. 1930.

48. Among the most popular songs of 1930, according to Roger Lax and Frederick Smith, *The Great Song Thesaurus* (New York: Oxford U.P., 1984), pp. 55–6.

49. EH–Henry Strater, c. Dec. 15, 1930, *SL*, p. 335.

50. MacLeish–Perkins, Jan. 4, 1931, *MacLeish Letters*, p. 31; Donaldson, *An American Life*, p. 207.

51. A letter from a Mr. Snooks quoted in Perkins–Henry Strater, [c. Dec. 1930], Baker Collection, PUL.

52. EH–Henry Strater, c. Dec. 15, 1930, *SL*, p. 335; EH–MacLeish, c. Dec. 15, 1930, LOC.

53. EH–Owen Wister, December 26, 1930, UVa. In his next book, *Green Hills of Africa*, he attempts what he says here cannot be done.

CHAPTER 3: 1931

1. *Citizen* and *Post*, Jan.–May 1931.

2. EH–Mary Pfeiffer, Jan. 28, 1931, PUL.

3. *Citizen*, Jan.–Feb. 1931; EH–Waldo Peirce, Jan. 17, 1931, MeW/JFK.

4. *Citizen*, Jan. 2 and 5, 1931.

5. *Citizen*, Feb. 3 and 10, 1931.

6. *Citizen*, Jan.–Feb. 1931.

7. *Citizen*, Feb. 3, 1931.

8. *Citizen*, April 28, 1931.

9. *Citizen*, Feb. 25, 1931.

10. *Citizen*, March 9, 1931.

11. *Citizen*, Jan. 9, 1931.

12. *Citizen*, Feb. 27, 1931.

13. *Citizen*, Jan. 27, 1931.

14. Baker, pp. 219–21; Hemingway Fishing Log, 1931, JFK.

15. EH Fishing Log, 1930–34, JFK; *Citizen*, February 4, 1931.

16. *Citizen*, Feb. 4, 1931.

17. Elinor Langer, *Josephine Herbst* (Boston: Little, Brown, 1983), pp. 106–12.

18. Isidor Schneider, "The Fetish of Simplicity," *Nation*, Feb. 18, 1931, 184–6.

19. *Citizen*, March 14, 1931. The Sidleys owned a large cabin at the L-Bar-T.

20. Item 624, Hemingway Collection, JFK.

21. EH–FSF, April 12, 1931, *SL*, p. 339.

22. EH–Perkins, April 12 and 27, 1931, Scribner Collection, PUL. See *Reading*.

23. Uncorrected typed carbon, MCL; EH–MacLeish, April 19, [1931], LOC.

24. Item 754, JFK.

25. *Citizen*, April 30, 1931.

26. Monroe County Deed Book, D-3, p. 153; Toby Bruce interview, Aug. 1, 1965, MCL; PPH–EH, May 11, 16, 1931, JFK.

27. *Tribune*, May 11, 1931.

28. EH–Waldo Peirce, May 14, 1931, JFK.

29. *Tribune*, May 15–18, 1931.

30. Quintana–EH, May 23 and June 26, 1931, JFK.

31. *DIA*, pp. 276–7.

32. *Tribune*, May 28, 1931.

33. *DIA*, pp. 218–9.

34. *Tribune*, May 31, 1931.

35. *Tribune*, June 17, 1931.

36. *Tribune*, June 26–27, 1931.

37. EH–Dos Passos, June 26, 1931, *SL*, p. 341.

38. *Tribune*, June 29–July 1, 1931.

39. EH–Perkins, Aug. 1, 1931, PUL.

40. Quintana–EH, June 25, 1931, JFK.

41. *DIA*, pp. 87–90.

42. Paul Mowrer–EH, June 27, 1931, JFK; Winifred Mowrer note, undated, JFK.

43. EH–Guy Hickok, July 15, [1931], private collection; EH–MacLeish, July 28, [1931], LOC.

44. *Tribune*, July 1931.

45. EH–Perkins, Aug. 1 and Dec. 9, 1931, PUL.

46. EH Notebook, inventory, JFK; bills, 1931, Galerie Simon, JFK.

47. Beach Collection, PUL; *Reading*.

48. Don Brown, "Hemingway Back in Paris; Sails for New York in Week," *Tribune*, September 20, 1931.

49. "The Ghost of a Writer," *Kansas City Star*, Oct. 21, 1931.

50. Wambly Bald, "La Vie de Bohème," *Tribune*, Sept. 23, 1931.

51. EH–L.H. Cohn, [Nov. 16, 1931], UDel.

52. EH–Waldo Peirce, c. Nov. 1, 1931, *SL*, p. 343.

53. Hickok–EH, Dec. 30, 1931, JFK.

54. EH–Hickok, Dec. 12, 1931, private collection.

55. EH–MacLeish, Dec. 9, 1931, LOC.

56. *DIA*, p. 232.

57. *DIA*, p. 91.

58. *DIA*, p. 222.

59. *DIA*, pp. 273–5.

60. EH–Perkins, Dec. 9, 1931, PUL.

61. EH–MacLeish, Dec. 9, 1931, LOC.

62. *DIA*, galley 79, UDel.

63. *New York Times*, Dec. 10, 1931.

64. EH–Perkins, Dec. 26, 1932, *SL*, 346–8; EH–MacLeish, Dec. 23, 1931, LOC; *Citizen*, Dec. 23, 1931.

CHAPTER 4: 1932

1. EH–George Albee, Jan. 31, 1932, UCal.

2. EH–Mary Pfeiffer, Jan. 5, 1932, *SL*, pp. 348–50.

3. "Death in the Afternoon," holograph notes in a private collection.

4. Perkins–EH, Jan. 5, 1932, JFK.

5. EH–Perkins, Jan. 5–6, 1932, *SL*, pp.351–2.

6. *DIA*, p.95.

7. Parish baptismal index, Key West; baptismal certificate, JFK; EH–MacLeish, Jan. 14, [1932], LOC; EH–MacLeish, Jan. 28, [1932], LOC; EH–Perkins, Feb. 7, 1932, PUL.

8. EH–Perkins, Feb. 7, 1932, PUL.

9. *New York Times*, Feb. 4, 1932.

10. EH–MacLeish, Feb. 9, [1932], LOC.

11. MacLeish–EH, [Feb. 29, 1932], *Letters of Archibald MacLeish* (Boston: Houghton Mifflin, 1983), p. 246.

12. Dos Passos–EH, [Feb. 1932], *Fourteenth Chronicle*, pp. 402–3.

13. EH–MacLeish, Dec. 9, 1931, LOC.

14. Item 22, JFK; corrected galleys, UDel.

15. [Feb. 1932], JFK, fragment unmailed.

16. A. G. Pfeiffer–EH, Feb. 24, 1932, JFK.

17. *Miami Daily News*, [no date], clipping in MCL. Passenger and crew number was reported variously between 400 and 488. The ship apparently sank on September 12, 1919.

18. Items 226a and 226b, JFK; MS Am 1199, Houghton, Harvard; *WTN*, p. 9. See Susan Beegel, *Hemingway's Craft of Omission* (UMI Press, 1988), Chap.4, for full account. See also Paul Smith.

19. *WTN*, p. 67.

20. *WTN*, pp. 75–88.

21. *True Gen*, p. 91.

22. MacLeish–EH, [April 7, 1932], *Letters*, p. 247.

23. See Scott Donaldson's *MacLeish: An American Life* for the most complete analysis of this relationship.

24. EH–Perkins, April 5, 1932, JFK.

25. EH–Perkins, April 5, 1932, JFK.

26. Perkins–EH, April 19, 1932, PUL, Amory Blaine is the hero of Fitzgerald's novel *This Side of Paradise*.

27. Grace Hemingway–EH, April 5, 1932, JFK.

28. Grace Hemingway–EH, March 13, 1932, JFK.

29. EH–Grace Hemingway, April 8, 1932, Lilly.

30. See *Young Hemingway* and *Homecoming*. EH–Robert Coates, Oct. 5, 1932, in *New Yorker*, Nov. 5, 1932, pp. 86–7.

31. Item 355, JFK. Use of "niggers" is not meant to be inflammatory,

rather to remind the reader that white Americans in the 1930s used this term as casually as salt.

32. "Log of the HMS *Anita*," JFK; *New York Times*, April 27, 1932.

33. "Incoming, Outgoing Ships," *Post*, April 27, 1932; John Unterecker, *Voyager: A Life of Hart Crane* (1969), pp. 754–9.

34. EH–Waldo Peirce, June 6, 1932, JFK.

35. EH–Perkins, May 14, 1932, JFK; EH–Strater, c. May 22 and June 10, 1932, PUL.

36. "Log of the HMS *Anita*" and typescript, JFK.

37. *Anita* log, JFK.

38. *Post*, April 28, 1932.

39. *New York Times*, May, 1932.

40. *Post*, May 16, 1932.

41. *Post*, May 3, 1932.

42. EH–Perkins, May 14, 1932, PUL.

43. EH–Perkins, June 2, 1932, PUL; EH–Bud White, June 2, 1932, JFK.

44. EH–MacLeish, June 2, 1932, LOC.

45. EH–Henry Strater, June 10, 1932, PUL.

46. *Post*, June 8–10, 1932.

47. EH–MacLeish, June 2, 1932, LOC; First Union Trust of Chicago–EH, June 13, 17, and 18, 1932, Tulsa.

48. PH–EH, four letters, May 1932, JFK.

49. PH–EH, letters May and June, 1932, JFK.

50. Memoir of Josephine Wall Merck, undated, JFK.

51. Item 548, 549, JFK; Scott Donaldson, "The Case of the Vanishing American," *Hemingway Notes*, Spring 1981, pp. 16–19; *Young Hemingway*, 104–5.

52. Hemingway Hunting Log, 1930–34, JFK.

53. EH–Bill Lengel, misdated as c. Aug. 15, 1932, *SL*, p. 367. More likely first week in July.

54. EH–Perkins, Aug. 9, 1932, PUL.

55. EH–Paul Romaine, July 6, 1932; Aug. 9, 1932, *SL*, pp. 363–5.

56. "An Autopsy and a Prescription," *Hound & Horn*, July–Sept. 1932, pp. 520–39.

57. EH–MacLeish, [Aug. 27, 1932], LOC.

58. "Correspondence," *Hound & Horn*, Oct.–Dec. 1932, p. 135.

59. *DIA*, pp. 70–72.

60. Hemingway Fishing Log, 1930–34, JFK.
61. EH–MacLeish, July 31, 1932, LOC.
62. Murphy–MacLeish, Sept. 8, 1932, *Lost Generation*, pp. 63–5; Donnelly, pp. 66–8.
63. Murphy–MacLeish, Sept. 8, 1932, *Lost Generation*, p. 65.
64. "Dissertation on Pride," *New York Sun*, Sept. 23, 1932, p. 34.
65. Herschel Brickell, "What Bullfighting Means to the Spaniards," *New York Herald Tribune*, Sept. 25, 1932, p. 12.
66. R. L. Duffus, "Hemingway Now Writes of Bull-fighting As an Art," *New York Times*, Sept. 25, 1932, pp. 5, 17.
67. Robert M. Coates, "Bullfighters," *New Yorker*, Oct. 1, 1932, pp. 61–3; Granville Hicks, "Bulls and Bottles," *Nation*, Nov. 9, 1932, p. 461; Malcolm Cowley, "A Farewell to Spain," *New Republic*, Nov. 30, 1932, pp. 76–7.
68. Hemingway Hunting Log, JFK; EH–MacLeish, Oct. 13, 1932, LOC; EH–Henry Strater, Oct. 14, 1932, *SL*, p. 370.
69. Nordquist bill dated Oct. 15, 1932, Tulsa.
70. Mario Sanchez's painted bas-reliefs, Martello Tower, Key West Historical Society.
71. *Citizen*, Nov. 8–10, 1932; PH–EH, Nov. 8, 1932, JFK; Hemingway family papers, UTex; *New York Times*, Nov. 12, 1932.
72. Ralph Stitt–EH, c. Dec. 2, 1932, JFK.
73. *New York Times*, Dec. 6, 1932, p. 27.
74. Stitt–EH, Dec. 6, 1932, JFK.
75. Gus Pfeiffer–EH, Dec. 8 and 10, 1932, JFK.
76. EH–Perkins, Dec. 7, 1932, *SL*, p. 379. This blurb appeared as quoted in *Washington Post* early in 1933, JFK.
77. EH–MacLeish, Dec. 22, 1932, LOC; Hemingway Hunting Log, 1930–34, JFK.
78. EH–MacLeish, Dec. 22, 1932, LOC; Hemingway Hunting Log, 1930–34, JFK; various newspapers.
79. *WTN*, pp. 13–17.

CHAPTER 5: 1933

1. EH–Perkins, Jan. 4 and 7, 1933, PUL.
2. Berg, p. 215–25.

3. EH notebook, Jan. 1933, private collection; EH–Eric Knight, Jan. 31, 1933, PUL.

4. Josephine Merck, "Stray Comments About Ernest Hemingway," unpublished, JFK.

5. *Nation*, Jan. 18, 1933, pp. 63–4.

6. *True Gen*, pp. 89–90; EH notebook; Kert, pp. 245–6.

7. Gingrich, *Nothing but People* (Crown, 1971), pp. 85ff. Memoir less than accurate in the details.

8. EH notebook; *Citizen*, Jan. 23, 1933.

9. *New York Times*, Feb. 16, 1933; *Citizen*, March 10, 1933.

10. EH–Dos Passos, c. March 10, 1933, PUL.

11. EH–Albee, Feb. 16, 1933, UCal.

12. Shevlin–EH, Feb. 7, 1933, JFK; *Citizen*, Jan. 31, 1933.

13. *WTN*, p. 147.

14. Items 648a, 648b, and 529a, JFK. See Donald Junkins, "Philip Haines Was a Writer" and "Hemingway's Paris Short Story," *Hemingway Review*, Spring 1990, pp. 2–48.

15. EH–Perkins, Feb. 23, 1933, PUL. This novel has been misidentified elsewhere as the beginning of *THHN*.

16. Gingrich–EH, Feb. 24, 1933, private collection; Gingrich–EH, April 24 and May 26, 1933, JFK.

17. EH–Gingrich, March 13, 1933, *SL*, pp. 383–4. For a more romantic version of the negotiations, read Gingrich's *Nothing but People*, which is right in everything but the accuracy of chronology, dialogue, and places.

18. EH–Gingrich, March 17, 1933, private collection.

19. EH–Gingrich, April 3, 1933, *SL*, p. 384.

20. Mary Post–EH, Feb. 24, 1933, private collection.

21. Item 813, JFK.

22. The three villages mentioned, Fornaci, San Dona, and Zenzon, are all roughly eight kilometers from Fossalta, enclosing it in a triangle, one leg of which is the Piave River.

23. For a detailed analysis of the story's structure, see Paul Smith, pp. 268–75.

24. Gaby Delys and Harry Pilcer had a nightclub act in Paris before the war, but Hemingway never saw her dance. See *Paris Years*, p. 82.

25. Item 815, JFK; *WTN*, p. 53.

26. See *Homecoming*, pp. 103–4.
27. *Citizen*, April 1, 1933.
28. Anthony Mason interview with MSR.
29. PH–EH, May 21 and 25, 1933, JFK.
30. In undated clipping from Daniel Lord's column in *The Sign*, [c. 1930s], JFK; Hemingway notebook in private collection.
31. *Citizen*, March 29, April 5, 1933.
32. EH–Dos Passos, c. March 10, 1933, PUL.
33. EH–Perkins, March 13, 1933, PUL.
34. Charles Scribner–EH, March 31, 1933, JFK.
35. *Citizen*, April 12, 1933; EH Fishing Log, 1930–34, JFK.
36. *Citizen*, April 14, 1933; EH Fishing Log, 1930–34, *New York Times*, April 14–15, 1933.
37. *New York Times*, April 15, 1933.
38. EH calendar log, 1933, JFK.
39. Jane Armstrong, "Ernest Hemingway Returns in Quest of Giant Marlin," *Post*, April 14, 1933.
40. *New York Times*, April 21, 1933.
41. See Carleton Beals, *The Crime of Cuba* (Lippincott, 1933), photo #28.
42. Anthony Mason interview.
43. *Post*, May 25, 1933.
44. Anthony Mason interview.
45. Grace Hemingway–EH, JFK.
46. PH–EH, May 27, 1933, JFK.
47. *Post*, May 27, 1933. The *Anita* log puts marlin 30, 31, and 32 on May 25.
48. Anthony Mason interview; *Post*, June 4, 1933.
49. *Post*, July 5, 1933.
50. *Post*, "Waterfront Gossip," June 9, 1933.
51. EH–MacLeish, July 27, 1933, LOC.
52. Jane Mason–EH/PH, Sept. 2, 1933, JFK; Dr. K.P.A. Taylor–EH, July 19, 1933, JFK.
53. See *Anita* log, 1933, JFK, pp. 62–4.
54. EH notebook on *WTN* in Baker Collection, Box 17, Folder 6, PUL; *Anita* log, 1933, JFK, p. 62; EH–Gingrich, June 7, 1933, *SL*, p.393. Another copy of this letter in a private collection adds, "Have come down the coast for a while at Cabanas," not in *SL*.

55. Perkins–EH, June 19, 1933, JFK.
56. See *Young Hemingway*, pp. 77–87; *Homecoming*, pp. 100–201, 206–7.
57. Item 384, JFK.
58. MSS are simplifed here: see Items 222, 382, 383, 384, 385, 513, 522, and 816, JFK, and *WTN*, pp. 151–62; see Paul Smith, pp. 307–17, for best entry to the MSS.
59. EH–Perkins, July 13, 1933, PUL and Maryland.
60. Gertrude Stein, *The Autobiography of Alice B. Toklas* (Harcourt Brace, 1933).
61. EH–Janet Flanner, April 8, 1933, *SL*, p. 388.
62. "Bull in the Afternoon," *New Republic*, June 7, 1933, pp. 94–7.
63. Scribner-1, Box 2, Folder 12, PUL.
64. Perkins–EH, wire, June 12, 1933, JFK; EH–Perkins, June 13, 1933, *SL*, p. 394.
65. Letter attached to EH–MacLeish, June 12, 1933, LOC.
66. EH–MacLeish, June 28, 1933, LOC.
67. EH Fishing Log, 1933, JFK.
68. "Town Tales Told in Tabloid," *Post*, July 8, 1933.
69. *Post*, July 19, 1933.
70. John Raeburn, *Fame Became of Him* (Indiana U. Press, 1984), pp. 45–50.

CHAPTER 6: 1933–34

1. *Post*, Aug. 3 and 4, 1933; *New York Times*, Aug. 4–13, 1933.
2. EH–Perkins, Aug. 10, 1933 (mailed in Bermuda on August 11), Scribner-1, PUL.
3. Anthony Mason interview and *Post*, Aug. 13, 1933.
4. See *Homecoming*, pp. 145–57, and *Hemingway: Up in Michigan Perspectives*, eds. F. J. Svoboda and J. J. Waldmeir (Michigan State U. Press, 1995), pp. 105–26. This MS has never been published. Also Item 617, JFK.
5. *GHOA*, MS-309-10, UVa.
6. Hadley Mowrer–EH, Aug. 23, 1933, formerly in the private John and Marsha Goin Collection.
7. Waring Jones Collection, Xerox copy in Baker Collection, PUL; Goin Collection: dinner bill at Hotel Roma (La Coruna), Aug. 17, 1933; let-

ters received at Hotel Avenida (San Sebastián), Aug. 22, 1933; Kert, pp. 250–1.

8. Hanneman, Vol. 1, p. 36.

9. Items 222-1 and 222a, JFK; EH–Perkins, Aug. 31, 1933, Scribner-1, PUL. Alternate titles were "Long Time Ago Good," "Tomb of a Grandfather," and "Indian Summer."

10. Cass Canfield–EH, Oct. 19, 1933, Goin Collection.

11. EH–Perkins, Sept. 18, 1933, Scribner-1, PUL.

12. EH–Gingrich, Sept. 26, 1933, private collection.

13. "The Friend of Spain: A Spanish Letter," *Esquire*, Jan. 1934.

14. Pound–EH, Aug. 13 and Sept. 29, 1933, copies in JFK.

15. Story published in *Cosmopolitan*, April 1934, pp. 20–3, 108–22. EH–Mrs. Mary Pfeiffer, Oct. 16, 1933, *SL*, pp. 396–9.

16. EH–PH, Oct. 16, 1933, JFK.

17. EH–PH, [Oct. 24, 1933], JFK.

18. *Tribune*, Oct. 9, 1933.

19. EH–Gingrich, Sept. 26, 1933, private collection.

20. Item 265a, JFK, unpublished; this overheard incident will reappear years later in *A Moveable Feast*. In EH–PH, Oct. 17, 1933, JFK, he says the sketch was written to submit to *The New Yorker*.

21. Jonathan Cape–EH, Oct. 2, 1933, JFK, refers to sending Hemingway four books, *While the Billy Boils*, Sean O'Faolain's *Midsummer Night Madness*, *Brazilian Adventure*, and William Plomer's *The Child of Queen Victoria*. The hunt was canceled because of rain.

22. EH–Mr. Hall, Oct. 16, 1933, JFK, enclosed in a letter to PH on Oct. 19.

23. EH–Mrs. Paul Pfeiffer, Oct. 16, 1933, *SL*, pp. 396–9.

24. EH–PH, Oct. 16, 1933, JFK.

25. EH–Clifton Fadiman, Nov. 26, 1933, PUL.

26. This Protestant conundrum affects more than one American writer, including, at times, Hawthorne, Melville, and Twain.

27. EH–Mr. Hall, Oct. 16, 1933, JFK.

28. EH–PH, Oct. 19, 1933, JFK.

29. PH–EH, Oct. 22, 1933, JFK.

30. *Tribune*, Oct. 16, 1933.

31. In 1995 dollars, the safari cost close to $200,000.

32. Hotel bill, October 1933, JFK.

33. To-do list, Tulsa; Pauline's safari notebook, Stanford.

34. EH–Gingrich, Nov. 21, 1933, private collection.

35. Morrill Cody–Carlos Baker, Sept. 18, 1962, PUL.

36. Wambly Bald, "A Farewell to Montparnasse," *Tribune*, July 25, 1933.

37. *Esquire*, Feb. 1934, p. 156.

38. Gingrich–EH, Oct. 13, 1933, JFK.

39. Perkins–EH, telegram, Oct. 26, 1933, JFK.

40. MacLeish–EH, telegram, Oct. 31, 1933, JFK.

41. Perkins–EH, telegram, Nov. 11, 1933, JFK.

42. Perkins–EH, Nov. 6, 1933, JFK.

43. See *Reception*, pp. 135–47.

44. Louis Kronenberger, "Hemingway's New Stories," *New York Times Book Review*, Nov. 5, 1933.

45. EH–Perkins, Nov. 16, 1933, *SL*, pp. 399–401.

46. EH Passport, JFK.

47. EH Notes, CO-365, Box 17, Folder 6, PUL; hotel bill, Dec. 9–10, 1933, JFK; Daniel Streeter, *Denatured Africa* (Garden City Pub., 1926); McLendon, p. 99.

48. Elspeth Huxley, *Out in the Midday Sun* (Viking, 1985).

49. *Young Hemingway*, pp. 228–9.

50. Jane Mason–EH, Nov. 1, 1933, JFK.

51. Paid bill for 550 pounds, Dec. 14, 1933, Tulsa; EH–J. F. Manley, Nov. 6, 1933, JFK; *Young Hemingway*, pp. 228–33.

52. *Young Hemingway*, pp. 29–30; *SAR*, p. 10.

53. EH–Gingrich, Dec. 19, 1933, private collection.

54. "Ernest Hemingway's Introduction," Jimmy Charters and Morrill Cody, *This Must Be the Place* (Herbert Joseph, 1934), pp. 1–3.

55. Bill Lengel–EH, Jan. 26, 1934, JFK.

56. *East African Weekly Times*, Dec. 15, 1933.

57. *East African Weekly Times*, Dec. 1, 1933–Jan. 19, 1934.

58. *Esquire*, April 1934, p. 19.

59. Hemingway hotel bill, Jan. 16–22, 1933, Goin Collection.

60. EH–Perkins, Jan. 17, 1933, PUL.

61. H. Kortischoner–EH, Dec. 22, 1938, JFK.

62. Pauline Hemingway's safari journal, Stanford. The total kill was probably larger, but these are all she recorded. The details of the safari, unless otherwise noted, all come from this journal.

NOTES

CHAPTER 7: 1934

1. *Citizen*, April 12, 1934.
2. EH–Gerald Murphy, April 27, 1934, *Lost Generation*, p. 83.
3. Brentano's book bill, March 23, 1934, JFK. See also *Reading* and *Library*.
4. EH–Gingrich, April 12, 1934, private collection.
5. Contract dated April 18, 1934, *Pilar* papers, JFK. A black boat at sea is difficult to see during the day and impossible at night.
6. EH–Perkins, April 30, 1934, Scribner-1, PUL.
7. EH–Gingrich, March 24, 1934, private collection.
8. EH–Gingrich, April 12, 1934, private collection.
9. *Green Hills of Africa* holograph MS, UVa; M.A. theses of David LeDuc and Robert Trogdon, N.C. State University; Barbara Lounsberry, "The Holograph Manuscript of *Green Hills of Africa*," *Hemingway Review*, Spring 1933, p. 36.
10. *Vanity Fair*, March 1934, p. 29.
11. Charles Cadwalader–EH, March 6, 1934, and EH–Cadwalader, April 2, 1934, Baker Collection, PUL.
12. Several telegrams in early April 1934, JFK.
13. "Out in the Stream: A Cuban Letter," *Esquire*, Aug. 1934, pp. 19, 156, 158.
14. "The Law of the Jungle," *New Yorker*, April 14, 1934, p. 31.
15. EH–Sara Murphy, April 27, 1934, *Lost Generation*, p. 84.
16. *Citizen*, April and May, 1934.
17. Lawrence Conrad, "Ernest Hemingway, " *The Landmark*, Aug. 1934, p. 397.
18. EH–Perkins, April 30, 1934, Scribner-1, PUL.
19. *Post*, May 2–5, 1934.
20. Ibid., May 4, 1934.
21. *Pilar* papers, May 5, 1934, JFK.
22. *Citizen*, May 1934.
23. FSF–EH, May 10, 1934, JFK.
24. EH–FSF, May 28, 1934, *SL*, pp. 407–9.
25. *Citizen*, May 10, 21, and 23, 1934.
26. *Citizen*, July 5, 1934.
27. *Citizen*, July 6–18, 1934.
28. *Pilar* papers, JFK.

29. "To Get for Cuba" shopping list, Goin Collection; EH–Gingrich, July 14, 1934, private collection; EH–MacLeish, c. July 11, 1934, LOC.

30. Samuelson, pp. 64–68. Samuelson's book, edited posthumously, is filled with small errors (names, dates, places); where we differ my sources may be checked against his text.

31. *Post*, July 21, 1934.

32. *Post*, July 25, 1934.

33. "Genio After Josie: A Havana Letter," *Esquire*, Oct. 1934, p. 21.

34. *Post*, August 1–15, 1934.

35. Photograph, JFK.

36. *Post*, Aug. 7, 1934.

37. *Post*, Aug. 28, 1934.

38. *Post*, Aug. 14 and 17, 1934.

39. EH–Mary Pfeiffer, Aug. 20, 1934, PUL.

40. *Post*, Sept. 4 and 5, 1934; EH–Cadwalader, Sept. 6, 1934, PUL.

41. See PH–EH letters of September, 1934, JFK.

42. EH–Gingrich, Sept. 13, 1934, private collection.

43. Tourist Identification Card, Sept. 14, 1934, JFK. PH–EH, Sept. 15, 1934, JFK.

44. EH–Perkins, Oct. 3, 1934, PUL.

45. Perkins–EH, Oct. 6, 1934, PUL.

46. EH–Lester Ziffin, Nov. 23, 1934, Baker Collection, PUL.

47. *Post*, Oct. 4 and 5, 1934.

48. EH–Cadwalader, Oct. 18, 1934, Baker Collection, PUL. In the May 1936 *Esquire* letter, Hemingway used the experience for "There She Breaches! Or Moby Dick off the Morro," pp. 35, 203–05.

49. Ludington, pp. 329–30.

50. *Post*, Oct. 21, 1934.

51. *Post*, Oct. 26, 1934; EH–Gingrich, Oct. 25, 1934, private collection; Oct. 16, 1934, *Post* in the Hemingway Collection, Tulsa; EH–Murphys, Nov. 7, 1934, *Lost Generation*, p. 96.

52. PH–EH, Oct. 5, 1934, JFK; "She Was Papa's Washerwoman," *Miami Herald*, Aug. 30, 1964.

53. *Miami Herald*, Dec. 12, 1976.

54. EH–Gingrich, July 15, 1934, *SL*, p. 410.

55. Robert Frost to friends, Dec. 1934, *Selected Letters of Robert Frost*, ed. Lawrence Thompson (Holt, Rinehart & Winston, 1964), pp. 413–15.

56. *Citizen*, Oct.–Nov. 1934; Garry Boulard, "State of Emergency: Key West in the Great Depression," *Florida Historical Quarterly*, Oct. 1988, pp. 166–83.

57. *GHOA*, MS-308, UVa.

58. Kert, p. 269, based on interviews with all three sons. Ada's possibly lesbian nature became apparent to the boys only years later.

59. Gregory Hemingway interview with MSR.

60. Katy Dos Passos–Murphys, Dec. 2, 1934, *Lost Generation*, p. 100.

61. Perkins–EH, Nov. 10, 1934, PUL.

62. EH–Murphys, Nov. 16, 1934, *Lost Generation*, p. 97; EH–Gingrich, Nov. 16, 1934, *SL*, p. 410; EH–Perkins, Nov. 16, 1934, PUL.

63. Perkins–Owen Wister, Nov. 21, 1934, PUL.

64. *Time*, Nov. 1934, reprinted in *Citizen*, Dec. 4, 1934.

65. "Notes on Life and Letters," *Esquire*, Jan. 1935, p. 21; EH–Gingrich, Nov. 19, 1934, private collection.

66. *GHOA*, p. 21.

67. EH–Perkins, Nov. 20, 1934, PUL.

68. Perkins–EH, Nov. 22, 1934, PUL.

69. Perkins–EH, Nov. 28, 1934, PUL.

70. *Citizen*, Dec. 5, 7, and 8, 1934.

71. EH–Perkins, Dec. 14, 1934, PUL.

72. *Citizen*, Dec. 19, 1934; Hotel Peabody bill for EH, wife, and one son, Dec. 22, 1934, PUL.

CHAPTER 8: 1935

1. *Citizen*, Jan.–March 1935.

2. *Citizen*, Dec. 20, 1934, Jan. 11, 1935.

3. *Citizen*, March 1, 1935.

4. *Citizen*, March 4, 1935.

5. *Citizen*, April 11, 1935.

6. Katy Dos Passos–Sara Murphy, Jan. 1935, *Lost Generation*, pp. 109–10.

7. PH–Sara Murphy, Jan. 1935, *Lost Generation*, p. 102.

8. *Papa*, p. 19.

9. EH–Perkins, Jan. 16, 1935, PUL; Burt MacBride–EH, Jan. 21, 1935, JFK; Perkins–Lawrence Kubie, Jan. 22, 1935, PUL.

10. Burt MacBride–EH, Jan. 23 and 25, 1935, JFK; *Citizen*, Jan. 24, 1935.

11. *Citizen*, Feb. 2, 1935; Berg, photographs.

12. Perkins–EH, Feb. 4, 1935, PUL.

13. EH–Gingrich, Feb. 4, 1935, private collection.

14. EH–Perkins, telegram, Feb. 18, 1935, PUL; Perkins–EH and EH–Perkins telegrams, Feb. 19, 1935, PUL.

15. Several telegrams and letters back and forth between Hemingway and Perkins, Feb. 19–22, 1935, PUL.

16. EH–Perkins, Feb. 22, 1935, PUL; Sara Murphy–Hemingways, Sept. 12, 1935, *Lost Generation*, p. 142.

17. Murphys–Hemingway and Dos Passos, March 14, 1935, Waring Jones Collection, copies in PUL.

18. Donnelly, pp. 88–90; telegrams in Waring Jones Collection, copies in PUL.

19. EH–Gerald and Sara Murphy, March 19, 1935, *Lost Generation*, p. 118.

20. Ernest Hemingway, "The Sights of Whitehead Street: A Key West Letter," *Esquire*, April 1935, p. 25.

21. EH–Patrick Murphy, April 5, 1935, *Lost Generation*, pp. 126–9; to-do list, Hemingway notebook previously in Goin Collection.

22. "On Being Shot Again: A Gulf Stream Letter," *Esquire*, June 1935, pp. 23, 156–7.

23. Numerous Hemingway letters, JFK; Algernon Aspinall, *The Pocket Guide to the West Indies*, rev. ed. (London: Sifton, Praed, 1935), p. 71; "The Wet Way from Bimini to Florida," *Literary Digest*, Feb. 15, 1930, p. 17; EH–Perkins, June 3, 1935, PUL; EH–MacLeish, June 2, 1935, LOC.

24. John Dos Passos, *The Best of Times*, pp. 208–14.

25. Katy Dos Passos–Gerald Murphy, June 20, 1935, *Lost Generation*, pp. 131–2.

26. Mary Hemingway–Carlos Baker, Baker Collection, PUL.

27. EH–Perkins, May 1, 1935, PUL.

28. EH–MacLeish, June 2, 1935, LOC.

29. EH–Gingrich, June 4, 1935, SL, pp. 414–5; Mary Hemingway–Carlos Baker, March 12, 1962, Baker Collection, PUL.

30. *Papa*, pp. 35–37.

31. Meyers, p. 285; Mellow, pp. 469–70.

32. EH–Perkins, July 4, 1935, PUL.

33. EH–Perkins, April 14, 1935, PUL.

34. EH–Perkins, July 2, 1935, PUL.

35. Perkins–EH, July 9, 1935, PUL.

36. *GHOA*, p. 150.

37. EH–Perkins, June 19, 1935, PUL.

38. Perkins–EH, June 28, 1935, PUL.

39. EH–Perkins, July 30, 1935, PUL. "Pursuit and Failure" was added later.

40. EH–Perkins, July 30, 1935, PUL; various notes in Goin Collection; "The President Vanquishes: A Bimini Letter," *Esquire*, July 1935, p. 167.

41. *Citizen* Aug. 5, 1935.

42. EH–Perkins, c. Aug. 15, 1935, PUL; EH–Gingrich, Aug. 23, 1935, PUL.

43. *Citizen*, Aug. 20 and 31, 1935.

44. "The 1935 Labor Day Hurricane," *Coral Tribune*, week of September 11, 1954, MCL.

45. EH–Perkins, Sept. 7, 1935, PUL.

46. *Citizen*, Sept. 5, 1935.

47. *Coral Tribune*, week of Sept. 11, 1954.

48. *Coral Tribune*, week of Sept. 4, 1954.

49. *Coral Tribune*, week of Sept. 18, 1954; *Citizen*, Sept. 5–7, 1935.

50. *Citizen*, Sept. 5–8, 1935; EH–Perkins, Sept. 7, 1935, PUL.

51. Maurine Williams, "Weep Twice for Them," *Citizen*, Sept. 6, 1935.

52. EH–Perkins, Sept. 7 and 12, 1935, PUL; EH–Sara Murphy, Sept. 12, 1935, *Lost Generation*, pp. 142–3.

53. Ernest Hemingway, "Who Murdered the Vets?" *New Masses*, Sept. 17, 1935, pp. 9–10.

54. EH–Perkins, Sept. 7, 1935, PUL.

55. "Million Dollar Fright: A New York Letter," *Esquire*, Dec. 1935, pp. 35, 190B. A year later Max Schmeling defeated Louis.

56. Subtitled "A Serious Topical Letter," *Esquire*, Sept. 1935, pp. 19, 136.

57. Sara Murphy–PH, Oct. 18, 1935, *Lost Generation*, p. 148. Hemingways at the Westbury Hotel, East 69th.

58. See Hanneman, Vol. 1, Item A-39.

59. *Newsweek*, Oct. 26, 1935, pp. 39–40; DeVoto, "Hemingway in the Valley," *Saturday Review of Literature*, Oct. 26, 1935, p. 5; Charles Poore, "Ernest Hemingway's Story of His African Safari," *New York Times Book Review*, Oct. 27, 1935, pp. 3, 27; Carl Van Doren, "Ernest Hemingway, Singing in Africa," *New York Herald Tribune Books*, Oct. 27, 1935, p. 3; "Hunter's Credo," *Time*, Nov. 4, 1935, p. 81.

60. Reader's letter, May 9, 1935, JFK.

61. Qualified voters list, *Citizen*, Nov. 1, 1935; Election results, *Citizen*, Nov. 13, 1935.

62. EH–Ivan Kashkin, Aug. 19, 1935, *SL*, p. 419.

63. EH–Dos Passos, Dec. 17, 1935; EH–Mr. Green, Dec. 21, 1935, private collection.

64. EH–FSF, Dec. 16, 1935, *SL*, pp. 424–5.

65. EH–Dos Passos, Dec. 17, 1935, *SL*, pp. 425–7.

66. EH–Perkins, Dec. 17, 1935, PUL.

67. Perkins–EH, Dec. 20, 1935, PUL.

68. EH–Mr. Harris, Dec. 12, 1935, private collection.

69. 1934–35 Hemingway notebook, internal dating, Goin Collection.

70. See Paul Smith, pp. 321–6. EH–Sara Murphy, March 19, 1935, *Lost Generation*, p. 118. The question, older than literature, was most clearly stated in Housman's poem "To an Athlete on Dying Young."

71. EH–Gingrich, Dec. 9, 1935, private collection.

72. Published, with several words blanked out, in the Feb. 1936 *Esquire* as "The Tradesman's Return," pp. 27, 193–6.

73. EH–Mr. Green, Dec. 24, 1935, private collection.

74. EH–Mr. Hopkins, Dec. 31, 1935, private collection.

CHAPTER 9: 1936

1. *Citizen*, Jan.–March and Jan. 11, 1936.

2. EH–Ivan Kashkin, Jan. 12, 1936, *SL*, p. 432.

3. EH–Mary Pfeiffer, Jan. 26, 1936, *SL*, p. 436.

4. Feb. 11, 1936, *Lost Generation*, p. 156.

5. See "The Short Happy Life of Francis Macomber" and "The Snows of Kilimanjaro." Many argue for an affair with Jane Mason, but corroborative evidence is less than convincing. For every affair he did have–with

Pauline, Martha Gellhorn, Mary Welsh–evidence is plentiful.

6. F. Scott Fitzgerald, *The Crack-up*, reprint, ed. Edmund Wilson (New York: New Directions, 1945), pp. 69–74.

7. EH–Dos Passos, Jan. 13, 1936, *SL*, p.433.

8. *Citizen*, Jan.–Feb. 1936; EH–Mary Pfeiffer, Jan. 26, 1936, *SL*, pp. 433–7.

9. Baker, p. 617.

10. EH–Sara Murphy, Feb. 27, 1936, *SL*, pp. 438–40; EH–Dos Passos, April 12, 1936, *SL*, pp. 446–7.

11. EH–FSF, Nov. 24, 1936, *SL*, p. 232.

12. *The Crack-up*, pp. 75–80.

13. EH–Perkins, Feb. 7, 1936, *SL*, p. 438.

14. *Esquire*, Aug. 1936, pp. 27, 194–201.

15. FSF–EH, July 16, 1936, JFK; EH changed the name to Julian.

16. Item 692, JFK.

17. *Citizen*, March 11, 1936.

18. *Ladies' Home Journal*, June 1933, p. 35. Hemingway Collection, MCL.

19. *Citizen*, March 16, 19, and 20, 1936; EH–Perkins, April 9, 1936, *SL*, p. 443.

20. O. O. McIntyre, "New Eyes on Key West," *Kansas City Star*, June 2, 1936.

21. EH–John Weaver, April 12, 1936, PUL; EH–Gingrich, April 19, 1936, private collection.

22. EH–Perkins, April 19, 1936, PUL.

23. *Citizen*, April 22–26, 1936.

24. Arturo Suarez, "Waves from the Waterfront," *Post*, April 28, 1936.

25. *Post*, May 13, 1936; PH–Gerald Murphy, July 17, 1936, *Lost Generation*, p. 171; EH–Sara Murphy, June 13, 1939, *Lost Generation*, p. 227.

26. *Post*, May 10, 1936; Sara Murphy–EH, May 20, 1936, *Lost Generation*, p. 165.

27. *Post*, May 5, 1936; Sara Murphy–PH, May 11, 1936, *Lost Generation*, pp. 164–5; *True Gen*, p. 98, friend unidentified.

28. PH–EH, May 22, 1936, JFK.

29. *Citizen*, May 23–28, 1936; EH–Dos Passos, June 10, 1936, PUL; EH–MacLeish, May 31, 1936, LOC. Baker, who may not have seen the MacLeish letter, misread the Dos Passos letter, placing the experience between Miami and Bimini with Patrick Hemingway on board.

30. Granville Hicks, "Small Game Hunting," *New Masses*, Nov. 19, 1936, p. 23.

31. Baker Collection, Box 24, Folder 2, PUL.

32. Pound–EH, June 12, 1936, JFK.

33. EH–Abner Green, June 18, 1936, private collection. Green worked for the American Committee for the Protection of the Foreign Born. In EH–Green, July 2, 1936, private collection: "You can sign my name to any protest telegrams when there is an emergency to help anybody in a jam."

34. Baker Collection, Box 24, Folder 1, PUL.

35. Marjorie K. Rawlings–Perkins, June 18, 1936, PUL.

36. Arnold Gingrich, *Nothing but People* (Crown, 1971), p. 276.

37. PH–Gerald Murphy, July 17, 1935, *Lost Generation*, pp. 170–1.

38. Marjorie K. Rawlings–Perkins, June 18, 1936, Baker Collection, PUL.

39. "The Revolutionist" first appeared as vignette 11, *in our time*; Item 239a, paragraph beginning "In Paris there was a revolution being plotted . . ."; so-called Jimmy Breen MS, Item 529b, JFK, working title "A New Slain Knight." See *Homecoming*, pp. 145–57, and *Hemingway: Up in Michigan Perspectives* (MSU Press, 1995), pp. 105–28.

40. EH–Perkins, July 11, 1936; EH–Abner Green, June 18, 1936, private collection.

41. EH–Perkins, July 11, 1936 (Cat Cay), *SL*, pp. 447–8.

42. Item 211, JFK.

43. EH–Grace Hemingway, July 18, 1936, private collection; Thomas, pp. 131–8.

44. EH–Gingrich, July 21, 1936, private collection; EH–Nordquist, July 25, 1936, Baker Collection, PUL; *Citizen*, July 27, 1936; Harry Burns–Carlos Baker, April 29, 1963, PUL.

45. "Literary Felonies," *Saturday Review of Literature*, Oct. 3, 1936, p. 3.

46. EH checks, Waring Jones Collection, copies at PUL, Aug. 10–Oct. 29, 1936; Hadley H. Mowrer–Jack Hemingway, Aug. 24, 1936, Baker Collection, Box 17, Folder 11, PUL.

47. *True Gen*, pp. 98–100.

48. EH–Gingrich, Sept. 16, 1936, *SL*, p. 451.

49. EH–Gingrich, Aug. 25, 1936, Baker Collection, PUL; EH–Gingrich, Sept. 16, 1936, *SL*, p. 451; EH–Perkins, Sept. 26, 1936, *SL*. p. 454.

50. Item 204, *THHN* MS, JFK, p. 178–9, 190.

51. See Item 212-3, *THHN* typescript, JFK, p. 61.

52. Item 204-8, pp. 230–32, JFK, quoted in Robert Fleming, "The Libel of Dos Passos in *To Have and Have Not*," *Journal of Modern Literature*, Spring 1989, pp. 588–601.

53. See Carr, pp. 350ff.

54. Item 212-3, typescript, JFK.

55. M. K. Rawlings–EH, Aug. 1, 1936 (arrived Aug. 16), JFK.

56. EH–Rawlings, Aug. 16, 1936, *SL*, pp. 449–50.

57. EH–Mary Pfeiffer, Aug. 11, 1936, Baker Collection, PUL.

58. *True Gen*, p. 98.

59. EH–MacLeish, Sept. 26, 1936, *SL*, p. 453.

60. EH–Perkins, Sept. 26, 1936, *SL*, p. 454; Perkins–EH, Oct.1, 1936, Scribner-1, PUL.

61. Checkbook, copies of Waring Jones Collection, PUL; EH–Harry Burns, Oct. 24, 1936, and (taxidermists) Jonas Brothers–EH, Nov. 9, 1936, Baker Collection, PUL.

62. *Citizen*, Nov. 12, 1936. Toby Bruce claims to have driven Ernest, Pauline, and both sons to Key West, but all evidence says otherwise. Two undated letters, PH–EH, [Nov. 1936], JFK; *Citizen*, Nov. 21 and 30, 1936. Later EH said the pool was Pauline's folly, but he was planning it before she returned to Key West.

63. John Peale Bishop, "Homage to Hemingway," *New Republic*, Nov. 11, 1936, p. 40.

64. EH–Richard Armstrong, July 25, 1936, Christie's East auction catalog, Feb. 21, 1996, item 137.

65. Richard Armstrong–EH, Aug. 27, 1936, JFK; Richard Armstrong–EH, Sept. 2, 1936, Baker Collection, PUL; Christie's East catalog.

66. EH–Gingrich, Oct. 3, 1936, private collection.

67. Deleted "Interlude in Cuba," *THHN* MS, p. 460, renumbered p. 416, JFK.

68. *Post*, Dec. 6, 1936; EH–Perkins, Dec. 14, 1936, Scribner-1, Box 3, Folder 15, PUL; check stubs, Waring Jones Collection, copies PUL.

69. Harry Sylvester, "Ernest Hemingway: A Note," *Commonweal*, Oct. 30, 1936, p. 11. The tall tale must have come from Hemingway.

70. EH–Sylvester, Dec. 15, 1936, Baker Collection, PUL.

71. *The Diaries of Dawn Powell*, ed. Tim Page (Steerforth Press, 1995), p. 203.

72. *Citizen*, Dec. 28 and 31, 1936. See McClendon and other biographies.

CHAPTER 10: 1937–38

1. Kert, 282–92; Rollyson, pp. 1–62; *Saturday Review of Literature*, Sept. 26, 1936; Eleanor Roosevelt, syndicated column, "My Day," Sept. 16, 1936.
2. Martha Gellhorn, *The Face of War* (Atlantic Monthly Press, 1988), "1959 Introduction," p. 1.
3. Gellhorn–Eleanor Roosevelt, Jan. 5, 1937, cited in Kert, p. 291.
4. Gellhorn–Eleanor Roosevelt, Jan. 13, 1937, FDR.
5. *Citizen*, Jan. 8 and 11, 1937; Gellhorn–Pauline Hemingway, Jan. 14, 1937, PUL. All references to Martha Gellhorn letters are from notes made before she closed her correspondence and from citations in earlier biographies.
6. PH–EH, Jan. 13 and 17, 1937; *New York Times*, "Writer to Aid Loyalists," Jan. 12, 1937; Baker, p. 299.
7. PH–EH, Jan. 12, 13, 16, and 17, 1937, JFK.
8. Gellhorn–Eleanor Roosevelt, Jan. 13, 1937, FDR.
9. Quoted in *Citizen*, Jan. 20, 1937.
10. *True Gen*, pp. 101–2.
11. *Citizen*, Jan. 25, 1937.
12. The Hemingway letter has been lost. Patrick died on Jan. 30, 1937. Journal entry, Jan. 16, 1937, in Donnelly, pp. 114–20.
13. See Baker, p. 300, and MacLeish–EH telegrams, Feb. 11, 15, and 16, 1937, JFK.
14. EH–Pfeiffers, Feb. 9, 1937, *SL*, pp. 457–8. Addressed "Dear Family," this letter is one of the few he did not address only to Mary Pfeiffer. Also EH–Harry Sylvester, Feb. 5, 1937, *SL*, pp. 456–7.
15. Gellhorn–EH, Feb. 8, 1937, quoted in Kert, p. 294.
16. PH–Perkins, March 6, 1937, Scribner-1, Box 3, Folder 17, PUL; Gellhorn–Eleanor Roosevelt, Feb. 9, 1937, FDR; *New York Times*, Feb. 28, 1937. Hemingway sailed on the *Paris* on Feb. 27. PH–EH, three letters early March 1937, JFK; EH checkbook, March–May 1937, Baker Collection, PUL.

17. Samuelson, pp. 16, 22.

18. Gellhorn–EH, Feb. 15, 1937, quoted in Kert, p. 294.

19. Joris Ivens, *The Camera and I* (International Publishers, 1969 [written in 1943–44]), p. 111. For complete Ivens–Hemingway relationship see William Brasch Watson, "Joris Ivens and the Communists: Bringing Hemingway into the Spanish Civil War," in *Blowing the Bridge*, ed. Rena Sanderson (Greenwood Press, 1992).

20. Louis Fisher–Geikas, Feb. 25, 1937, formerly in the Goin Collection.

21. Watson 1982 interview with Ivens, "Joris Ivens and the Communists," p. 49.

22. Kert, pp. 294–6.

23. See Hugh Thomas, *The Spanish Civil War*; Robert Rosenstone, *Crusade on the Left*; Herbert Matthews, *Half of Spain Died*; Ronald Fraser, *The Blood of Spain*; Alvah Bessie, *The Heart of Spain*.

24. Gellhorn, *The Face of War*, p. 11.

25. Josephine Herbst, *The Starched Blue Sky of Spain* (Harper Collins, 1991), p. 132.

26. *True Gen*, pp. 111, 116. Josephine Herbst, more accurately, puts Hemingway's rooms at the three hundred level, which would have been the fourth floor in Europe.

27. Hemingway checkbook, March–May 1937, Goin Collection, shows the following payments in francs: 1500, Evan Shipman: canned goods for Madrid; 4000 Sidney Franklin: Sidney and Evan; 400 Sidney: cash loan; 750 Shipman: cash loan. Exchange rate: 29 francs to the dollar.

28. Shipman information due to Sean O'Rourke's research into Shipman's 1954 testimony before the Subversive Activities Control Board.

29. Herbert Matthews, *The Education of a Correspondent* (Harcourt, Brace, 1946), p. 68, hereafter Matthews.

30. "Hemingway Sees Dead Strewing Battlefield," March 22, 1937, in William Brasch Watson's meticulously edited "Hemingway's Spanish Civil War Dispatches," *Hemingway Review*, Spring 1988, p. 19, hereafter cited as Watson, "Dispatches."

31. Watson, "Ivens and the Communists," pp. 48–9.

32. Hemingway NANA dispatch #10, Watson, "Dispatches," p. 38. As in all news stories written from Hemingway cables, the original was more terse.

33. Gellhorn, "Only the Shells Whine," *Collier's* (July 17, 1937), pp.12–13, 64–65.
34. *Tribune*, May 11, 1937.
35. Francis Smith, "Hemingway Curses, Kisses, Reads at Sylvia Beach Literary Session," *Tribune*, May 14, 1937. Several secondary sources have mistakenly said he read "Fathers and Sons."
36. *Tribune*, May 13, 1937.
37. Martha Gellhorn, "A Reporter at Large: Madrid to Morata," *New Yorker*, July 24, 1937, p. 31.
38. These letters, which are closed to quotation, are in the JFK and the PUL.
39. See EH dispatches in Watson, "Dispatches," pp. 24–42.
40. *Citizen*, May 26, 1937.
41. See Gellhorn–Roosevelt correspondence, June 1937, FDR.
42. An insert crossed out on *THHN* MS, p. 356, JFK.
43. Item 208, JFK. Underlined words added later.
44. "Fascism Is a Lie," *New Masses*, June 22, 1937, p. 4. The *New York Times* buried the story on p. 9, covering it in three column inches, less than it gave to a local meeting of the Notre Dame alumni association. *Time*, June 21, 1937, pp. 79–81, gave it five full columns with five photographs, including one of Hemingway.
45. Dawn Powell–John Dos Passos, undated, UVa, quoted in Ludington, pp. 376–7.
46. Paul Romaine–Carlos Baker, Feb. 4, 1963, PUL; Prudencio De Pereda–Carlos Baker, June 2, 1967, PUL.
47. EH–Perkins, Thursday, [June 10, 1937], Scribner-1, PUL; Berg, pp. 324–5.
48. PH–EH, [June 21 and 22, 1937], JFK; Prudencio de Pereda–Carlos Baker, June 2, 1967, PUL.
49. EH–Mary Pfeiffer, Aug. 2, 1937, *SL*, p. 460.
50. PH–Sara Murphy. July 8, 1937, *Lost Generation*, pp. 194–5.
51. EH–Mary Pfeiffer, Aug. 2, 1937; dinner clothes: EH–PH wire, July 6, 1937, Tulsa; Gellhorn–Eleanor Roosevelt, Sunday, [July 11, 1937], FDR. Finally Hemingway read the narrative himself for the film.
52. Ernest Hemingway, "The Heat and the Cold," reprinted in *The Spanish Earth*, limited edition published by Jasper Wood (Cleveland, 1938), from *Verve*, Spring 1938, p. 46.

NOTES

53. Herbst, *Starched Blue Sky of Spain*, pp. 154–57; Carr, pp. 365–75; Ludington, pp. 366–72; MacLeish interview with Carlos Baker, PUL.
54. EH–Dos Passos, c. March 26, 1938, *SL*, pp. 463–5.
55. EH–Mary Pfeiffer, Aug. 2, 1937, *SL*, pp. 459–61.
56. *New York Times*, Aug. 14, 16, and 17, 1937; *Newsweek*, Aug. 21, 1937, p. 4; *Time*, Aug. 23, 1937, p. 66; and many columnists.
57. "Talk of the Town," *New Yorker*, Nov. 27, 1937.
58. Cape–EH, Aug. 10, 27, and 30, 1937, JFK and Goin Collection.
59. Bank accounts: Guaranty Trust–EH, Aug. 26 and Sept. 2, 1937, and Guaranty account statement, Sept. 1, 1937, Goin Collection. Wallach: doctor's prescription for Mr. Hemmingway [sic], Aug. 26, 1937, Tulsa.
60. John Sommerfield, *A Volunteer in Spain* (Knopf, 1937), p. 104.
61. Watson, "Dispatches," p. 49.
62. Martha Gellhorn, "Men Without Medals," *Collier's*, Jan. 15, 1938, p. 10. Poet Edwin Rolfe's account of Belchite, where he fought with the Lincoln Battalion, curiously does not mention Merriman in the final assault, where Rolfe was present. Merriman appears throughout Rolfe's book, *The Lincoln Battalion* (Veterans of the A. Lincoln Brigade, 1939). See Baker, p. 623.
63. Rooms 113/114 at a special group price of thirty pesetas (about $5) a day: Hotel Florida bills, PUL and JFK.
64. Basics: Grocer's bill delivered to Hemingway at the Foyot, Waring Jones Collection; extraordinaries: Sara Murphy–EH, Sept. 20, 1937, JFK.
65. Watson, "Dispatches," p. 54; Hanneman, p. 155.
66. See Copyright, General Index 1938–45, Entry No. D unpub 54650, LOC. Subtitled "But Not for Love."
67. With Morris Musselman, EH wrote youthful farces "Hokum" and "Jomeo and Ruliet." His sister, Marcelline Sanford, copyrighted a one-act farce, "Be Seated," in 1938, D unpub 39510, LOC. Fitzgerald, Faulkner, Dos Passos, and Wilder all wrote plays, with varying success.
68. The longest attempt at theater was "The Dictator—A Play," 30 pages, Item 365, JFK, probably done in the late 1920s. A substantial amount of his known reading was focused on theater. See *Reading* and *Library*.
69. See *Reading* and *Library*.

70. Item 80, JFK.

71. Ernest Hemingway, "Preface," *The Fifth Column and the First Forty-nine Stories* (Scribner's, 1938).

72. Ernest Heminway, *The Fifth Column and Four Stories* (Scribner's, 1969), p. 44.

73. EH–FSF, July 1, 1925, *SL*, pp. 165–6.

74. *The Fifth Column and Four Stories*, pp. 80–3.

75. *Time*, Oct. 18, 1937, pp. 80–1, 83–5; portrait by Waldo Peirce; fifteen captioned photos documenting EH's life from Oak Park to the war in Spain.

76. Lewis: *Newsweek*, Oct. 18, 1937, p. 34; *Nation*, Oct. 23, 1937, pp. 439–40; Cowley: *New Republic*, Oct. 20, 1937, pp. 305–6; *New Masses*, Oct. 26, 1937, pp. 22–3. Sales: Hanneman, p. 41.

77. *Tribune*, Dec. 25, 1937.

78. The *Normandie* departed Dec. 18, arriving New York Dec. 23. Martha writes EH on board, thus could not have been at Teruel as most biographers have her. The *Europa*, from which PH writes Sara Murphy, left New York Dec. 16, arriving Cherbourg Dec. 21. *Tribune*, Dec. 22, 1937.

79. Watson, "Dispatches," pp. 67–8.

80. *Lost Generation*, p. 203.

81. Baker, pp. 323–4; Baker Collection, Box 18, Folder 8, PUL. The Hotel Elysée marks the first time Hemingway moves from the Left to the Right Bank. Sara Murphy–EH, Sept. 20, 1937, *Lost Generation*, p. 201: three of Hemingway's trunks were stored at this hotel by Sara.

82. Books: Waring Jones Collection, Brentano's book bill for 3,168.50 francs paid in January 1938 (approximately $110), PUL. Wallach: Baker Collection, Box 18, Folder 8, has prescription for Drainochol (extract of jaborandi and artichoke), Chophytol, and Belladinol. Translation: pneumatic, Jean Gardner(?)–EH, Jan. 12, 1938, JFK.

83. Pauline's passport shows Southampton date, Baker Collection, PUL; *Gripsholm* did not stop in a French port, *Tribune*. Reporters: PH–EH [Aug. 17, 1937], JFK. *New York Times*, Jan. 26–9, 1938.

84. *Citizen*, Jan. 29, 1938.

85. "Hemingway Tells of War, New Play, in Interview," *Citizen*, Feb. 1, 1938.

86. EH–Hadley Hemingway Mowrer, Jan. 31, 1938, *SL*, pp. 462–3. I and

others have said EH took the *Pilar* to Havana around Feb. 1. The *Gripsholm*, en route from New York, docked in Havana about Feb. 2; he may have gone over to pick up freight from France.

87. "Spain and Her Lesson of War," *Oak Leaves* (Oak Park, Ill.), Feb. 3, 1938, on meeting of Jan. 31.

88. Grace Hemingway–EH, [Feb. 3, 1938], JFK, included another clipping of the marriage of his sister Madelaine (Sunny) to Kenneth Mainland.

CHAPTER 11: 1938–39

1. Gregory Hemingway interview; *Homecoming*, pp. 124–6.

2. Bowers urged the implementation of this plan in a March 30 cable and in an April 3 confidential letter to the U.S. Secretary of State, cited in Jeffrey Shulman, "Hemingway's Observations on the Spanish Civil War," *Hemingway Review*, Spring 1988, pp. 147–9. Edgar Mowrer is the brother of Paul Mowrer, second husband of Hadley Hemingway Mowrer.

3. Vincent Sheean, *Not Peace but a Sword* (Doubleday, 1939), pp. 235ff. EH and Pauline were still married when book appeared. *New York Times*, April 25, 1938, says raid came five minutes into film; also EH got a five-minute ovation when introduced.

4. Matthews, *Education of a Correspondent*, pp. 132–3; Watson, "Dispatches," pp. 73–5; Gellhorn–Eleanor Roosevelt, "Barcelona, April 24 or 25" [1938], FDR.

5. Gellhorn, "On Apocryphism," *Paris Review*, Spring 1981, p. 284.

6. Kert, pp. 315–6.

7. See Watson, "Dispatches," pp. 75–82.

8. EH–John Wheeler, June 2, 1938, in Watson, "In Defense of His Reporting from Spain," *Hemingway Review*, Spring 1988, p. 120.

9. See John Raeburn, *Fame Became of Him* (Indiana U. Press, 1984), pp. 87–91. Will Watson, "The Pravda Article," *Hemingway Review*, Spring 1988, p. 115.

10. Ernest Hemingway, in Watson, "Dispatches," p. 86.

11. See Claude Bowers–Secretary of State, May 17, 1938, in Schulman, *Hemingway Review*, Spring 1988, pp. 149–50. "Hemingway Returns, Tired of War in Spain," *New York Times*, May 31, 1938.

12. *Citizen*, May 31, June 2 and 3, 1938.
13. Florida Auto Registration card, Waring Jones Collection, CO365, Box 17, PUL.
14. Paul Smith, pp. 369–74.
15. See Jay Allen–EH, July 8, 1938, JFK.
16. EH–Perkins, July 12, 1938 [two letters same date], *SL*, pp. 467–71.
17. EH–MacLeish, c. mid-July 1938, JFK, quite possibly not mailed, but does reflect his state of mind. See MacLeish's measured response, MacLeish–EH, Aug. 6, 1938, *MacLeish Letters*, pp. 294–5; EH–Ralph Ingersoll, July 18 and 27, 1938, JFK.
18. *Citizen*, June 18 and July 13, 1938.
19. McLendon, pp. 182–7.
20. [Gellhorn]–EH, JFK.
21. CO365, Box 24, Folder 1, PUL.
22. EH–Mary Pfeiffer, Aug. 18, 1938, Baker Collection, PUL; hotel bill, JFK.
23. Kert, p. 317, interview with Patrick.
24. EH–Mary Pfeiffer, Aug. 18, 1938, Baker Collection, PUL.
25. Baker, p. 333. The book was published without a dedication.
26. Gellhorn–Eleanor Roosevelt, Aug. 14, 1938, FDR. Address on stationery: 18 Square du Bois de Boulogne, XVI.
27. PH–EH, [Sept. 1–5], 10, and 28, 1938, JFK. Sept. 10 letter misdated at JFK as 1936.
28. Hanneman, pp. 46–7; *Saturday Review of Literature*, Oct. 15, 1938, p. 5; *New York Times Book Review*, Oct. 23, 1938, p. 4; *Nation*, Dec. 10, 1938, pp. 628, 630; *Time*, Oct. 17, 1938, p. 75; *New Masses*, Nov. 22, 1938, pp. 21–2; *New Republic*, Nov. 21, 1938, pp. 367–8.
29. EH–Perkins, Oct. 28, 1938, *SL*, pp. 473–5.
30. Hadley Richardson–EH, Jan. 8, 1921, JFK.
31. Grace Hemingway–EH, Dec. 25, 1938, JFK.
32. *New York Daily Mirror*, Jan. 15, 1939, p. 3.
33. *New York Daily Mirror*, Jan. 17, 1939.
34. Kert, pp. 322–3.
35. PH–Sara Murphy [Jan. 1939], *Lost Generation*, pp. 219–20, misdated as Dec. 1938.
36. EH–Mrs. Paul Pfeiffer, Feb. 5, 1939, *SL*, pp. 475–7, misdated Feb. 6; Gellhorn–Mrs. Roosevelt, Feb. 3, 1939, FDR.

37. The *Pilar* remains temporarily in Key West: see PH–EH, [Feb. 28, 1939], JFK.
38. EH–Perkins, Feb. 7, 1939, *SL*, p. 479. Twelve years later the story became *The Old Man and the Sea*.
39. Pauline's letters are being sent to the Ambos Mundos, but the *For Whom the Bell Tolls* manuscript says it was written first in the Hotel Sevilla-Biltmore. Waring Jones Collection, PUL, CO365, Box 17 confirms the Biltmore. EH–Tommy Shevlin, April 4, 1939, *SL*, p. 484.
40. PH–EH, [Feb. 28, 1939], JFK; PH–Sara Muprhy, [March 10, 1939], *Lost Generation*, p. 222.
41. Bill from Sevilla-Biltmore Hotel, March 18, 1939, Waring Jones Collection, PUL.
42. Item 83, JFK.
43. EH–Perkins, March 25, 1939, *SL*, pp. 482–3.
44. Kert, pp. 325–6.
45. Gellhorn–Eleanor Roosevelt, May 17, 1939, FDR.
46. Martha Gellhorn, *A Stricken Field* (Duell, Sloan & Pearce, 1940), p. 87.
47. Lionel Trilling, "Hemingway and His Critics," *Partisan Review*, Winter 1939, p. 53.
48. EH–Grace Hemingway, May 28, 1939, private collection; EH–Patrick Hemingway, June 30, 1939, *SL*, pp. 486–8; PH–EH, July 12, 1939, JFK; EH–Mrs. Paul Pfeiffer, July 21, 1939, *SL*, pp. 491–2.

INDEX